THE ODES OF HORACE

THE ODES OF HORACE

A CRITICAL STUDY

BY STEELE COMMAGER

NEW HAVEN AND LONDON
YALE UNIVERSITY PRESS, 1962

Set in Times Roman type and printed
in the United States of America by the
Vail-Ballou Press, Inc., Binghamton, N.Y.

Library of Congress catalog card number: 62-8241

PARENTIBUS OPTIMIS

PREFACE

Poeta nascitur non fit. But though poets may be born, poems are made. Few poets have been more explicit about that than Horace, for whom an eye in fine frenzy rolling was less compelling evidence of genius than were bitten fingernails. The critical emphasis he gave to technical accomplishment demands a corresponding respect from us, and suggests that it is here that any investigation of his poetry should start. Criticism need not, of course, wait upon direct invitation. A text must itself be persuasive. If it is not, the author's assurances of craftsmanship remain irrelevant. In Horace's case his critical insistence on the poet's technical *labor* confirms what we independently recognize in the Odes themselves. That covenant between critic and poet commands our attention.

Perhaps the chief distraction in reading the Odes as poetry is our fondness for regarding them as a repository of home truths. The tendency is one Horace himself encourages by presenting us with phrases that seem too apposite to remain in their context. Thackeray was content if his hero could "quote Horace respectably through his life"; Horace is, we all know, the most miscellaneously relevant of poets. His gleaming lines have illuminated a disproportionate bulk of the volumes of Golden Hours with Latin Authors. *Carpe diem, aurea mediocritas,* and *simplex munditiis* are practically household terms. We seem to feel that the range of his formulations can best be displayed by detaching them at either end. His conciseness and apparent clarity phrase by phrase tempt us into believing that there is an equally concise and clear meaning to be assigned to a poem as a whole, or even to his thought as a whole. Yet Horace had no systematic philosophy to impart; he was coating no doctrines with the honey of verse. His poems record only an imaginative apprehension of the world, and an Ode's meaning, like that of any other poem, does not lie in a phrase or a paraphrase. It inheres in the sounds, the figures, the tone, the emotional coloring; in many cases, the logic is less important than the mood. Each Ode is a calculated assault on our sensibilities, a deliberate invasion of our consciousness. Only by yielding to each in its entirety can we momentarily share Horace's characteristic vision. And his willingness to share that vision is the only "message" he has.

But though a reading of the Odes must begin, and perhaps ultimately end, by taking each poem as a distinctive entity, such an approach need not preclude a more general interpretation. Each of the Odes is, to be sure, a whole, and it may be that we violate its integrity even by regarding it in conjunction with any other. Yet each is also an integer in Horace's total output, and the temptation to add them together is almost irresistible, even if no two readers are likely to come out with the same result. Certain themes and images are persistent and point to what seem to be the abiding concerns or habits of his imagination. Without trying to capture his Protean intelligence in a net of categories it may at least be possible to define the shapes it can take.

The bulk of the literature on Horace is enormous. Yet since the Odes will continue to be greater than the sum of their interpretations there is no need to apologize for adding to it. This book is limited in its scope. My aim has been to examine some, though by no means all, of the Odes, with particular attention to their language and structure, and to the effect a poem as a whole is intended to produce or does produce. With this focus it is, I hope, legitimate to treat the Odes with only incidental references to the Satires and Epistles. I do not pretend to have made a comprehensive survey of Horace's work or of the intellectual, philosophical, and historical background, but have tried, rather, to introduce only such material as is specifically relevant to a particular poem. It is legitimate to maintain that any poem should be read as a timeless document of the creative intelligence. Yet every author lives in a specific time and place, and though Horace built his *monumentum aere perennius* for the ages he intended it to be admired first by his contemporaries. Frequently his text demands a context of knowledge which he could assume but we must rediscover. We miss a good deal in *C.* 3.21 unless we are aware of its hymnic form, and in *C.* 3.14 if we do not know in what year the consulship of Plancus fell. And it is interesting, if not crucial, to remember when reading the third Roman Ode that Augustus aspired to the character of Romulus, or to know that Horace was ten years older when the fourth book of Odes appeared than he was when the first three did. To be aware of his achievement in his own time it is similarly helpful to have some idea of his literary precedents, not so much because they constitute a source for his work as because they provide a convenient measure of what he was attempting to do. The same is true of his theoretical assumptions about poetry and the poet, and by locating his position in terms of previous and contemporary literary beliefs it is easier to recognize the distinctive qualities of his own convictions.

Every student of Horace must be grateful for the appearance of Eduard Fraenkel's monumental *Horace* (Oxford, 1957), and to his affluent learning I am heavily indebted. Often when I depart from his interpretations it is only as a result of the discoveries he has made. He has, moreover, treated many of the Odes (such as the hymns) in such detail that I felt any further comment would be superfluous. Of the other recent works on Horace the one I have found most congenial is that of L. P. Wilkinson, *Horace and His Lyric Poetry* (Cambridge, Eng., 1946), and I am grateful to him on many points of explication. To master all the specialized writings on Horace would be an endless task, and the Siren voices of criticism have an uncanny way of diverting us from our destination, the text. I have tried simply to acknowledge whatever influenced me directly, without pretending to a full survey of the critical material. The most convenient recent bibliography, by Erich Burck, is in the ninth edition of Kiessling-Heinze, *Q. Horatius Flaccus, Oden und Epoden* (Berlin, 1959), 569 ff. Others are E. Norden, *Die römische Literatur* (Leipzig, 1954), 175 ff., and R. J. Getty, *Classical World 52* (1958–59), 167 ff., 246 ff. In citing the various works on Horace, I have made an effort to avoid the atmosphere of easy acrimony which sometimes haunts footnotes. Since we have inevitably to stand upon the shoulders of previous scholars, it ill becomes us to step on their toes in getting there. The text used throughout is that of F. Klingner, *Horatius, Opera* (Leipzig, 1959). The abbreviations used for classical authors' names and works are those listed in Liddell and Scott's *Greek Lexicon* and

Lewis and Short's *Latin Dictionary*. The translations are my own. I have tried to make them quite literal, and they have no pretensions to elegance. If they seem stiff and wooden, it should be remembered that they are intended only as a crutch.

I should like to thank the Society of Fellows at Harvard for the grant which enabled me to write this book, and the Ford Foundation which assisted in its publication. My thanks are due also to Professors Wendell Clausen, Cedric Whitman, Mason Hammond, Dr. Kenneth Reckford, Seth Benardete, and Christian Wolff for their criticism of individual chapters, and in particular to Professor Eric Havelock, for his suggestions both on individual points and on the structure of the whole. To those who have been my students during the past few years, I am grateful for showing me repeatedly that no interpretation of Horace can aspire to finality. I am deeply obliged, finally, to Dorothy Dean and Ann Reynolds for their indefatigable efforts in typing and proofreading the manuscript, and to Julee Stone MacGowan, of the Yale University Press, for her painstaking and sympathetic editing.

Portions of this book have appeared, in different form, in the *American Journal of Philology*, the *Transactions and Proceedings of the American Philological Association,* and the *Phoenix*. My thanks are due to the editors of these publications for permission to use some of the material again.

The quotation from Robert Frost on page 291 is from "Reluctance" in *Complete Poems of Robert Frost,* copyright 1935 by Holt, Rinehart and Winston, Inc.; reprinted by permission of Holt, Rinehart and Winston, Inc. The quotation from T. S. Eliot on page 328, is from "East Coker" in *Four Quartets,* copyright 1943 by T. S. Eliot; reprinted by permission of Harcourt, Brace and World, Inc.

S. C.

Boston, Massachusetts
January 1961

CONTENTS

PREFACE vii

ABBREVIATIONS xiii

I LITERARY CONVENTIONS AND STYLISTIC CRITICISM IN THE AUGUSTAN AGE 1

The Descent of the Muses 2
Horace's Use of Traditional Formulas 16
Ars and *Ingenium* 20
Horace and Alexandrianism 31
Horace's Stylistic Criticism 42

II STRUCTURAL CHARACTERISTICS OF THE ODES 50

Patterns of Words 50
Architectural Patterns and the Use of Metaphor 58
The Cleopatra Ode 88

III QUALITIES OF IMAGINATION 99

Balance of Attitude 104
Tension between Form and Subject: Parody 120
The Amatory Odes 141

IV THE POLITICAL ODES 160

Early Work 160
Longer Odes of the Early Twenties 172
Later Odes 226

V THE WORLD OF NATURE: TIME AND CHANGE 235

Nature as a Moral Metaphor 235

The Ethics of Change 255
Nature's Decorum and Death 265
Book Four 291

VI THE WORLD OF ART 307

REGISTER OF CITATIONS FROM HORACE 353

INDEX 361

ABBREVIATIONS FOR PRINCIPAL PERIODICALS

AC	*L'Antiquité Classique*
AJP	*American Journal of Philology*
CJ	*The Classical Journal*
CP	*Classical Philology*
CQ	*Classical Quarterly*
CR	*Classical Review*
CW	*Classical Weekly*
Eos	*Eos. Commentarii Societatis Philologae Polonorum*
Eranos	*Eranos. Acta Philologica Suecana*
F&F	*Forschungen und Fortschritte*
Gnomon	*Gnomon. Kritische Zeitschrift für die gesamte klassische Altertumswissenschaft*
G&R	*Greece and Rome*
HSCP	*Harvard Studies in Classical Philology*
Hermes	*Hermes. Zeitschrift für klassische Philologie*
Historia	*Historia. Zeitschrift für alte Geschichte*
JHS	*Journal of Hellenic Studies*
JRS	*Journal of Roman Studies*
JPh	*Journal of Philology*
Klio	*Klio. Beiträge zur alten Geschichte*
LEC	*Les Études Classiques*
MAAR	*Memoirs of the American Academy in Rome*
MEFR	*Mélanges d'Archéologie et d'Histoire de l'École Française de Rome*
MH	*Museum Helveticum. Revue Suisse pour l'Étude de l'Antiquité classique*
Mn	*Mnemosyne*
NJA	*Neue Jahrbücher für das klassische Altertum*

NJW	*Neue Jahrbücher für Wissenschaft und Jugendbildung*
Philologus	*Philologus. Zeitschrift für das klassische Altertum*
Phoenix	*The Phoenix. The Journal of the Classical Association of Canada*
PMLA	*Publications of the Modern Language Association*
REA	*Revue des Études Anciennes*
RevArch	*Revue Archéologique*
RevBelge	*Revue Belge de Philologie et d'Histoire*
RhM	*Rheinisches Museum*
TAPA	*Transactions of the American Philological Association*
WienStud	*Wiener Studien. Zeitschrift für klassische Philologie*
WJA	*Würzburger Jahrbücher für die Altertumswissenschaft*
YCS	*Yale Classical Studies*
ZRPh	*Zeitschrift für Romanische Philologie*

ABBREVIATIONS FOR HORACE'S WORKS

A.P.	*Ars Poetica*
C.S.	*Carmen Saeculare*
C.	*Carmina*
Ep.	*Epistles*
Epod.	*Epodes*
S.	*Satires*

THE ODES OF HORACE

I

LITERARY CONVENTIONS AND STYLISTIC CRITICISM IN THE AUGUSTAN AGE

HORACE is among the most professional of poets in the sense that he is among those most thoroughly aware of and committed to art as a distinctive discipline. The son of a provincial auction crier, he became through his poetry alone a spokesman for the world's greatest power. His work was not only the most important fact of his life but in a sense was his real life, and he was forever contrasting his origins and tangible possessions with his intangible achievement.[1] Yet he did not rest content with negative formulations alone. For the poet to translate his private awareness of himself into a public image a special language is demanded, one that is more likely to be allusive than explicit, symbolic than literal. The customary terminology was that bequeathed by the Greeks, and the Augustans duly invoked the Muse, declared their role as her priest, and boasted of the springs and holy groves through which they received their inspiration. Yet each reiteration of these poetic formulas enlarged, qualified, or repudiated their original intent, until the continuity of expression became hardly more than a measure of the difference in actual belief. To look at the manner in which Horace's contemporaries employed that traditional language is to see how available it was generally for meaningful statements. And it is

1. *C.* 2.18.10, 2.20.5–6, 3.30.12; *Ep.* 1.20.20–22; see below, 330 ff.

to understand, too, why Horace was to seek more adequate terms for formulating his private conception of his calling.

If few classical poets were more aware of their own distinct personality as an artist, none has left us a comparable body of criticism. Horace's objective statements on the craft of poetry, like his subjective ones about being a poet, are intimately involved with the contemporary poetic situation. Along with the decline in the validity of poetic formulas, a progress largely negative in spirit, there was emerging a positive poetic couched in more technical terms. Horace wrote in an age agitated by literary disputes, and the different traditions represented had roots running back through Cicero's generation to the Alexandrians, and in some cases even to Aristophanes and Pindar. There was the hoary question of *ars* and *ingenium,* reproduced by the skirmishes of "water drinkers" and "wine drinkers"; there were different views on the kind and the quantity of verse a poet should aim for, and on the audience he should seek. And at the same time that Horace's position on these issues reflects certain historical tendencies it also illuminates the aims and bias of his own work.

The Descent of the Muses

Nearly every poet has confessed to an element other than craftsmanship in his work, whether he term it divine inspiration, genius, felicity, grace, luck, or, as the French critic Bonhours hospitably labeled it in an essay of the same title, "le je ne sais quoi." Did Homer's, Hesiod's, and Pindar's "Muse" have an objective divine reality independent of their own use of her? Or was she merely a projection, a familiar and convenient shorthand for the creative process? How can we be sure when "the Muse" has become "my Muse"? Even to divide objective fact from symbol ignores the lack of conceptual language which then existed. If the "Muse" of the early poets was a metaphor, she was, probably, one only in the sense that language itself is a metaphor for reality. Nice distinctions are virtually impossible; happily they are largely irrelevant here. More to the point is the extent to which such vitality as the Muse possessed was to pale into an abstraction. One might, indeed, characterize her biography as the history of a fading metaphor. Just as individual Roman poets consistently invoked their individual Greek prototypes, so they were willing to depend upon Greek conventions in formulating more general beliefs about poetry. Yet the conventions of any period represent only "what is agreed upon," and hence their value is likely to change with time. From embodying an agreed-upon reality, common poetic motifs came to signify an agreed-upon indulgence toward the past: they became "conventional" in a pejorative sense. Forms are notoriously more resistant to innovation than are ideas, and the statements made by the Augustans differ little from those which poets had made for centuries. The distinctions are primarily those of tone and emphasis, but the chronological change they reveal is profound.

Μῆνιν ἄειδε, θεά: *arma virumque cano.* The opening lines of the *Iliad* and the *Aeneid* define the attitudes not only of two authors but of two epochs. To Homer, embarking upon such a task without first assuring oneself of the Muse's sustaining power would seem overweening.[2] Vergil, however, even in imitating Homer's invocation, relegates it to a secondary position (8 ff.), while beating out a strong personal assertion in his opening words. The contrast is still more striking if, with Servius and Donatus,[3] we accept the following four lines as the beginning of the poem:

> ille ego, qui quondam gracili modulatus avena
> carmen, et egressus silvis vicina coegi
> ut quamvis avido parerent arva colono,
> gratum opus agricolis; at nunc horrentia Martis
> arma virumque cano . . .

I am he who formerly played my song upon a slender reed;
then leaving the forests I compelled the neighboring fields

2. Cf. Hom., *Od.* 1; Hes., *Op.* 1–2; *Th.* 1 ff. The fact that Greek poets tended to think of themselves as the servants, messengers, or interpreters of the Muse (for references, see O. Falter, *Der Dichter und sein Gott* [Würzburg, 1934], 64 ff.; 74 ff.) may explain why they so rarely declare their own immortality, as distinct from that of their subject; see below, 310.

3. Servius, in his preface, and Donatus (163 ff., Brummer) preserve the tradition that Varius and Tucca removed the first four lines of the *Aeneid* after Vergil's death. Cf. Suet., *Vit. Verg.* 65 (Reifferscheid).

to obey the settler, however greedy he might be—a work welcome to farmers; but now of the bristling arms of Mars and of the man I sing . . .

An elaborate self-identification commands the opening position, with the poet invoking his own past before turning to the deity. The lines would seem to have been excised for reasons of taste rather than piety—it was, at least, on aesthetic grounds alone that Horace objected to neglect of the customary Homeric form:

quanto rectius hic, qui nil molitur inepte:
"dic mihi, Musa, virum, captae post tempora Troiae
qui mores hominum multorum vidit et urbes."
[*A. P.* 140–42]

How much better this man begins, who undertakes nothing ineptly: "Tell me Muse, of the man, who after the fall of Troy saw the customs and cities of many peoples." (A translation of the opening lines of the *Odyssey*.)

Even the cautious Varro betrays how mechanical the form had become ("and since, so they say, the gods aid those who call upon them, first I will invoke them"), while Quintilian was soon to praise Homer's invocations as a means of insuring the audience's good will.[4]

The merely decorative status of the Muses appears still more dramatically in the widespread disposition to seek substitutes for them. Cicero (*Tusc.* 5.23.66) had allegorized the Muses into a symbol of the humanistic life—*cum Musis, id est, cum humanitate et cum doctrina*—but it remained for the elegiac poets to reincarnate them in specific human beings. The Homeric or Pindaric ("Be my oracle, Muse, and I will be your interpreter," *Fr.* 150, Schroeder) appeal to the goddess reappears, in drastically altered form, in Tibullus:

usque cano Nemesim, sine qua versus mihi nullus
verba potest iustos aut reperire pedes. [2.5.111–12]

4. Varro, *R. R.* 1.1.4; Quintilian, 10.1.48. In general, see E. R. Curtius, *ZRPH, 59* (1939), 129 ff.

> Unceasingly I sing of Nemesis, without whom no verse of mine can find its words nor its proper meter.

Propertius is even more explicit, declaring his mistress Cynthia to be an elegant sufficiency for inspiration:

> non haec Calliope, non haec mihi cantat Apollo,
> ingenium nobis ipsa puella facit.[5]

> Not Calliope, not Apollo, sings these things to me; my mistress herself inspires my genius.

The Muse has become a lovely lady whose stooping to folly now provides both source and subject for new epics:

> seu nuda erepto mecum luctatur amictu,
> tum vero longas condimus Iliadas. [2.1.13–14]

> Or if, her tunic snatched off, she struggle unclothed with me, then in truth I set down vast Iliads.

Few poets were privileged to find so felicitous a source of inspiration, and more common was the invocation of the ruler. Vergil sought a Zeuslike nod of approval from Octavian,[6] and the accompanying extravaganza (*G.* 1.24 ff.) drew from a later poet a stringent comment. "What think you of the Scorpion drawing his arms in, that Octavius may have room enough? or the despair of Tartarus at missing such a treasure? or the backwardness of Proserpine to follow her mother? Here are together eight such verses as I would give eighty bushels of wheat to eradicate from the poetry of a friend." [7] The enthusiasm of Vergil, writing in the early excitement of the *Pax*

5. Prop., 2.1.3–4; cf. 2.30.37–40; Ov., *Am.* 1.3.19, 2.17.34, 3.12.16; *Tr.* 4.10.59. Martial (8.73) asserts that Catullus, Gallus, Tibullus, and Propertius all drew their inspiration from a mistress, and he promises to write immortal verse himself, given the same conditions.

6. *G.* 1.40; cf. Ps.-Verg., *Cul.* 24–26.

7. W. S. Landor, *Imaginary Conversations of Greek and Roman Authors* (London, 1853), 452.

Augusta, is less suspect than that of later poets, whose increasingly fulsome tributes suggest little more than a lively sense of self-preservation. Lucan, banishing the divine machinery of epic, discovered in Nero a more than adequate substitute:

> sed mihi iam numen; nec, si te pectore vates
> accipio, Cirrhaea velim secreta moventem
> sollicitare deum Bacchumque avertere Nysa:
> tu satis ad vires Romana in carmina dandas. [1.63–66]

> But to me you are even now a divinity; and if I as a bard receive you in my breast, I would not wish to rouse the god who inspires the secret rites of Delphi, nor to draw Bacchus from Nysa—you are enough to give strength in Roman songs.

Seneca illustrates how far poets were prepared to go. His assertion that Nero equalled Apollo not only in voice but in beauty was, if we remember the portrait busts of that emperor, scarcely less extreme than Lucan's fear that the new weight of Nero's divinity might upset the very equipoise of the universe.[8]

"What have I to do with you, O Phoebus and the nine sisters?" Martial's question was that of a whole century. The pragmatic Juvenal found the customary formulas not only irrelevant to, but incompatible with, his own experience: "nor indeed can Poverty, unhappy and short of cash, grasp the thyrsus and sing in the Pierian cave, when night and day the body's needs are unfulfulled: Horace's stomach was well filled when he cried 'evoe!' "[9] Persius' repudiation of the Muses was even more thorough:

> Nec fonte labra prolui caballino
> nec in bicipiti somniasse Parnaso
> memini, ut repente sic poeta prodirem.
> Heliconiadasque pallidamque Pirenen

8. Sen., *Apocol.* 4.1.22–23; Lucan, 1.56 ff. For the tributes of later writers, see F. Knickenberg, *De deorum invocationibus* (Marburg, 1889), 43 ff.

9. Juv., 7.59–62; cf. Mart., 1.76.

illis remitto, quorum imagines lambunt
hederae sequaces. [*Prol.* 1–6]

I never wet my lips in the nag's spring, nor do I remember having any dream on twin-peaked Parnassus, so that I might suddenly burst forth a poet. The Muses and the pallid fountain of Pirene I leave to those whose statues the pliant ivy caresses.

As a student of philosophy Persius may have found divine inspiration theoretically implausible, but as an empirical observer he knew for certain that a more compelling incentive was a hungry stomach: *magister artis ingenique largitor venter* (10). Petrarch abstracted part of the phrase for his Coronation Oration: "I do not deny that in the struggle I have had the advantage of a certain genius given to me on high by the giver of all good things, by God himself—that God who may rightly be called, in the words of Persius, *magister artis ingenique largitor*." [10] His disastrous misconstruction in the interests of traditional piety is perhaps the best comment on the change from Homer's Greece to Imperial Rome.

Where some poets banished the Muse entirely, most were content merely to diminish her status. Catullus' editors have been struck by his promise to tell the Muses of a friend's kindness in order that the Muses might then pass the story on to posterity (68.45). Clearly Catullus violates the normal procedure; dictation should come from above. Startling in terms of the past, Catullus' inversion was mild in terms of what was to follow. The Muses begin appearing as often to forbid poets from certain themes as to encourage them. The device could not be more frankly transparent.[11] Invocations are increasingly egalitarian, not to say domestic. Once the goddesses arrive to remind Propertius of his mistress Cynthia's birthday (3.10.1), while elsewhere he acknowledges their reality—*sunt igitur Musae*—only because his poetry has dissuaded Cynthia from a projected trip (1.8.41).

10. As edited and translated by E. H. Wilkins, *PMLA, 68* (1953), 1246.

11. Verg., *E.* 6.3 ff.; Hor., *Epod.* 14.6; *C.* 1.6.9 ff., 4.15.1 ff.; Prop., 3.3.13 ff., 37 ff.; Ov., *Am.* 2.18.15 ff. The motif goes back to Callimachus (*Aitia* 1.1.21 ff.), and became a favorite method for refusing uncongenial (usually military) themes.

Equally revealing is the gap between Pindar's devout "our mother, the Muse," and Propertius' casual assumption of parentage: *a me nata Musa.*[12] The poet no longer feels himself the creature of some higher power, but assumes that his own creative potency is sufficient. Petronius spoke of the mind's ability "to conceive or give birth," while Ovid proclaimed a proud parthenogenesis:

> Palladis exemplo de me sine matre creata
> carmina sunt; stirps haec progeniesque mea est.[13]

> My songs, following the precedent of Pallas Athene, are born from me alone, without a mother. This offspring and progeny is all mine.

Such intellectual deviationism never became quite respectable, and most poets continued to admit the Muse at least sporadically as a partner to their acts of creation. She might, though, become simply a synonym for "poetry," signifying a crystallization of the poet's own power rather than an appeal to a higher one. An indulgent *mea Musa* is common, and we hear of Catullus' "learned Muse," Vergil's "rustic Muse," and Ovid's "wanton Muse."[14] Correspondingly, the Muse's "holy breath" which Hesiod and Democritus had celebrated,[15] and which lies behind the word "inspiration," came to be thought of as the poet's own. Tibullus preserves the older idea of a breath from above

12. Pi., *N.* 3.1; Prop., 3.1.9–10. Greek poets rarely referred to their poems as offspring, and when they did the emphasis was likely to fall on something other than their own creativity: Pi., *O.* 10.85 ff.; cf. Plato, *Smp.* 209d.

13. Petr., *Sat.* 118; Ov., *Tr.* 3.14.13; cf. *Tr.* 1.7.35, 3.1.66. Vergil implies the analogy in comparing his method of writing with the labor of a mother bear licking her young into shape (Suet., *Vit. Verg.* 59, Reifferscheid; Aulus Gellius, 17.10.3). In Augustan poetry there is also a frequent use of metaphors of natural fertility; see the examples collected by G. Riedner, *Typische Äusserungen der römischen Dichter* (Nürnberg, 1903), 61–62.

14. Cat., 65.2; Verg., *E.* 6.8; Ov., *Rem. Am.* 362.

15. Hes., *Th.* 31; Democr., 18 (Diels). Cf. A. DeLatte, *Les conceptions de l'enthousiasme* (Paris, 1934), 28 ff. Hobbes, in a less sympathetic age, was to upbraid the poet who "loves to be thought to speak by inspiration, like a Bagpipe"; see J. E. Spingarn, *Critical Essays of the Seventeenth Century* (Oxford, 1957), *2,* 59.

(2.1.35), as does Horace in one Ode (*C.* 4.6.29). But the carelessness with which poets handled the belief indicates how rarely they consulted its original meaning.[16] Propertius even termed Callimachus *non inflatus.* The primary idea has become so faint that to be breathed into or "inflated" is now a pejorative (2.34.32).

In separating the sixteenth century's view of the world from that of the seventeenth, Marjorie Nicolson pointed out that where to the first the correspondence of macrocosm and microcosm was a fact, to the second it was a metaphor.[17] The transition is not unique, and the change between Classical Greece and Augustan Rome is eloquent of the fact that one age's convictions harden into another's conceits. Hesiod's initiation by the Muses at the foot of Mount Helicon (*Th.* 22 ff.) was to become an archetype of the poetic experience, but if he felt himself to be relating an actual event his successors saw in it only a symbol to be manipulated for their own purposes. Callimachus suggests the metaphorical character of his own experience by casting his encounter with the Muses into a dream.[18] His imitation of Hesiod is a personal tribute rather than a spiritual reaffirmation. Yet Callimachus at least accepts Hesiod's terms, for the relationship still lies between Muses and poet, with divine assistance at issue. With the Romans, the poet became less of a pilgrim, more of a pioneer. Of Ennius' famous visit to the haunts of the Muses we know little for certain, but his attitude betrays a suggestive shift in emphasis: *cum neque Musarum scopulos . . . / . . . nec dicti studiosus quisquam erat ante hunc. / Nos ausi reserare . . .* (215–17, Vahlen [2]). Lucretius confirms the emphasis on primacy:

16. The breath often becomes thought of as the poet's own: Verg., *E.* 4.54; Hor., *S.* 1.4.46; *C.* 4.3.24; *Ep.* 2.1.166. DeLatte, *Les conceptions,* 31, cites these passages from Horace as though they still referred to a divine πνεῦμα, thus ignoring the inversion that has taken place. In Longinus (8.4) emotion sometimes takes the place of a divinity.

17. *The Breaking of the Circle* (Evanston, 1950).

18. *Anth. Pal.* 7.42; cf. Prop., 2.34.32, and H. E. Butler and E. A. Barber, *The Elegies of Propertius* (Oxford, 1933), xl ff. Ennius also seems to have cast his meeting with the Muses and/or Homer into a dream; see J. H. Waszink, *Mn,* 4th Series, *3* (1950), 221 ff. On Hesiod's experience see K. Latte, *Antike und Abendland, 2* (1946), 152 ff.

Ennius ut noster cecinit qui primus amoeno
detulit ex Helicone perenni fronde coronam. [1.117–18]

As our Ennius sang, who first bore down from fair Helicon
a wreath of immortal leaves.

The derivative character of Latin literature tended to make it self-conscious, and poets were quick to announce themselves the first in attempting specific genres. Lucretius, Vergil, and Propertius all exploited the trip to Helicon, or sometimes Parnassus, as a convenience in asserting priority:

avia Pieridum peragro loca nullius ante
trita solo. [Lucr., 1.926–27]

I wander through the wildernesses of Pieria, places where
no one before has set his foot.

primus ego in patriam mecum modo vita supersit
Aonio rediens deducam vertice Musas;
primus Idumaeas referam tibi, Mantua, palmas.
[Verg., *G.* 3.10–12]

I shall be the first, if my life but last, to return to my own
country bringing down with me the Muses from the Aonian
peak; I shall be the first to bring back the Idumaean palms
to you, Mantua.

sed me Parnasi deserta per ardua dulcis
raptat amor; iuvat ire iugis qua nulla priorum
Castaliam molli devertitur orbita clivo.
[Verg., *G.* 3.291–93]

But sweet desire sweeps me through the deserted heights of
Parnassus; I love to go upon ridges where there is no track
of anyone before me turning down over a gentle slope towards Castalia.

sed quod pace legas, opus hoc de monte Sororum
detulit intacta pagina nostra via. [Prop., 3.1.17–18]

But, for something to read in time of peace, our page has brought down this work from the Muses' mountain by a virgin path.

The interest displayed is largely topographical. The holy mountain is no longer a place of inspiration, but a symbolic locale on which to stake out a claim previously unexplored. Poets think no longer in terms of the divine, but in terms of their relations with their compeers as founders of literary genres. The various parts of Helicon have come to resemble some antique Everest, metaphorically scaled not for what is to be found there, but simply because no one else had done so previously.

Associated with the trip to the Muses' mountain was a draught from the holy spring to be found there. The connection of poetry and water is ancient and complex, and there is some evidence for believing that the Muses may once have been water nymphs.[19] Hesiod was reputed to have found inspiration in the pure waters of Hippocrene (*καθαραὶ λιβάδες, ἔνθεον ὕδωρ*).[20] But like the visit to the holy mountain, the poet's spring soon acquired a purely secular reference:

avia Pieridum peragro loca nullius ante
trita solo. iuvat integros accedere fontis
atque haurire, iuvatque novos decerpere flores

19. See Pauly-Wissowa, *Real-Encyclopädie, s. v. Musai;* O. Kern, *Die Religion der Griechen* (Berlin, 1926), *1,* 208. Hesiod (*Th.* 3 ff.) imagines the Muses dancing near and bathing in various springs.

20. *Anth. Pal.* 7.55, 9.64, 11.24; Persius, *Prol.* 1 (though this may refer rather, or as well, to Ennius). Cf. W. Kroll, *Studien zum Verständnis der römischen Literatur* (Stuttgart, 1924), 28–29; M. Ninck, *Die Bedeutung des Wassers im Kult und Leben, Philologus Suppl., 14* (Leipzig, 1921), 90 ff. If the Muses were indeed originally water nymphs, the belief that inspiration came with a drink from certain springs might be explained as a variation on the primitive notion that one could absorb the powers of other creatures by eating them; see G. Murray, *Five Stages of Greek Religion* (London, 1935), 21 ff.

> insignemque meo capiti petere inde coronam
> unde prius nulli velarint tempora musae.
> [Lucr., 1.926–30]

> I wander through the wildernesses of Pieria, places where no one before has set his foot. I love to draw near the untouched fountains and drink from them, I love to pluck fresh flowers and weave a glorious garland for my head from a place whence the Muses have crowned no man's temples before.

Integros translates, but does not reproduce the meaning of καθαρός. The latter means divine purity, the former signifies only the poet's primacy in his chosen genre. The expeditions of Roman poets produce a cumulative image not unlike that of a picnic on Parnassus. References in Vergil (*sanctos fontis*), Horace (*fontibus integris*), and Propertius (*puro de fonte*) all neglect the original meaning of the image they exploit.[21] The adjectives, like those commonly used of the holy mountain—*deserta, vacuum, loca nullius ante trita solo, avia, intacta*—proclaim not so much the poet's necessary isolation in nature as his literary uniqueness. For those poets who could not claim priority, the holy spring could serve as a means to indicate their literary genealogies, and we hear of Pindaric draughts (Hor., *Ep.* 1.3.10) and Homeric streams (Ov., *Am.* 3.9.25). As early as the third century writers began specializing in springs much as they were to parcel out plots on Parnassus or Helicon. Moschus (3.77) suggested that the heady water of Hippocrene should be allowed to epic poets alone, leaving Arethusa to supply the humbler needs of the writer of pastorals. From the various springs and streams there grew up an elaborate if often arbitrary topography. Vergil seems to connect the streams of Permessus with erotic verse (*E.* 6.64 ff.), and in these terms Propertius drew a contrast between Hesiodic verse and elegy:

> nondum etiam Ascraeos norunt mea carmina fontes,
> sed modo Permessi flumine lavit Amor. [2.10.25–26]

21. Verg., *G.* 2.175; Hor., *C.* 1.26.6; Prop., 3.1.3.

> Not yet do my songs know the springs of Hesiod, but Love has bathed them only in the waters of Permessus.

He incorporated a similar opposition into a graceful *recusatio.* His patron Maecenas had frequently urged grander themes upon him, and finally Propertius made his way to the fountain of epic:

> parvaque tam magnis admoram fontibus ora,
> unde pater sitiens Ennius ante bibit. [3.3.5–6]

> And I brought my modest lips to the great fountains from which father Ennius, thirsting, had drunk before.

But if Pegasus could be led to water, not even Maecenas could make him drink. Propertius withdrew, declaring the waters of erotic poetry more to his taste:

> talia Calliope, lymphisque a fonte petitis
> ora Philitea nostra rigavit aqua. [3.3.51–52]

> Such things Calliope said, and then with water drawn from the fountain she annointed my lips with the drink known to Philetas.

The general confusion regarding the different fountains gives a certain urgency to Propertius' question: "Tell me"—he is addressing the shades of Callimachus and Philetas—"in what cave did you weave your song? With what foot did you enter? Or what water did you drink?" (3.1.5–6) [22]

As the Muses became increasingly fanciful, and the appurtenances of inspiration increasingly secular, the analogies used for the poet's calling suffered a corresponding metamorphosis. Greeks of the sixth and fifth centuries had found cogent an analogy between the poet

22. For a discussion of the vexed problem of assigning different springs and streams to different types of poetry, see Butler and Barber, *Elegies of Propertius,* xli–xlii, 209; Z. Stewart, *HSCP, 64* (1959), 193; G. Luck, *The Latin Love-Elegy* (London, 1959), 131 ff.

and the prophet, both being intermediaries between gods and men.[23] The Romans' use of *vates* for "poet" might be thought to signal the same exalted conception. The word does not, however, occur in that sense before Horace and Vergil, where it probably represents to a great extent the wishes of Augustus.[24] If poets were to be one vehicle for his program of reform, the term might well recommend itself as possessing an antique dignity superior to that of the customary *poeta* (cf. Tac., *Dial.* 9.3). Yet a society sophisticated enough to enjoy Ovid's *expedit esse deos, et, ut expedit, esse putemus* (*A. A.* 1.637) was not likely to be impressed by so pious a regression. Ovid, who invokes the name of *vates* or *sacerdos* repeatedly, typifies the response of the elegists:

> vatibus Aoniis faciles estote, puellae,
> numen inest illis; Pieridesque favent.
> est deus in nobis; et sunt commercia coeli:
> sedibus aetheriis spiritus ille venit. [*A. A.* 3.547–50]

> Be kind, maidens, to Aonian bards; there is a divine power in them, and the Muses favor them. There is a god in us, and we have dealings with the heavens. Our inspiration comes from the ethereal seats above.

Commercia coeli aptly describes the elegists' view of their privileges. Their much advertised inspiration became a commodity to be offered in competition for mistresses.[25] In these terms Ovid elsewhere ex-

23. The association is common in the early stages of poetry, and several languages had a common name for both professions; see H. M. and N. K. Chadwick, *The Growth of Literature* (Cambridge, Eng., 1932), *1,* 617 ff., 637–38. Cf. Bacchylides, 8.3; Pi., *Pae.* 6.1–6; *Fr.* 104c, 5–6; 150 (Schroeder); E. Fascher, *Prophetes* (Giessen, 1927), 11 ff. Plato used the comparison between poet and prophet to prove that both were irrational: *Phdr.* 244c ff.; *Ap.* 22c; *Men.* 99d; *Ion* 534c.

24. M. Runes, *Festschrift für Paul Kretschmer* (Wien, 1926), 202 ff. See also A. Sperduti, *TAPA, 81* (1950), 219–20, H. Dahlmann, *Philologus, 97* (1948), 337 ff.

25. Ov., *Am.* 3.8.23 ff.; Tib., 2.4.15 ff. For references to the elegists' contrast between the poet's riches and those of his habitual rival, the *dives amator,* see K. F. Smith, *The Elegies of Tibullus* (New York, 1913), *ad* 1.4.61.

pressed his surprise that any girl's door should be closed to him (*Am.* 3.8.23 ff.), and even the less obstreperous Tibullus adopted the same attitude:

> at tu, nam divum servat tutela poetas,
> praemoneo, vati parce, puella, sacro. [2.5.113–14]

> But, maiden, I warn you, spare the sacred bard, for the protection of the gods gaurds them.

In turning the concept of the *vates* to their own uses the elegists did not so much deprecate as insult its original value:

> non ego, Phoebe, datas a te mihi mentiar artes:
> nec nos aëriae voce monemur avis:
> nec mihi sunt visae Clio Cliusque sorores,
> servanti pecudes vallibus, Ascra, tuis.
> usus opus movet hoc: vati parete perito;
> vera canam: coeptis, mater Amoris, ades!
> [*A. A.* 1.25–30]

> I shall not, Phoebus Apollo, lyingly assert that my arts were given by you. I have been given no advice by the voice of birds in the sky; Clio and her sisters never appeared to me while I was guarding sheep in your valleys, Ascra. Experience inspires this work; pay attention to an experienced bard. I shall sing the truth. Mother of Cupid, aid what I have begun!

The image of a bard which Ovid substitutes is but a parody of the one he rejects. Discernible beneath the lineaments of the *peritus vates*—which here signifies no more than one experienced in love—are the traditional features of the poet endowed with a more than mortal wisdom. Ovid invokes Venus, the "mother of Cupid," to aid him with his compendium of courtship much as Homer had implored the Muse's support during the catalogue of ships. Repudiating any traditional form of inspiration, Ovid nevertheless asserts an almost oracular infallibility: *vera canam.* The responsibility felt by Hesiod when embarking upon the cosmology of the gods (*Th.* 26 ff.) is now directed toward a different end, that of revealing and ordering the earthly world of amatory experience.

Horace's Use of Traditional Formulas

Where the elegists put on the robes of a *vates* to protect an amatory undress, Horace saved them for more sober ends. His language, on occasion formal to the point of the ritualistic, has tempted readers to think of his role in quasi-religious terms. A. Y. Campbell, the most prominent spokesman for that view, thinks that Horace "feels his function as Poet to be of a sacerdotal kind, to be, though not identical with, yet strictly analogous to, that of the Priest." [26] His appraisal is provocative rather than persuasive. Horace's claim to be *Musarum sacerdos* has primarily the local purpose of isolating the so-called "Roman Odes" (*C.* 3.1–6) from the body of his work:

> Odi profanum volgus et arceo.
> favete linguis: carmina non prius
> audita Musarum sacerdos
> virginibus puerisque canto. [*C.* 3.1.1–4]

> I hate the profane crowd and I keep it at a distance. Be reverent in your speech—as priest of the Muses I sing to maidens and youths songs never heard before.

Horace's seemingly religious boast of *carmina non prius audita* refers not to any arcane doctrines but only to his own priority in using Latin lyric for national songs.[27] Similarly, his priestly vestments are a metaphorical warning of the public role he temporarily adopts, one which the charming first sentence of *C.* 3.7 stamps as finished: *Quid fles, Asterie?* [28] Vergil had risen to a comparable solemnity to dis-

26. *Horace, A New Interpretation* (London, 1924), 80; cf. 68.

27. Cf. Prop., 3.1.1 ff., where Propertius uses similar symbolic language (it seems, in fact, an imitation of Hor., *C.* 3.1.1 ff.) to represent the fact that he is the first poet to use elegiac verse for national themes.

28. See below, 111.

tinguish the fourth Eclogue from its fellows—*Sicelides Musae, paulo maiora canamus*—and Propertius was to exploit the language of ritual to mark off the nationalism of one elegy (4.6). But none of the three poets intended his lines to be an index to the whole of his work.

Horace's fullest statement of his devotion to the Muses lies in the proem of the fourth Roman Ode. He gives a virtual catalogue of traditional motifs, professing the *amabilis insania* of inspiration and recalling his miraculous protecton both in childhood and throughout his life. Yet these claims can be explained by the fact that in that Ode he wished to be recognized as the spokesman of the *almae Musae* for a specific purpose.[29] Even if we grant that Horace's intense commitment here to a special vision of poetic and political harmony makes meaningful his role as a Pindaric bard, it must also be conceded that the poem is in a class by itself. When he invokes the traditional gods of poetry elsewhere it tends to be in terms which seem little more than honorific:

> spiritum Phoebus mihi, Phoebus artem
> carminis nomenque dedit poetae. [*C.* 4.6.29–30]

> Apollo gave me inspiration, Apollo gave me the art of song
> and the name of poet.

It is hard to agree with the judgment that "beyond doubt Horace was conscious that the god spoke from his lips." [30] Neither the tone nor the context of the lines suggests that piety was any more important a motive than was diplomacy. The Ode is in effect the public announcement of Horace's appointment to compose the *Carmen Saeculare,* destined to honor particularly Apollo and his sister Diana.[31] The *nomen poetae* would seem more at issue than the *ars carminis,* for the poem signals Horace's achievement of what was virtually the poet laureateship. Here, for the only time in the Odes,

29. See below, 195, 207–08.
30. F. Altheim, *A History of Roman Religion* (London, 1938), 383.
31. The only other Ode in which Horace invokes Apollo at length (*C.* 1.31) was written for an equally formal occasion; see below; 332–33.

Horace mentions himself by name: *vatis Horati* (44). The term *vates* hovers between the badge of a quasi-divine function and that of a political appointment. It is not hard to suspect that here, as in the *Carmen Saeculare* itself, Apollo has as strong affiliations with the Augustan house as with the Olympic Pantheon.[32]

The manner in which Horace deals with more general beliefs about the poet is hardly more persuasive. At the same time that he terms poets divine (*A. P.* 400) he cheerfully rationalizes away the beliefs that made them so. Though he designates Orpheus, son of Calliope, as *sacer interpres deorum* (*A. P.* 391), he euhemeristically explains away (*dictus ab hoc,* 393) Orpheus' magical power of taming wild beasts as evidence merely that he was a primitive peacemaker. In his hymnic Defense of Poetry (*Ep.* 2.1.119 ff.), convincing evidence for Campbell of Horace's sacerdotal convictions, Horace seems to have assembled all the miscellaneous virtues ever attributed to a poet without scanning them very carefully. His opening assertion, that no poet ever stoops to cheat his ward, is hardly overpowering, while the claim that the poet "fashions the tender lisping lips of the child, and steers the ear from indecent words," carries little conviction coming from the author of the Epodes. And how many Augustans would be impressed by his boast that the poet averts disease and brings good crops?

Horace's piety did not inhibit references to *Musa pervicax* or *Musa procax,* nor deter him from his blithe *quo, Musa, tendis?* [33] His ceremonial addresses seem little more than a ceremony, a convenient way to define his role for the public. In the first Ode the gestures toward Polyhymnia and Euterpe are perfunctory. Any private significance he feels in his calling seems reserved for the allusion to Bacchus, though even that remains formal: [34]

> me doctarum hederae praemia frontium
> dis miscent superis, me gelidum nemus
> Nympharumque leves cum Satyris chori
> secernunt populo, si neque tibias

32. On the identification of Apollo and Augustus, see below, 187, 200.
33. *C.* 2.1.37 ff., 3.3.69 ff.
34. See below, 331, 337 ff., 341 ff.

Euterpe cohibet nec Polyhymnia
Lesboum refugit tendere barbiton.
quodsi me lyricis vatibus inseres,
sublimi feriam sidera vertice. [*C.* 1.1.29–36]

The ivy, reward of learned brows, raises me to the gods above. The cool grove and the light bands of Nymphs and Satyrs separate me from the people, if only Euterpe does not withhold the flute nor Polyhymnia refuse to tune the Lesbian lyre. But if you place me among the lyric bards, then will I strike the stars with my uplifted head.

In the last two lines, addressed to Maecenas, the heavenly image expresses only a worldly ambition. The same is true of the Ode to Melpomene, Horace's longest invocation of the Muse outside the fourth Roman Ode:

Romae, principis urbium,
dignatur suboles inter amabilis
vatum ponere me choros,
et iam dente minus mordeor invido.

o testudinis aureae
dulcem quae strepitum, Pieri, temperas,
o mutis quoque piscibus
donatura cycni, si libeat, sonum,

totum muneris hoc tui est,
quod monstror digito praetereuntium
Romanae fidicen lyrae;
quod spiro et placeo, si placeo, tuum est.
[*C.* 4.3.13–24]

The youth of Rome, first among cities, deems me worthy to be placed among the lovely chorus of bards, and already now I am bitten less by the tooth of envy. O Pierian Muse, you who temper the sweet sound of the golden lyre, you who may give, if you please, the voice of swans even to

> mute fish, it is by your gift alone that I am pointed out by the finger of passers-by as minstrel of the Roman lyre; that I breathe songs and please, if please I do, is all your gift.

The poem reads like an answer to *C.* 1.1. Not only Maecenas but the youth of all Rome has now ranked Horace among the canonical lyric bards (*vatum choros*). The apparently devotional language is in reality profoundly secular; to be "pointed out by the finger of passers-by" is his definition of his priestlike state. Cynically we might say that Melpomene, like Euterpe and Polyhymnia in *C.* 1.1, simply symbolizes Horace's worldly success. Yet the feeling behind the lines suggests something more private, and perhaps we should say that Melpomene is a metaphor of the singularity Horace felt. The lines then become an apostrophe to his own peculiar genius. His overwrought humility, which makes his own ability no more important than that of a mute fish, acts as a tactful framework for his pride. Certainly the denial of responsibility for his work is alien to his more objective estimates, and to the whole spirit of the *Ars Poetica*. Horace's sense of independent achievement is perhaps stronger than that of any poet in antiquity. He stands as the prototype of the self-made man: "as much as you take from my birth you must add to my talents" (*Ep.* 1.20.22). What his birth was is well known, but what his talents meant to him remains more obscure. By invoking the Muse of tradition and proclaiming himself her *vates,* Horace succeeded in establishing his role only in public terms. Although the conventional language suggests the presence of special qualities, it fails to define or communicate them. Its usefulness seems to have been vitiated for him by the constant abuse it had received at the hands of his contemporaries, particularly the elegists. To convey his sense of what it meant to be a poet he was to find more private symbols, and more expressive figures.[35]

Ars and Ingenium

The years between Pindar and Horace have seen poetry's conventions change as new ideas forced themselves upon static forms. The

35. See below, 328 ff.

Muses have become a literary curiosity, the appurtenances of inspiration operate only as a sophisticated shorthand, and the sacred bard appears most frequently now as a political or an amatory figure. Each poet's experience qualifies and to some extent deprecates these generalities, and certainly the changes reflect a difference not in the way poets wrote but in the way they publicly spoke of their writing. That any poet was more painstaking than Pindar is dubious, but it is hard to imagine Pindar speaking, as Horace did, of scratching his head and biting his nails.[36] Though Pindar knew that "the ways of art are steep" (*O.* 9.107), he knew too that the divinity which had made them so would aid him in surmounting them, and he could imperially define the poet as "one knowing much by nature" (*O.* 2.86). Nor does the historical change represent simply a growth in the poet's self-consciousness; for, again, what poet is more proudly prominent in his writings than Pindar? The development is rather one aspect of a broader movement, an assertion not so much of the individual as of individual responsibility. Bruno Snell [37] has charted the movement from the grand fatality of Homer to the self-willed individuals of Euripides, from the pious awe of Hesiod to the introspective concern of Callimachus, and the poet's gradual emancipation from the Muses confirms the pattern. The Olympic Pantheon had itself suffered a disheartening decline. In the fifth century Protagoras

36. Hor., *S.* 1.10.71. The idea of the poet as a craftsman is of course common in early Greek literature, but this skill is itself conceived of as attributable to a divine agency; see Hom., *Od.* 8.43–45, 479–81, 488; Solon, 1.49 ff., Diehl, and compare the attitude toward other such arts as carpentry, metalworking, or weaving: Hom., *Il.* 5.59–61, 15.411–12; *Od.* 6.232–34, 7.108–11, 8.493; *Hom. Hymn* 5.12–13; Pi., *O.* 7.50–51. This skill is conceived of as quite different from that learned only from other mortals; hence Pindar's scorn: *O.* 2.86–88, 9.100–104; cf. Hom., *Od.* 22.347–48. Thus the idea of poetry as something woven (Pi., *O.* 6.86; *N.* 2.2, 4.44) emphasizes less the labor that goes into the weaving than the beauty of the finished product; contrast the typical Augustan use of the same metaphor, below, 38, 46.

The idea that the poet received special help from the gods should be distinguished from the idea that the poet wrote in a kind of manic ecstasy, which seems to be no older than the late fifth century; see E. R. Dodds, *The Greeks and the Irrational* (Berkeley, 1956), 82. Plato, probably elaborating upon Democritus, is largely responsible for establishing this idea. By showing that poets wrote irrationally, he hoped to diminish their authority as compared to the rational precepts of philosophy.

37. *The Discovery of the Mind* (Oxford, 1953), especially chap. 3.

admitted that he did not know if the gods existed, and later writers treated them even more cavalierly. The Stoics reduced them to Mind, the Cynics neglected them to glorify animal nature, and the Epicureans banished them entire to an immensity of indifference. Man had indeed become the measure of all things. By the Alexandrian age the hymn was a secular form, and in Rome writers as different as Cicero and Ovid could agree that the gods were a political rather than a religious necessity.[38] Such dubious divinity as remained was more often thought of as achieved than as derived. Hesiod's conviction that kings were divinely inspired had by the third century yielded to the theory of Euhemerus that the divinities themselves were only remarkable men, posthumously apotheosized.

The body of poetic theory remained fluid enough to reflect these changes in the heavens, and as the gods retired more attention was paid to qualities inherent in the poet. Pindar had already begun to speak of the poet's special "nature" or φύσις. But, being committed to a belief in divine inspiration, he continued to objectify φύσις by the "godlike" bird of Zeus.[39] Democritus united both qualities in his praise of Homer as possessing a "god-inspired nature" (21, Diels), while Plato discovered poets to compose "by a certain nature and because they are inspired" (*Ap.* 22c). Aristotle was apparently the first to dispense altogether with the divine, holding that poets composed either through madness or "a happy gift of nature." [40] In quoting Democritus on "god-inspired nature" Horace (*A. P.* 295) significantly forgets, or omits, the adjective, for if "divine nature" never came to seem an oxymoron it was by the Augustan age felt to be an anachronism. Writers preferred to describe themselves in terms of such words as *ingenium* or *natura* rather than ἐνθουσιασμός or ἔνθεος; talent, they assumed, was innate, not inspired. (The transfer in language and concept corresponds roughly to that between Spenser's

38. Cic., *Div.* 2.12.28; Ov., *A. A.* 1.637; cf. Cic., *Div.* 2.24.51; *N. D.* 1.26.71. The idea can be traced back through Polybius (6.56.7) to Critias; see H. J. Rose, *Ancient Greek Religion* (London, 1946), 99.

39. Pi., *O.* 2.86 ff.; cf. *O.* 9.100 ff.; *N.* 3.40 ff.

40. Arist., *Po.* 1455a, 35–36 (Butcher's translation). Cf. Longin., 34.4. Epicharmus (40, Diels) contrasted only φύσις, not divine inspiration, with learning. Elsewhere Aristotle comes close to making inspiration seem little more than a pathological state: *Prob.* 953a; cf. Cic., *Tusc.* 1.33.80.

statement that poetry is "poured into the witte by a certain enthousiasmos and celestial inspiration" and the Romantic notion of Wordsworth that poetry is "the spontaneous overflow of powerful feelings.") By Cicero's time adjectives like *divinus* had to be hedged with careful qualifiers. Even in the defense of Archias, where he is willing to exploit any traditional argument for the poet's glory, Cicero nevertheless guards himself with an *aliquis, quasi,* or *quidam.*[41] And when an Augustan professed a belief in divine inspiration he was careful to seek examples almost exclusively from the remote past,[42] just as, in a later Augustan age, Dryden was to look back to the "giant race before the flood."

With poets increasingly free to consider themselves as possessing a special ability rather than as possessed by it, certain problems arose which had been previously irrelevant. It became legitimate to inquire whether the poet's innate ability (*natura* or *ingenium*) or the skill he acquired by training (τέχνη or *ars*) was the more important, a question which would have seemed impertinent as long as a divine force demanded recognition. Pindar is usually called the first to oppose nature and art, yet Pindar does not so much pose a question as answer one. Φύσις meant to him "divinely inspired nature," and with that assumption he could not but exalt god-given ability over that which was man-learned.[43] Not until poets relinquished their franchise upon the divine could the debate be staged in such a way as to allow alternate conclusions. It was probably orators and prose writers who first made explicit the demand for mundane qualities like industry and training. Oratory had never boasted so intimate an association with the gods as had poetry, for its great period of development came after the sense of a divine immanence was considerably impaired. Although Pericles implored the aid of the goddess Persuasion before each speech, fourth-century Sophists were readier to advertise their own resources. Isocrates let it be known that he had spent ten years laboring on his *Panegyric,* while the many reworkings of the opening of

41. Cic., *Arch.* 8.18; cf. *N. D.* 2.66.167; *Tusc.* 1.26.64; *De Or.* 2.47.194.

42. See J. Tate, *CQ, 22* (1928), 72, n. 2. Comparing Augustan writers with primitive examples of inspired poets was a popular literary exercise; see J. F. D'Alton, *Roman Literary Theory and Criticism* (London, 1931), chap. 5.

43. See above, n. 39.

Plato's *Republic* were to become equally famous. "Both alike," approved Dionysius of Halicarnassus, "produced discourses which suggested not writing but carving and chasing" (*Comp.* 25). Demosthenes, according to Plutarch,[44] was scorned for his unwillingness to speak when unprepared; yet criticism did not remain so unreconstructed. A certain Simylus, probably in the fourth or third century, reminded his contemporaries of the inadequacy of a poetic nature if unaccompanied by art, practice, and the supervision of a discerning critic.[45]

By the Alexandrian age poets too were quick to take a formal stand in terms that were practical rather than devotional. Poetry, they reminded their readers, did not spring full born from the mind to the page, but emerged only after prolonged labor pangs. In the third century Philetas defined the poet as one "skilled in the arrangement of words and toiling much." Callimachus hailed his contemporary Aratus for his night-long vigils in polishing his work, and Callimachus himself was admired for his "chiselled" productions. Erinna's *Distaff,* three hundred lines of exquisite verse, was a characteristic product of the period, and the numerous tributes from the writers of the *Greek Anthology* evidence the favor that such writing found.[46]

To the poet of fifth-century Greece the city-state or πόλις offered an imaginative as well as a physical center. His poetry, like the sculpture on the Parthenon, made explicit its glory. The Alexandrians, living by and large in an adopted city, felt no such allegiance. The Muses had emigrated from Helicon to a new home in the great library, the Museum, which now became the quickening source upon which poets drew. All were official members, maintaining themselves by the

44. Plu., *Dem.* 8.849d; cf. D.H., *Comp.* 25.

45. P. Shorey has demonstrated that Simylus' statement was no more than "a résumé of current truisms"; see *TAPA, 40* (1910), 185 ff. The fragment of Simylus is from Stobaeus, *Floril.* 18.4 (Wachsmuth and Hense, *4,* 407). For the date, see J. W. H. Atkins, *Literary Criticism in Antiquity* (London, 1952), *1,* 179–80.

46. Philetas: Stobaeus, *Floril.* 2.4.5 (Wachsmuth and Hense, *2,* 27); Callimachus on Aratus: *Epigr.* 27.3 (Pfeiffer); cf. Ps.-Verg., *Cir.* 46; Ov., *Tr.* 2.11; *A. A.* 3.412; Sonnenburg, *RhM, 66* (1911), 477 ff.; praise of Callimachus: *Anth. Pal.* 9.545; cf. Prop., 3.1.8; praise of Erinna: *Anth. Pal.* 7.11, 7.12, 7.13, 9.26, 9.190. For a more general discussion, see A. Couat, *Alexandrian Poetry* (London, 1931), 517 ff.

patronage of the Ptolemies, and the "priest of the Muses" was now identified with the chief librarian—the offices were formally joined. Writers cultivated a learned coterie, for under a dictatorship their work was necessarily divorced from public affairs. Poetry became increasingly esoteric. Lycophron was christened Σκοτεινός, "the Obscure," Philetas compiled a lexicon of unusual poetic words, and Euphorion was reproached as *nimis obscurus*.[47] The isolation from a great national tradition, the unavailability of any real political issues, and the learned, cosmopolitan audience for which Alexandrians wrote forced their work into new molds. Poets retreated to obscure corners of the mythological world, indulged an introspective curiosity in psychology, or fled to a fabulous pastoral existence, often populated by the masks of urban literati. No longer the expression of a national consciousness, poetry had become simply a reflection of the poet's ingenuity. He wrote not as the educator of his people but as the pupil of his art, and his verse, from being a means to express an allegiance, now became its object.

The Alexandrian age is often stigmatized as the original *l'art pour l'art* school of poetry, and the Roman reception of it was not dissimilar to the English welcome of its nineteenth-century French descendant. It came to Rome, most specifically, with Parthenius in 73 B.C., whereupon its tenets were vociferously adopted by the so-called νεώτεροι or "new poets."[48] The movement has suffered from a bad press. Little of the poetry remains, and we have become used to seeing the school through Cicero's skeptical eyes. Cicero is hardly the glass we should choose to tell learning from pedantry, subtlety from obscurity, or cleverness from preciosity. He once confessed, in whatever context, that if life were twice as long it would still be too

47. Suidas, *Lex.*, *s. v.* Λυκόφρων; Cic., *Div.* 2.64.133. Cf. the epigrams attacking Callimachus and his followers for their obscurity: *Anth. Pal.* 11.20, 11.321, 11.322. Cf. F. Susemihl, *Geschichte der griechischen Literatur in der Alexandrinerzeit* (Leipzig, 1891), *1*, 394 ff.

48. The phrase is Cicero's: *Att.* 7.2.1; *Or.* 48.161. Usually recognized as belonging to the school are such writers as Catullus, F. Bibaculus, Cinna, Q. Cornificius, Calvus, Cornelius Gallus, P. Terentius Varro, and some of the poems of the *Vergilian Appendix.* See A. Gandiglio, *Cantores Euphorionis* (Bologna, 1904); E. A. Havelock, *The Lyric Genius of Catullus* (Oxford, 1939), 161 ff.

short to read lyric poetry (Sen., *Ep.* 49.5); and it was Cicero, too, who felt that the blunt Lucilius approached the limits of sophistication (*De Or.* 1.16.72). Yet, in all fairness, the skill of the neoterics may have been not only consciously invoked but self-consciously paraded. A commentator boasted that Cinna's nine-year labor, the *Zmyrna,* of which only three neat but innocuous verses remain, could not be read without notes.[49] Cinna's commentator had, of course, a vested interest, but his assertion seems plausible enough in light of the neoterics' determination for learning. Their ideal was that of the *doctus poeta,* one which was to captivate the elegiac poets in Horace's lifetime.[50] The Muses themselves were sent to school and graduated as *doctae,* and even Catullus confessed that his passion must sometimes wait upon a library.[51]

Classical theorists have always been ready to assign a corresponding virtue to every vice, and with all its much publicized faults Alexandrianism did give a new elegance to the poet's labor. Nor was it long before the respect for *ars* became so general as to evade the limits of any particular school. The last word of the anonymous treatise *ad Herennium,* probably from the middle of the first century before Christ, is *exercitationes.* Quintilian austerely reminded future orators that affection for a first draft was as suspect as that for a newborn child (10.4.2); but by then the idea of labor had become so glamorous that he felt it equally important to warn against the excesses of perfectionism (10.4.4). By asserting that technical mastery was no less important than genius, poets threw down a challenge which critics were quick to take up. Less self-conscious than the poets, they bear more detached witness to the changes that were taking place in literary theory. The Platonic or Aristotelian concentration upon the source, function, or psychology of poetry yielded to a preoccupation, even if couched largely in mechanical terms, with its architecture and verbal effects. The categorizing of different styles still played a major part, but occasionally critics found time to talk

49. Suet., *Gram.* 18; cf. Mart., 10.21.

50. For references, see W. Kroll, *Studien,* 37.

51. *Doctae Musae:* Cat., 65.2; Ps.-Verg., *Cat.* 9.2; Ov., *A. A.* 2.425, 3.411–12; *Tr.* 2.13; Stat., *S.* 1.2.259. For the dependence on a library, see Cat., 68.33; Ov., *Tr.* 3.14.37; Petr., *Sat.* 5, 118; cf. Hor., *A. P.* 268–69.

about the techniques of verse in more specific ways. Writers like Dionysius of Halicarnassus, a contemporary of Horace, and Demetrius, probably somewhat later in date, devoted themselves to exploring the virtuoso techniques underlying poetry's grand harmonies. Dionysius was so bold as to affirm that Homer, that prodigy of nature, sometimes displayed more art than genius, as in his onomatopoetic description of Sisyphus (*Comp.* 20). Sappho's Hymn to Aphrodite owes its preservation to the same critic, who subjected it to a careful technical analysis (*Comp.* 23). The very fact that a poem was quoted as a whole marks a significant advance over what had seemed the previous alternatives, philosophical speculations or the peeping and botanizing of grammarians on antique graves. Even Longinus, more often remembered for his title than his precepts, insisted that sublimity was a product not of genius alone.[52] If poetry was nothing but a divine gift, what need to write a hortatory treatise upon it?

Although the first century saw the champions of *ars* securely entrenched, it witnessed as well a reviving admiration for supposed children of nature such as Ennius. The situation was not unlike that in the eighteenth century, when the "coldly correct" lays of contemporaries were invidiously distinguished from the work of those such as Homer and Shakespeare, "prodigies of mankind, who, by the mere strength of natural parts, and without any assistance of art or learning, have produced works that were the delight of their own times, and the wonder of posterity." [53] Wiser critics since at least the time of Simylus had insisted that nature and art were affiliated, not opposed, and a judicious blend of the two was recommended by Neoptolemus, Horace, Longinus, Quintilian, and Plutarch.[54] Yet the very frequency with which the interdependence of the two had to be asserted suggests how persistently popular canons must have opposed them. Cicero, in his famous judgment on Lucretius, unconsciously illustrates the hold which the antithesis exercised upon the

52. See especially Longin., chap. 2 passim, and 22.1.

53. Addison, *Spectator Papers,* 160. "Untaught" was a favorite word for Shakespeare in Dryden's prefaces to his plays; cf. Milton's "sweetest Shakespeare, fancy's child, warble his native woodnotes wild" (*l'Allegro*).

54. Neoptolemus, in *Philodemus über die Gedichte, Buch V,* ed. Jensen (Berlin, 1923), 21, 29; cf. 99–101, 122; Hor., *A. P.* 408 ff.; Longin., 22.1, 36.4; Quint., proem 27; Plu., *Moralia* 2a ff.; cf. Tac., *Dial.* 33.

imagination of his generation. *Lucretii poemata ut scribis ita sunt multis luminibus ingenii multae tamen artis.*[55] Confronted by *tamen,* many editors have resorted to the panacea of emendation, adding a *non* before either *multis* or *multae.* Yet for Cicero's contemporaries it was all but instinctive to oppose *ingenium* and *ars,* and *tamen* simply betrays Cicero's surprise that the two should be found united.

The confrontation of *ars* and *ingenium* was reproduced in the quarrel of the so-called "wine drinkers" (*οἰνοπόται*) and "water drinkers" (*ὑδροπόται*). As confidence in a definable source of poetic genius had faded, intoxication had become increasingly acceptable as a token of inspiration, until some Alexandrian writers boldly declared that the waters of the holy spring were now available as a bottled commodity. In the idea we may see a deterioration of the *furor poeticus,* a belief that poetic natures might be most felicitous when uninhibited by rational control. Anxious to give the theory a reputable, or, at any rate, an antique derivation, its proponents adopted Cratinus as their spirited ancestor. They could recall the story that he had died from the shock of seeing a wine cask shattered (Aristophanes, *Pax* 700 ff.), and they were careful to remind contemporaries that he had declared wine a "swift horse to the poet" (*Anth. Pal.* 13.29). By construing all praise of wine as a confession that the author wrote only when drunk, they might mount any poet upon the same Pegasus. Archilochus, Anacreon, Alcaeus, and Aristophanes were soon conscripted, while Sophocles' praise of Aeschylus for writing *οὐκ εἰδώς* was similarly vulgarized.[56]

The movement may have taken its impetus from protest against what seemed the affected precision of Callimachus and his school—"dry dogs," they were termed. Callimachus referred to Archilochus as "wine smitten" (544, Pfeiffer), and Callimachus' followers seem to have maintained that mounting the Muses' chariot was only a more elegant confession of being on the wagon. The foolishness of the ensuing dispute was exceeded only by its acrimony. It passed down

55. Cic., *Q. Fr.* 2.11; cf. H. A. J. Munro, *Lucretius* (Cambridge, Eng., 1893), 2, 17.

56. Athenaeus, 1.22a, 10.428 f., 10.429a, 10.430a ff., 14.628a; Ov., *A. A.* 3.330; Sen., *Ep.* 88.37. In general, see H. Lewy, *Sobria Ebrietas* (Giessen, 1929), 46 ff.

to the Augustans through such writers as Antigonus, Nicaenetus, and Antipater of Thessalonica, and Horace preserves a record of its vitality: [57]

> Prisco si credis, Maecenas docte, Cratino,
> nulla placere diu nec vivere carmina possunt,
> quae scribuntur aquae potoribus. ut male sanos
> adscripsit Liber Satyris Faunisque poetas,
> vina fere dulces oluerunt mane Camenae.
> laudibus arguitur vini vinosus Homerus:
> Ennius ipse pater numquam nisi potus ad arma
> prosiluit dicenda. "forum putealque Libonis
> mandabo siccis, adimam cantare severis";
> hoc simul edixi, non cessavere poetae
> nocturno certare mero, putere diurno.
> quid? siquis voltu torvo ferus et pede nudo
> exiguaeque togae simulet textore Catonem,
> virtutemne repraesentet moresque Catonis?
>
> [*Ep.* 1.19.1–14]

If learned Maecenas, you believe old Cratinus, no poems written by water drinkers are able to please for long or to survive. Ever since Bacchus enrolled poets with his Fauns and Satyrs, the sweet Muses have generally smelled of wine in the mornings. Homer, by his praise of wine, is convicted of addiction to it; father Ennius himself never leaped forth to tell of battles unless he had drunk well. "I shall hand over the Forum and Libo's well to the dry and sober; the abstemious I shall prohibit from song." Once I had said this, poets did not cease to strive in drunkenness at night, and in reeking of wine by day. What? If anyone with fierce and savage aspect, barefoot and with scanty toga, were to imitate Cato, would he then be an example of Cato's virtue and morals?

57. For the quarrel, see *Anth. Pal.* 9.406, 11.20, 11.31, 11.322, 13.29; and for playful references to it, Prop., 4.6.75; Ov., *Met.* 7.432.

The apostrophe to Maecenas—*si credis*—is not a Horatian *credo*. He is satirizing a popular attitude, not endorsing it, as is sometimes claimed.[58] Cato's virtue is not available to those aping his costume. Why then should poetic genius be the reward of those reproducing only a fabled incoherence? Though Horace may have casually forbidden non-drinkers from song (8–9), his bias was surely convivial rather than aesthetic, as was that of Catullus in banishing water *ad severos* (27.6). Horace's own indulgence was at most an accident of his life, not an essential element of his creativity. The only thing poetic about poets, he held, should be their poetry. Though he did not join battle professionally with the οἰνοπόται, his sympathies with *male sanos poetas* are not discernible:

> ingenium misera quia fortunatius arte
> credit et excludit sanos Helicone poetas
> Democritus, bona pars non unguis ponere curat,
> non barbam, secreta petit loca, balnea vitat.
> nanciscetur enim pretium nomenque poetae,
> si tribus Anticyris caput insanabile numquam
> tonsori Licino conmiserit. [*A. P.* 295–301]

> Because Democritus believes genius more blest than wretched art, and excludes sane poets from Helicon, a good number do not cut their nails or beard, but seek out secluded spots and avoid the baths. Indeed one can win the name and esteem of being a poet simply by never entrusting to the barber Licinus a head so incurable that even three Anticyras could not cure it.

His slave Davus' diagnosis of "th' hysteric or the poetic fit" (*S.* 2.7.117) is a jibe at contemporary poetasters rather than an analysis of Horace's own habits, to which Damasippus bears detached and hostile witness: *adde poemata . . . quae siquis sanus fecit, sanus facis et tu* (*S.* 2.3.321–22). Horace would have approved the spirit if not the scholarship of Dryden, who emended Aristotle's "by a happy gift of nature or madness," to "by a happy gift of nature and not by

58. See B. Otis, *TAPA, 76* (1945), 179, n. 8.

madness." [59] The two Odes (*C.* 2.19, 3.25) professing to be written in a Dionysiac frenzy are remarkably calculated, and no one to my knowledge has suggested that Horace's feet were ever incapable of treading a perfect line.

Horace and Alexandrianism

It is always difficult to carry on a polemic in abstract terms, and the polarity of nature and art tended to become a contest between champions of the Alexandrian movement and defenders of more vigorous writers like Ennius. Cicero must confess to a prominent part in agitating the quarrel. Aroused by neoteric carping at Ennius' technical lapses, he turned to hail the older poet's native power: "O best of poets! though he is despised by those singers of Euphorion" (*Tusc.* 3.19.45). By the Augustan age the antithesis between the dry and precise Alexandrians and the rough and reputedly convivial Ennius had become axiomatic. *Ennius ingenio maximus, arte rudis,* judged Ovid, and he found Callimachus to reverse the distinction: *quamvis ingenio non valet, arte valet.*[60] The dispute was exacerbated both by a powerful archaizing taste,[61] and, more importantly, by the official sanction Ennius enjoyed. Augustus, as part of his effort to revive a feeling for the national past, encouraged an admiration for Rome's first truly national poet, much as Cicero had done two generations before. The elegiac poets, who were the most explicitly Alexandrian of the Augustans, also tended to be indifferent to the political and moral program of the emperor. Recent critics have been tempted to confound the twin antagonisms as a convenience in locating Horace's position. "The elegists," we are told "—both in fact and in theory—were unsympathetic to the Augustan and Horatian

59. Dryden, preface to *Troilus and Cressida;* see E. Sikes, *The Greek View of Poetry* (London, 1931), 96.

60. Ov., *Tr.* 2.424; *Am.* 1.15.14; cf. Ov., *Tr.* 2.259; *Am.* 1.15.19; Prop., 4.1.61; Stat., *S.* 2.7.75; Quint., 1.8.8, 10.1.40. For a more general discussion, see F. Wehrli, *Phyllobolia für Peter von der Mühll* (Basel, 1946), 9 ff. Horace (*S.* 1.4.60–61) chooses Ennius to represent the lofty, inspired poetry most unlike his own Satires.

61. On Augustan archaizing see Hor., *Ep.* 2.1.18 ff. (cf. below, 256–59), and R. Marache, *La critique littéraire* (Rennes, 1952), 29 ff.

program: they offended both its literary and its moral ideals, which were more or less inseparable." Or again, "the reaction against the 'official' view (of both Horace and Maecenas as well as—inferentially—Augustus) is apparent in all the elegists." [62] Both the identifications suggested and the oppositions struck are convenient rather than precise. Though Augustus might find the submission of aesthetic to moral standards expedient, to Horace the two remained eminently distinct. He was never constrained to accept Ennius' national virtues as compensation for his literary lapses. In one Satire, it is true, he points to Ennius as the obvious example of the true poet, gifted with *ingenium* and an *os magna sonaturum.* Yet Horace here, for strategic reasons, seeks to establish a gulf between poetry and his own prosy Satires, and hence he cites for the former the writing most unlike his own.[63] More detached estimates find Ennius a poor imitator of Homer (*Ep.* 2.1.50 ff.), with his metrical roughness and vagaries of diction arousing Horace's alarm rather than his admiration (*A. P.* 261). Like most poets, Horace knew that a writer's national or political sentiments are no touchstone for his technical accomplishment. His recommendation to hold back each work nine years before publishing was taken, plausibly enough, as a compliment to the *Zmyrna.*[64] Whatever Horace's objections to Cinna's politics, he was not equally ready to tear him for his bad verses.

The easy identification of the "Augustan and Horatian program" implies that Horace was a great poet—or at least a great political poet—insofar as he was a great Augustan. So to regard him is to rob even his political verse of its true distinction. The same is true of the *Aeneid.* If we read it only as a celebration of Rome, *pulcerrima rerum,* and ignore Vergil's somber reservations—*sunt lacrimae rerum*—we destroy an essential quality of its greatness. Augustus tried to make Horace his secretary, but in vain; [65] and to see Horace simply as a supporter of the Augustan program is to succeed retrospectively

62. B. Otis, *TAPA, 76* (1945), 185, 180, n. 10; cf. T. Higham, *CR, 48* (1934), 110.

63. See below, 42.

64. Hor., *A. P.* 388; cf. Ps-Acro and Porphyrio, *ad loc.*

65. Suet., *Vit. Hor.* 45 (Reifferscheid).

where the emperor failed. Nor do we do Horace a service by pretending that the most explicitly patriotic verse—early jeremiads such as *C.* 3.6 and *C.* 3.24, the enforced eulogies of the fourth book,[66] or state performances such as the *Carmen Saeculare*—is the most distinguished. It is, rather, the great Odes such as *C.* 1.37, *C.* 1.2, and C. 3.4, that are both morally and imaginatively the most powerful. And if they offer the best parallel in Latin poetry to the *Aeneid,* it is by virtue of their massive reservations and ambiguities no less than by their commitment to Augustus and to the Roman state.

The political hostility between Horace and the elegists has surely been exaggerated. It was not their style of politics but their style of life that Horace viewed skeptically. By avoiding the meter they used he suggests as much. The world, he implies, may be better viewed from a perspective grander than the closed room of their couplets—*exiguos elegos* (*A. P.* 77). Several times Horace gently satirizes the elegiac conventions of love. Yet he was aware of their charm as well as their fragility, and that, indeed, their very fragility was a main source of their charm. We have lately [67] come to realize how well Horace knew the *lepidus versus* of Catullus, the lampooner of Caesar; and against Tibullus and Propertius we can discover no really damaging attacks. For Tibullus, insulated from politics by the very denseness of his dreams, Horace expresses only critical respect or affectionate reproof.[68] And what of his famous quarrel with the politically recalcitrant Propertius? The recent attempt to locate a common mistress over whom they might have fought [69] betrays how slender the actual evidence is. Only in one place can we find a possible animus, and it is not markedly severe:

66. Suetonius (*Vit. Hor.* 46, Reifferscheid) states that Augustus "compelled" (*coegerit*) Horace to add a fourth book of Odes built around the poems celebrating the victories of the emperor's stepsons (*C.* 4.4, 4.14).

67. See especially R. Reitzenstein, *Hermes, 57* (1922), 357 ff.; C. W. Mendell, *CP, 30* (1935), 289 ff.; J. Ferguson, *AJP, 77* (1956), 1 ff.; and below, 57, 132–35, 144–46, 150, 153, 248, 275, 280.

68. *Ep.* 1.4.1 (*candide iudex sermonum*); *C.* 1.33. The elegist Valgius, though averse to political themes (*C.* 2.9), was nevertheless one of the few people whom Horace hoped to please (*S.* 1.10.82). On Horace's more general objections to the elegiac view of the world see below, 132, 239–40.

69. L. Herrmann, *REA, 35* (1933), 281 ff.

discedo Alcaeus puncto illius; ille meo quis?
quis nisi Callimachus? [*Ep.* 2.2.99–100]

I come off an Alcaeus in his judgment; who is he in mine?
Who but Callimachus?

Horace describes a mutual admiration society. Praised as another Alcaeus, he compliments his counterpart by terming him a new Callimachus.[70] There is nothing more invidious in the allusion to Propertius (if we admit the identification) than in his description of himself. There must have been a certain amount of rivalry between the two; both were members of Maecenas' circle.[71] Yet that hardly constitutes a profound antipathy. And if we look at the programmatic poems of each the congruences are striking. Propertius' reluctance to decorate Augustus rather than Cynthia with his talents produced a series of playful *recusationes.* Customarily they depend upon a contrast between the *magnus, grandis, tumidus,* and *vastus* nature of the task and his own *parvus, mollis, tenuis,* or *parcus* talent. The antitheses are too familiar in elegy to need rehearsal, but it may surprise us to find Horace adopting the same ideas and language.[72] Here is the opening of his final statement of the glories of Rome and of Augustus:

Phoebus volentem proelia me loqui
victas et urbis increpuit lyra,

70. The reference to Callimachus has usually been taken, with fair certainty, as an allusion to Propertius, the self-styled (3.1.1) disciple of Callimachus; see Butler and Barber, *Elegies of Propertius,* xxxix ff.

71. For the efforts of Horace and Propertius to imitate and improve upon one another see F. Solmsen, *CP, 43* (1948), 103 ff. Although the rivalry was sharper and certainly less affectionate than that between Horace and Vergil, it was not, in literary terms, altogether dissimilar. For the mutual imitations of Horace and Vergil, see G. Duckworth, *TAPA, 87* (1956), 281 ff.

72. *C.* 1.6, 2.1.37–40, 2.12, 3.3.69–72, 4.2.31 ff.; *Ep.* 2.1.250 ff. On the antitheses of styles in general, and in the elegists in particular, see A. Guillemin, *LEC, 8* (1939), 336 ff.; J. Hubaux, *Les thèmes bucoliques* (Bruxelles, 1930). Maecenas himself avoided national themes to write in the style of the neoterics, a fact which both Horace (*C.* 2.12.9–10) and Propertius (3.9.29–30) used in their own defense. On Maecenas' verse see H. Bardon, *La littérature latine inconnue* (Paris, 1956), *2,* 13 ff.

ne parva Tyrrhenum per aequor
vela darem. tua, Caesar, aetas
fruges et agris rettulit uberes . . . [*C.* 4.15.1–5]

As I was wishing to sing of battles and conquered cities, Apollo struck upon his lyre in warning, lest I should spread my tiny sails upon the Tyrrhenian sea. Your age, Caesar, has restored fertile crops to the fields . . .

Apollo's prohibition has antecedents running back through Vergil's sixth Eclogue to Callimachus, while the sailing image might have come straight from Propertius.[73] If it be urged that the Horatian *recusatio* is but a rhetorical device, and that poems embodying a plea of insufficient strength often go on to refute it, one can only reply that the same is true of the elegist.[74] And a comparison between the two poets' treatment of Actium should give us pause as to which was prepared to be the more loudly chauvinistic.[75]

The whole question of Horace's relations to Alexandrianism needs re-examining. Where some critics have postulated a political or personal hostility toward the elegists, others have pointed to the insulating effect of a Classical Greek influence. "Horace much preferred classical Greek to Hellenistic and Alexandrian models"; "the least open to Alexandrian influences of all the Latin classic poets"; "Horace despised the Alexandrians . . ." [76] The eagerness to regard distinct influences as necessarily hostile receives no encouragement from Horace himself. He was always willing to explore both Classical and Alexandrian poetry, and the work of Pasquali and Reitzenstein, in particular, has demonstrated how much he owed to those "despised"

73. Verg., *E.* 6.3 ff.; Call., *Aitia.* 1.1.21 ff. (quoted below, 36); Prop., 3.3.13 ff., 3.9.3–4.

74. On the Horatian *recusatio,* see below, 112 ff., and compare Prop., 2.1.17 ff., 2.10.12 ff., 3.1.25 ff., 3.3.7 ff., 40 ff., 3.4.1 ff., 3.9.37 ff., 49 ff., 4.1.1 ff.

75. Cf. Hor., *C.* 1.37 with Prop., 3.11 and 4.6, and see my article, *Phoenix, 12* (1958), 47 ff.

76. J. I. M. Tait, *Philodemus' Influence on the Latin Poets* (Bryn Mawr, 1941), 66; A. Y. Campbell, *Horace,* 139; T. Glover, *Horace* (Cambridge, Mass., 1932), 69.

Alexandrians.[77] Quintilian praised Horace for "rising occasionally" (*insurgit aliquando*); he betrayed his bias in rebuking Alcaeus for "descending" to love poetry.[78] We too may prefer Horace's loftier utterances, but we need not depreciate his slighter poems to do so. Such a division between solemn *vates* and playful *poeta* can be fatal to an appreciation of his major work as well as to a sympathy with his minor, for it makes it easy to forget that the most immensely conceived Odes preserve an equal fineness of control. Fundamental to Alexandrianism was the search for formal perfection, and though often vitiated by the triviality of its practitioners, it could become a powerful instrument in the hands of greater poets. The fact that Horace and Vergil made a means of what may often have been for the Alexandrians an end should not blind us to the similarities between them. In composing Rome's greatest national poem Vergil would write a few lines each morning, then spend the day in polishing them. He compared his labor with that of a mother bear gradually licking her young into shape (Gell., 17.10). What could be more Alexandrian? Unless it be Horace's identification of himself as a small and laborious bee, slowly creating the sweet structure of his verse (*C.* 4.2.27 ff.).

The best document for Alexandrian literary ideas is Callimachus' recently discovered prologue to the *Aitia:*

> Judge poetry by its art, not by the Persian measure, nor look to me for a loudly resounding song. It is not mine to thunder; that belongs to Zeus. For, when I first placed a tablet on my knees, Lycian Apollo said to me: "Poet, feed the victim to be as fat as possible, but, my friend, keep the Muse slender (λεπταλέην). This too I bid you: tread a path which carriages do not trample; do not drive your chariot upon the common tracks of others, nor along a wide road,

77. G. Pasquali, *Orazio lirico* (Firenze, 1920), 141–641; R. Reitzenstein, *NJA, 21* (1908), 81 ff., 365 ff.; *49* (1922), 24 ff.; see also E. A. Havelock, *Lyric Genius of Catullus,* 162 ff.; L. P. Wilkinson, *Horace and His Lyric Poetry* (Cambridge, Eng., 1946), 116 ff.

78. Quint., 10.1.63, 10.1.96. In praising Alcaeus' political verse alone, Quintilian is more exclusive than Horace, who gives Alcaeus' lighter work equal weight; cf. *C.* 1.32.4 ff., and see below, 110–11, 339.

but on unworn paths, though your course be more narrow. For we sing among those who love the shrill voice of the cicada and not the noise of asses." Let others bray like the long-eared beast, but let me be the dainty, the winged one. [*Aitia* 1.1.17–32]

The oppositions were to become familiar in Latin. Vergil adopted them in contrasting epic and pastoral-erotic poetry:

> cum canerem reges et proelia, Cynthius aurem
> vellit et admonuit: "pastorem, Tityre, pinguis
> pascere oportet ovis, deductum dicere carmen."
> nunc ego (namque super tibi erunt qui dicere laudes,
> Vare, tuas cupiant et tristia condere bella)
> agrestem tenui meditabor harundine Musam. [*E.* 6.3–8]

When I was about to sing of kings and battles, Apollo plucked my ear and warned me: "A shepherd, Tityrus, should raise fat sheep, but sing a fine-spun song." There will be others, Varus, who will be eager to sing your praises and write of grim wars; now I shall meditate the rustic Muse on a slender reed.

In the Satires Horace touched upon the contrast in passing—

> hac prece te oro:
> pingue pecus domino facias et cetera praeter
> ingenium— [*S.* 2.6.13–15]

This I pray of you: Make fat the flocks for their master, and everything else save his wits.

and he may have glanced at it again in opposing Grosphus' large herds with his own slender Muse:

> mihi parva rura et
> spiritum Graiae tenuem Camenae
> Parca non mendax dedit et malignum
> spernere volgus. [*C.* 2.16.37–40]

> To me Fate, sparing yet not deceiving, has given modest lands and the slender spirit of the Greek Muse, and a disdain for the envious crowd.

Tenuis was the translation of the Greek λεπτός, and it had come to bear an almost technical allusion to the Callimachean style.[79] Whether or not Horace intends a direct reference, the similarity of concept is unmistakable. Even Fate's name (*Parca*) becomes a punning synonym for "sparing," carrying out the modesty of *parva rura,* and suggesting the same stylistic qualities as Callmachus' ὀλίγος.[80] Vergil imported a metaphor of weaving by joining *deductum carmen* ("woven song") to *tenui harundine,*[81] and Horace likewise united the two in praising the poet's "fine-spun song" (*tenui deducta poemata filo*), and in his warning to be *tenuis cautusque serendis.*[82] The image of the poet as weaver which stretched back to Pindar has now become a specific recommendation of fineness and delicacy.

Callimachus' defense of a "slender" style took shape elsewhere as an attack upon the epic poet Antimachus, whose *Lyde* he termed "fat and inelegant." [83] The opposition has a precedent in the contest of Aeschylus and Euripides in the *Frogs,* but it was the Alexandrian poets who first made it formal.[84] Later, Catullus, Vergil, Horace, Propertius, and the writers of the highly Alexandrian *Vergilian*

79. For the translation of λεπτός into *tenuis* see Cat., 51.9, translating Sappho, 2.9 (Diehl). For other uses of λεπτός see Call., *Epigr.* 27.3 (Pfeiffer); *Anth. Pal.* 9.25.1. For *tenuis* see Prop., 3.1.8, 3.9.29. *Lepidus, gracilis,* and *angustus* are also used to suggest the same qualities of style; see E. Reitzenstein, *Festschrift Richard Reitzenstein* (Leipzig, 1931), 23 ff., especially 35–36.

80. Call., *Aitia* 1.1.9; *Hymn to Apollo* 112.

81. Verg., *E.* 6.5–8; cf. *E.* 1.2. Quintilian (8.2.9) cites *deductum carmen* as an example of a maximum of meaning in a minimum of space.

82. *Ep.* 2.1.225; *A. P.* 46. Propertius uses *tenuare* as meaning "weave" in his invocation of Callimachus and Philetas (3.1.5), and the author of the *Culex* compares himself to a spider spinning a *tenuem* web (2). For other Horatian uses of *tenuis* see *C.* 1.6.9, 3.3.72.

83. Call., *Fr.* 398 (Pfeiffer); cf. *Aitia* 1.1.23. Catullus also attacks Antimachus as *tumidus* (95.10), and Horace mocks Antimachus in *A. P.* 136, according to Ps.-Acro, *ad loc.* Ps.-Verg. (*Cat.* 9.61 ff.) ties the approach to Callimachus with a rejection of the *pinguis populus.*

84. See B. Snell, *Discovery of the Mind,* 117; for the stylistic oppositions among the Latin poets, see A. Guillemin, *LEC, 8* (1939), 336 ff., and J. Hubaux, *Les thèmes bucoliques,* 1 ff.

Appendix all reject writing which is *pinguis, tumidus, inflatus, crassus,* or *turgidus.* Not because a poem is modern, but because it is *crassus et inlepidus,* Horace reminds the archaizers, should it be censured.[85] When the tragic writer wishes to touch his hearers' hearts he must find new bottles for old wine, and toss aside his "swelling tones (*ampullas*) and Brobdingnagian words." [86] The idea, notes Porphyrio, comes from Callimachus. *Professus grandia turget,* Horace knew (*A. P.* 27), and he could cite a certain Furius in proof:

> pingui tentus omaso
> Furius "hibernas cana nive conspuet Alpis."
> [*S.* 2.5.40–41]

> Furius, stuffed with fat tripe, "bespews the wintry Alps with white snow."

Callimachus had proclaimed that "it is not mine to thunder; that belongs to Zeus," [87] and Horace seems to be parodying the thunderous style Callimachus rejected. In the verse of Furius that he quotes Horace has substituted the author's name for what Quintilian (8.6.17) tells us was originally the first word, *Iuppiter.* Furius, in Horace's version, is convicted of thundering like the Zeus he had so ludicrously described.

A failure to distinguish clearly between quantitative and qualitative terms often clouds ancient criticism, probably because of the lack of a developed technical vocabulary. Catullus' reference to Antimachus (*at populus tumido gaudeat Antimacho,* 95.10) would seem to be a reflection upon Antimachus' thick style, yet the unflattering contrast with Cinna's *parva monumenta* (9) makes it likely that Catullus is attacking rather the amount Antimachus wrote. Such impreciseness is less important in practice than in theory. An overblown style, we might guess, would appear in a poem of inordinate length, one very likely addressed to a popular audience and on grandiose themes. At the end of the *Hymn to Apollo* Callimachus appends some programmatic

85. *Ep.* 2.1.76. The implicit opposition here of *crassus* and *lepidus* suggests that Horace may associate *lepidus* and λεπτός; cf. *S.* 2.4.52.

86. *A. P.* 97; cf. *Ep.* 1.3.14.

87. Call., *Aitia.* 1.1.20; cf. Prop., 2.1.39–40.

lines which recall the diagrammatic oppositions of the prologue to the *Aitia:*

> Envy spoke secretly into the ear of Apollo: "I do not admire the poet who fails to sing things as great in number as the sea." Apollo struck Envy with his foot and replied: "Great is the flow of the Assyrian river, but it bears upon its waters much of the earth's filth and much refuse. The Melissae do not bear to Demeter every kind of water, but only that from the slender stream, pure and undefiled, which springs up from a holy fountain, the very flower of waters."
>
> [*Hymn* 2.105 ff.]

The scholiasts tell us that Envy represents those who accused Callimachus of being unable to write a large poem, and Callimachus' retort is in effect an expansion of "judge poetry by its art, not by the Persian measure." [88] Quantitative and qualitative standards tended to coalesce: swollen rivers are naturally the muddiest. So Horace was to learn, from Lucilius among others. *Flueret lutulentus:* Lucilius' grittiness is a consequence of his excessive flow, reputedly two hundred verses an hour.[89] Cassius Etruscus, an Augustan disciple of Lucilius, displays his admiration by affecting the same turgidity:

> Etrusci
> quale fuit Cassi rapido ferventius amni
> ingenium, capsis quem fama est esse librisque
> ambustum propriis. [*S.* 1.10.61–64]

> Such was the genius of the Tuscan Cassius, more fervid than a rushing river, who was burned, as the story goes, upon a funeral pyre made of his own books and cases.

Opposed to such undisciplined effusions is the distilled talent of the true poet, *puroque simillimus amni* (*Ep.* 2.2.120). We might surmise

88. Call., *Aitia.* 1.1.17; cf. *Fr.* 465 (Pfeiffer), and the contrast between long and short works in the prologue to the *Aitia.* Cf. also Cat., 14, 22, 95.

89. Hor., *S.* 1.4.9 ff.; cf. *S.* 1.10.50, 60. It has been suggested that Horace was indebted to Callimachus directly for the images of clear and muddy streams; see F. Wehrli, *MH, 1* (1944), 69 ff.

that Damasippus' accusation—"so rarely do you write"—is but inverted praise (*S.* 2.3.1). So much would seem to be guaranteed by the boast of the notorious Bore, no less a literary than a social menace: "for who is able to write more, or more quickly than myself?" (*S.* 1.9.23–24). A certain Crispinus propounds the Bore's question more systematically. His claim to exceed Horace's slender output provokes a reply which reads like a vulgar recasting of Apollo's retort to Envy:

> Look, Crispinus challenges me at long odds: "take a tablet, if you will; I shall take mine. Let us appoint a place, an hour, and judges; let us see which of us is able to write more." The gods did nobly when they made me of a tiny and impoverished spirit, and of rare and infrequent speech; but you, if you wish, imitate the hot air shut up in the goat-skin bellows, always laboring away until the fire softens the iron. [*S.* 1.4.13 ff.]

"You write with ease to show your breeding," protests Sheridan's Clio: "But easy writing's vile hard reading."

Among the coterie audiences of the Alexandrian age, readers were often as learned as writers, and the neoteric and elegiac ideal of the *doctus poeta* celebrated the same narrowness of appeal. It was, probably, the young Vergil (*Cat.* 9.64) who bade farewell to the "fat-headed populace," much as Catullus had ridiculed the affection of the masses for the bombastic Antimachus (95.10). Horace was equally quick to reject the *malignum vulgus* as an audience for his *tenuis spiritus*—let only a handful of learned friends approve his verse! [90] In the Satires, such declarations remain suspect insofar as Horace is trying to disassociate himself from the image of a public prosecutor. Yet his pleas are not merely personal and defensive. The efforts of Lucilius and Plautus to please too large a number are singled out as undermining the quality of their work.[91] And elsewhere, addressing his book of Epistles as though it were a freed slave, Horace gives it a parting reminder that it was not brought up to hate keys and seals, and the hearing of a modest number (*Ep.* 1.20.3 ff.).

90. Hor., *S.* 1.10.81 ff.; cf. *C.* 2.16.39–40.
91. Hor., *S.* 1.10.73–77; *Ep.* 2.1.175–76.

Horace's Stylistic Criticism

Like Vergil, Horace was not consistently *contentus paucis lectoribus* (*S.* 1.10.74), any more than he consistently refused heroic themes. But both poets, even when writing most directly for the eyes of a larger public, still intended their verse to stand up under the scrutiny of a chosen few. Their standards of craftsmanship continued to reflect those of the Alexandrians, even when their themes and tone reflected upon the uses to which the Alexandrians had put their craft. Yet to establish a direct influence of Callimachus upon Horace is less important than to sense a community of stylistic intent. If Horace embodied the stronger aspect of Alexandrianism, an insistence upon formal elegance, it was because his views were instinctive rather than doctrinaire. We frequently find explicit what his work everywhere confirms, the necessity of *labor.* Petronius' famous tribute—*curiosa felicitas*—has encouraged quotation more often than consideration. *Felicitas* has a root meaning of "fertile," while *curiosa,* the adjective of *cura,* does not mean "curious" but "painstaking." The phrase thus conveys the union of imposed discipline and inborn creativity, of *ars* and *ingenium.* Though Horace would have rejoiced in their identification it is the adjective he himself chose to emphasize, as his scholiast's comment on his criticism of Lucilius reminds us: *non cessat autem Lucilium tangere, quasi incuriose scripserit.*[92]

Horace's assertion that poetry demands *ingenium,* a *mens divinior,* and an *os magna sonaturum* is often abstracted and developed in more ample terms than its context encourages. It occurs in the course of his defense against being a poetic slanderer (*S.* 1.4.38 ff.). He sophistically replies that what he writes does not deserve the name of poetry. By insisting upon the necessity of a *mens divinior* he means to write off his own *sermoni propiora,* as though that freed his verse from accusations of slander as well. The argument is patently calculated to confuse the issue with definitions rather than answer the charges. The lines have a tactical rather than a theoretical origin, and should not be wrenched from the situation that produced them. Quintilian's title for the Epistle to the Pisos—the *Ars Poetica*—

92. Porphyrio *ad S.* 1.10.71.

recognizes a truer emphasis. Implicit in the very writing of such a treatise is the belief that poetry is an art which can and should be learned. In praising a blend of art and nature Horace merely endorsed accepted doctrine, but his development of it is interesting:

> natura fieret laudabile carmen an arte,
> quaesitum est: ego nec studium sine divite vena
> nec rude quid prosit video ingenium: alterius sic
> altera poscit opem res et coniurat amice.
> qui studet optatam cursu contingere metam,
> multa tulit fecitque puer, sudavit et alsit,
> abstinuit venere et vino; qui Pythia cantat
> tibicen, didicit prius extimuitque magistrum.
> nunc satis est dixisse "ego mira poemata pango;
> occupet extremum scabies; mihi turpe relinqui est
> et quod non didici sane nescire fateri." [*A. P.* 408–18]

> It is often asked whether a praiseworthy poem is made by nature or by art. I myself do not see what good study is without a rich natural vein, nor what use genius is that remains unpolished; so much does each demand the help of the other, and amicably ally itself. The man who is eager to touch the longed-for goal in the race course endured and did as much as a child—he sweated and shivered, he abstained from love and wine. The flute player who celebrates the Pythian games learned from his teacher and lived in fear of him. But now it is enough to have said, "What marvelous poems I write: pox take the hindmost! To me it is shameful to be outstripped, and to confess that I am indeed ignorant of what I have never learned."

The careful balance of the first four lines lapses to allow further treatment of *ars,* and the distribution is symptomatic. We may measure the distance we have come from Pindar's divinely inspired bard by the athletic metaphor, for to Pindar too the analogy was impressive. He saw the point of contact in an equal reliance upon heaven-sent strength (*N.* 2.1. ff.). For Horace it lies in the equal need of training.

His slighting references to poetry as a game [93] are but conventionally deprecatory, and fail to convince us that he approached it with any less seriousness than one would approach an Olympian contest. He suggests as much in comparing the poet with the dancer, beneath whose apparent sporting lies the tension of artifice: *ludentis speciem dabit et torquebitur* (*Ep.* 2.2.124). The unembarrassed assertion of struggle anticipates characteristic modern admissions, Flaubert's cry of "the agonies of art," or Eliot's well-documented confession of "the intolerable wrestle with words."

Sir Joshua Reynolds once laid it down that to be self-taught was to be taught by a very bad master. He might have cited Horace in support, who reminded the hopeful poet not only to apply the touchstone of the past—"handle Greek models by night, handle them by day"—but to seek out as well the sternest minds of the present:

> Quintilio siquid recitares, "corrige sodes
> hoc" aiebat "et hoc." melius te posse negares
> bis terque expertum frustra: delere iubebat
> et male tornatos incudi reddere versus. [*A. P.* 438–41]

> If you recited anything to Quintilius he would say, "Correct this, my friend, and this." If, after trying two or three times in vain, you should say that you could do no better, then he would tell you to strike it out, and return the ill-made verses to the anvil.

"A good poet's made as well as born," wrote Ben Jonson in his preface to Shakespeare's first folio, and the emphatic word is "good." Horace, like Reynolds, accepted the claim to be self-taught as the proclamation of only a Pyrrhic victory:

> si defendere delictum quam vertere malles,
> nullum ultra verbum aut operam insumebat inanem,
> quin sine rivali teque et tua solus amares. [*A. P.* 442–44]

93. Hor., *S.* 1.10.37; *Ep.* 1.1.10; and possibly *Ep.* 1.14.36, 2.2.56.

If you should prefer defending your fault to repairing it,
then he would not waste any further words or vain efforts
to stop you from admiring yourself and your creations,
alone without any rival.

Doctus now has a pejorative sense, largely through its specialized association with the neoterics, and we are more likely to remember Horace's one scornful use of the word than other more typical ones.[94] To be *indoctus* was to be guilty of a more serious and far more widespread failing:

navem agere ignarus navis timet, habrotonum aegro
non audet nisi qui didicit dare; quod medicorum est
promittunt medici, tractant fabrilia fabri:
scribimus indocti doctique poemata passim.[95]

He who is ignorant of a ship fears to steer one, nor does anyone who has not studied medicine dare give southernwood to a sick person. Doctors deal in what has to do with doctoring, workmen handle tools, but all of us, taught or untaught, turn out poems on every side.

The lines reaffirm the concept of the poet as craftsman which ran back to Solon but which usually played a subsidiary role. Where Classical Greek theory took for granted the poet's specialized labor, preferring to pay tribute to his special nature, Horace assumed the second and devoted himself to inculcating the first. He addressed himself not to the source of *ingenium* but to the ways in which it might be improved. Pindar thought in terms of the things which could not be

94. *S.* 1.10.19. The often quoted words have been built up into evidence of a deep-seated hostility toward Catullus, despite the eloquent protest of E. K. Rand, *HSCP, 17* (1906), 15 ff.

95. *Ep.* 2.1.114–17. Cf. *A. P.* 416–18 for the false shame that prevents men from learning, and *A. P.* 441 for an analogy between poet and blacksmith. Persius was equally skeptical of those who "suddenly step forth a poet" (*Prol.* 1 ff.). Cf. Persius' insistence (1.106), probably in imitation of Horace (*S.* 1.10.71), that bitten fingernails are a surer sign of the true poet.

learned, Horace in terms of those which had to be. The shift in emphasis is not confined to literary theory alone, and there is an instructive contrast between the two poets' tributes to a more general ἀρετή. "It is by gift of nature," held Pindar, "that there stands forth to view the noble spirit, which passes from fathers to sons." But Horace, praising the stepsons of Augustus for their native *virtus,* was quick to supplement his tribute: *doctrina sed vim promovet insitam.*[96]

The ability to write great poetry seemed to Horace less a gift than a calling. The concept of inspiration had yielded to that of nature, and now nature had come to seem no more important than nurture. *Incultum* was for Horace as sharp an accusation of verse as it was for the elegists of their mistress. It was Horace's distinguished contribution to give dignity to the poet's labor. Plato complained that poets were the most incompetent critics of their own work (*Ap.* 22b), but what he chose to construe as proof of inspiration Horace banished as a vice. The fanciful derivations of *vates* from *vesania* or *carmen* from *carere mente* that Plato's judgment encouraged could find no sanction in Horace.[97] In his hands the time-honored image of poetry as something woven became a specific claim of rewriting: *scriptorum quaeque retexens.*[98] Matching his call to a training as strenuous as any athlete's, as specialized as any doctor's, is his reminder that the poet's task is retrospective as well. He must use the stylus' blunt eraser as often as its point: *saepe stilum vertas, iterum quae digna legi sint scripturus* (*S.* 1.10.72–73). Lucilius was the most prominent example of what happened when that axiom was ignored. His superior *ingenium* was never submitted to a sufficiently intense discipline, and Horace rebukes him as "too lazy to bear the labor of writing—of writ-

96. Pi., *P.* 8.44–45; Hor., *C.* 4.4.33. Each poet develops the theme characteristically. Pindar reminds Xenarces that "victory does not depend on men, but a god gives it" (*P.* 8.76), while Horace emphasizes the "unknowing" state of youths before they are trained (*C.* 4.4.5 ff.). On Pindar's view of nature as against learned skill see W. Jaeger, *Paideia, 1* (New York, 1939), 217 ff. Although Horace's emphasis in *C.* 4.5 is conditioned by the special relation of Augustus to Tiberius and Drusus, it is of a general validity.

97. For Plato, see the references in n. 23 above, and for the derivations of *vates* and *carmen,* see Varro, *L. L.* 6.52; Isidore, *Orig.* 1.39.4. Cf. Horace's scorn for the *vesanus poeta* (*A. P.* 453 ff.).

98. *S.* 2.3.2; cf. *Ep.* 2.1.225; Ov., *Pont.* 1.5.13.

ing well, I mean: as to quantity, I let that pass." [99] Pope's judgment on Dryden, that he lacked "the last and greatest art—the art to blot," was urged by Horace against a whole race. The Romans' familiar evil was not a lack of genius but a failure to control it:

> natura sublimis et acer;
> nam spirat tragicum satis et feliciter audet;
> sed turpem putat inscite metuitque lituram.
> [*Ep.* 2.1.165–67]

> A nature sublime and vigorous: for the Roman breathes tragic strains well enough and is creatively bold, but in his ignorance he thinks an erasure base and fears it.

> nec virtute foret clarisve potentius armis
> quam lingua Latium, si non offenderet unum
> quemque poetarum limae labor et mora. vos, o
> Pompilius sanguis, carmen reprehendite, quod non
> multa dies et multa litura coercuit atque
> praesectum deciens non castigavit ad unguem.
> [*A. P.* 289–94]

> Nor would Latium be more powerful in valor and in its famous feats of arms than in language, if the labor and time in using the file did not offend every one of our poets. Yet spurn, O descendants of Pompilius, the poems that many days and many rewritings have not ten times over forced into a shape able to pass muster beneath a close-cut nail.

Multa dies ideally expands to a large figure. The true poem, he suggests, is more likely to be a nine years' than a nine days' wonder: *nonumque prematur in annum membranis intus positis* (*A. P.* 388).

"Harp? Lyre? Pen and ink, boy, you mean!" So Coleridge's schoolmaster addressed his most famous pupil, and Horace was no less

99. *S.* 2.1.75 (Lucilius' *ingenium*); *S.* 1.4.12 (his laziness). Cf. *S.* 1.4.7 ff., 1.10.1 ff., 50 ff.; *Ep.* 2.1.50–52, 170 ff.

severe. Informing his criticism is a concern with the physical act of writing rather than with any metaphysical concept of literature, a perception into means rather than a vision of ends. So much has been written on the possible sources and arrangements of the *Ars Poetica* that we are in danger of forgetting its real distinction. It is, after all, remarkable less for the number of stylistic theories it treats than for the summary manner in which it treats them. The familiar question of whether it be poetry's function to please or to instruct leads Horace no further than the customary compromise. He invokes the problem only to dismiss it (*A. P.* 333 ff.). The work is most interesting as our first example of one craftsman's message to another.[100] It has been eloquently maintained that the articulating ideal of the poem is τὸ πρέπον, *decorum*. If that be so, we must acknowledge that τὸ πρέπον is conceived in practical rather than speculative terms. At issue is the fitness of diction, of meter, of invocation, of the parts to the whole, of theatrical character. Any comparison between Horace's treatment of drama and that of Aristotle cannot but enforce our sense of the limitations Horace instinctively sought.

When Swift characterized the poet as a creature of sweetness and light whose emblem was the bee, he invoked an image which ran back to Homer. There the honeyed sweetness of poetry was formulated, and in Pindar we meet everywhere the analogy between the divine sweetness of his own writing and that of the bee.[101] Plato, in a famous passage in the *Ion* (534a ff.), enlarged upon the comparison, declaring that the bee was also sufficiently unpredictable and irresponsible to represent the efforts of that "light, winged, and airy thing," the poet. Horace took over the image, and deliberately inverted its Platonic associations. In his hands the analogy expresses the poet's painstaking care: *ego apis Matinae more modoque . . . per laborem plurimum*

100. W. Wimsatt and C. Brooks, in *Literary Criticism, A Short History* (New York, 1957), 94, find in the *Ars Poetica* "snatches of studio wisdom." The estimate need not be pejorative.

101. Pi., *O.* 11.4; *N.* 11.18; *I.* 2.32; *Fr.* 152 (Schroeder). Bees were fabled to have woven a honeycomb on Pindar's mouth in his infancy (*Anth. Pal.* 2.386; Paus., 9.23.2). Cf. the similar story about Homer (*Anth. Pal.* 2.342). See also Bacchy., 9.10; *Anth. Pal.* 2.110, 128–30, 7.13; Pauly-Wissowa, *Real-Encyclopädie, s. v. Biene;* Robert-tornow, *De apium mellisque significatione* (Berlin, 1893), 105 ff.

. . . *operosa carmina fingo.*[102] The explicit emphasis on *labor* stands as the most characteristically Horatian element in his criticism. It forms the burden of his strictures upon Lucilius, it provides the refrain of his message to the Pisos, it animates his suspicion of Plautus and Ennius. The reminder that older poets would write differently were they Augustans is not a reproach to former generations, but an incitement to contemporaries, a warning that an admiration for the archaic is less a tribute to the past than a disservice to the present (*Ep.* 2.1.88). Horace stepped forward as the most distinguished spokesman for what has since become axiomatic, that inspiration is in large part perspiration. It was his critical triumph finally to banish the *demens poeta* to some other Elysium, and to show that *ars* finds its true opposite not in *ingenium* but in *iners.* "When industry builds on nature," wrote Sir Thomas Browne, "we may expect pyramids." *Exegi monumentum.*

102. *C.* 4.2.27 ff. Even in casual references the idea of labor is as important as that of sweetness: *Ep.* 1.3.21, 1.19.44. Lucretius had hinted at the same idea of labor, but the idea of sweetness remained for him the more powerful: 3.10 ff.

II

STRUCTURAL CHARACTERISTICS OF THE ODES

Patterns of Words

> Up to this day I have not had an artistic delight in any poet similar to that which from the beginning an Ode of Horace gave me. What is here achieved is in certain languages not even to be hoped for. This mosaic of words, in which every word, by sound, by placing, and by meaning, spreads its influence to the right, to the left, and over the whole; this minimum in extent and number of symbols, this maximum thereby achieved in the effectiveness of the symbols, all this is Roman, and believe me, elegant par excellence.

Analogies between literary style and a lapidary pattern are familiar, but Nietzsche's [1] application of it is peculiarly apt. Being an inflected language and lacking any articles, Latin might achieve certain effects to perfection. The relationship between subject, object, and modifiers is defined by their endings, and not, as is normally the case in English, by their position. Poets might thus neglect sense sequence to build stanzas in accordance with arbitrary aesthetic ideas, provided they were metrically amenable. Milton's attempt at a literal translation of Horace's Ode to Pyrrha (*C.* 1.5) illustrates by its failings the special advantages Roman poets enjoyed:

1. *Werke, Taschenausgabe* (Leipzig, 1906), *10,* 343.

What slender youth bedew'd with liquid odours
Courts thee on roses in some pleasant cave,
  Pyrrha, for whom bind'st thou
  In wreaths thy golden hair,

Plain in thy neatness? O how oft shall he
On Faith and changed Gods complain: and seas
  Rough with black winds and storms
  Unwonted shall admire:

Who now enjoyes thee credulous, all gold,
Who alwayes vacant, alwayes amiable
  Hopes thee; of flattering gales
  Unmindfull. Hapless they

To whom thou untry'd seem'st fair. Me in my vowed
Picture the sacred wall declares t' have hung
  My dank and dripping weeds
  To the stern God of Sea.

Who is credulous? and who all gold? No such problems perplex the Latin, but in a close English translation such syntactical chaos and ambiguity are almost inevitable. If we look at the first and last stanzas of the original we can see how poets exploited the resources of their grammar in a way unavailable to English:

Quis multa gracilis te puer in rosa
perfusus liquidis urget odoribus
  grato, Pyrrha, sub antro?

In contrast to the necessarily logical word order of Milton's version, here the sequence of words is a visual representation of the scene. The central position of *te,* which opens the second half of the line after the caesura, focuses our attention. Surrounding it on the page is *gracilis . . . puer;* already we feel some of the implications of *urget,* a word far less abstract than Milton's "courts." Enclosing both Pyrrha and the slender youth is *multa . . . in rosa:* the bowered scene is visually complete. The question set up by the initial *quis?* is furthered by the puzzling order of the words that follow: many – slender – you – boy – on – rose. The very piling up of these words prepares us for the sensuous image that follows: flowing perfumes in the rose-strewn recesses of "some pleasant cave."

The last stanza is equally inimitable:

> me tabula sacer
> votiva paries indicat uvida
> suspendisse potenti
> vestimenta maris deo.

In the arrangement of words, two interlocking pairs on either side of the main verb, we can see the very design of a *tabula votiva*.[2] English, with its articles and greater reliance on explanatory prepositions, baffles so direct an effect. The necessity for words like "in," "to," "the," and "of" clutters any clear pattern, while to retain the emphatic *me* and the terse sequence of words we are forced to such awkwardnesses as Milton's "me in my vow'd picture." In the Latin, moreover, no adjective falls in the same line as the noun it modifies. The words are rather "suspended," as it were, like the clothes to which Horace refers. We realize that he has not so much described a scene as created one, and that the "temple wall" is the page itself.

In commenting upon the effectiveness of Latin's "symbols" or "words" (*Zeichen*), Nietzsche formalized abstractly what was instinctive to the poet. In Horace's hands words assume an almost tactile reality, and each, like a mosaic tile, achieves an integrity of its own:

> illi robur et aes triplex
> circa pectus erat, *qui fragilem truci*
> *conmisit pelago ratem*
> *primus* . . . [*C.* 1.3.9–12]

> That man had oak and triple bronze about his heart, who first committed his fragile bark to the fierce sea.

If we read the stanza as we are taught to, seeking to approximate the English order by looking first for subject, verb, and object, and then matching substantives and modifiers, the stanza's impact is diffused. The order of the words is contrived for a special effect. The central

2. See W. Wili, *Horaz* (Basle, 1948), 249, and below, 324.

position of *conmisit* makes the clause follow the pattern of a Golden Line: "two substantives and two adjectives, with a verb betwixt to keep the peace." [3] The device was common at moments of gnomic solemnity,[4] and Horace appropriates some of the grandeur associated with it. By arbitrarily juxtaposing *fragilem* with *truci, pelago* with *ratem,* he visually forces upon us man's heroic confrontation of nature's power. A similar consideration dictates the postponing of *primus* from its normal position. The special quality of the achievement is held suspended, accumulating force through the description of the voyage's dangers, to break only upon the final word.

Since word patterns could thus confirm meaning, poets might achieve the visual equivalent of onomatopoeia. Although conspicuously available to Latin, the device has remained anonymous. Experiment dates back at least to Ennius' notorious phrase *saxo cere comminuit brum,* in which the verb "split" actually falls between the halves of "head." [5] Horace carried the mannerism to a sophisticated extreme:

> nunc et latentis proditor intumo
> gratus puellae risus ab angulo
> pignusque dereptum lacertis
> aut digito male pertinaci. [*C.* 1.9.21–24]

> Now [seek] the enticing laugh that betrays some girl hiding in her secret corner, and the pledge snatched from her arm or finger, scarcely resisting.

Deliberate self-betrayal and feigned resistance are ambiguities natural to love, and the complexities of Horace's syntax reflect or even compound them. Four modifiers without substantives initiate us into the

3. The definition is Dryden's, as quoted by Wilkinson, *Horace,* 146.

4. See, for instance, *S.* 2.2.136; *Epod.* 13.11; *C.* 3.1.16, 4.2.25; Propertius, 1.8.46; Vergil, *G.* 1.468.

5. *Ann.* 609 (Vahlen²) Cf. *Ann.* 572, with its imitations by Furius Bibaculus (*Frag. Poet. Rom.* 319, 11, Baehrens) and Vergil, *A.* 10.361. Horace gets an effect similar to that of *cere comminuit brum,* though more chaste, in his praise of Pollio as *maestis praesidium reis* (*C.* 2.1.13). Pollio is visually also a "bulwark" to his clients, standing between them and their grief.

confusion; the arrangement of words is as intricate and as puzzling as the event itself. Our very effort to overcome the difficulty of the lines involves us in them, and the text becomes a context of reality.

Fortune's capriciousness was proverbial, but in subscribing to it Horace retains unmistakably individual terms:

> Fortuna saevo laeta negotio et
> ludum insolentem ludere pertinax
> transmutat incertos honores,
> nunc mihi nunc alii benigna. [*C.* 3.29.49–52]

> Fortune, delighting in her savage business and persistent in playing her capricious game, shifts about her fickle favors, now kind to me, now to another.

The last two lines do little more than explicate what is inherent in the verbal arrangement of the first two, where tight contrasts jar us in the manner of Fortune's own reverses. *Fortuna . . . pertinax* approaches an oxymoron: "random change . . . holding fast." The jolting sequence "savage – joyful – business – pleasure" presents a double incongruity. Fortune joys in savage business and is stubborn in her play. We would expect the pairing to be reversed, but for Fortune *negotium* and *ludus* are identical. Her business is but sport, and to disport herself is her business. *Insolens* carries its primary sense of "unwonted" rather than merely "insolent" or "wanton." It is capricious sport (*ludum insolentem*) to which Fortune steadfastly holds (*pertinax*). Verbal incongruities hurl us from one extreme to the other; the lines do not so much describe an experience as reproduce it. "Poetry," Robert Frost has said, "is what is lost in translation."

Horace forces us to grant every word its individual weight. Often the very sounds virtually become the meaning. The movement from life into death struck him as an almost physical contraction:

> Te maris et terrae numeroque carentis harenae
> mensorem cohibent, Archyta,
> pulveris exigui prope litus parva Matinum
> munera . . . [*C.* 1.28.1–4]

> Archytas, measurer of the sea and of the earth and of the sands without number, now the scanty gift of a little earth confines you . . .

The open sonorities of *o* and *a* yield to narrow *i*'s and *u*'s. Catullus' mockingly solemn catalogue of kisses, *quam magnus numerus Libyssae harenae* (7.3) is no more deliberate in its rhetoric than *numeroque carentis harenae*. The specific fact of the tomb arrests Archytas' vague immensities of knowledge. Measurer of the universe, he has his measure taken by a tiny heap of sand, and the reaches of human accomplishment sink into a little, little, grave.[6]

In virtuoso passages like these Horace compels us to an awareness of the words as they lie on the page much as a Van Gogh exhibits the tactile reality of paint. The technique, however, was not confined to isolated stanzas, and on one occasion Horace devoted a whole Ode to exploring it:

Donec gratus eram tibi
  nec quisquam potior bracchia candidae
cervici iuvenis dabat,
  Persarum vigui rege beatior.

"donec non alia magis 5
  arsisti neque erat Lydia post Chloe,
multi Lydia nominis
  Romana vigui clarior Ilia."

me nunc Thressa Chloe regit,
  dulcis docta modos et citharae sciens, 10
pro qua non metuam mori,
  si parcent animae fata superstiti.

"me torret face mutua
  Thurini Calais filius Ornyti,
pro quo bis patiar mori, 15
  si parcent puero fata superstiti."

6. For Horace's strongly spatial sense of death, cf. *C.* 1.4.16–17 (and below, 269); *C.* 2.14.7–9, 2.18.36 ff. (and below, 83).

quid si prisca redit Venus
  diductosque iugo cogit aeneo,
si flava excutitur Chloe
  reiectaeque patet ianua Lydiae? 20

"quamquam sidere pulcrior
  ille est, tu levior cortice et inprobo
iracundior Hadria,
  tecum vivere amem, tecum obeam lubens." [*C.* 3.9]

While I was still pleasing to you, and no other youth, more favored, put his arms about your fair neck, then did I flourish more blest than the king of the Persians.

"While you burned more fiercely for no other woman, and Lydia was not ranked behind Chloe, then I, Lydia, flourished more glorious in my great fame than Roman Ilia."

Now Thracian Chloe, versed in sweet measure and skilled upon the lyre, rules me; for her I would not fear to die, if only the Fates spare her and let her live.

"Now Calais, son of Thurian Ornytus, scorches me with a mutual passion; for him I would suffer twice to die, if only the Fates spare him and let him live."

What if the old love returns and unites beneath her brazen yoke those who were parted; if fair Chloe is dismissed and the door opened again to slighted Lydia?

"Although he is fairer than a star, and you more fickle than a tossing cork and more wrathful than the wanton Adriatic, with you I would love to live, with you I would gladly die."

So precise are the repetitions and contrasts as to produce an almost tessellated effect. Philodemus' repartee between prostitute and prospective client (*Anth. Pal.* 5.46) is often cited as a precedent, but the two poems have almost nothing in common save the dialogue structure. The only ornament of Philodemus' lines is their cheerful vulgarity; they lack anything of the Ode's intricate formality. Using the lovers' words as though they were bits of tile, Horace constructs a single dazzling pattern, binding boast and counterboast through echoes at once rhythmic and verbal—the repetitions are too obvious to need rehearsal. Yet despite the powerful pairing of stanzas the two figures remain distinct, since an equally powerful verbal pattern maintains the independence of each lover. Each relies upon an individual rhetoric; even the difference between the confident *non metuam mori* (11) of Horace (presuming him to be the anonymous male) and Lydia's submissive but no less proud *bis patiar mori* (15) is indicative. Horace speaks throughout in social terms—kingship, servitude, expulsion—while Lydia turns to the natural images of fire, stars, and water. The verbal structure thus becomes itself the structure of experience, the coupling of each pair of stanzas being imposed upon the distinct pattern of each sex's individuality. Only with the last line's symmetrical refrain does the tensely intertwined arrangement resolve itself. *Tecum vivere* recalls and re-establishes the memories of a happy past (*vigui . . . vigui*); *tecum obeam* recalls and transforms the brief boasts of estrangement (*non metuam mori . . . bis patiar mori*). Summarizing the passion of both lovers, the final line reshapes it for the future.

As the Ode moves by prearranged steps from elegiac memory through vaunts of altered attachment to the promise of renewed allegiance, it does not so much record an actual amatory situation as propose an ideal form for one. In this it recalls Catullus' dialogue between Septimius and Acme (45), a poem equally abstract in mood, if more sensuous in detail, and of a comparable if less elaborate finish. Horace has fragmented the arrangement of the Septimius-Acme poem, exploiting more fully the possibilities of the dialogue form. Catullus' two speeches of competitive devotion have split into a three-part progression; dialectic replaces duet. Catullus' poem, we might say, simply develops the concentration implicit in the first two words. With the phrase *donec gratus eram tibi,* on the other hand, alternatives are already present. We are confronted not only by present intensity but by a movement between past and present, happiness and estrangement; by a changing as well as a charged atmosphere. Where one poem has the static intensity of an embrace, the other's formal pattern of alternating repetition and variation suggests the shifting coyness of a minuet. Horace's two lovers derive as much satisfaction from their own cleverness as from the end to which it is directed, not so much permitting us to overhear their confessions as demanding that we attend to their every intonation. Though Horace is Lydia's partner he stands at a distance as well, pointing at the pair of lovers rather in the manner of Prospero drawing back the curtain on Ferdinand and Miranda at chess. And the lovers, in turn, manipulate their words as though they were the very chessmen, placing them carefully in prearranged and co-responsive patterns. The great sixteenth century scholar, Scaliger, perhaps intoxicated by the grandiose manifestos of the Ode, proposed to barter the kingdom of Aragon to have written it. The impulse behind so Marlovian a gesture is suggestive—for surely, if confronted by the Septimius-Acme poem, we would offer the same riches in order to know the happiness of the figures themselves. The most significant love affair in Horace's poem, we feel tempted to say, is that between Horace and the Latin language.[7]

Architectural Patterns and the Use of Metaphor

Horace, if we may believe his editors and critics, found it all but impossible to follow the advice about composing that he gave to the younger Pisos: *sit quodvis, simplex dumtaxat et unum* (*A. P.* 23). "No reader of the Odes," wrote Tyrrell, "however careless, can have failed to notice the extraordinary difficulty of discovering in them anything like a connected train of thought." [8] Horace's particular Pegasus would seem to display its closest affinities with Leacock's famous horse, who when mounted galloped off rapidly in all directions. Porphyrio already knew of attempts to split difficult poems into separate parts, and the expedient remained popular. Peerlkamp's edition of the Odes, first published in 1834, carried the divide-and-conquer theory to a systematic extreme. Whatever he felt to be a lapse of logic or of taste he repaired by wholesale transpositions, rejections, and emendations. Horace's champions have been scarcely more reassuring than his critics, though the explanations they have devised for his waywardness have been both ingenious and various. Macaulay

7. On *C.* 3.9, see also below, 141 ff.
8. R. Y. Tyrrell, *Latin Poetry* (Boston, 1895), 192–93.

thought it simply a perverse desire to start as far as possible from the subject in hand; A. Y. Campbell traced it to the "oracular" style which he considered natural to Horace as *vates* of the Roman people; and a French critic has enthusiastically proclaimed it to be a defining prerogative of *"le lyrisme."* [9]

These glamorous explanations are not very satisfactory. A few of the Odes may remain ultimately obscure, but before rewriting Horace or seeking excuses for him, we might ask if our own lapses are not more relevant than his. By examining some of the poems it is possible to discern certain persistent techniques and structural patterns. And from these, in turn, we may discover what kind of logic, if any, underlies his seemingly disheveled progress.

An Ode which has given a good deal of trouble is the well-known one which opens with a salute to Pindar (*C.* 4.2). The very brilliance of some of the individual passages seems to have had the effect of casting the connections between them into obscurity. Certainly the stanzas in praise of Pindar seem a dazzling whole:

Pindarum quisquis studet aemulari,
Iulle, ceratis ope Daedalea
nititur pinnis, vitreo daturus
  nomina ponto.

monte decurrens velut amnis, imbres 5
quem super notas aluere ripas,
fervet inmensusque ruit profundo
  Pindarus ore,

laurea donandus Apollinari,
seu per audacis nova dithyrambos 10
verba devolvit numerisque fertur
  lege solutis . . .

9. Macaulay as quoted by C. Cary, *A Life of Horace* (New York, 1904), 170; Campbell, *Horace,* 81; P. Colmant, *LEC, 9* (1940), 418. Cf. H. Toll, *Phoenix, 9* (1955), 153 ff.; H. L. Tracy, *Studies in Honour of Gilbert Norwood* (Toronto, 1952), 203 ff. Even so good a poet as Landor frequently confessed himself baffled by Horace's transitions; see below, 267. Some of the Odes which have caused particular trouble are *C.* 1.4, 1.7, 1.9, 2.18, 3.4, 3.14, 4.2. See below, as indicated by Register.

> Whoever tries to emulate Pindar, Iullus, stuggles on wings fashioned from wax by the art of Daedalus, and is destined to give his name to a glassy sea. Like a river rushing down a mountainside which the rains have swollen above its customary banks, Pindar seethes and rushes along unrestrained with deep-voiced roar, worthy to be awarded the laurel of Apollo whether he rolls new words through bold dithyrambs and is borne along in measures free of any rules . . .

To echo the writer one praised was to pay an ultimate compliment,[10] and Horace's tribute, extending in a single sentence through some five stanzas, is Pindaric in its rhetoric. More specifically, the analogy between poetry and water, nowhere else in the Odes so elaborately developed, seems to have been dictated by Pindar's fondness for the comparison.[11] A pause, either of meter or of sense, falls after *decurrens, amnis, imbres, notas,* and *ripas*. The choppy rhythm, enforced by the sibilant at the end of each of these words, conveys the image of seething and violent plunges, which lengthen into the powerful and virtually unbroken impetus of the stanza's last two lines. The closeness with which the sounds and rhythms echo the sense strengthens the idea that Pindar's verse is itself a creation of nature, and the same is implicit in the ambiguity of *profundo ore* (7–8), *devolvit* (11), and *fertur* (11), which can apply equally well here to a natural phenomenon or to artistic creation. The supposition that the water-poetry simile is borrowed from Pindar is strengthened by Horace's later use of *Dircaeum* (25), rather than the equivalent and more common *Thebanum,* as an epithet for Pindar. Dirce was a river near Thebes which, according to Pindar (*I.* 6.74–76), owed its origin to the Muses, and in offering that Ode to Lampon, Pindar speaks of himself as giving him "a drink of the pure water of Dirce"

10. Another example of such tribute through imitation is Vergil, *G.* 2.490 ff., where Lucretian phrases reinforce Vergil's praise of Lucretius. (Propertius alters and develops the passage: 2.34.71 ff.) Dante, in describing the Provençal poet Arnaut Daniel, begins writing in Daniel's dialect (*Purg.* 26.139 ff.).

11. For the association of poetry and water see above, 11 ff., and for Pindar's special linkage of the two see J. Finley, *Pindar and Aeschylus* (Cambridge, Mass., 1955), 52–53.

(74). Horace's use of "Dircaean" recalls, then, the opening simile's fusion of water and poetry, and, like it, underlines the Pindaric quality of natural genius which Horace here chooses to emphasize.

In the famous stanzas contrasting his own talent with that of Pindar, Horace again seems to turn to the Greek poet for his terms:

> multa Dircaeum levat aura cycnum, 25
> tendit, Antoni, quotiens in altos
> nubium tractus: ego apis Matinae
> more modoque,
>
> grata carpentis thyma per laborem
> plurimum, circa nemus uvidique 30
> Tiburis ripas operosa parvos
> carmina fingo.

A swelling breeze uplifts the Dircaean swan, Antonius, whenever he turns toward the loftiest regions of the sky; but I, according to the mode and manner of the Matine bee, which through incessant toil gathers the pleasant thyme, humbly fashion my laborious songs amid the grove and banks of moist Tibur.

Pindar had distinguished, invidiously enough, between the high-flying eagle (the poet by nature) and the lowly jackdaw (the poet by learning alone).[12] Though Horace's bias is apologetic rather than aristocratic, he endorses for his own purposes the Pindaric antithesis between φύσις and τέχνη. *Levat aura* (25) insists upon the conspiracy between Pindar and nature already suggested by *fertur* (11); standing in painful contrast is Horace's laborious struggle (27–32). Although the image of the Matine bee strikes a primary contrast with that of Pindar as a swan, it looks back as well to the opening comparison

12. Pi., *O.* 2.86–88. In lines 22–24, Horace again invokes a Pindaric comparison between the blackness of oblivion and the golden renown given by the poet; cf. Pi., *N.* 7.12 ff.; *I.* 4.40–44, 5.56–57. The stanza may look back to the phrase *lege solutis* (12): Pindar is able to free his subjects from the normal laws of life and death. As if to emphasize the relevance of the earlier phrase, Horace himself, in lines 22–23, is *numerisque fertur lege solutis,* allowing an elision at the end of both lines—something very rare in the Odes.

between Pindar and a flooding river. Just as it was difficult to tell whether *profundo ore, devolvit,* and *fertur* were to be taken literally or figuratively, so Horace again uses a kind of overlapping simile, to the point that editors disagree as to whether *circa . . . nemus* should be taken with what precedes or with what follows. But though the language is as ambiguous in its reference as that used in the second and third stanzas, the intention of the simile is very different. *Per laborem plurimum, operosa, parvos*—the idea is diametrically opposed to that embodied in *profundo ore, devolvit,* and *fertur.* The landscape associated with Horace represents not nature uninhibited and essential, but nature labored over and transformed—the domain of art. Further contrasts point the distinction. Horace's limited talent is implicit in the specific and local landscape he describes. A placid stream has replaced the overflowing river; the sheltered banks and woodland of "moist Tibur" stand at a safe remove from Pindar's mighty flow. The homely tautology *more modoque* (28) not only draws us down to earth from the swan's huge freedom, but also suggests a tiny precision as against the Greek poet's careless profusion, *inmensusque ruit* (7). Outclassed by such natural grandeur, the laborious bee can do no more than cultivate his garden.

Hellenists have been quick to quote with approval the description of Pindar as a soaring swan, while Horatian scholars have seen in the Matine bee a symbol too apposite to remain in its context. Although the analogies have proven a fertile text for discourse, we should not forget that Horace intended them to be considered first in terms of the poem itself. The contrast prefigures a crucial one between Horace and Iullus Antonius, to whom the Ode is dedicated. Iullus, a son of Mark Antony and Fulvia, was a favorite of Augustus, and he seems to have suggested that Horace write a triumphal Ode in the manner of Pindar to welcome the emperor home from Gaul in 16 B.C.[13] *C.* 4.2, Horace's reply to Iullus' proposal, is technically a *recusatio,* and recalls Propertius' refusal (3.9) to oblige Maecenas with a poem celebrating Augustus. Just as Propertius answers Maecenas with a sly *te duce* (3.9.47), so Horace deftly turns Iullus' invitation back upon Iullus himself:

13. See E. Fraenkel, *Horace* (Oxford, 1957), 432 ff.

concines maiore poeta plectro
Caesarem, quandoque trahet ferocis
per sacrum clivum merita decorus (35)
fronde Sygambros.

> You, a poet of loftier style, will sing of Caesar, whenever, adorned by his well-deserved triumphal wreath, he leads the fierce Sygambri along the Sacred Way.

The emphatic *concines* (which is repeated in line forty-one) follows immediately upon Horace's description of himself as a low-flying bee, and the practical motive behind the contrast between Pindar and himself now becomes apparent. Iullus was also a poet, and he seems to have been willing to attempt the grand style. Ps.-Acro, at least, attributes to him an epic on Diomede, one which doubtless demonstrated the *maius plectrum* (33) praised by Horace. Iullus' talent, Horace suggests, is of a kind comparable to Pindar's, and quite unlike his own *parvos* (31) ability. And as he had contrasted Pindar's lonely exaltation with his own obscure efforts, so he now leaves to Iullus the task of celebrating Augustus, content himself to be an anonymous bystander:

tum meae, si quid loquar audiendum,
vocis accedet bona pars et "o sol
pulcer, o laudande" canam recepto
Caesare felix. [45–48]

> Then, if I can say anything worth listening to, a goodly part of my voice shall swell the refrain, and "O glorious, O praiseworthy day," I shall sing, happy that Caesar has returned.

The rustic formula *o sol pulcer* may possibly remind us of Icarus, for the "fair day" of Augustus' homecoming is fraught with equal danger for those who would rise too high. If anyone should aspire to make a name for himself by a Pindaric celebration of the emperor, he is likely to find that it will be a name principally reminiscent of disaster: *daturus nomina ponto*. The bee's creation can at best reflect the splendor of Augustus' Golden Age (39–40), but to rise properly to the occasion demands the sure flight of a swan. Attempts to confuse the two kinds of talent, the two kinds of poetry, will be fatal—as the struggles of Icarus, wearing swan's feathers stuck on with the wax of bees (2), have proved.[14] Iullus, if he so wishes, may attempt Pindaric flights, but for Horace discretion remains the better part of patriotism. His pride is not so great as to lead him to such a fall. His art knows when to yield to nature.

The two concluding stanzas have often struck readers as indecorous as well as unrelated. Specifying ten bulls and ten heifers for Iullus to sacrifice in honor of the ruler's return, Horace trails away upon the nice details of the single *tener vitulus* which will "free" him from his vows:

> fronte curvatos imitatus ignis
> tertium lunae referentis ortum,
> qua notam duxit, niveus videri,
> cetera fulvos. [57–60]

> Imitating with his forehead the crescent fire of the three-day-old moon, snow-white where it is marked, but otherwise tawny.

Peerlkamp was characteristically severe: *quam putida diligentia in describenda vetuli immolandi forma!* He complains that "no reason appears why Antonius should sacrifice so many victims; Horace [only] a calf," and forthwith he excises the offending lines.[15] Aristotle insisted that proportion was the basis of metaphor, and the last stanzas here are best taken as metaphors of a sort, the sacrifices being proportionate to the styles of the donors. Iullus' grand gesture incarnates his grandiloquence, while Horace's slender talent is implicit in the tiny calf he offers, the detailed affection of his description being itself calculated to prove the humble industry of the Matine

14. For a description of Icarus' flight, see Ovid, *A. A.* 2.33 ff.; *Met.* 8.183 ff.

15. Modern critics have been equally uneasy. A. Y. Campbell, *Horace*, 227, catalogues the Ode among those which "in their various ways end 'off.' " Cf. H. Toll, *Phoenix*, 9 (1955), 153.

bee. Perhaps the disproportionate attention he gives to the calf's moon-shaped spot also emphasizes Horace's reluctance to associate himself with the sun in any form. His sacrifice, like his modest position in the crowd, marks him as one content with merely the reflected glory of Iullus'—or any other poet's—lofty, and perilous, attempt to Pindarize. In his contrast of victims Horace may glance as well at a familiar literary distinction, the *tener vitulus* insinuating his own *tenuis spiritus,* and Iullus' herd suggesting an almost *pinguis* mode.[16] The hint could never become explicit without insulting Augustus as well as Iullus, and we need not make it so precise. In any case, the exaggerated modesty of the comparison recalls the terms of the contrast between Pindar's style and Horace's own, and that between Iullus' *maius plectrum* and Horace's *parvos* talent. The Ode progresses through these antithetical similes and metaphors, and its logic lies in terms of the various tensions it so maintains.[17]

In a poem of this length the distinction between our momentary reactions as we read and our final awareness of the total structure becomes acute. Every word and sound demands an immediate response, and the temptation is great to devote all our attention to the particular felicities of each line or group of words. Yet only when we view the poem from a certain distance, recognizing how each part functions in terms of the others, does the shape of the whole emerge—and then we are likely to substitute the intellectual construct at which we arrive for the poem itself. Even in the shorter Odes it is hard to maintain a hospitable balance between the two responses, so imperious are the claims of each. A good example is the Ode to Pyrrha, one of the loveliest of the amatory poems (for Milton's translation see above, p. 51):

> Quis multa gracilis te puer in rosa
> perfusus liquidis urget odoribus

16. Cf. *C.* 2.16.33 ff., and above, 36 ff. For the general contrast of sacrifices, see *C.* 2.17.30–32.

17. Like most of Horace's *recusationes,* this one is not altogether binding. In the next Ode (*C.* 4.3) we discover that the Muse can give the voice of swans even to mute fish such as Horace, and the following poem, if not precisely swanlike, is at least one of Horace's most Pindaric efforts. The sequence of the three Odes is surely deliberate.

grato, Pyrrha, sub antro?
cui flavam religas comam

simplex munditiis? heu quotiens fidem 5
mutatosque deos flebit et aspera
nigris aequora ventis
emirabitur insolens,

qui nunc te fruitur credulus aurea,
qui semper vacuam, semper amabilem 10
sperat, nescius aurae
fallacis. miseri, quibus

intemptata nites: me tabula sacer
votiva paries indicat uvida
suspendisse potenti 15
vestimenta maris deo. [*C.* 1.5]

The Ode's decorative charm, from the description of the slender youth, drenched in words as in perfumes, to the untranslatable *simplex munditiis,* to the visual reproduction of the *tabula votiva,* makes it easy to gloss over its fineness of structure. The storm of love was a well-worn conceit, while the comparison between a woman and the sea had been current at least as early as Semonides:

> The sea often stands without motion and harmless, a great joy to sailors in summer, and yet often it rages, driven to and fro with waves loudly roaring: to this sea such a woman is most like. [7.37–41, Diehl]

Love, it was universally acknowledged, was "bittersweet," (γλυκύπικρος), and there were no guarantees that in a moment sweet perfumes would not change to bitter brine. But where most writers granted a precarious equilibrium of fair and foul, Horace views Pyrrha in the more cynical terms of fair appearance and dark reality. Her golden hair (4), her gleaming beauty (13), and the fact that her lover believes her "all gold" (9) confirm the fair aspect that her name (from πῦρ, "fire") implies. But beauty is only skin deep, and behind the deceptively shining surface waits the certainty of black winds. To recognize that *aura* (11) hides beneath *aurea* (9)—the pun, emphasized by the words' identical positions in the line, is surely deliberate—is the prerogative of only the experienced mariner. The youth is *insolens* (8), unaccustomed to change; in this context it is easy to suspect that the word contains a reference as well to *insolo,* "to place in the sun." Like Catullus, Horace has learned that the suns that shine brightest shine briefest: *fulsere quondam candidi tibi soles* (Cat., 8.3). The lulling sounds of *semper vacuam,*[18] *semper amabilem* can give only a false sense of security, for to expect peaceful constancy from a woman is as fatuous as to hope that the sea remain forever calm.

Such a poem makes all its supposed precedents seem blunt and artistically naïve.[19] A mosaic metaphor, while plausible, is inadequate to such an Ode, for while the technique is similar to that used in various virtuoso passages, its effect is less confined. As in the Ode to Iullus, the different correspondences and contrasts provide not a decorative pattern but the supporting poles of the architecture. The Ode to Iullus assumes lines both spacious and formal, but even in a poem on apparently so slight a theme as the storm of love, Horace found room for the same kind of intricate polarities. Again the form is basically that of an antithesis, now intensely compressed rather than extended through several variations. Where the Ode to Iullus poses different images against one another, that to Pyrrha makes literal description itself a part of the controlling metaphor. Pyrrha's gleaming beauty is real enough; *aurea* proclaims only what our eyes could record. But when opposed to the "black winds" of her violence, her serene beauty tends to become figurative as well, to present itself in terms of a fair day before the storm strikes.

Classical criticism gives us little help in dealing with such devices as a structural technique. The standards were largely formal, and

18. *Vacuam* (10) and *intemptata* (13) both keep up the sea analogy. *Vacuus* may have the sense of "unclouded" (cf. *C.* 1.3.34), and *temptare* is sometimes used of seafaring (cf. *C.* 3.4.31). Perhaps *urget* (2) has something of the same idea; cf. *C.* 2.10.2. The *insolens puer* in fact exemplifies one of the extremes described in *C.* 2.10; he is *altum semper urgendo,* unmindful of the *procellas.* Zielinski's proposed emendation of *deo* (*C.* 1.5.16) to *deae* is tempting, for Venus could be goddess of the sea as well as of love; cf. *C.* 1.3.1, 3.26.5, 4.11.15. For further discussion of *C.* 1.5, see below, 144 ff., 238.

19. Cf. *Anth. Pal.* 5.156, 190, 12.156, 167, and the examples collected by B. Lier, *Ad topica carminum amatoriorum symbolae* (Stettin, 1914), 34–35.

discourage response to Horace's demands by failing to provide a category for them. Philosophers and rhetoricians contributed the bulk of stylistic discussion, and while we have a good deal about the psychological implications of figures of speech or about the practical occasions for their use, we have almost nothing on their possible structural function. The traditional approaches all shared the debilitating assumption that a figure was self-contained and might be adequately discussed in isolation. Puttenham instructed his sixteenth-century contemporaries that "figures . . . be the flowers, as it were, and colours that a Poet setteth upon the language of arte, as the embroderer doth his stone and perle or passements of gold upon the stuffe of a Princely garment." [20] In appealing to an analogy with clothing he confirmed a basic prejudice of classical doctrine. In theory, as distinct from practice, figures were treated as an arbitrary decorative device. Aristotle might term metaphor "the mark of genius," Cicero might inquire as to the pleasure it produced, and Longinus might speculate upon its relation to passion, but all tacitly accepted what the grammarians maintained, that metaphor was one of the *exornationes verborum* (*Auct. ad Her.,* 4.13.18). Like clothing, figures were something an author might fit on or strip off, depending upon the demands of the occasion.[21] How many metaphors are proper to poetry? How many to prose? And how many to the gradations of style in each, from the low to the middle to the grand? On the one hand, critics feared, metaphors might become so bold as to be indecorous. In such cases conversion to simile was recommended.[22] Metaphors threatened other dangers as well, among which frigidity (ψυχρότης), affectation (κακοζηλία), and vulgarity (τὰ ἐπιπόλαια) were the most conspicuous. On the other hand, metaphors promised inestimable advantages. Aristotle praised their "foreign air," and they were similarly favored for adding vividness (ἐνάργεια), majesty (σεμνότης), and charm (χάρις), while the *Auctor ad Herennium* waxed even more

20. G. Puttenham, "The Arte of English Poesie" (1589), III, 1, in G. Smith, ed., *Elizabethan Critical Essays, 2* (Oxford, 1904), 143.

21. Cf. Arist., *Rh.* 3.2.10; Cic., *De Or.* 3.38.155.

22. Cic., *Or.* 24.81–82, 39.134; Demetr., *Eloc.* 80; Longin., 32.3; Quint., 11.1.6.

hospitable: "Metaphor is used for the sake of placing something vividly before the eyes . . . for the sake of brevity . . . for the sake of avoiding obscenity . . . for the sake of making something larger . . . for the sake of making something smaller . . . for the sake of decorating." [23]

The terms are not likely to aid us in understanding a poem. When not given over to speculative categorizing, critics devoted themselves to practical legislation, and, between the two, little attention went to metaphor as something intrinsic to meaning and structure. Yet Horace's Odes, to a greater extent than any other classical body of short poems save perhaps Pindar's Odes, demand such attention. The ease with which he moves between literal and figurative might justifiably be called the most distinctive element of his verse. Often it solicits our interest only to frustrate it. How do we classify his treatment of Pyrrha, which hovers between description and metaphor? Such manipulation of fact and figure is characteristic, and in it Horace found not merely a striking device but an important principle of organization. Traditional conceits suggest the simplest means of defining it more precisely, for where custom has established the terms of comparison we can better chart an individual's exploitation of them.

The bow with which Eros was armed gave fair warning that love was a kind of warfare, and by the Augustan age the possible variations on that theme had all become exquisitely familiar.[24] On several occasions Horace referred to the conceit in passing, and in two poems he gave it structural importance:

23. 4.34.45. In general, see W. B. Stanford, *Greek Metaphor* (Oxford, 1936), 35 ff.

24. See Sophocles, *Ant.* 781; Euripides, *Med.* 531, 632–34; *Fr.* 430 (Nauck [2]); Lucretius, 1.34; Vergil, *A.* 4.1–2, 93–95. For references to the bow of Eros, see Lier, *Ad topica carminum,* 31–32. The *castra amoris* were a commonplace; Ovid's elaborate version (*Am.* 1.9.1 ff.) is a catalogue of motifs. See also R. Pichon, *De sermone amatorio* (Paris, 1902), *s. v. arma, bella, castra;* for occurrences in comedy, see K. Preston, *Studies in the Diction of the Sermo Amatorius in Roman Comedy* (Chicago, 1916), 50. Horace plays upon the theme in *C.* 3.26.1 ff., 4.1.1–2, 15–16. Poets rang the final change by insisting that the conceit was not merely literary, pointing to their torn hair, scratched cheeks, and bitten necks as evidence; cf. *C.* 1.13.9–12, 1.17.21–28; for further references, see K. F. Smith, *The Elegies of Tibullus, ad* 1.6.73.

Scriberis Vario fortis et hostium
victor Maeonii carminis alite,
quam rem cumque ferox navibus aut equis
  miles te duce gesserit.

nos, Agrippa, neque haec dicere nec gravem 5
Pelidae stomachum cedere nescii
nec cursus duplicis per mare Ulixei
  nec saevam Pelopis domum

conamur, tenues grandia, dum pudor
inbellisque lyrae Musa potens vetat 10
laudes egregii Caesaris et tuas
  culpa deterere ingeni.

quis Martem tunica tectum adamantina
digne scripserit aut pulvere Troico
nigrum Merionen aut ope Palladis 15
  Tydiden superis parem?

nos convivia, nos proelia virginum
sectis in iuvenes unguibus acrium
cantamus vacui, sive quid urimur,
  non praeter solitum leves. 20

[*C.* 1.6]

You will be celebrated by Varius, a poet of Homeric flight, for your bravery and your victories over the enemy, whatever deeds the soldiers, formidable on ship or horseback, have performed with you as their leader. I, Agrippa, shall attempt to sing neither of these things, nor of the destructive spleen of Achilles not knowing how to yield, nor of shifty Ulysses' voyages, nor of Pelops' savage house, since I am too slender in talent for such grand themes, while shame and the Muse who rules the unwarlike lyre forbid me to lessen your own glory and that of noble Caesar by my want of genius. Who could write fittingly of Mars clad in his adamantine corselet, or of Meriones black with Trojan dust, or of Diomede, with Pallas Athene's help a match for the gods above? In a light vein as always, whether I be unengaged or fired with love, I sing of banquets, I sing of the battles of maidens fiercely attacking youths with their trimmed fingernails.

Like *C.* 4.2, the Ode is a tactful *recusatio.* As Horace leaves Iullus to celebrate Augustus in Pindar's swanlike strains, so he recommends Varius, "a bird of Homeric song," as more suitable than himself for praising Agrippa. *Grandia* (9) embraces both the actual battles of Agrippa (3–4) and also (6–8) standard epic and tragic themes. (*Saevam Pelopis domum* probably alludes also to Varius' own tragedy *Thyestes,* produced soon after Actium.) By implicitly ranking Agrippa's accomplishments with such exalted subjects, Horace pays him a graceful compliment. He also dissociates himself from both legendary and contemporary themes of that sort. As it takes a Homer to describe an Achilles, so it will demand at least "a bird of Homeric song" to describe an Agrippa. And Horace certainly is not that,[25] any more than he is willing to be thought of as a Pindaric swan. In describing his own talent as *tenuis* (9) he appeals to Callimachus' Μοῦσα λεπταλέη, appearing here as the *inbellis lyrae Musa potens* (10). Scenes of Homeric warfare (13–16) suggest the type of *grandia* which any panegyric would be bound to include,[26] while the amatory topics of the final stanza reassert the imperatives of the "slender" style. Horace will treat only festive, if acrimonious, banquets. Varius can

25. In passing, we should notice Horace's characteristic slyness. The apparently objective catalogue of unsuitable subjects (5–8) is itself a proof of his inability to deal with them. By describing Achilles as "ignorant of how to yield" (6), Horace in effect destroys the moral structure of the *Iliad;* we need only contrast Homer's οὐκ ἐθέλει (*Il.* 9.678). Nor does *stomachum* (6), a word customarily reserved for the Satires, add anything to Achilles' grandeur. The grammarian Charisius (cited by E. C. Wickham, *The Works of Horace* [Oxford, 1896], *ad loc.*) gives it as an example of deliberate lowliness (ταπείνωσις). Similarly, *duplicis* (7) subtly devalues Ulysses. The way in which Horace treats these epic examples seems intended as a warning to Agrippa of how, on a larger scale, he would botch any similar theme. For other examples of a similar technique see below, 324 ff.

26. The rhetorical questions have caused some difficulty, as *quis* (13) appears to refer to no one. See Fraenkel, *Horace,* 233–34. Probably we should see in them a reminder of Varius, as all three subjects (13–16) are from the *Iliad,* and Varius has been termed a "bird of Homeric flight" (2). Cf. *S.* 1.10.43–44: *forte epos acer / ut nemo Varius ducit.*

describe the grimmer family dinners of tragedy. *Nos proelia virginum . . . cantamus:* figurative battles alone fit themselves to Horace's "unwarlike lyre," and trimmed nails are the only weapons he allows his fierce Amazons. Rejecting the martial theme of Agrippa's conquests, Horace proclaims himself a military historian of the wars of love.[27]

The arrangement of the different antitheses recalls the plan of *C.* 4.2. But in the Ode to Agrippa Horace also relies upon a contrast of the sort he used in the Ode to Pyrrha, a dialectic of literal and figurative terms. In the opposition of *bella* and *bella amoris* he apparently found a convenient scheme, for he turned to it again in an Ode of a quite different type:

Natis in usum laetitiae scyphis
pugnare Thracum est: tollite barbarum
morem verecundumque Bacchum
sanguineis prohibete rixis.

vino et lucernis Medus acinaces 5
immane quantum discrepat: inpium
lenite clamorem, sodales,
et cubito remanete presso.

voltis severi me quoque sumere
partem Falerni? dicat Opuntiae 10
frater Megyllae, quo beatus
volnere, qua pereat sagitta.

cessat voluntas? non alia bibam
mercede. quae te cumque domat Venus,
non erubescendis adurit 15
ignibus, ingenuoque semper

amore peccas. quidquid habes, age
depone tutis auribus. a miser,
quanta laborabas Charybdi,
digne puer meliore flamma. 20

27. Another *recusatio* using the contrast of real and figurative *bella* is *C.* 2.12. Horace rejects savage historical and mythical themes to celebrate Licymnia, who struggles only in jest and whose savagery is mere pretense. Propertius too uses the contrast (1.6.29–30, 3.5.1–2).

quae saga, quis te solvere Thessalis
magus venenis, quis poterit deus?
vix inligatum te triformi
Pegasus expediet Chimaera. [*C.* 1.27]

To fight with cups destined for joy is a habit fit only for Thracians. Away with this barbarous custom; keep modest Bacchus from bloody brawls. The Persian sword is a poor match for wine and lamps. Soften your impious shouting, comrades, and settle back upon your elbows. Do you wish me to take my share of the strong Falernian? Then let the brother of Opuntian Megylla declare by what wound he is blest, by what arrow he perishes. He refuses? On no other condition will I drink. Whatever Venus conquers you, she burns you with fires you need not blush for; you sin always with a freeborn love. Come now, whisper whatever it is to ears that will not betray their trust.—O wretched boy, in what a Charybdis you were caught, you who are worthy of a better flame! What witch, what magician with Thessalian drugs, what god can free you? Scarcely Pegasus himself will set you free, so entangled are you with this triple-formed Chimera.

Sensus sumptus est ab Anacreonte, Porphyrio dutifully reminds us, and we have a fragment which looks like the model:

Come, boy, bring me a cup, so that I may have a large draught, ten parts of water to five of wine, since I would play the Bacchant in decorous fashion. Come, no longer let us practice this Scythian drinking with uproar and noise over the wine, but drink modestly among fair songs. [43, Diehl]

Civil harmony rebukes barbaric outrage; the "sense" of the poems is indeed the same. Yet precedent for Horace's form eludes all attempts at *Quellenforschung. Laetitiae . . . pugnare* erects a tension between festivity and battle, joy and pain, which the juxtaposition of *vino et lucernis* with *Medus acinaces* intensifies. The jarring effect recalls that produced by *tenues grandia* (*C.* 1.6.9). In neither case is Horace straining for an isolated effect, but stating a structural and conceptual conflict. Departing from the generality of Anacreon's terms, he appeals to a tighter antithesis between real and figurative *bella,* exploiting for a different purpose the contrast of *C.* 1.6. Despite the gnomic remoteness of the first sentence, the battles it rebukes are actual ones, if we may judge from the alarmed imperatives which follow (2–8). Horace seems to imagine himself addressing some carousers who have gotten out of hand, and *barbarum* (2), *sanguineis rixis* (4), *Medus acinaces* (5), and *inpium clamorem* (6–7) keep before us the martial violence he castigates.[28]

In the calmer lines which follow, Horace retains the military vocabulary, compelling us to measure the two scenes against one another more precisely. The brother of Megylla "perishes," wounded by Cupid's arrow and "conquered" by Venus' earthly counterpart (11–12). His blushing cheeks (*erubescendis,* 15), evidence his injuries and match the bloody results of more serious battles, *sanguineis rixis* (4). A subsidiary religious reference strengthens the contrasts. "Blest" in his wounds (*beatus,* 11), the lover sins (*peccas,* 17) in venial fashion merely.[29] Such peccadillos are but proper to the god of the vine, unlike the "impious" clamor (6) which signals heretical departure from his service. Banishing the atmosphere of violence, Horace encourages us to feel an epitome of civilized harmony in the genial scene that follows (9 ff.). The banqueters leave the orgiastic realm of Thracian Dionysus for the serener rule of a *verecundus Bacchus,* and the only battles, injuries, or conquests which remain are metaphorical ones. Literal and figurative meanings range themselves as polarities, and upon the resulting tension Horace builds a moral dialectic.

The final two stanzas seem to lead us away from the oppositions which have been so carefully constructed. Yet, in slightly different terms, they epitomize and finally resolve them. The triple-formed Chimera with whom the hapless youth is entangled (*inligatum,* 23)

28. Fraenkel, *Horace,* 180–81, emphasizes the dramatic quality of the scene, and A. L. Wheeler, *Catullus and the Traditions of Ancient Poetry* (Berkeley, 1934), 204–05, writes out actual stage directions.

29. *Peccare* sometimes had a specific sexual meaning in the erotic vocabulary; cf. *C.* 3.7.19, and see the references given by R. Pichon, *De sermone amatorio,* 227–28. *Pereo* (12) could also have an erotic sense, as did "die" in Elizabethan English; cf. Propertius, 1.4.12, 1.10.5; Ovid, *Am.* 2.7.10.

represents a chaotic mingling of dissimilars; the image is anticipated by the previous stanza's contrast of water and fire (19–20). Both look back to the unnatural union of joy and savagery, wine and swords with which the poem opens. (The idea of a discordant joining is brought out visually by the way in which *scyphis* is caught, *inligatum,* as it were, between *laetitiae* and *pugnare.*) Even the colloquial *immane quantum discrepat* (6)—"a stereotyped phrase," comments Shorey—enforces the Ode's basic antithesis, if we remember the primary meaning of *immane,* "monstrously." And just as it is only Pegasus (24) who may be able to free the youth from his Chimera, so it is only the poet who, through the poem itself, can set free the banqueters from the union of dissimilars in which they are enmeshed.

The metaphor of inner riches was as familiar in a philosophical context as that of the lover as warrior was in an amatory one, and in an Ode to Sallustius Crispus (*C.* 2.2) Horace explored its structural possibilities in a similar way. The poem, which is probably early, is somewhat mechanical, and Horace's imagination seems to have been engaged as much by the technical opportunities the theme afforded as by its moral significance.

Nullus argento color est avaris
abdito terris, inimice lamnae
Crispe Sallusti, nisi temperato
  splendeat usu.

vivet extento Proculeius aevo (5)
notus in fratres animi paterni;
illum aget pinna metuente solvi
  Fama superstes.

latius regnes avidum domando
spiritum quam si Libyam remotis (10)
Gadibus iungas et uterque Poenus
  serviat uni:

crescit indulgens sibi dirus hydrops
nec sitim pellit, nisi causa morbi

fugerit venis et aquosus albo 15
corpore languor.

redditum Cyri solio Prahaten
dissidens plebi numero beatorum
eximit Virtus populumque falsis
dedocet uti 20

vocibus, regnum et diadema tutum
deferens uni propriamque laurum,
quisquis ingentis oculo inretorto
spectat acervos. [*C.* 2.2]

There is no luster to silver hidden away in the greedy earth, Sallustius Crispus, you who are hostile to metal unless it shine by a temperate use. Proculeius shall live through the long ages to come, famous for his paternal spirit toward his brothers; undying Fame shall lift him upon wings that never falter. You will rule more widely by conquering a greedy spirit than if you should join Libya with distant Gades and make the Carthaginian settlers on either side of the channel serve a single master. Dreadful dropsy grows by feeding upon itself, nor can thirst be banished unless the cause of the disease has left the veins and the watery weakness departed from the body. Virtue, dissenting from the judgment of the people, removes Prahates from the number of the truly rich, even though he has been restored to the throne of Cyrus, but instead, teaching the people not to use false names, she hands over kingship, the secure diadem, and the truly earned laurel wreath to that man alone who can look upon huge piles of treasure unmoved, without casting any jealous glance at it over his shoulder.

Sallustius Crispus was reputedly lavish with the fortune he had inherited from his great-uncle, the historian Sallust, and we may surmise that he would be less impressed by the warning against burying silver than by the injunction implicit in *temperato* (3). The personal application remains somewhat obscure, in part because of the syntactical ambiguity of the first stanza.[30] Fortunately the historical context does not define the Ode's general intent. Yet even as an abstract statement it has caused difficulty. Tyrrell was unnecessarily severe:

> When we read how "Virtue will refuse the name of *happy* [italics his] to kings, and will give (not the name of *happy* but) the kingly throne and diadem to him who, without turning to gaze again, can look on huge heaps," we cannot help asking ourselves whether the poet has really said what he wished to say.[31]

The stanzas are not really so inarticulate, but they depend on our recognizing that *beatus* (18) may mean "rich" as well as "happy" or "blessed." The ambiguity was familiar,[32] while the concept of inner riches was neither obscure nor esoteric. The broad contrast of inner and outer had been basic to Plato, and the Stoics were not long in making it axiomatic. "Only the wise man is rich," they argued, "only the wise man is king." [33] Though Horace was not above ridiculing their paradoxes in the Satires, he is willing enough to endorse their terms here, and the presence of *Virtus* (19), the chief Stoic deity, may suggest a doctrinaire bias to the Ode. Yet the concept was by then a commonplace. *Effugere cupiditatem regnum est vincere,* deposed Publilius Syrus (154, Woelfflin), a writer of the Caesarian age whose handbook gave the illusory status of epigram to what were no more than proverbs. Like most philosophical maxims, the contrast between inner and outer riches had long since become a τόπος. A pertinent example is a contemporary epigram dedicated to the same Sallustius which applauds the "great riches of your heart" (*Anth. Pal.* 16.40). Horace simply generalizes the encomium, balancing earthly possessions with the more stately mansions of the soul,

30. I.e. whether we should take *nisi . . . usu* with *nullus . . . terris* or with *inimice lamnae*. See W. H. Alexander, *TAPA, 74* (1943), 192 ff.; W. M. Calder, *CP, 56* (1961), 175 ff.

31. R. Y. Tyrrell, *Latin Poetry,* 194.

32. See the references given by Lewis and Short's *Latin Dictionary;* and for *beatus* as "rich" in Horace, see *C.* 1.29.1, 3.7.3. Horace seems to play upon the double sense of *beatus* in *C.* 3.16.32, 4.9.46; *S.* 1.3.142, 2.6.74; *Ep.* 1.16.20, 2.1.139. Cf. especially *C.* 3.16.25 ff., 39 ff.

33. See Cic., *Par.* 42 ff., and the references in P. Lejay, *Oeuvres d'Horace, Satires* (Paris, 1911), *ad S.* 1.3.125.

wealth physical with wealth metaphysical. One may master great riches, even to the proverbial lordship of both shores of the Mediterranean, or one may master the desire for them (9–12). Such self-sufficiency represents greater riches and a grander kingship: *latius regnes* (9). Proculeius, by his splendid generosity toward his brothers (5–8), exemplifies such a conquest and rules a richer kingdom than the miser enslaved by his buried silver (1–4). He enjoys the conquest of time, *extento aevo* (5), a possession that outlasts merely spatial riches.

A specific historical example of kingly wealth appears in Prahates (17), who corresponds to the hypothetical ruler of the linked shores of the Mediterranean (10–12). Prahates has conquered the kingdom of Cyrus, but "the victor," in Fitzgerald's words, "belongs to the spoils." Prahates cannot rule his *avidum spiritum,* and Virtue hence rejects him from the number of the truly, the inwardly, the metaphorically rich: *numero beatorum eximit* (18–19). The true or figurative king is he who can afford to ignore merely physical wealth. *Regnum et diadema tutum* (21) looks back to *domando* (9), while the laurel crown of the conquering general (22) points a contrast with the man who has literally conquered both shores of the Mediterranean (10–12). The repetition of *uni* (12, 22), with opposed applications, emphasizes the contrast. The true king's disdain for money, even when heaped up before him (23–24), binds the Ode by a final contrast with the miser's servitude to his buried wealth (1–4).[34]

The urgency of self-rule was a commonplace, and the metaphor dormant if not dead. Horace revives its meaning, as far as was possible, by making us aware of the implicit but rarely explicated comparison with external kingship, incorporating contemporary political history to illustrate the latter. The emphasis which falls upon *vocibus* (21), the only stanzaic enjambment, suggests that the Ode's principal concern is with the right use of names, and by maintaining an identical terminology for both sides of his antithesis Horace achieves a succinct

34. Lines 13–16 look like an inheritance from the Satires, and are one reason for thinking the Ode early. But though distinct from the Ode's principal contrasts, the lines reproduce them in different terms. To indulge avarice is to increase it (13); we have almost a diagnosis of the miser enslaved by his buried silver. One must eradicate the disease completely (14–16), as one must entirely depose an *avidum spiritum.*

poetic logic. Yet it is not a very exciting one, and in exploring the various contrasts between true and false riches, riches metaphorical and physical, Horace never really raises the poem from the level of frigid ingenuity.

By comparison with *C.* 2.18, on a closely related theme, the Ode to Sallustius reads like an exercise. In *C.* 2.18 Horace relies upon the same type of antithesis between figure and fact, but now only as a concealed framework for a more passionate statement. His control is equally sure, but he has abandoned the air of someone making a geometrical demonstration.

Non ebur neque aureum
  mea renidet in domo lacunar,
non trabes Hymettiae
  premunt columnas ultima recisas

Africa neque Attali 5
  ignotus heres regiam occupavi
nec Laconicas mihi
  trahunt honestae purpuras clientae.

at fides et ingeni
  benigna vena est pauperemque dives 10
me petit: nihil supra
  deos lacesso nec potentem amicum

largiora flagito,
  satis beatus unicis Sabinis.
truditur dies die 15
  novaeque pergunt interire lunae:

tu secanda marmora
  locas sub ipsum funus et sepulcri
inmemor struis domos
  marisque Bais obstrepentis urges 20

submovere litora,
  parum locuples continente ripa:
quid quod usque proximos
  revellis agri terminos et ultra

limites clientium 25
salis avarus? pellitur paternos
in sinu ferens deos
et uxor et vir sordidosque natos.

nulla certior tamen
rapacis Orci fine destinata 30
aula divitem manet
erum. quid ultra tendis? aequa tellus

pauperi recluditur
regumque pueris, nec satelles Orci
callidum Promethea 35
revexit auro captus. hic superbum

Tantalum atque Tantali
genus coercet, hic levare functum
pauperem laboribus
vocatus atque non vocatus audit. 40

[*C.* 2.18]

No ivory nor gilded ceilings shine in my home; no beams carved from Hymettian marble rest on pillars quarried from distant Africa; I have not, as an unwitting heir, seized upon the palace of an Attalus; nor do wellborn clients spin gowns of Laconian purple for me. But faith and a rich vein of genius are mine, and the wealthy seek me out, poor as I am. I importune the gods for no more, nor do I demand anything further from my powerful friend, happy enough in my Sabine farm alone.

Day treads upon day, and new moons hasten forward to die. You let out contracts for cutting marble even upon the very verge of death, and, unmindful of the tomb, you build your houses and hasten to thrust back the boundary of the sea that roars at Baiae. What of the fact that you rip up the markers of your neighbor's field, and in your greed leap over the bounds of your clients? The husband, holding in his arms the household gods, is driven out with his wife and

> destitute children. Yet no hall waits more certainly for the rich man than the destined bourne of greedy Orcus. Why do you always strive for more? The impartial earth opens alike for the pauper and the children of kings, nor is the minion of Orcus bribed by gold to release the artful Prometheus. He confines proud Tantalus and the race of Tantalus, and, invoked or not invoked, he attends to free the poor man done at last with his labor.

Pronouncing the Ode early, the Kiessling-Heinze edition maintains that "the individual parts are as yet hardly bound together in organic fashion." The criticism seems to have some justice. Horace might have ended the poem at line fourteen, after the satisfying paradox of *pauperemque dives me petit* and the play on *beatus.* The lines achieve an almost sonnetlike completeness in working out the antithesis of inner and outer riches, of golden halls as against the "rich vein of genius" which has only the humble Sabine farm for its external setting.[35]

The couplet that follows (15–16) appears to introduce an unrelated theme, raising the poem from a social to an ultimate context. The calendar itself was originally lunar—*menstruo metiens iter annuum,* Catullus apostrophized Diana (34.17–18)—so the moon might be a guaranteed symbol, as it were, for life's passing. Heraclitus and Empedocles had designated the moon's orbit as dividing the eternal heavens from the terrestrial world of death and decay (*1,* 294, 35 ff., Diels). Its imperfections such as discolorations, wanings, and waxings tie it to the latter, but its perpetual renewal links it with the former. In a sense the moon mediates between eternal and transient, and Horace found both aspects peculiarly evocative. *Novaeque pergunt interire lunae* (16): the line is both epitaph and promise of continuity. The moon's changes (*pergunt interire*) predict the mortality of all sublunar nature,[36] but *novae* separates the persistence of na-

35. The tone of *C.* 2.18 is more personal than that of *C.* 2.2, for in *C.* 2.18 it is specifically Horace's poetry rather than some conventional "inner riches" that constitutes his secret wealth. On the relation of this contrast to his attempts to define his poetry see below, 332 ff.

36. Cf. *C.* 2.11.5 ff., and the fragment of Sophocles (*Fr.* 787, Nauck [2]) in Plutarch, *Dem.* 45.911c.

ture's changes from the finality of human death.[37] The steady procession of days and months reminds us that the alternation of life and death is the only permanent thing in nature—a proposition that the anonymous *avarus* ignores. In titling the Ode *"de continentia"* Ps.-Acro might have been proposing, or even acknowledging, a pun which would have both etymological and poetic sanction. By breaking through the *continente ripa* (22) to build out upon the sea, the *parum locuples*[38] convicts himself of an incontinence so profound as to defy nature's own limits. *Sepulcri inmemor struis domos:* the line between land and sea is a token of nature's final line between life and death, for in neglecting the former the *avarus* shows himself blind to the latter. The image of building into the sea was one Horace returned to persistently, with a mixture of fascination and outrage.[39] And on at least one other occasion he attributed to it a similar symbolic value:

> Intactis opulentior
> thesauris Arabum et divitis Indiae
> caementis licet occupes
> terrenum omne tuis et mare publicum:
>
> si figit adamantinos
> summis verticibus dira Necessitas
> clavos, non animum metu,
> non mortis laqueis expedies caput. [*C.* 3.24.1–8]

Though your wealth exceeds the untouched treasures of Arabia and the riches of India, and you may seize with your buildings all the land and the public sea, once dread Necessity plants her adamantine nails in your roof, you

37. Cf. *C.* 4.7.13 ff.

38. The use of *locuples* (literally, "full of space," from *locus* and *plenus*) in this context provides a good example of the way Horace refreshes our sense of a word's radical meaning. Cf. *canities* (*C.* 1.9.17; see below, 271) or *exilis* (*C.* 1.4.17; see below, 269).

39. Cf. *C.* 3.1.33–36, and perhaps *C.* 2.3.17–20, where *exstructis in altum divitiis* may refer to the same idea; see A. R. Anderson, *CP, 10* (1915), 456. Cf. also Sallust, *Cat.* 20.11; Vergil, *A.* 9.710 ff.; Ov., *A. A.* 3.126; Pliny, *H. N.* 35.13.166 (Mayhoff); Martial, 10.30.

will not free your soul from fear nor your head from the noose of death.

In *C.* 2.18 the assault upon the sea by the *avarus* and his disregard for the sanctioned boundary lines of property (23–28) betrays the same blindness. In neither passage are social effects alone at issue, for in both Horace addresses himself to those who ignore the inevitable dimensions of the grave.

If we keep in mind Horace's very concrete manner of presenting abstractions the Ode's logic becomes clearer. *Nulla certior . . . aula* (29–31) invites us to compare the "hall of death" with the spreading mansion of the *avarus*. Again we have a dialectic of figurative and literal.[40] The *parum locuples* will change his extravagant holdings for the tomb's narrow walls:

Much you had of land and rent,
Your length in clay's now competent,

runs the dirge for the Duchess of Malfi. *Coercet* (38) receives an additional emphasis from the convulsively violent verbs that Horace used in describing the overreaching *avarus: urges submovere* (20–21), *revellis* (24), *salis* (26), *pellitur* (26).[41] Defiance of nature's limits yields to the limit of death (*fine,* 30), and human rapacity falls prey to *rapax Orcus* (30). You can't take it with you—*quid ultra tendis?* The formulation (32) recalls *ultra limites* (24–25), and, by contrast, Horace's description of himself: *nihil supra lacesso . . . satis beatus* (11 ff.). The spatial expressions of sufficiency, extravagance, and containment themselves define a moral comment. The house of ivory and gold rejected by Horace (1 ff.) prefigures in general terms the home of the *avarus* (17 ff.). We are encouraged to compare the two by the repetition of *domus* (2, 19), by the similarity of archi-

40. Although the syntax of 29–31 is ambiguous, the meaning varies little, for in either case the image of a "house of death" remains. See Wickham, *Works of Horace, ad loc.* For the traditional use of the metaphor, cf. Homer, *Od.* 10.512; Aes., *Pers.* 924; Eurip., *Alc.* 260; Verg., *A.* 6.269; Hor., *C.* 1.4.17. For the frequent occurrence in epitaphs, see R. Lattimore, *Themes in Greek and Latin Epitaphs* (Urbana, 1942), 165 ff.; F. A. Sullivan, *TAPA, 70* (1939), 507 ff.

41. For Horace's spatial sense of death, see above, 55.

tectural details (4, 17), and by the distinction drawn between the absence of *clientae* (8) and the expulsion of them (25). Horace rests content within the boundaries of the Sabine farm, which displays no riches save those of his own nature, *ingeni benigna vena* (9–10). The humble dimensions of his farm are a token of his acceptance of the human estate with its limits, and his contentment reflects his knowledge of the ultimate equality of every man's dwelling in the grave, *aequa tellus* (32).

The poem rests, then, upon a series of antitheses, the principal one being that between the figurative house of death and the actual house of the *avarus,* with a further contrast lying between the house of the *avarus* and the Sabine farm. In terms of the relations maintained between these different images we can see that the various parts of the Ode are in fact "bound together in organic fashion," and that its disjointedness is no more than superficial.

Although the poem is not itself fragmentary, it attracts a fragmentary approach. Many readers have been tempted to isolate the description of the *avarus* and see it in the context of social history. We are frequently reminded that the foundations left along the shore at Baiae prove Horace's lines to be no fantasy, that Cicero's generation had already seen comparable land greed, and that Sallust and Tacitus protested against similar iniquities. The Ode has appealed more successfully to egalitarian, or at least chivalric, sentiments than to critical ones: "It has a strangely modern ring, and might have been written by some socialist poet who had watched a body of Highland crofters being expelled from their holdings that the land be made into a deer forest." [42] To establish the authenticity of Horace's descriptions is neither to explain nor to negate their possible further relevance within the poem. Symbols need not be at odds with reality. They are rather a product of it, a "throwing together" of two elements, a union, usually, of actual fact and some further meaning. As in the treatment of Prahates in the Ode to Sallustius (*C.* 2.2.15 ff.), the poet does not abdicate to become a historian, but history becomes

42. R. S. Conway, *New Studies of a Great Inheritance* (London, 1921), 53. The sociopolitical background is also emphasized by G. Carlsson, *Eranos, 42* (1944), 16; V. Pöschl, *Horaz und die Politik* (Heidelberg, 1956), 21.

woven into the poetic structure. Like the building out upon the sea, the expulsion of tenants betokens an individual refusal to accept the limits of human life; thus *ultra limites* (24–25) here has a special significance beyond that of historical documentation.

The private bias of *C.* 2.18 is more apparent if we look at *C.* 2.15, the Ode most frequently compared with it:

Iam pauca aratro iugera regiae
moles relinquent, undique latius
extenta visentur Lucrino
stagna lacu platanusque caelebs

evincet ulmos. tum violaria et 5
myrtus et omnis copia narium
spargent olivetis odorem
fertilibus domino priori,

tum spissa ramis laurea fervidos
excludet ictus. non ita Romuli 10
praescriptum et intonsi Catonis
auspiciis veterumque norma:

privatus illis census erat brevis,
commune magnum; nulla decempedis
metata privatis opacam 15
porticus excipiebat arcton

nec fortuitum spernere caespitem
leges sinebant, oppida publico
sumptu iubentes et deorum
templa novo decorare saxo. 20

In a short time now the kingly buildings will leave few acres for the plow, and on all sides the fishpools will be seen spreading broader than the Lucrine lake, and the unwed plane tree will conquer the elms. Then violets and myrtles and the whole company of perfumes will scatter their scent upon the olive groves that once bore fruit for

> their former master; then will the densely grown laurel exclude the burning rays of the sun. Not thus was it prescribed by the rule of Romulus and unshorn Cato and by the custom of our ancestors. Their private income was modest, and that of the community great. No private portico, measurable in ten-foot lengths, captured the cooling northern breeze, nor did the laws allow them to spurn the turf found anywhere for building their huts, commanding them to adorn at public expense the towns and the temples of the gods with new-cut stone.

Buildings and private fishponds encroach upon the public land much as the *avarus* takes over the sea and the land of his clients. Again wealth is made to seem a violation of nature, but now it is allied with sterility and engaged in a virtual war of occupation. Artificial pleasures such as private lakes (*stagna,* 4) have taken over the land once available for crops, while the "unwed" (4) plane tree "conquers" (5) the elm, and exotic perfumes overpower the "fertile" (8) and indigenous olive. Newly planted thickets beat back the "blows" of the sun (10), and private porticos "capture" (16) the very winds. In sharp contrast was the natural life of the early Romans. Cato, Horace somewhat fancifully recalls, was himself unshorn (11), and the earth then provided material for homes to rise wherever a natural site offered (17).

C. W. Mendell, concentrating upon the satiric element in *C.* 2.18, points out that both *C.* 2.18 and *C.* 2.15 "refer emphatically to the extension of large estates as a national scandal." [43] Yet the general similarity should not be allowed to override the important distinction between the two. The very fact that *C.* 2.18 is addressed to an individual, anonymous though he may be, while *C.* 2.15 addresses no one, indicates the difference in Horace's perspective. *C.* 2.18 treats the extension of large estates not only as a national scandal but as an individual folly as well, an aspect that *C.* 2.15 ignores. Both Odes describe the effects of wealth in terms of an assault of the artificial upon the natural, and both use equally violent verbs. But where in *C.* 2.15 the concept of nature provides a premise, an unquestioned standard, in *C.* 2.18 it offers a logical symbolic argument. In the former poem trespassing

43. *YCS, 11* (1950), 290.

upon nature is wrong per se; in the latter it is wrong because it betrays a culpable blindness to the natural phenomenon of mortality.[44]

The more private concern of *C.* 2.18 suggests that an equally valid comparison might invoke a poem such as that to Postumus, *C.* 2.14. The contrast there between the *brevis dominus* of life (24) and the final rule of *indomita mors* (4) recalls, structurally if not emotionally, the dialectic in *C.* 2.18 between earthly mansion and ultimate home. "A worthier heir," Horace warns Postumus, "will drink up your Caecuban now guarded by a hundred keys, and will stain the tiled floor with proud wine, richer than that drunk at the pontiffs' banquets" (25–28). Locking up vast cellars of wine betrays the unworthy assumption that one will live indefinitely,[45] as does the building of a house out upon the sea: *sepulcri inmemor struis.* Both Odes have a bias which is individual rather than public. Death, after all, is the ultimate privacy. As we come into the world alone, we leave it alone: Ajax withdraws for his suicide, and Everyman's friends abandon him on his way to the grave. Reminders of death hardly decorate public denunciations of greed—or so, at any rate, it seemed to Horace. The Satires, his most public poetry, generally avoid the subject in arguing against avarice, whereas the Odes and Epistles rely on it. Satire marshals objections practical and immediate rather than ultimate: buried money is useless; rich men essentially need no more than poor; no one is rated by what he owns; everyone hates the rich; there is always someone richer (*S.* 1.1). Only rarely in the Satires does Horace touch upon the argument that is his favorite in the Odes and Epistles, that money neither survives death nor saves anyone from it.[46] The argument of *C.* 2.18 distinguishes the poem from both the

44. *C.* 3.24, which is also often compared to *C.* 2.18, lies halfway between *C.* 2.18 and *C.* 2.15. Although the first two stanzas and the last focus, as does *C.* 2.18, on the individual's state of mind, the bulk of this sprawling Ode is concerned with public wrongs and public remedies, more in the manner of *C.* 2.15. The concept of nature in *C.* 3.24 is social and external, with the Getae and Scythians having a function similar to that of Cato and the early Romans in *C.* 2.15.

45. Cf. *S.* 2.3.122–23, and below, 264.

46. *C.* 1.4.13–14, 2.3.17 ff., 2.14.11 ff., 2.18.29 ff., 3.24.1 ff., 4.7.15 ff.; *Ep.* 1.6.20 ff., 1.16.73 ff., 2.2.175 ff. For the Satires' infrequent use of death as an argument against avarice, see *S.* 2.2.129 ff., 2.3.122–23. It is indicative that in *S.* 2.5, an extended treatment of legacy seeking, Horace avoids treating

Satires and the Odes of social protest. Although it incorporates elements of each, its primary concern is the individual's private relations with himself.

THE CLEOPATRA ODE

From the various Odes discussed in this chapter, certain techniques seem constant enough to be termed characteristic. Most obvious is Horace's fondness for an antithetical arrangement of themes and ideas, and we can watch the verbal contrasts and repetitions that he so often exploits in individual stanzas develop into an architectural control for whole poems. This is not altogether to deny the popular theory of Reincke that each Ode tends to fall into three distinct parts.[47] Such a dismembering of stanzas is always possible, but usually a more important type of organization can be seen in the balance of ideas and images that an Ode maintains throughout.

In the second place, we notice that Horace consistently employs similes and metaphors not as ornaments of thought, but as methods of thought. To the generations trained on Shakespeare and Donne Horace's figures are not likely to seem remarkable, but if we compare the Odes with the short poems of Catullus, say, or with the works of Tibullus, we must be struck both by the profusion and by the intricacy of Horace's usage. Often he achieves a special economy by counterpointing literal and figurative meanings, thus allying his fondness for antithetical and metaphorical structures. Perhaps, indeed, he found congenial a style based heavily on metaphors precisely because they invited antithetical treatment.

Finally, we may remark a third characteristic, though it is less constant than the other two. That is his genius for weaving history into a poem's essential structure and making a unified fabric of the two. Agrippa's conquests, Prahates' kingdom, and the outrageously evident mansion and land seizures of the *avarus* all become assimilated

---

death as anything but a motive for a social comedy. On the similar distinction between the treatment of nature in the Satires and in the Odes, see below, 236 ff.

47. G. Reincke, *De tripartita carminum Horatianorum structura* (Berlin, 1929).

as structural elements, and, in each case, as the literal term of an antithesis.

In pushing these various techniques to a delicate extreme, the so-called "Cleopatra Ode" (*C.* 1.37) offers a paradigm of certain important elements of Horace's imagination. Like *C.* 2.18, it has more often excited attention as a historical document than as a literary one. We are frequently urged to contemplate its "Weltgeschichtliche Bedeutungsschwere," and are reminded that Horace treats the conflict not only of Cleopatra and Octavian but of Egypt and Rome, East and West, the old and the new.[48] The number of ideological reverberations have obscured the individual quality of Horace's tones:

Nunc est bibendum, nunc pede libero
pulsanda tellus, nunc Saliaribus
ornare pulvinar deorum
tempus erat dapibus, sodales.

antehac nefas depromere Caecubum 5
cellis avitis, dum Capitolio
regina dementis ruinas
funus et imperio parabat

contaminato cum grege turpium
morbo virorum, quidlibet inpotens 10
sperare fortunaque dulci
ebria. sed minuit furorem

vix una sospes navis ab ignibus
mentemque lymphatam Mareotico
redegit in veros timores 15
Caesar ab Italia volantem

remis adurgens, accipiter velut
mollis columbas aut leporem citus
venator in campis nivalis
Haemoniae, daret ut catenis 20

48. See W. Wili, *Horaz,* 136–37; H. U. Instinsky, *Hermes, 82* (1954), 126–28. T. Birt, *Horaz' Lieder, 2* (Leipzig, 1925), 59, speaks of Horace's "politische Muse." For fuller treatment of *C.* 1.37, and of the criticism of it, see my article, *Phoenix, 12* (1958), 47 ff.

fatale monstrum: quae generosius
perire quaerens nec muliebriter
  expavit ensem nec latentis
    classe cita reparavit oras,

ausa et iacentem visere regiam 25
voltu sereno, fortis et asperas
  tractare serpentes, ut atrum
    corpore conbiberet venenum,

deliberata morte ferocior:
saevis Liburnis scilicet invidens 30
  privata deduci superbo
    non humilis mulier triumpho. [*C.* 1.37]

Now is the time to drink, comrades, now with unfettered foot to strike the ground, now to honor with Salian feasts the couch of the gods. Before this it was forbidden to draw forth the Caecuban wine from ancestral cellars, as long as a Queen, together with her band of men stained with foul perversion, was preparing mad destruction for the Capitol and ruin for our rule, she being so abandoned as to hope for anything imaginable, drunk as she was upon sweet fortune. But when scarcely a single ship escaped from the flames it lessened her madness, and Caesar reduced her thoughts, inflamed by Mareotic wine, to the stern reality of fear, pursuing her with his galleys as she fled from Italy, like a hawk pursuing soft doves or a swift hunter the hare in the fields of snowy Haemonia, so that he might cast into chains that prodigy of fate. She, seeking to die nobly, did not like a woman tremble at the sword, nor did she repair with her swift fleet to hidden shores. She dared to look upon her fallen palace in serenity, and bravely took to herself the harsh-scaled serpents so that she might drink in their black poison with her whole body, growing fiercer in her premeditated death. She, no humble woman, scorned indeed to be led as a private citizen on board the haughty Liburnian galleys for a proud triumph.

Nunc est bibendum: the opening words at once issue a literal command and state the Ode's articulating image, one that has gone oddly unremarked.[49] The pun on *libero* (suggesting Liber or Bacchus) prolongs the sense of the Romans' intoxicated joy, which becomes explicit again with the reference to the long-stored-away Caecuban wine (5). The description of Cleopatra, *fortunaque dulci ebria* (11–12) recalls her notorious carousing, yet the phrase's primary force is figurative. Before Actium Cleopatra had been, as it were, drunk with power, and *dementis* (7), *inpotens* (10), *furorem* (12), and *lymphatam Mareotico* (14) insist upon her heady illusions. Her final drink hovers between literal and figurative—*conbiberet venenum* (28). Drunken irresponsibility has become a higher freedom. She celebrates a triumph as surely as do the Romans, and her drink to yesterday is no less splendid than their toast to tomorrow.

The Ode's moral progress is remarkable. In all the previous poems Horace's sympathies have been unequivocal. We are in no doubt as to whether wars of love are to be preferred to actual wars, inner riches to outer, Sabine farm to spreading mansion. But in the Cleopatra Ode—the name by which we remember it is itself suggestive—antithetical structure implies a double moral commitment. We move from Cleopatra's drunken illusions to her steady-eyed draught of reality, from a public Roman triumph to an individual Egyptian one. The images of hawk and tender dove, hunter and fleeing rabbit, are crucial in that word's truest sense, for they mark the point at which poetic intentions cross (17–24). The comparisons are better calculated to arouse pity than fear, and Caesar's role, in terms of the similes, is not particularly heroic.[50] The lines act as a kind of pivot to divert our sympathies from Caesar to Cleopatra, and a straightforward song of triumph slides into what has been justly termed a "panegyric of the vanquished queen."[51] Horace's manipulation of fact confirms such an interpretation, for he deliberately magnifies the moral force of Cleopatra's final defiance. He neglects the year which

49. M. Andrewes, in the fullest recent study of Horatian imagery, remarks only on the hunting simile in 17 ff. See *G&R, 19* (1950), 110.

50. All critics have not agreed with this interpretation. W. H. Alexander finds Horace "self-propagandized by name calling," and reproaches him for "bad taste in the field of 'applied patriotism.'" See *CJ, 39* (1944), 233.

51. Wilkinson, *Horace,* 133.

actually elapsed between Actium and her suicide; she seems to rise directly from defeat to noble death. He assigns her proud refusal to be led in Caesar's triumph as the sole motive for her suicide, one which other accounts by and large play down.[52] And finally, he ignores her attempts to cajole Octavian, as she had Caesar and Antony before him. Horace's Cleopatra witnesses her defeat with stoic fortitude, *voltu sereno* (26), and then embraces a death worthy of Cato himself.[53]

The transition from triumphal shout to elegy is meditated rather than impulsive, and the Ode's second half answers the first in contrapuntal detail. In altering the import of the drink imagery, Horace points to a more general shift in attitude. Cleopatra's world, as we first see it, verges on the fantastic. Her notorious band of eunuchs (9–10) or *semi-viri* appears as a disease (*morbo*) or deformation of nature, and furthers the air of unreality surrounding her. To be challenged by a woman's rule was sufficient affront to the Romans, but for Cleopatra's very men to be unmanned added biological insult to political injury. With Actium, Cleopatra's unreal world and dreams of glory shatter upon the fact of Caesar's victory. True fears (15) overwhelm fanciful hopes. Caesar's sober strength crushes the queen's intoxicated fantasies; the juxtapositions are clear, and our sympathies unequivocal.

Horace makes of Actium no less a moral than a military watershed, and the first words after the central similes compel us to qualify, if not reverse, the Ode's initial distinctions. *Generosius . . . nec muliebriter expavit:* Cleopatra assumes the prerogatives of her conquerors. *Generosius* implies a specifically Roman sense of "wellborn," and with *nec muliebriter* she sheds the effeminacy of the Egyptian court. She abandons (*nec reparavit,* 24) her dreams of conquest (*funus parabat,* 8),[54] and her serenity in defeat is the more impressive for

52. Cf. Verg., *A.* 8.709; Prop., 4.6.64 ff.; Vell., 2.87; Suet., *Aug.* 17. Only Plutarch (*Ant.* 84.954b ff.) is close to Horace in his conception of the situation.

53. The similarity to Cato's noble suicide after his defeat at Thapsus is striking; cf. *C.* 1.12.35–36, 2.1.23–24.

54. The contrast is probably deliberate, and dictates the use of *reparavit* (24), an odd word in such a context. It has been frequently emended; see L. Mueller, *Q. Horatius Flaccus, Oden und Epoden* (St. Petersburg, 1900), *ad loc.*

her previous agitation. If her daring remains it is founded on reality: *ausa et iacentem visere regiam voltu sereno*. As her delusions diminish (*mentem . . . redegit in veros timores Caesar,* 14–16) her presence expands (*invidens privata . . . non humilis mulier*), and a rise in her personal stature counterpoints the decline of her public fortunes. Dr. Johnson praised Milton for his "weightily embodied" descriptions, and in Horace's portrayal of Cleopatra's final acceptance of reality we find a comparable denseness of verbal suggestion (26–28). We feel the snake's harsh scales, see its black venom, hear its hiss in the repeated sibilants, and almost taste the poison which Cleopatra "drinks in" with her whole body. *Conbiberet* (28) insists upon the physical immediacy of her final act, and marks how far behind lie the intoxicated dreams of the poem's opening (10–12). *Deliberata* (29) repudiates her previous fantasies, while austere negations (*nec muliebriter, nec reparavit,* culminating in *non humilis*) reflect upon her former indulgence. *Superbo non humilis mulier triumpho*—the final sequence of words produces an effect almost impossible to convey in translation, one that epitomizes the double impact of the poem. *Superbo* and *non humilis* are practically identical, and as we read the last line it is easy to forget that *mulier* and *triumpho* are logically opposed. The verbal arrangement suggests that the triumph belongs with Cleopatra as well. "Her life would be eternal in our triumph," declares Shakespeare's Caesar, and Cleopatra's death becomes eternal in her own, for it is she who finally shatters Caesar's dream of leading her a captive.

A comforting rationalization proposes that Horace exalts Octavian's enemy only to magnify Octavian.[55] Yet not until her defeat does Cleopatra become formidable; it is the change in her character that is responsible for our respect. In the second stanza *regina* and *ruinas* (7) seem practically synonyms rather than subject and object. But the Cleopatra we leave is very different from the one to whom we are introduced. Intoxicated hopes have sobered into a meditated draught; by embracing reality she has overtopped her lofty illusions.

55. See Wickham, *Works of Horace, ad loc.* Wickham believes that Horace, by his admiration for Cleopatra, is merely "bringing out in stronger relief the danger from which Rome has been freed, and the glory of Octavianus, who has conquered no unworthy foe."

Waking from a dream of Roman rule she achieves a Roman nobility; casting off her unnatural world she dies a more than natural heroine. Public catastrophe and private renascence are simultaneous. Cleopatra's final wrought serenity signals her triumph over Fortune's reverses, and, Phoenixlike, she rises from the ashes of her own defeat.

Horace's divided sympathies complicate a characteristic technique. The balance of figurative and literal is familiar from other poems, though the antitheses are more elaborate than usual. The Romans' festive drink is opposed to Cleopatra's finally triumphant one, which contrasts as well with her earlier intoxication. Paradoxically, it is her literal drunkenness which produces her illusions, while her figurative drink (*conbiberet venenum,* 28) represents her final awareness of reality. The correspondences and ironies are as intricate as those between the Sabine farm, the mansion of the *avarus,* and the *aula Orci* in *C.* 2.18. By maintaining a single image and refracting it into different aspects, both literal and figurative, Horace shapes the Ode into a tense unity.

The poem provides a model, not only of a characteristic structural technique, but of Horace's alchemy of history as well. The elements were all common knowledge. Propertius needed only to refer to Cleopatra's notorious fondness for drink:

> "non hoc, Roma, fui tanto tibi cive verenda!"
> dixit et assiduo lingua sepulta mero. [3.11.55–56]

> "You need not have feared me, Rome, with such a citizen as this to protect you!" So spoke the tongue which constant draughts of wine had overwhelmed.

Her band of eunuchs had an equally bad reception. Horace himself, in an Epode written either during or immediately after the battle of Actium, dwelt upon them in fascinated detail:

> Romanus eheu—posteri negabitis—
> emancipatus feminae
> fert vallum et arma miles et spadonibus
> servire rugosis potest

interque signa turpe militaria
  sol adspicit canopium. [*Epod.* 9.11–16]

A Roman, alas—you who come in later times will deny it—having surrendered himself to a woman, carries stakes and arms for her, and, though a soldier, he can bring himself to serve withered eunuchs, and among the military standards the sun shines upon the shameful Egyptian pavilion.

Here Horace mentions the eunuchs only for the sake of invective. The Ode does more than recollect the same emotions in greater tranquillity. Cleopatra's intervening suicide compelled Horace to a fresh consideration which distinguishes the Ode from its predecessor. The Epode's pure cry of triumph (*io Triumphe . . . io Triumphe,* 21, 23) modulates into the ambiguity of *superbo triumpho* (31–32); abuse of the effeminate Egyptian court becomes balanced by Cleopatra's rejection of womanly fear; festive invitation (*capaciores adfer huc, puer, scyphos,* 33) ramifies into a dialectic of symbolic drinks. The two poems provide an instructive example of the way narrative elements in the Epodes tend to become structural ones in the Odes. Blending the familiar tales about Cleopatra's drinking and about her retinue of eunuchs with other equally well-known facts—her hopes of Roman rule, her final repudiation of womanhood, her royal death—Horace transmutes all alike into an organic whole. We cannot, as we can with Propertius, isolate the references to drinking. Remove them and the poem collapses. History has been concentrated into image, and image has become inseparable from the poem's structure and meaning.

For a parallel, whether of technique or of attitude, we must look not to Horace's contemporaries but to Shakespeare's retrospective vision in *Antony and Cleopatra.* As Horace builds the Ode upon different types of drinking, so Shakespeare concentrates the opposition of social values and human ones in the single image of melting or dissolution. In these terms we see Antony's downfall, as he becomes "the ebb'd man." "Our fortune sinks most lamentably," he cries; or again, "authority melts from me!" Yet there is a melting with as well as a melting from, and in the idea's sexual suggestion Shakespeare conjures up the individual rebirth which Antony achieves with Cleopatra:

> the higher Nilus swells
> The more it promises: as it ebbs, the seedman
> Upon the slime and ooze scatters his grain,
> And shortly comes to harvest.

On Shakespeare's boards the conflict is played out principally in terms of Antony, in whom love vies with honor, East with West. Horace could hardly share the Englishman's distanced perspective, and even had he felt free to treat the subject in the same way it is unlikely that he would have anticipated Shakespeare's tacit verdict, and Dryden's explicit one, that the world was well lost. Yet both Horace and Shakespeare recognized the interplay between Caesar's national victory and Cleopatra's individual one. Taking from North's Plutarch the events Horace knew at first hand, Shakespeare built them into the structure of his work by a technique reminiscent of Horace's own. His antitheses echo those of the Ode even as they elaborate upon them. A public sense of history informs the play. We watch an emerging empire triumph over a decaying dynasty, masculine Roman over effeminate Egyptian, land force over sea power, grave sobriety over light sport, foursquare *virtus* over devious love, youth over age—the contrasts are all the playwright's own. Yet private lives play against public issues, and the counterpoint is familiar. Leaving aside her womanhood—

> My resolution's plac'd and I have nothing
> Of woman in me—

Cleopatra rises by "a Roman death" to an ultimate victory over Rome's very founder:

> Where souls do couch on flowers, we'll hand in hand,
> And with our springly port, make the ghosts gaze.
> Dido and her Aeneas shall want troops,
> And all the haunt be ours.

Horace's perspective, both because of his historical involvement and because of the necessarily more restricted range of lyric, makes any comparison with Shakespeare seem indecorous. Yet the similarities in structural technique are striking, while the differences are more profound quantitatively than qualitatively. Nor is Horace's attitude, Roman though he was, so far from that of the dramatist. For he was, we should remember, the first poet to recognize what history was to confirm, that in Cleopatra the world had borne a "lass unparalleled."

In a well-known study, J. Middleton Murray defined "the problem of style" as one of communication.[56] How can we make words adequate to experience, how give instead of describe, convey rather than flatly state? Murray found the best if necessarily evasive answer in Stendhal, whose definition at least preserves the terms of the problem:

> Le style est ceci: ajouter à une pensée donnée toutes les circonstances propres à produire tout l'effet que doit produire cette pensée.

If Horace's Odes demonstrate anything, it is the radical integrity of "pensée donnée" and "circonstances." The time-honored opposition of the *utile* and the *dulce* is pernicious in implication, for it assumes a split between an essential meaning and some decorative means used in conveying it. For a poem the length of the *De Rerum Natura* the sugared pill may prove an efficacious mode of discourse, but it can hardly be effective in shorter works, where our imagination must be compelled at the same time as our reason. Yet attempts to separate the formal elements of an Ode—structure and figures, sounds and rhythms—from its "meaning" are persistent. We hear, for instance, that the appeal of Horace is twofold: "the forms in which he expressed himself, and the substance of which they are the garment. We shall find him distinguished in both; but in the substance of his message we shall find him distinguished by a quality which sets him apart from other poets ancient and modern." [57] Had Horace believed in such a division between form and substance he would probably have written prose. In protesting against the "purple patch" (*A. P.* 15–16) which authors sewed onto their work, Horace reproached a whole of theory of style, and in offering instead the analogy

56. *The Problem of Style* (Oxford, 1922), 71 ff.
57. G. Showerman, *Horace and His Influence* (New York, 1931), 3.

of a living creature (*A. P.* 1 ff.) he anticipated the nineteenth century's concern for organic form. Wordsworth and Coleridge insisted that language be the "Flesh-Garment, the Body, of Thought," and De Quincey expatiated upon their identity:

> The more closely any exercise of mind is connected with what is internal and individual in the sensibilities,—that is, with what is philosophically termed subjective,—precisely in that degree, and the more subtly, does the style or the embodying of the thoughts cease to be a mere separable ornament, and in fact the more does the manner, as we expressed it before, become confluent with the matter . . . If language were merely a dress, then you could separate the two; you could lay the thoughts on the left hand, the language on the right. But, generally speaking, you can no more deal thus with poetic thoughts than you can with soul and body. The union is too subtle, the intertexture too ineffable,—each co-existing not merely *with* the other but each *in* and *through* the other. An image, for instance, a single word, often enters into a thought as a constituent part. In short, the two elements are not united as a body with a separable dress, but as a mysterious incarnation.[58]

And so it is with the Odes, where the ideas work not merely "with" but "in and through" Horace's specific language. If we change any element of his language a different idea remains—or no idea at all. To speak of a lyric poet's "message" is meaningless except in terms of the forms in which he creates it. Art, in one sense, is simply the form we impose on life, and once we forget Horace's, or any poet's, medium in the search for his message, we may as well cease reading poetry altogether.

58. *Collected Writings,* Masson, ed., *10* (London, 1890), 229. Cf. M. H. Abrams, *The Mirror and the Lamp* (New York, 1953), 290–91.

III

QUALITIES OF IMAGINATION

THE question of "the man and the work" is perennially tempting. With Horace the balance between the two has proved precarious. Enthusiasm for the author of the Odes frequently leads us to neglect its cause and justification, the Odes themselves:

> The man Horace is more interesting than his writings, or, to speak more correctly, the main interest of his writings is in himself. We might call his works "Horace's Autobiography." To use his own expression about Lucilius, his whole life stands out before us as in a picture. Of none of the ancients do we know so much, not of Socrates, or Cicero, or St. Paul. Almost what Boswell is to Johnson, Horace is to himself. We can see him, as he really was, both in body and soul. Everything about him is familiar to us. His faults are known to us, his very foibles and awkwardnesses . . . He seems almost as a personal friend.[1]

Though this was written in the late nineteenth century, its assumptions have shown themselves persistent. We have all become familiar with the image of a man rotund and balding, convivial if sometimes irascible; of a gentleman farmer and urbane socialite who moved placidly through life. The Satires and Epistles tell us enough about the facts of Horace's existence to encourage us to draw upon our intuition for the gaps, and to use the result as a context in which to read the Odes. "He never thought of marrying, he was never in love;

1. J. Lonsdale and S. Lee, *The Works of Horace* (London, 1887), 9–10.

he never deceived himself as to the nature of his emotions; his soul was never touched." [2] We know him as the good neighbor, the adviser of youth, the clubman; we wonder whether he would have smoked a pipe or a cigar had he the choice; we even go back a generation to observe a twinkle in his father's eye. These matters are all, perhaps, of a legitimate interest, yet to pursue them with too importunate a fancy is to risk a serious dislocation of emphasis. We tend to forget that incomparably the most important fact of Horace's life is his poetry, and that only because he wrote great poetry do we care about the rest. Everything, or almost everything, we can learn about him is valuable, but only as long as we remember that it is peripheral and that the text is central. When he predicted his immortality—*non omnis moriar*—it was the Odes that he was thinking of, and to resurrect his personal habits is a dubious vindication of his boast.

Implicit in the Odes themselves is a more important biography, the biography of the poet's imagination. In this context alone does the phrase *le style est l'homme même* become meaningful. Its usefulness lies in directing our attention to similarities between specific qualities of style and wider tendencies of the writer's imagination, to his "poetic" rather than his "practical" personality, in Croce's terms.[3] Here is a typical passage from Ovid:

> illo saepe loco capitur consultus Amori:
> quique aliis cavit, non cavet ipse sibi.
> illo saepe loco desunt sua verba diserto:
> resque novae veniunt, causaque agenda sua est.
> hunc Venus e templis quae sunt confinia ridet.
> qui modo patronus, nunc cupit esse cliens.
>
> [*A. A.* 1.83–88]

2. H. D. Sedgwick, *Horace* (Cambridge, Mass., 1947), 65.

3. Attempts to reconstruct an artist's life from his works have usually ended in manifest confusion. The most prominent example in recent years has been Caroline Spurgeon's *Shakespeare's Imagery and What It Tells Us* (Cambridge, Eng., 1935). In general see R. Wellek and A. Warren, *Theory of Literature* (New York, 1949), 215 ff.

> There the lawyer is often captured by Love; he who guarded the interests of others fails to guard himself. There words often fail him despite all his eloquence. New cases come on, and it is his own cause that he must plead. Venus laughs at him from the temples that are her precincts: he who was just recently an advocate now wishes to become a client.

The lines tell us nothing, really, about Ovid's interest in or knowledge of law. But his fascination with the change of a lawyer into a client does suggest an imagination that might find a congenial subject in famous transformations. Looking at the characteristically facile manipulation of words and rhythms we might even say that Ovid's mind was such as to make everything he wrote in a sense a *Metamorphosis.*

In his inaugural lecture at Oxford, W. H. Auden said that the two questions that interested him most in reading a poem were: "1) Here is a verbal contraption, how does it work? and 2) What kind of a guy inhabits this poem?" The second question clearly depends to some extent upon the first. In applying both to Horace we may ask what habits of style characterize the "verbal contraptions" examined in the last chapter, and what they in turn suggest as to the more general qualities of the "inhabitant's" imagination.

The most striking element in those Odes, particularly if they are compared with their models or with other contemporary works, is the intricacy of verbal correspondences and antitheses that they present. So elaborate and so pervasive is the mannerism that it marks itself off qualitatively from the similar techniques common to nearly every poet. The instinct is as marked in Horace's slightest linguistic devices as it is in the structure of whole poems. Oxymorons and puns, a juxtaposing of dissimilars or an identifying of them, are habitual mechanics of his verse. Only Lucretius had shown a comparable willingness to explore the possibilities of puns, and for Lucretius the game was burdened with a weight of philosophical conjecture. He considered resemblances between words to be not merely fortuitous. If the letters (*elementa*) were similar, might it not be that the atoms (*elementa*) of the substances the words represented were also related? Thus *ignis* and *lignis* echoed one another, he believed, because there were certain atoms common to wood and fire—and for that reason, plausibly enough, wood burns (1.901 ff.).

Without so doctrinaire a conception, Horace allowed to verbal devices a comparable responsibility. They are less often a rhetorical flourish than a means of conveying a poem's logic in miniature. An oxymoron like *tenues grandia* (*C.* 1.6.9) stands as an index to the poem's intent, summarizing the contrast between slender talent and epic theme. The fanciful names he employs are by and large a case of *nomen et omen;* thus in citing *pauper Opimius,* the ancestor of our "poor little rich boy," Horace directs attention to a central moral problem.[4] The same is true of that phrase's lyric equivalent, *magnas inter opes inops* (*C.* 3.16.28). The double standard implicit in *beatus* provides the ethical structure for at least two poems (*C.* 2.2, 3.16), and puns like *Parca non mendax* (*C.* 2.16.39) or *rex-recte* (*Ep.* 1.1.59 ff.) are equally significant, one adumbrating a whole philosophy of style, the other a fundamental moral issue. Such wordplay commonly involves a tension of ideas rather than merely verbal gymnastics, and even the most blatant exercise in ingenuity is likely to have a serious point. The last Epistle of the first book is in effect a sustained pun likening Horace's collection of poems, then ready for publication, to a slave eager to escape. Nearly every verb has a double application. Yet even in so sustained a display of wit Horace found room for an important literary manifesto.

"By far the greatest thing," proposed Aristotle, "is the use of metaphor. That alone cannot be learnt from another; it is the sign of genuis. For the right use of metaphor means an eye for resemblances" (*Po.* 22.1459a). We might wish that he had seen fit to expatiate on the intimacy between metaphor and genius, but his observation that metaphor entails an "eye for resemblances" needs no philosophical sanction. His reminder enforces the fact that Horace's penchant for metaphor and simile, which Aristotle regards as essentially the same (*Rh.* 1406b), partakes of the same double awareness that measures Horace's response to so many specific situations. Nearly all the Odes examined in the last chapter explored metaphor as a structural

4. *S.* 2.3.142; cf. *inmitis Glycerae* (*C.* 1.33.2), below, 240.

principle, if only in the working out of a traditional conceit. In many of the political Odes, divine myth operates as a kind of prolonged metaphor, and it is rare that his so-called "nature Odes" are simply descriptive.[5] The dialectic so prominent in these two groups of poems occurs constantly elsewhere in less noticeable form. We see it in his fondness for rationalizing mythology and, conversely, in his tendency to mythologize reality. The golden rain of Danae becomes a lover's bribe (*C.* 3.16.1 ff.), Orpheus and Amphion are reduced from miracle workers simply to benefactors (*A. P.* 391 ff.), and the monsters of hell appear as Lucretian avatars of our daily existence (*S.* 1.1.68 ff.). Nor, on the other hand, is any incident too small to assume the dimensions of epic or tragedy.[6] Myth and reality forever impinge upon one another, and frequently an Ode's principal effect depends on our simultaneous awareness of each.

In the Satires, more explicitly ethical than the Odes, moral and stylistic patterns combine in Horace's constant deploying of antithetical paradigms. The second Satire of the first book, probably the earliest poem in the collection, finds the familiar pairs already assembled. Prodigal is yoked to miser; the man who walks with his cloak raised to an indecent height paces one whose toga drags upon the ground; an overly perfumed gentleman companions another of hircine rankness; adulterer competes with the less demanding frequenter of the *olens fornix:*

> si quis nunc quaerat "quo res haec pertinet?" illuc:
> dum vitant stulti vitia, in contraria currunt. [23–24]

> If anyone should now ask, "To what does all this pertain?"
> it is to this: while fools are avoiding one vice, they rush
> to the opposite extreme.

The prolix delight Horace takes in cataloguing the embarrassments of adulterers suggests that the philosophic cast of the introduction may be perfunctory. Yet it remains significant that he chooses an

5. On the political Odes see below, 172 ff.; and on the nature Odes, chap. 5, passim.

6. See below, 120 ff.

antithetical framework for his presumably edifying tales.[7] Frequently Horace seems to pursue life through a series of μέν and δέ clauses, charting his own course by the derelictions to either side: "This person goes off to the left, that one to the right." [8] Antithesis appears as fundamental to his moral constructs as to his artistic ones, and we might guess that his doctrine of a Golden Mean (*C.* 2.10) has a more vital source in his own habits of thought than in the philosophical tradition of the μεσότης.

Virtually everything Horace treated presented itself to him in a double aspect. He forever compels us to seek similarities or to acknowledge oppositions, to discriminate and yet maintain a balance. His structural and verbal habits tell us nothing about his daily life. They allow us to say only that his imagination is drawn to correspondences and alternatives, that his awareness tends to be inclusive rather than concentrated, and that his reactions are likely to be both complex and controlled. For the sake of clarity it is perhaps simplest to postulate two categories. There are those poems in which Horace balances or reconciles two attitudes toward his subject, and there are those in which he deliberately creates a tension between the subject and the form. Any arrangement that is so general admittedly covers rather than illuminates the individual Odes, and the distinction is meant only to be convenient, not absolute. Many of the poems clearly fit both categories, and the amatory Odes in particular combine the two in a manner as elusive as it is characteristic.

Balance of Attitude

Whereas in the Satires Horace tends to think in terms of negative extremes, in the Odes he is often willing, less prescriptively, to allow for opposed alternatives without dismissing either. Sometimes his judiciousness renders his own moral position precarious. "Destitute, I seek the camp of those who desire nothing, and fleeing to it, I rejoice to leave the side of the rich as a more splendid lord of the wealth that I despise than if I should be said to hide away in my barns

7. The subject matter of the *fornix* section may have come from Lucilius; see G. C. Fiske, *Lucilius and Horace* (Madison, 1920), 256 ff. There is, however, no evidence that Lucilius used the same kind of antithetical philosophical framework for his description.

8. *S.* 2.3.50; cf. *S.* 1.1.1 ff., 101 ff., 2.2.53 ff.; *Ep.* 1.18.86 ff., 2.2.201 ff.

whatever the tireless Apulian ploughs—a poor man amid mighty wealth" (*C.* 3.16.22–28). His spiritual flourish is impressive only until we come to its climax, addressed to Maecenas: "Nor, if I wished more, would you deny it to me" (38). Even the famous *dulce et decorum est pro patria mori* (*C.* 3.2.13) loses something of its luster when we read on and find that flight is impractical as well as ignoble (14–16). Horace's tendency to look upon both sides of any question occasionally makes life seem a glorified balance sheet: "as much as you take from my birth you add to my merits" (*Ep.* 1.20.22); "time will assign to her the years it exacts from you" (*C.* 2.5.14–15).

Somewhat similar is the equable inclusiveness with which Horace catalogues the various professions, often the better to define his own. The technique was not unusual ("some say the fairest thing on the black earth is a host of cavalry, others a host of foot soldiers, and still others a fleet of ships, but to me the fairest thing is my beloved," wrote Sappho [9]), but Horace is remarkable for the tolerance with which he views those not equally admiring of his own beloved, the Muse. Athlete, statesman, merchant, farmer, sailor, trader, soldier, hunter—all are viewed with an indulgent, if complacent, eye.[10] Horace loves the country, his bailiff, the city (*Ep.* 1.14). Though we are left in no doubt as to which is morally superior, both preferences remain valid, and elsewhere Horace could show himself altogether incapable of deciding between the two: "inconstant as the wind, at Rome I love Tibur, at Tibur, Rome." [11] *Laudabunt alii:* some prefer Rhodes and some Mytilene, some Ephesus and some Corinth, some Thebes and some Delphi (*C.* 1.7.1 ff.). If Horace himself is struck by Tibur, his own choice does not rebuke that of others. Even Tibur has nothing absolute about it. Should the Fates prohibit him from spending his old age there, Tarentum will do equally well:

> Tibur Argeo positum colono
> sit meae sedes utinam senectae,
> sit modus lasso maris et viarum
>   militiaeque.

9. 27 (Diehl). In general, see B. Snell, *Discovery of the Mind,* 47 ff., and below, 330 ff.

10. *C.* 1.1.3 ff.; cf. *C.* 4.3.1 ff.

11. *Ep.* 1.8.12; cf. *S.* 2.7.28–29.

unde si Parcae prohibent iniquae,
dulce pellitis ovibus Galaesi
flumen et regnata petam Laconi
  rura Phalantho. [*C.* 2.6.5–12]

Would that Tibur, founded by an Argive colony, might be the home of my old age! Might there be a final rest for me there, weary of the sea, of travel, of warfare! But if the unfair Fates forbid it, thence I shall seek the river of Galaesus, dear to its sheep clad in their blankets of skin, and the fields once ruled over by Spartan Phalanthus.

Can we imagine Catullus equally amenable if he had been told he might not return to Sirmio?

The balances Horace strikes sometimes become peculiarly elusive. "Happy is he who far from business cares . . ." For some sixty-five lines the second Epode conjures up a countryside hardly distinguishable from that of Vergil's Arcadians:

vel cum decorum mitibus pomis caput
  Autumnus agris extulit,
ut gaudet insitiva decerpens pira
  certantem et uvam purpurae,
qua muneretur te, Priape, et te, pater
  Silvane, tutor finium.
libet iacere modo sub antiqua ilice,
  modo in tenaci gramine:
labuntur altis interim ripis aquae,
  queruntur in silvis aves
fontesque lymphis obstrepunt manantibus,
  somnos quod invitet levis. [17–28]

Or when in the fields, Autumn raises his head, adorned with ripe fruits, how the farmer rejoices, plucking the grafted pears and the grape that rivals the color of the purple dye, with which he may honor you, Priapus, and you, Father Silvanus, keeper of boundaries. It is pleasant to lie now

> under some ancient ilex, now in the matted grass; meanwhile the waters glide on between high banks, the birds sing in the trees, and the springs are loud with their flowing streams, a sound inviting soft sleep.

The lovely sounds and images are themselves an invitation, lulling us into an unquestioning sentimental acceptance. Only with the poem's last four lines do we discover that the speaker is not the poet but the usurer Alfius, and not until the final word does his pastoral vision shatter upon the continuing realities of his profession:

> haec ubi locutus faenerator Alfius,
> iam iam futurus rusticus,
> omnem redegit idibus pecuniam,
> quaerit kalendis ponere. [67–70]

> When thus the usurer Alfius had spoken, just about to become a farmer, he gathered in all his money upon the Ides —and seeks, upon the Kalends, to lend it out once more!

In thus withdrawing from the scene, Horace inadvertently (or perhaps gleefully) laid it open as a literary battlefield where subsequent scholars might tilt at one another over his "sincerity." Does Horace express a genuine love of the country? Or is he satirizing the fashionably extravagant praises it received? ("He is laughing at what we should now call the Lake school of poets and their admirers," writes Tyrrell.[12]) Yet the essence of the poem lies in the fact that Horace shows himself neither exclusively a sentimentalist nor exclusively a cynic. He is simply aware that two attitudes exist—and may collide.

Behind Horace's pairing of antithetical figures in the Satires lies a more interesting balance, arising from his reluctance to commit himself to any single attitude. His preference for the dialogue form is in itself significant. Thus to deliver some traditional γνῶμαι on the virtues of modest living he adopts the mask of a country neighbor, Ofellus:

12. *Latin Poetry* (Boston, 1895), 192; cf. G. Boissier, *Nouvelles promenades archéologiques* (Paris, 1904), 18–19. For the opposite view see G. A. Simcox, *A History of Latin Literature, 1* (New York, 1883), 295.

> Quae virtus et quanta, boni, sit vivere parvo
> —nec meus hic sermo est, sed quae praecepit Ofellus
> rusticus, abnormis sapiens crassaque Minerva—
> discite . . . [*S.* 2.2.1–4]

> Learn, my good friends, what a virtue it is, and how great, to live on little—nor is this my own talk, but rather what the peasant Ofellus taught me, a philosopher unschooled and of a roughhewn wisdom . . .

Horace employs an argumentative structure not merely for dramatic interest but as a means of evading responsibility for the morality he retails. In the longest of the Satires, and the most formal philosophically, it is the Stoic Damasippus who speaks (*S.* 2.3). Nearly all of the neophyte philosopher's pontifications could as well have come from the poet, but Horace does not permit us to make the identification. Both the opening and the close present a miniature ἀγών, and the humorous exchanges emphasize the gap between the two participants. It would be difficult in any circumstances to prove the author of *S.* 1.3 a committed Stoic, and in *S.* 2.3 Horace does not neglect to remind us that the sect Damasippus represents is subject to the lapses it condemns: "O greater madman, spare, I pray, the lesser!" (326).

Nec meus hic sermo est: it may equally well be Horace's slave Davus who propounds doctrines we would not be amiss in taking as Horace's own (*S.* 2.7). Yet Davus, like Damasippus, is represented as merely serving up crumbs from the philosophical table of Crispinus. He stands, in fact, at an even further remove than Damasippus, for, in a kind of low-life parody of the relationship of Damasippus and Crispinus, Davus merely repeats what Crispinus' porter has overheard and relayed to him. Nor is Crispinus an impeccable source of wisdom. Elsewhere he is christened *ineptus,* and he seems to have been himself only a hanger-on of the Stoics (*S.* 1.3.138). Almost proverbial for the profusion of his writings (*S.* 1.1.120), Crispinus was on one occasion foolish enough to challenge Horace to a contest of productivity, and Horace's opinion of him was not flattering: "But do you, if you wish, imitate the air shut up in goat-skin bellows, always laboring away until the fire softens the iron" (*S.* 1.4.19–21).

Davus' moralizing, then, comes third-hand from a near idiot. Yet as though this were not enough, Horace removes himself further, as he did with Damasippus, by casting the Satire as a running debate. The scene is laid during the Saturnalia, and Billingsgate alternates with Davus' lofty pronouncements. *Furcifer . . . pessime,* Horace abuses his slave (*S.* 2.7.21–22), and Davus interjects a lively reminder that the two persons are anything but identifiable: "Cease trying to scare me by your looks! Restrain your hand and temper while I tell you what the porter of Crispinus taught me" (43–45). The Satire ends with a threat to deport Davus to the Sabine farm unless he promptly remove himself from sight. Over the whole episode lingers an air of holiday unreality. Horace seems to assure us that Davus' address, which is at times as serious as anything in the Epistles, represents no more than an amusing and isolated incident.

By thus detaching himself from convictions that he largely shares, Horace enjoys license to preach while remaining able to disclaim any philosophic pretensions. His apologies for essaying the grand style demonstrate a comparable unwillingness to take a definitive stand. *Insurgit aliquando,* judged Quintilian (10.1.96); yet if we glimpse the poet in flight it is often only to have him refer us to the ground beneath. Soaring, Horace refuses to surrender his pedestrian self. In an Ode to Asinius Pollio (*C.* 2.1) Horace salutes his friend's forthcoming history of the civil wars with a full organ roll of rhetoric: *iam nunc minaci murmure cornuum / perstringis auris, iam litui strepunt* . . . (17–18). For five stanzas the tempo mounts, only to subside into an almost domestic rebuke:

sed ne relictis, Musa, procax iocis
Ceae retractes munera neniae,
mecum Dionaeo sub antro
quaere modos leviore plectro. [37–40]

But lest, Muse, shamelessly abandoning jesting themes, you attempt again the task of the Cean dirge, seek with me measures of a lighter style in the cave of Venus.

"Better without," wrote Landor in his copy. Horace's reversals have more often embarrassed his admirers than they did the poet himself, for whom heroic and mundane worlds could exist in easy harmony.

The third Roman Ode, one of Horace's most solemn productions, follows the same course. Juno's speech to the assembled gods occupies a large part of the poem, and she parades before us a pageant of Trojan and Roman history. The august occasion is Romulus' apotheosis—Juno will admit him to divinity only on condition that Rome renounce any return to Troy. Her diatribe mounts to an apocalyptic vision of the doom that awaits any disobedience of her edict:

"ter si resurgat murus aeneus
auctore Phoebo, ter pereat meis
excisus Argivis, ter uxor
capta virum puerosque ploret."

non hoc iocosae conveniet lyrae.
quo, Musa, tendis? desine pervicax
referre sermones deorum et
magna modis tenuare parvis. [*C.* 3.3.65–72]

"If thrice the bronze wall should rise under the auspices of Phoebus Apollo, then thrice should it perish, cut down by my Argives, thrice should the captive wife mourn her husband and children."

But this does not become the jesting lyre. Whither, Muse, are you headed? Cease so boldly to report the words of the gods and to belittle great matters with trifling measures.

The Ode's final stanza gently banishes Juno's oracular rhythms together with the whole council of gods. Such withdrawals, like the conclusion of the second Epode, are not really palinodes, nor do they repudiate all that has gone before. They merely remind us that another world exists, the world of the *iocosa lyra,* the *levius plectrum,* and the *tenuis* style. The last stanza of *C.* 3.3 falls in the center of the Roman Odes, and between the two longest and most grandiloquent of the group. The lines, aside from their function in that poem,[13] seem intended, more generally, as a pledge that Horace's abandonment of his usual lighter role is only temporary. The opening sentence of *C.* 3.7 redeems his promise: *quid fles, Asterie?* The words give a casual fillip to the gloomy prognostications ending *C.* 3.6, and recall us to a world of less exaltation and intensity. Like the last stanzas of *C.* 2.1 or *C.* 3.3, *C.* 3.7 as a whole reminds us that the panorama of history yet includes each day's frivolities, and that even the plains of high endeavor are scattered with peaceful retreats. The patriotic Alcaeus, Horace pointedly observes elsewhere, found time amid battles to sing of Bacchus, the Muses, Venus and Cupid (*C.* 1.32.5 ff.).

Nowhere does Horace convey his sense of alternate worlds more beautifully than in the delicate diminuendo of the Regulus Ode (*C.* 3.5). The story of Regulus was a commonplace of heroism, and by the middle of the first century it had received the final accolade, admission to the debates of the rhetorical schools.[14] Regulus, captured by the Carthaginians during the first Punic War, was dispatched to Rome to hasten an exchange of prisoners. In return, he was to receive his own freedom. *Magnitudo animi et fortitudo negat,* wrote Cicero (*Off.* 3.26): Regulus advised against any compromise, choosing instead, over the protests of his friends, to return to torture and death in Carthage:

atqui sciebat, quae sibi barbarus
tortor pararet: non aliter tamen
  dimovit obstantis propinquos
    et populum reditus morantem,

quam si clientum longa negotia
diiudicata lite relinqueret,
  tendens Venafranos in agros
    aut Lacedaemonium Tarentum. [49–56]

13. See below, 223, n. 124.

14. Cic., *De Or.* 3.28.109; cf. *Att.* 16.11.4; *Off.* 3.26.99 ff.; Livy, Epitome of book 18; Gell., 6.18; Val. Max., 2.9.8; see T. Frank, *CP, 21* (1926), 311 ff.; E. Silk, *YCS, 13* (1952), 145 ff. On the emotional effect of the Ode's close, see Campbell, *Horace,* 226.

> And yet he knew what the barbarian torturer was preparing for him. Nevertheless he pushed aside the relatives blocking his way and the people who would delay his return, just as though he were leaving behind the tedious business of his clients, the lawsuit finished, and heading for the fields of Venafrum or Lacedaemonian Tarentum.

In the poem's close Nietzsche might have found an example of "*der Pathos der Distanz.*" Regulus' splendid act fades into a crepuscular familiarity, and the framework of daily routine provides a context in which the heroic becomes meaningful. The tension between the quiet simplicity of language and the enormity of the event it describes gives the lines their chief power. In a sense our emotions are relieved as we return to the commonplace. Yet in another way they are intensified, for the comparison obliquely reminds us that for Regulus the *longa negotia* of life are in fact finished, and that he is truly returning to his final home.

The mock recantations at the end of the Ode to Pollio (*C.* 2.1) or the third Roman Ode are characteristic, but even more common than Horace's apologies for displaying the grand style are his protests that he cannot attain it. Here again he insists on having it both ways at once. The *recusatio* was of course a common form,[15] but in Horace's hands it usually becomes equivalent to the rhetorician's *praeteritio,* of which the anonymous *Auctor ad Herennium* gives examples under the heading of *occultatio: "Occultatio* arises when we say that we are passing by (*praeterire*) or do not know or do not wish to say what we actually are saying, in the following manner: 'For indeed, concerning your childhood, which you gave to every sort of intemperance, I would speak, if I thought this the proper time; but for now I leave it aside advisedly. And this also I pass by, that the tribunes have said that you are delinquent in your military service . . . Of these things I say nothing.' Or again: 'I don't mention the fact that you have taken money from allies; I am not concerned with the fact that you have robbed the cities, the kingdoms, and the homes of all; your thefts and all your plunderings I omit' "

15. See above, 34, 65, and H. Lucas in *Festschrift für Vahlen* (Berlin, 1900), 319 ff.

(4.27.37). And so with Horace, the vow to avoid certain subjects is made only through a descriptive catalogue of them:

> "aut si tantus amor scribendi te rapit, aude
> Caesaris invicti res dicere, multa laborum
> praemia laturus."
> "cupidum, pater optime, vires
> deficiunt; neque enim quivis horrentia pilis
> agmina nec fracta pereuntis cuspide Gallos
> aut labentis equo describet volnera Parthi."
> [*S.* 2.1.10–15]

"Or if such a passion for writing seizes you, then dare to describe the deeds of unvanquished Caesar, and you will be sure to bear off many a prize for your work."

"My spirit is willing, O best of fathers, but my strength fails. Not everyone can describe the battle lines bristling with spears, nor the Gauls perishing with lance heads shattered, nor the wounds of the Parthian falling from his horse."

The plea of *vires deficiunt* may remind us of the Callimachean disclaimer, "Seek not from me a loud-sounding lay, for to thunder belongs not to me but to Zeus." Yet Horace normally enforces such protests by at least a few scattered claps:

> nec sermones ego mallem
> repentis per humum quam res conponere gestas
> terrarumque situs et flumina dicere et arces
> montibus inpositas et barbara regna tuisque
> auspiciis totum confecta duella per orbem
> claustraque custodem pacis cohibentia Ianum
> et formidatam Parthis te principe Romam,
> si quantum cuperem possem quoque. [*Ep.* 2.1.250–57]

Nor would I prefer my "talks," which creep along the ground, to composing tales of great deeds and to describing: lands and rivers; citadels set on mountaintops; bar-

> barian realms; the wars brought to an end throughout the whole world under your auspices; the bars that close the temple of Janus, guardian of peace; and Rome, with you its leader, dreaded by the Parthians—if only I were able to do as much as I would like.

Rejections of epic themselves become epic. "You would not wish the long wars of fierce Numantia, nor dread Hannibal, nor the Sicilian sea red with Punic blood to be wedded to the soft measures of the lyre, nor the savage Lapiths, and Hylaeus mad with wine . . ." So continues the list of things that Maecenas does not wish to hear (*C.* 2.12.1 ff.). In the Ode to Iullus Horace's "you will sing" gave him an opening for describing the themes (*C.* 4.2.33–44) to which he claimed to be inadequate, and in the Ode to Agrippa (*C.* 1.6) he manages with equal adroitness to demonstrate the very ability he disclaims. After proving conclusively, one would judge, his own ineptness,[16] he turns and shows us fools for believing him:

> quis Martem tunica tectum adamantina
> digne scripserit aut pulvere Troico
> nigrum Merionen aut ope Palladis
> Tydiden superis parem? [*C.* 1.6.13–16]

> Who could write fittingly of Mars clad in his adamantine corselet, or of Meriones black with Trojan dust, or of Diomede, with Pallas Athene's help a match for the gods above?

The rhetorical questions might, on the basis of the lines themselves, be answered with the name "Horace." Yet having made it impossible for us to believe his modest excuse of *culpa ingeni* (12), he then proceeds to reiterate it:

> nos convivia, nos proelia virginum
> sectis in iuvenes unguibus acrium
> cantamus vacui, sive quid urimur,
> non praeter solitum leves. [17–20]

16. See above, 71, n. 25.

> In a light vein as always, whether I be unengaged or fired with love, I sing of banquets, I sing of the battles of maidens fiercely attacking youths with their trimmed fingernails.

Heroic encounters have given way to lovers' quarrels. Having risen, Horace now insists that he could never leave the ground. In the last verse we hear an echo of the *levius plectrum* and the values it summarizes. By catching these values in the metaphor "wars of love," Horace not only achieves a special tightness of structure but also manages to retain a position that is not fully resolved. In the very act of reasserting his allegiance to a gentler world he steals a glance at a harsher one, commandeering his language from the subjects he rejects. And in the next poem (*C.* 1.7), as a final irony, he turns for the first time in the Odes to the epic hexameter, even using it to retell a heroic myth (21 ff.).

Horace's determination to have the best of both worlds is equally evident in an Ode written in 28 B.C. for the dedication of the temple to Actian Apollo:

> Quid dedicatum poscit Apollinem
> vates? quid orat de patera novum
> fundens liquorem? [*C.* 1.31.1–3]

> What does the bard ask from the newly dedicated Apollo? For what does he pray, pouring the fresh wine from his cup?

What the bard demands is simple enough: humble surroundings, enjoyment of what he possesses, a sound mind, and an old age not lacking the lyre (15 ff.). The list is not very compelling to the imagination, and Horace seems to acknowledge as much by stating his enthusiasm for a modest life in terms of a rejection of sumptuous riches:

> non opimae
> Sardiniae segetes feracis,
>
> non aestuosae grata Calabriae
> armenta, non aurum aut ebur Indicum . . . [3–6]

> Not the rich harvests of fertile Sardinia, not the prosperous herds of baked Calabria, not gold nor Indian ivory . . .

For some three stanzas Horace catalogues the earthly splendor to which he is indifferent, exploiting the aesthetic value of sensuous images without accepting moral responsibility for them. Because Milton's imagination could not resist Satan's grandeur, Blake proclaimed that Milton was "of the devil's party without knowing it." Blake's criticism only dramatizes the truism that moral and poetic appeal are not necessarily synonymous. Preachers and artists alike have found the punishments of the damned to be more effective propaganda than the vague emoluments of paradise. To make simple frugality imaginatively compelling is equally difficult, and Horace betrays as much by the rapidity with which he sketches it: *me pascunt olivae, me cichorea levesque malvae* (15–16). Instead he itemizes what he repudiates, adding up riches with one hand only to dismiss them with the other. Detailing the charms of Satan, he simultaneously marks his distance from them.

Horace stands as the classic example of the man who manages to eat his cake and have it too. Indulging the most extravagant of pastoral fantasies, he escapes charges of sentimentality; dispensing moral unction, he avoids the reproach of sermonizing; rising to an epic grandeur, he denies pretensions to sublimity; summoning all wealth's sensuous reality, he receives credit for banishing it. To maintain a single attitude throughout an Ode is frequently impossible—Horace does not so much confront any given subject as surround it.

In the majority of these poems Horace seems to stand detached from the alternatives he explores. At times he seems almost to be reading over our shoulder, and we suspect that we are identifying ourselves more closely with some attitude he strikes than he himself does. He continually escapes us, maintaining the distant irony of his viewpoint now through the dialogue technique of the Satires, now through his shifts from the pastoral to the satiric, now through his leaps from the grandiloquent to the frivolous. Yet he does not remain invariably aloof. The Cleopatra Ode (*C.* 1.37) is interesting precisely because it involves his sympathies fiercely, and in a way that runs counter to his formal attitude. The same is true of the

Odes on death and of some of the love poems, chiefly those of the fourth book. In the short poem after the Cleopatra Ode we can sense the same kind of split in lighter terms:

> Persicos odi, puer, adparatus,
> displicent nexae philyra coronae,
> mitte sectari, rosa quo locorum
> sera moretur.
>
> simplici myrto nihil adlabores
> sedulus curo: neque te ministrum
> dedecet myrtus neque me sub arta
> vite bibentem. [*C.* 1.38]

> I detest Persian finery, boy; crowns woven of linden please me not at all; cease to search out where the late rose lingers. I care nothing for you to labor diligently to enhance the simple myrtle; the myrtle disgraces neither you the servant nor me, as I drink beneath the slender vine.

So the first book ends, with a quietness comparable to the dying close of many of the Odes. It stands in marked contrast not only to the deliberate rhetoric of the opening poem, *Maecenas atavis edite regibus* (*C.* 1.1.1), but to the spirited tones of *C.* 1.37 as well. It is, indeed, almost a palinode, an explicit rejection of the Eastern finery to which he had virtually surrendered himself in the preceding poem. "A simple-life sermon in a nutshell," comments Campbell.[17] Yet here, as in *C.* 1.37, Horace's formal position is imperiled by an imaginative attachment to what he rejects. The exaggerated language of his repudiation—*Persicos odi adparatus . . . nihil adlabores . . . neque dedecet*—itself tends to devalue it. Nor is his austere pleasure in the *simplex myrtus* altogether convincing; in less guarded moments he was more likely to call for the headier fragrance of the *flores amoenae rosae*.[18] Cleopatra herself, a dying exoticism, was in a sense the last rose of summer, and just as it is the Egyptian queen who steals that poem, so it is the haunting sound of *rosa quo locorum*

17. Campbell, *Horace,* 223.
18. *C.* 2.3.14; cf. *C.* 1.36.15, 2.11.14, 3.19.22, 3.29.3.

sera moretur that beguiles our imagination now. The rose lingers in our memory longer than Horace's renunciation of it.

The tension of attitudes in *C.* 1.38 remains playful, but in other Odes it could become more somber. The *propempticon* for Vergil (*C.* 1.3) shows Horace less in control of two positions than caught between them. The poem has long embarrassed commentators, who have proposed such panaceas as dividing it into two or regarding it simply as a humorous extravaganza.[19] Certainly its progress is perplexing. After a conventional prayer for Vergil's safety, Horace passes to a consideration of the first mariner's bravery:

> illi robur et aes triplex
> circa pectus erat, qui fragilem truci
> conmisit pelago ratem
> primus . . . [9–12]

> That man had oak and triple bronze about his heart, who first committed his fragile bark to the fierce sea.

His admiration shifts suddenly to an accusation of the *inpiae rates* (23–24) which cross the seas in disobedience to divine fiat. It is then an easy transition from specific reproach to general condemnation:

> audax omnia perpeti
> gens humana ruit per vetitum nefas. [25–26]

> Bold to endure all things, humankind rushes through forbidden wrong.

Prometheus, Daedalus, and Hercules provide examples of man's impious *audacia* (27 ff.). Yet they seem at the same time to be paradigms of heroic freedom; consequently, as examples, they half undermine the moral they are meant to illustrate. The last stanza

19. K. Prodinger, *WienStud, 29* (1907), 171 ff.; E. A. Hahn, *TAPA, 76* (1945), xxxii. For a perceptive study of the Ode as a whole, see J. P. Elder, *AJP, 73* (1952), 140 ff.

yokes the two concepts, and the poem ends as both a hymn to man's achievements and a stern elegy upon his folly:

> nil mortalibus ardui est:
> caelum ipsum petimus stultitia neque
> per nostrum patimur scelus
> iracunda Iovem ponere fulmina. [37–40]

> Nothing is too arduous for man. We seek the sky itself in our folly, and through our sinfulness we do not allow Jove to lay aside his angry thunderbolts.

The first line suggests a paean upon the heroic flight of ἀρετή,[20] but behind it loom shadows of the Gigantomachia, a hubristic assertion of the irrational.[21] Man exerts power (*neque patimur*) over the gods themselves—but only through his evil. Horace seems to join, but not assimilate, two traditional views of man's unconquerable mind. He could look on the one hand to Theseus' praise of human inventiveness, or to the famous chorus from the *Antigone:* "This wondrous creature, crossing the gray sea, driven by stormy south winds, making his way half buried through the waves that would engulf him." [22] But on the other hand there were the philosophical commonplaces on the *improba navigii ratio* running back to Hesiod, which Horace himself was not above invoking elsewhere as a rhetorical prop for attacking greed.[23] In *C.* 1.3, it seems as though Horace's instinctive feelings were not amenable to the traditional requirements of the form he had chosen. The *propempticon* demanded that the subject's voyage, and the first voyager, be roundly cursed, but Vergil's trip excites quite different emotions in Horace. As a motive for Horace's

20. Cf. *C.* 3.2.21–22: *virtus recludens . . . caelum negata temptat iter via.*

21. Cf. *C.* 3.4.49 ff. (Yet even here there is a notable sympathy for the fallen Giants; see below, 200 ff.)

22. Eurip., *Supp.* 208 ff.; Soph., *Ant.* 332 ff.

23. *C.* 3.24.36 ff. Yet here again appears Horace's sneaking admiration for what he formally disapproves: *horrida callidi / vincunt aequora navitae.* For condemnations of sailing, including its banishment from the Golden Age, see Hesiod, *Op.* 236; Lucr., 5.1006; Verg., *E.* 4.32; Hor., *Epod.* 16.57–60; for further references, see P. Shorey, *Horace, Odes and Epodes* (Boston, 1898), *ad C.* 1.3; K. F. Smith, *The Elegies of Tibullus, ad* 1.3.37.

response we do not have to seek anything more particular than the admiration naturally aroused by the founder, the πρῶτος εὑρετής, of any new art. Yet we might guess as well that the crossing between Rome and Greece of a poet, a poet who was *animae dimidium meae* (8), might have been peculiarly evocative for Horace. It was, after all, on having made just this kind of crossing that Horace most prided himself (*C.* 3.30.13–14; *Ep.* 1.19.32–33).

Tension between Form and Subject: Parody

In parody and allegory we may logically see Horace's fondness for oxymorons and puns extend itself into a method of literary discourse. Like oxymorons, parody clarifies a contrast; like puns, allegory plays upon special resemblances. But where oxymorons and puns are built upon the contrast or identification of certain distinct ideas, parody and allegory are built upon the contrast or identification of an idea with the form that presents it. Where parody dramatizes the distance between some conceptual scheme and reality, allegory dwells upon their closeness. Allegory as Horace practiced it is so bound up with contemporary politics that it defies purely formal appreciation. These political Odes are in one way as complex as anything he wrote, for they involve both a formal tension and, usually, a tension of feelings, thus carrying on a massive dialectic, not only between present politics and myth, but between two attitudes toward the present as well.[24]

Parody presents fewer problems. Perhaps most significant is the frequency with which it engaged Horace's imagination. As early as the first book of Satires he was to indulge in casual burlesque:

> nunc mihi paucis
> Sarmenti scurrae pugnam Messique Cicirri,
> Musa, velim memores et quo patre natus uterque
> contulerit litis. [*S.* 1.5.51–54]

Now, Muse, recount to me in a few words the battle of Sarmentus the buffoon and Messius Cicirrus, and tell me, sprung from what father each came to the lists.

24. See below, 208–09.

By importing an epic invocation and account of pedigrees, Horace lends a Homeric dimension to the jesters' easy vulgarity, and we are entertained not only by the event but by its absurdity.[25] Town and country mouse venture forth in equally august garments. The fable, or αἶνος, was familiar,[26] but the form it assumes is characteristically Horatian. The mice's nocturnal foray to richer tables boasts philosophical sanction:

> "carpe viam, mihi crede, comes, terrestria quando
> mortalis animas vivunt sortita neque ulla est
> aut magno aut parvo leti fuga: quo, bone, circa,
> dum licet, in rebus iucundis vive beatus,
> vive memor, quam sis aevi brevis." [*S.* 2.6.93–97]

> "Seize the path, comrade, believe me. Since all terrestrial creatures are fated to mortality, and since there is no escape from death for either great or small, then, good friend, while it is permitted, live happily among pleasant surroundings; and live ever mindful of how brief is your span."

Behind *carpe viam* it is easy to catch the rhythm of some such formula as *carpe diem,* while the speculative cast and portentous language of what follows proves the mice to be philosophers if not rank Epicureans. As impressive as the trip's solemn metaphysic is the epic cast of its adventures. Behind the mice's outing loom such heroic expeditions as that of Diomede and Odysseus (*Il.* 10.272 ff.):

> iamque tenebat
> nox medium caeli spatium, cum ponit uterque
> in locuplete domo vestigia . . . [100–02]

> And now night held the mid-span of the sky, when the pair set foot in the rich home . . .

25. For the possibility that Horace may have drawn upon Lucilius for the battle of *scurrae,* see G. C. Fiske, *Lucilius and Horace,* 308 ff.

26. See P. Lejay, *Oeuvres d'Horace, Satires, ad loc.*

The high seriousness of language compels us to measure a homely fable against philosophic and epic grandeur. From our simultaneous awareness of each, and of the tension between them, comes the passage's chief effect.

Such easy burlesque is innocuous and isolated. The third Epode presents a more sustained example as Horace invokes the range of tragic experience to parallel his own misfortune, an overdose of garlic:

> ut Argonautas praeter omnis candidum
> Medea mirata est ducem,
> ignota tauris inligaturum iuga
> perunxit hoc Iasonem,
> hoc delibutis ulta donis paelicem
> serpente fugit alite.
> nec tantus umquam siderum insedit vapor
> siticulosae Apuliae
> nec munus umeris efficacis Herculis
> inarsit aestuosius. [9–18]

> When Medea was struck with love for the leader of the Argonauts, Jason, fair beyond all the others, she annointed him with garlic as he was about to lay upon the bulls the yoke they had never felt before; with gifts smeared with garlic she took vengeance upon his mistress, before fleeing upon her winged serpent. No vapor so fierce ever settled upon parched Apulia from any star, nor did the gift of Deianira burn more savagely into the shoulders of Hercules, famous for his labors.

In summoning up the παραδείγματα or *exempla* of Medea and Hercules, Horace exploits a technique traditionally associated with more serious occasions, an appeal to the stabilized moral history of the past. Phoenix exhorts Achilles with the story of Meleager; Achilles himself persuades Priam to cease from tears by pointing to Niobe; and the example of Orestes is repeatedly held up to Telemachus.[27] Homer's

27. *Il.* 9.524 ff.; *Od.* 1.296 ff. (cf. 1.32 ff.), 3.195 ff., 3.305 ff.; and see W. Jaeger, *Paideia, 1,* 31 ff. On the paradigm in general, see Cic., *Inv.*

heroes, drifting from history into myth, soon joined the forebears whom they had invoked, and were themselves cited as equally authoritative models. Exemplary gods, heroes, and men crowd Pindar's Odes, and the paraenetic poems of Alcaeus had already relied upon a similar technique.[28] Latin authors were equally ready to seek figures from more recent history, and handbooks like the *Facta ac Dicta Memorabilia* of Valerius Maximus were soon to provide a storehouse where poets and rhetoricians—the distinction became increasingly tenuous—might seek perspicuous instances.[29] With the elegiac poets the technique hardened into little more than a display of learning, but Horace tended to reserve it for more serious effects. The gravest passages invoke figures like the fallen Giants, Deucalion and Pyrrha, Ulysses, Achilles, Teucer, and Regulus; or there was that most familiar of the proofs of death, the catalogue of great men who had died.[30]

From so august a tradition Hercules and Medea emerge to take their place in Horace's warning against garlic. The solemn introduction—*ut Argonautas*—belongs with the stylized form of the paradigm, in which a *καὶ γάρ* or *namque* often precedes the illustration. The heavy sounds and portentous language—*inligaturum . . . perunxit . . . delibutis*—preserve an almost oracular tone, which is maintained by the ponderous *exempla* drawn from nature: *nec tantus umquam* (15). The concept and the language could hardly be at a further remove from the reality of the event, and the poem's substance is in a sense no more than the space between the two poles.

Horace's poems, instead of drawing us into their own emotional

---

1.30.49 ff.; Quint., 5.11.6; Victorinus, *Rhet. lat. min.* 239, 10 ff. (Halm); W. Jaeger, *Paideia, s. v. paradeigma* and *exempla;* R. Volkmann, *Die Rhetorik der Griechen und Römer* (Leipzig, 1885), 233 ff.; K. Alewell, *Über das rhetorische Paradeigma* (Leipzig, 1913); H. V. Canter, *AJP, 54* (1933), 201 ff.

28. See Fraenkel, *Horace,* 185.

29. Cicero, after citing the example of Priam, directs his readers to more recent history: *abeamus a fabulis, propiora videamus* (*Div.* 2.9.22; cf. *Off.* 3.26.99; *Tusc.* 1.48.116). For a catalogue of historical *exempla,* see H. W. Litchfield, *HSCP, 25* (1914), 1 ff.

30. *Epod.* 13.11 ff.; *C.* 1.2.5 ff., 3.4.49 ff., 3.5.13 ff.; *Ep.* 1.2.18. The last poem is a veritable index of *exempla* (1–30); cf. *Ep.* 1.6.63. The listing of those who have died (*C.* 1.28.7 ff., 2.18.32 ff., 4.7.15–16, 25 ff.) is the same technique that Dunbar elaborates in his "Lament for the Makaris."

context, frequently demand that we see those emotions in some other context. We are as often distanced as involved; he encourages us to observe his feelings rather than to share them. We cannot, for instance, read the tenth Epode, an attack upon a certain Mevius, in the same way we read an Archilochean, Lucilian, or Catullan invective. The quickest way to see what Horace is doing is to compare the Epode with what is generally accepted as its source, a fragment of Archilochus.[31] Archilochus hurls straightforward, if highly wrought, imprecations upon a treacherous friend who was probably identified in the missing lines, for the poem's bias is sharply specific. The fate assigned him is drastic: to be shipwrecked, tossed by the waves, and covered by the scum of seaweed; to lie upon the shore, stiff with cold, gnashing his teeth in helplessness; to be captured by the top-knotted Thracians, and fed upon the bitter bread of slavery. "This would I wish to see him suffer, he who wronged me and trampled underfoot his pledges, he who was once a friend." The person and his crime are specific; Archilochus asks our sympathy for a particular situation. Horace's *olens Mevius* has no such significance in terms of the Epode. Horace refers to no quarrel or injury, nor need we be at pains to find one.[32] Had Horace wished to enlist our feelings for a specific quarrel in the manner of Archilochus he could easily have done so. Like the sixth Epode, a fierce attack upon, probably, no one, the poem suggests an exercise in invective. It does not then, as Fraenkel emphasizes, belong among the autobiographical poems; in all probability it is rather a literary "cursing" (Ἀραί or *Dirae*). On the basis of this work we can readily believe what Horace was to assert in the Epistles, that his Epodes, unlike those of his master Archilochus, had driven no one to suicide.[33]

Granting, then, that Horace does not expect us to share his wrath, is the poem simply a proof of his ability to curse? Here its particular structure becomes important. The difference between the form of the Epode and that of Archilochus' poem is even more significant, and

31. 79 (Diehl). For full treatment of the fragment see Fraenkel, *Horace,* 27 ff. He considers the Epode's motive "the wish to produce a polished poetic invective reminiscent of Archilochus" (31).

32. For an attempt to identify Mevius, see T. Frank, *Classical Studies Presented to Edward Capps* (Princeton, 1936), 160 ff.

33. *Ep.* 1.19.25, 31; *Epod.* 6.13.

more easily demonstrable, than the difference we feel in their emotional content. Archilochus' curses have no special logic save that which his anger gives them, but Horace has imposed upon his abuse the formal structure of the *propempticon* or "send-off poem." The form was familiar by the Augustan age. What looks like an incipient example appears as early as Sappho, and in the Hellenistic age the genre became fairly popular. Erinna, Callimachus, Theocritus, and later Meleager and Dioscorides give us an approximate idea of the traditional elements, while Ovid and Statius display a veritable catalogue of motifs.[34] The most convenient summary is that of the rhetorician Menander.[35] He defines it as a farewell "with words of good omen" (εὐφημία). The two principal elements are grief at the voyager's departure (often accompanied by curses upon the inventor of ships and the first sailor), and—since the departure must take place—entreaties to the gods for a successful trip, together with praise of the traveler, prayers for his safety, and hopes for a quick return.

Horace was not unacquainted with the conventions, as his *propempticon* for Vergil demonstrates (*C.* 1.3). Unless we keep the form in mind, the chief effect of the Epode is lost. The poem is an elaborate exercise in inversion, beginning with the first word:

Mala soluta navis exit alite
ferens olentem Mevium. [*Epod.* 10.1–2]

Under evil auspices sets forth the ship bearing stinking Mevius.

We need only compare Callimachus' "Ship, you who bear off the only sweet love of my life," or the opening of Horace's Ode to Vergil's ship. The customary encomium of the voyager has sunk to

34. Sappho, 96.8–9 (Diehl); Erinna, 3 (Diehl); Callimachus, *Fr.* 400 (Pfeiffer); Theocritus, 7.52–70; Meleager, *Anth. Pal.* 12.52; Dioscorides, *Anth. Pal.* 12.171; Ovid, *Am.* 2.11; Statius, *S.* 3.2. On the form see F. Jäger, *Das antike Propemptikon und das 17. Gedicht des Paulinus von Nola* (Rosenheim, 1913); G. L. Hendrickson, *CJ, 3* (1908), 100 ff.; J. P. Elder, *AJP, 73* (1952), 145–46.

35. *Rhet. gr. 3,* 395 ff. (Spengel).

a single adjective *olentem,* while the traditional prayer that all winds be calm save favoring ones has become a demand that tempests alone hit Mevius' ship—only the favoring west wind is not invoked (3 ff.). The usual entreaty for the passenger's safety has turned to a prayer for his death, which if fulfilled will be honored by the usual sacrifice:

opima quodsi praeda curvo litore
porrecta mergos iuverit,
libidinosus immolabitur caper
et agna Tempestatibus. [21–24]

But if you will gladden the gulls as a fat prize stretched out upon the curved shore, then a wanton goat and a lamb will be sacrificed to the gods of storms.

In wedding the form of the *propempticon* to the substance of Ἀραί, Horace distinguishes his poem from its Archilochean predecessor, and suggests where the creative impulse for it lay. He does not invite us to share his hatred, but to observe his cleverness in expressing it. We must see his abuse, literary though it may be, in terms of the incompatible tradition of the *propempticon,* for in the tension between substance and form lies the point of the Epode.

That exuberant poem seems to have been done simply for the sake of the doing, and we may say the same of his Ode to a Wine Jar (*C.* 3.21). The poem is not, as it is frequently labeled, simply an "address." Rather it is an invocation in strict hymnic form, with the *pia testa* (4) replacing the deity.[36] The formal structure is carefully maintained: reminder of lineage (*O nata mecum consule Manlio*), catalogue of powers (*seu . . . seu . . . seu*), prayer to descend (7), recitation of past achievements (11–12),[37] threefold division of attributes (*tu . . . tu . . . tu*), and, finally, roll call of attendant deities (21–24). The sonorous opening introduces a series

36. Eduard Norden pointed out in great detail the formal elements of the Ode's structure, citing numerous parallels: *Agnostos Theos* (Berlin, 1913), 143–63.

37. In the reference to Cato (11 ff.) Horace again uses a paradigm for humorous effect. *Narratur* is a typically solemn introduction; cf. *S.* 2.6.80; *C.* 1.7.23, 3.5.41. For a parallel to the listing of the god's ἀρεταί, cf. *C.* 1.10. 13 ff.

of quasi-religious terms: *pia testa* (4), *quocumque nomine* (5), *moveri* (6), *bono die* (6), *descende* (7). *Quocumque nomine* looks like a deliberate reminiscence of Catullus' Hymn to Diana:

> sis quocumque tibi placet
> sancta nomine. [34.21–22]

May you be holy, by whatever name you will.

And it is surely no accident that a traditional invocation to Diana (*C.* 3.22) follows the Ode to the Wine Jar, as if to insure that we realize what Horace has done. Yet even so, many editors have failed to follow the poem's double reference, with the result that key phrases receive increasingly tortuous explanations. On *pia,* for instance, we find "the amphora has been faithful to its charge"; *quocumque nomine* becomes "a bookkeeping expression, 'on whatever account,' " and *bono die* "a red-letter day"; while *descende* is woodenly explained by "the *apotheca* was in the upper part of the house." [38] To ignore the ironic tension between social reality and religious formula is to lose one, and in fact the principal, source of enjoyment.

As is so often the case, the precedent to which we are referred, a poem by Poseidippus (*Anth. Pal.* 5.134), is chiefly useful in measuring the complexity of Horace's achievement. Poseidippus simply implores "the dewy rain of Bacchus." We have at most only a hint of the religious formulas Horace exploits. Horace directs our attention not merely to the jar, but to his manner of addressing it; *pia* is as important as *testa.* The Ode is in honor of Messalla Corvinus, who, if we may judge from the *Symposium* written by Maecenas, was noted for his fondness for the wine jar.[39] But Messalla was also patron of Tibullus, and famed for his own meticulous attention to style.[40] We

38. C. H. Moore, *Horace's Odes and Epodes* (New York, 1902), *ad loc.* Cf. C. L. Smith, *The Odes and Epodes of Horace* (Boston, 1899), *ad loc.*

39. Servius, *ad Aen.* 8.310, reports that in Maecenas' *Symposium* Messalla gave a speech *"de vino."* The effects ascribed to wine in Messalla's speech are not dissimilar to those described by Horace, though they are too conventional to prove a connection between the two works. Cf. H. Bardon, *La littérature latine inconnue, 2* (Paris, 1956), 15 ff.

40. Tactitus, *Dial.* 18; Quint., 10.1.113. Messalla was probably a poet himself, though what and how much he wrote remains uncertain; see H. Bardon, *La littérature latine inconnue, 2,* 22–23. On *C.* 3.21 see below, 337.

may surmise that he was no more likely to miss the skill of Horace's invitation than he was to refuse it.

Horace most often weaves such a counterpoint of tradition and fact around the events of his own life. His modern instances are likely to be old saws: the animals protecting him in his infancy are descended from those who gathered around Pindar and Stesichorus,[41] while in his flight from the formidable Bore he re-enacts Hector's escape from Achilles.[42] In the notorious account of his flight at Philippi (*C.* 2.7.9 ff.) it is hard to tell where history stops and literary fancy begins. The shield he claims to have abandoned looks suspiciously like those left behind by Archilochus, Alcaeus, and Anacreon,[43] and even if we ignore the literary context of this incident we can hardly take literally what follows. Horace solemnly assures his friend that divine intervention alone saved him. Mercury, in purloining Horace from the battle, reminds us that he is god of thieves as well as of poets:

> tecum Philippos et celerem fugam
> sensi relicta non bene parmula,
> cum fracta virtus et minaces
> turpe solum tetigere mento:
>
> sed me per hostis Mercurius celer
> denso paventem sustulit aere. [*C.* 2.7.9–14]

> With you I shared the experience of Philippi and our headlong flight there, my shield ingloriously abandoned, when Virtue was shattered and menacing hosts touched the base soil with their faces. But swift Mercury bore me away trembling through the enemy's midst, with a dense cloud around me.

Aphrodite's rescue of Paris (*Il.* 3.380 ff.) seems to have suggested the means of Horace's departure. The stanza's effect depends upon our

41. *C.* 3.4.9 ff. For the traditional nature of the tale see Pliny, *H. N.* 10.29.82 (Mayhoff); Pausanius, 9.23.2. See below, 207.

42. *Sic me servavit Apollo* (*S.* 1.9.78; cf. Hom., *Il.* 20.443). Lucilius had also quoted the passage in Homer, 231–32 (Marx).

43. Archilochus, 6 (Diehl); Alcaeus, 49 (Diehl); cf. Herodotus, 5.95; Anacreon, 51 (Diehl).

remembering Paris' elegant escape as we watch Horace's portly and trembling figure hurtling along in its protective myth.

Where Horace's martial career is invincibly Homeric, his amatory one is in the best elegiac tradition. In prostrating himself before the door of a coy mistress he testifies less clearly to an overwhelming passion than to a thorough schooling in conventional poetic forms (*C.* 3.10). The posture he adopts is that of the *exclusus amator,* the Ode being technically a *παρακλαυσίθυρον,* or "lament before the door." [44] The vast majority of Greek and Latin lovers seem to have lived lives of noisy desperation. They often accompanied their suits to a *dura puella* by beating upon the latter's portals, or in a milder mood they might merely deck them with garlands and verses. Those without the acumen or resources to provide a golden rain received harsh treatment from the *janitor,* and Plato mentions "sleeping upon the doorstep" as a matter of common practice (*Smp.* 183a). In the Epodes Horace showed himself familiar with the ritual,[45] and in *C.* 3.10 he displays exemplary thoroughness in recording the lover's traditional woes. He bolsters his plea for entrance with a mournful reminder of the cold and rain he is enduring (5–8), a climate apparently continuous in the world of the *exclusus amator,* if we may judge from the frequency of their complaints. The violet hue of his face (14) is calculated, understandably, to impress upon Lyce the extent of his sufferings. From here the transition is easy to the customary rebuke to the austerity of the *dura puella:*

> parcas, nec rigida mollior aesculo
> nec Mauris animum mitior anguibus. [17–18]

Relent, you who are no softer than the rigid oak, nor gentler in heart than Moorish serpents.

44. The term *παρακλαυσίθυρον* is itself late (Plu., *Moralia* 753b), but the procedure was familiar long before. For discussion and examples, see H. de la Ville de Mirmont, *Philologie et linguistique, mélanges offerts à Louis Havet* (Paris, 1909), 573 ff.; H. V. Canter, *AJP, 41* (1920), 355 ff.; F. O. Copley, *TAPA, 73* (1942), 96 ff., and *Exclusus Amator* (Baltimore, 1956).

45. *Epod.* 11.19–22. The weapons Horace abandons in *C.* 3.26 are those with which a lover might equip himself for attacking his mistress' door. See also *C.* 1.25.1–8, 3.15.8 ff.

Now, having rung the changes upon the theme, Horace in closing inserts a single cracked note:

> non hoc semper erit liminis aut aquae
> caelestis patiens latus. [19–20]

> Not always will my ribs endure your threshold or the rain from heaven.

We expect one of the usual warnings—a threat that, unless admitted, he will batter down the door, shortly and noisily expire, or, at the least, proclaim Lyce's harshness until dawn.[46] But instead of a final confession of enslavement, Horace delivers a quiet warning of his departure. The threat forms a gentle mockery of the whole situation, since the formalized world of amatory complaint shatters upon any recognition that it is not the only world and that one may leave it. Horace builds the poem upon the tension between his inflamed importunities and his cool awareness of their absurdity. He calls upon us to recognize both the charms of convention and the claims of reality.

Horace exercised his knowledge of literary forms, or even formulas, particularly in his autobiographical Odes on amatory themes. Here lay the most abundant opportunities, for by the Augustan age the language and sentiments of love had become elaborately stylized, offering a wealth of possible attitudes. That of the *exclusus amator* was merely one of the most obvious. A more delicate and complex amatory Ode is that declaring Horace's love for Lalage:

> Integer vitae scelerisque purus
> non eget Mauris iaculis neque arcu
> nec venenatis gravida sagittis,
> Fusce, pharetra,
>
> sive per Syrtis iter aestuosas 5
> sive facturus per inhospitalem

46. Cf. Aristophanes, *Ec.* 960 ff.; Theocritus, 3.53; *Anth. Pal.* 5.23; Propertius, 1.16.17 ff., 2.9.41, 2.5.22; Tibullus, 1.10.54; Ovid, *Am.* 1.9.7–8; Aulus Gellius, 4.14.

Caucasum vel quae loca fabulosus
  lambit Hydaspes.

namque me silva lupus in Sabina,
dum meam canto Lalagen et ultra 10
terminum curis vagor expeditis,
  fugit inermem,

quale portentum neque militaris
Daunias latis alit aesculetis
nec Iubae tellus generat, leonum 15
  arida nutrix.

pone me pigris ubi nulla campis
arbor aestiva recreatur aura,
quod latus mundi nebulae malusque
  Iuppiter urget, 20

pone sub curru nimium propinqui
solis, in terra domibus negata:
dulce ridentem Lalagen amabo,
  dulce loquentem. [*C.* 1.22]

The man who is pure of life and guiltless, Fuscus, does not need Moorish javelins, nor bow, nor quiver heavy with poisoned arrows, whether he be about to set off through the sultry Syrtes or through hostile Caucasus or through the regions that the storied Hydaspes washes. For while I was singing of my Lalage, wandering carefree in the Sabine forest beyond my usual boundaries, there fled from me, unarmed though I was, a wolf, such a monster as neither martial Daunia nourishes in its wide oak forests nor the land of Juba breeds, dry nurse of lions.

Set me in barren fields where no tree is refreshed by the summer breeze, a corner of the globe over which clouds and evil weather brood; set me under the chariot of the too-near sun, in a land denied to dwellings—still will I love my sweetly laughing Lalage, my Lalage sweetly speaking.

The poem has been commonly read for its edifying moral. At first it hardly appears to be on an amatory topic at all. The solemn tone of the opening could easily be taken at face value, and indeed, in the nineteenth century, Flemming set the Ode to a hymnlike accompaniment for organ. We become uneasy only at the exaggerated description of the wolf, *quale portentum* (13), where we would expect to find a traditional paradigm illustrating the gnomic proposition of the first stanza.[47] It is not, it appears, Horace's purity in any usual moral sense that makes him invulnerable, but rather his love for Lalage ("babbling one"). The shift from an apparently ethical to an erotic bias is underlined by the echoes of Catullus. If the second stanza does not remind us of the geographical catalogue that opens Catullus' eleventh poem, Horace's *dulce ridentem* (23) can hardly be missed as the repetition of a phrase in Catullus' only other poem in Sapphics (51.5).

The only moral values that the Ode proposes lie, we increasingly realize, in an amatory context. The whole poem may be seen as a wry but amused comment upon the lover's *pietas* and *fides* which Catullus constantly invokes. Even the seemingly austere language of the first line can bear a specialized erotic meaning.[48] Playing the part of a typical elegiac poet, Horace dramatizes their insulated concept of the world. He commands without embarrassment language that would be more appropriate in the mouth of an Elder Cato, cavalierly assuming it to have a particular amatory connotation as though there could be no other. Such a twisting of normal words to specialized meanings is no more parochial than the poem's central assumption, that even an animal will recognize and yield to the true lover. The Ode is in effect a comment from within on the world of elegy. What Horace parodies here is the same attitude he was to rebuke explicitly elsewhere,[49] the refusal to recognize any emotion or experience that is not amatory, the instinct for annihilating all that's made to a sentimental thought in a sentimental shade.

H. J. Munro, Catullus' great editor, saw the Ode as an unsuccessful attempt to elaborate upon part of Catullus' Septimius-Acme poem

47. See Fraenkel, *Horace*, 185.
48. G. L. Hendrickson, *CJ*, *5* (1910), 250 ff.
49. See above, 33; below, 239–40.

(45).[50] Sensitive to the Ode's incongruities, he was yet single-minded enough to dismiss them. His criticism is remarkable both for its sharpness and for its syntax:

> But what poet of high genius would ever imagine himself as actually wandering about amid Arctic ice and fogs, or again beneath the suns of the burning zone, and continuing the while to love his sweetly laughing Lalage? Did he dream that "sighing like furnace" would give him the heat too of a furnace, fired perchance by the inspiration of some "woful ballad made to his mistress' "—laugh? but then the torrid equatorial suns? Horace never really conceived the situation: he was simply trying to outdo what he remembered in his Catullus:
>
> Acmen Septimius suos amores
> tenens in gremio, "mea," inquit, "Acme,
> ni te perdite amo atque amare porro
> omnes sum assidue paratus annos
> quantum qui pote plurimum perire,
> solus in Libya Indiaque tosta
> caesio veniam obvius leoni."
>
> Septimius, holding his beloved Acme in his embrace, says, "My Acme, if I do not love you desperately, if I am not ready to go on through all the years to come loving you as much as the most desperate lover can love, then let me go alone to face the green-eyed lion in Libya or scorched India."

The answer to "what poet . . . ?" is "one who had read a good deal of love poetry written since the time of Catullus." Perhaps the most important difference in the two poems is the generation that fell between them. Septimius' hyperbolic protestations had since been absorbed into a world as formal as that of courtly love. Horace's

50. *Criticisms and Elucidations of Catullus* (Cambridge, Eng., 1878), 237–38. The translation below of Catullus 45 is mine.

vows no longer ring clear, for we are bound to be haunted by echoes of the intervening elegiac experience. Here is Vergil's description of the outburst of Gallus, Rome's first elegiac poet:

> "Our labors cannot change Cupid, not even if we should in the dead of winter drink of the Hebrus and endure the Sithonian snow and sleet, nor if, when the dying bark is drying up on the tall elm, we should drive about the sheep of the Aethiopians beneath the star of Cancer! Love conquers all: let us too yield to love." [*E.* 10.64–69]

And here is Tibullus:

> Lo, I wander distressed in the darkness through the whole city [and am not harmed. Venus protects me] nor does she allow anyone to waylay me and wound me, or to snatch away my garments for a prize. Whoever is held fast by love may go safely and with heaven's protection (*tutusque sacerque*) wherever he wishes: he need fear no ambush. Neither am I harmed by the sullen cold of the winter night; nor am I hurt by the rain's heavy downpour. [1.2.25–30]

And here Propertius:

> Nor is there anyone who would harm sacred lovers: they may go even on the road ruled by Sciron without being harmed. Whoever is a lover may walk upon the shores of Scythia and no one will be so barbarous as to wish to harm him. The moon shows him the path, the stars reveal the rough places; Cupid himself waves his flaming torch before him, and savagely raging dogs turn aside their gaping fangs: for lovers the road is safe at any hour. [3.16.11–18]

Septimius' passionate pilgrimage could be read by Horace's contemporaries only as a sentimental journey. Any Augustan who repeated Septimius' lonely expedition would find himself now on well-traveled roads, for hyperbole of feeling had become a conventional idiom. Horace unites Septimius' devotion with Gallus' sense of love's ineradicable power, compounding both with Tibullus' and Propertius' conviction of the lover's invulnerability. He has been suspected of writing a satire on Propertius' poem.[51] Yet the satiric intent, if we can call it that, plays rather about the whole world of elegy, summarizing the range of its fragile commonplaces.

Of Horace's Ode E. A. Havelock has observed that "his emotions are not equal to his conceptions."[52] The charge need not be a rebuke; we might find in it instead a perceptive definition of one kind of parody. The poem's point lies not in its closeness to the "truth and reality" that Munro demanded and found in Catullus, but in its distance from them. Catullus, despite his ironically indulgent view of Septimius and Acme, beguiles us nevertheless into the emotional world of the lovers, but Horace invites us instead into a literary tradition. Though the Ode claims to be autobiographical, Horace seems tacitly to ally himself with the reader rather than with the lover in the poem. Only by keeping his intentions in mind can we avoid both the sonorities of Flemming, and, alternatively, accusations of artificiality. Horace exaggerates the assumptions of elegy to the point where we cannot ignore the gap between so stylized a world and the actual world. Once we acknowledge that gap, the wolf-infested but still crystalline wilds of erotic sentiment shatter.[53]

Although Horace makes patent the absurdity of the situation, he betrays as well, perhaps, an ironic awareness of its reality. At the same time that he exposes the insulated and insulating quality of elegiac love, he also recognizes its validity as an image of human experience. In terms of ordinary social values the lover's stance is laughable. But measured by private emotional standards there is nothing inappropriate in his boasts, and we feel his desperate single-mindedness to be as enviable as it is ridiculous. Horace's parody allows him to adopt sentiments and gestures which he could indulge

51. R. M. Haywood, *CJ, 37* (1941), 28 ff.

52. *Lyric Genius of Catullus,* 180.

53. We may guess that Aristius Fuscus, to whom the Ode is addressed, would not have mistaken Horace's purpose. Known to the scholiasts as *grammaticus doctissimus* (Ps.-Acro *ad S.* 1.9.62), he was perhaps a writer of comedies (Porphyrio *ad Ep.* 1.10, though see Ps.-Acro *ad loc.*) and certainly a literary critic of high repute, one of the few whom Horace declared himself anxious to please (*S.* 1.10.83). A close friend of the poet (*Ep.* 1.10.3–4), he seems to have possessed an embarrassingly quick sense of humor, for it is he who heartlessly and knowingly abandons Horace to the Bore (*S.* 1.9.71 ff.).

only vicariously, as it were—for there are two people in the poem, one posturing on stage, the other laughing in the wings. Even his laughter remains gentle, since he perceives the beauty as well as the absurdity of the conventions he exploits. And he knew, too, that to demonstrate the latter is frequently to heighten our sense of the former. How else should we explain the perennial charm of Pope's Hampton Court? [54]

Frequently Horace uses parody for a discernible practical effect upon the person whom he addresses. The playful description of his flight at Philippi sets a mood that makes the substance of his message to Pompeius more acceptable,[55] and he draws upon a similar technique in the Ode to the famous *filia pulcrior* (*C.* 1.16). In the youthful excesses of the Epodes (*criminosis iambis,* 2–3), Horace had apparently injured a girl whom he leaves nameless.[56] He now recants his former *tristia* (26),[57] pleading that she abandon her resentment and readmit him to her good graces. Horace seems to be drawing upon the *Palinode* of Stesichorus, who, so the story went, had written a poem attacking Helen of Troy. The gods, judging that the abuse of beauty warranted banishment from it, promptly struck the poet blind. Stesichorus, being more perceptive than Homer (Plato, *Phdr.* 243a), required little time to grasp the cause of his blindness. He then penned his *Palinode* in praise of Helen, whereupon his sight was miraculously restored. Horace certainly knew of Stesichorus' poem; he refers to it as early as the seventeenth Epode (42 ff.). The fact that his Ode follows one which, if it does not abuse Helen, at least predicts the doom she will bring (*C.* 1.15.4 ff.), suggests that he may have had the sequence of Stesichorus' two poems in mind.[58] And it would be difficult to find a better description of Leda and Helen than *matre pulcra filia pulcrior* (1).

54. For the possible connection between *C.* 1.22 and the Odes on poetry, see below, 342.

55. See below, 171.

56. For some attempts to identify the *filia pulcrior* see T. Frank, *Classical Studies Presented to Edward Capps,* 159 ff.; E. A. Hahn, *TAPA, 70* (1939), 213 ff. See also Fraenkel, *Horace,* 207–08.

57. *Tristia* bears an almost technical reference to poems of invective; cf. *tristi laedere versu* (*S.* 2.1.21), where Horace is being reproached for his personal attacks.

58. Ps.-Acro *ad C.* 1.16 says that Horace is imitating Stesichorus.

It would, however, be misleading to emphasize the possible influence of Stesichorus. Horace's Ode is principally interesting for its mock-heroic technique, and for this we know of no precedent in the Greek poet. Portentously he describes the awfulness of anger: greater by far than the emotions felt by enraptured prophetess, by Bacchant, by Corybant; neither Noric sword nor savage waves can turn it; it outfaces Jupiter himself. Out of the insults that they had exchanged Horace spins what is virtually a hymn to *Ira,* complete with mythological pedigree and tributes to the deity's past accomplishments:

> fertur Prometheus addere principi
> limo coactus particulam undique
> desectam et insani leonis
> vim stomacho adposuisse nostro.
>
> irae Thyesten exitio gravi
> stravere et altis urbibus ultimae
> stetere causae, cur perirent
> funditus inprimeretque muris
>
> hostile aratrum exercitus insolens. [*C.* 1.16.13–21]

> Prometheus, it is said, was forced to add to our primal clay a portion taken from every animal, and placed in our breast the rage of the maddened lion. Wrath laid low Thyestes with dreadful destruction; wrath stands as the ultimate cause that lofty cities have perished entirely, and the exulting enemy has ploughed under their fallen walls.

The solemn citations [59] are not intended to ridicule mythology, any more than the town and country mouse belittle epic event, or the dose of garlic makes tragedy absurd. For analogies we must look not to such a work as *Tom Thumb,* which lampoons the conventions of opera, but to "The Rape of the Lock," which exploits for its own purposes the conventional forms of epic and religion without depreci-

59. In Thyestes (17) Horace again uses a solemn paradigm for burlesque effect; cf. Medea in *Epod.* 3.9 ff. and *C.* 2.13.8, or Cato in *C.* 3.21.11–12. Cicero (*Tusc.* 4.36.77) cites Thyestes as a standard example of *ira.*

ating their independent validity. Mock-heroic mocks not the heroic but the illusion of the heroic. Thus, in Spence's *Anecdotes* we discover that Pope, whose "imitations of Horace" provide explicit evidence of the affinity he felt, attempted to conciliate an equally wrathful beauty by the same technique:

> The stealing of Miss Belle Fermor's hair was taken too seriously, and caused an estrangement between the two families, though they had lived so long in great friendship before. A common acquaintance, and well-wisher to both, desired me to write a poem to make jest of it, and laugh them together again. It was with this view that I wrote "The Rape of the Lock."

Parody is a way of looking at life, or at least of correcting our view of it. Horace, like Pope, grafts domestic skirmish onto the stable dimension of myth in order that we may measure the gap between them. The exaggerated terms in which he describes her former wrath are intended to make the *filia pulcrior* realize how disproportionate her feelings were. To measure reality against a conceptual scheme here has a practical end. By investing a petty event with the garments of a giant Horace calls the girl's attention to how small is actually is.

The gap between the way things are and the way they seem to be can be viewed in a variety of ways. In one perspective it is tragic; it is Lear's discovery of his daughters' true natures. In another it is ironic, and the eighteenth century officially christened the gap between pretense and actuality "The Ridiculous." [60] By suggesting how much at variance with reality was the girl's reaction, Horace, like Pope, attempts to "make a jest" of the episode, and "laugh together" the two principal actors. Only after she has, we presume, adjusted her emotions to reality does Horace relax the tension he has built and return to a unified view:

> compesce mentem: me quoque pectoris
> temptavit in dulci iuventa
> fervor et in celeres iambos

60. The preface to *Tom Jones* elaborately formulates the idea of "The Ridiculous." See also J. Bullitt, *Jonathan Swift and the Anatomy of Satire* (Cambridge, 1953), 24 ff.

misit furentem: nunc ego mitibus
mutare quaero tristia, dum mihi
  fias recantatis amica
    opprobriis animumque reddas. [22–28]

Calm your spirit. Anger tried me too in my sweet youth, and sent me raging to swift iambics. Now I would change bitterness for sweetness, provided that, once I have taken back my attacks, you become my friend and give me your heart again.

In banishing the apparatus of parody Horace gracefully pleads that the girl likewise abandon her sullen anger that drew it forth. He sets her an example by repudiating his own *tristia* (26), the unhappy product of his former wrath and the cause of her *tristes irae* (9). In the lovely final phrase *animumque reddas* he reveals to her the serious intention upon which his mockery was built.

Parody acts in this poem as a kind of mitigating medium, and the same is true of the Ode recounting Horace's narrow escape from a falling tree (*C.* 2.13). Here his motives are less apparent, for no second person is involved. The Ode is in fact an apostrophe to himself, the tree being no more than a formal addressee:

Ille et nefasto te posuit die,
quicumque primum, et sacrilega manu
  produxit, arbos, in nepotum
    perniciem opprobriumque pagi;

illum et parentis crediderim sui
fregisse cervicem et penetralia
  sparsisse nocturno cruore
    hospitis; ille venena Colcha

et quidquid usquam concipitur nefas
tractavit, agro qui statuit meo
  te, triste lignum, te caducum
    in domini caput inmerentis.

quid quisque vitet, numquam homini satis
cautum est in horas . . . [1–14]

> Whoever first planted you did so on an ill-omened day, and with sacrilegious hand brought you up, O tree, to be a menace to posterity and a disgrace to the countryside. I could believe him to have broken the neck of his own father, and to have scattered his hearth with the blood of a guest at night; he had traffic in Colchian poisons and in whatever wickedness was anywhere conceived, he who set you out in my field, baneful log, to fall down upon the head of your undeserving master.
>
> Man never takes enough care from hour to hour as to what he should avoid . . .

The awful paradigms unite with a religious solemnity of language (*nefasto die, sacrilega manu, perniciem opprobriumque, nefas*) to render absurd a commonplace of rural life. The themes of parricide and the Colchian sorceress reappear from the third Epode, where we find the same overwrought vocabulary. Yet the resemblance between the two poems is merely formal. Horace's complaint about garlic had no motive other than his pleasure in so charming a stylization of a social misfortune. But in the Ode to the *triste lignum,* as in that to the *filia pulcrior* (*C.* 1.16), there is a more serious intention. Parody implies distance, for we must stand sufficiently far away to see simultaneously both extremes, the original and the author's distortion of it. Horace's travesty of his near misfortune suggests just such an attempt at perspective, but not so much for his audience as for himself. By blowing up a trivial event to absurd dimensions he seems to seek relief from it by assuring himself of its triviality. Just as he sought to persuade the *filia pulcrior* of the foolishness of her reaction, so he now seeks to free himself from what he knows to be an excessive concern. Yet the mock-heroic tone of *C.* 2.13 is less sustained than that of *C.* 1.16; perhaps we should even say that it is less successful, presuming that the *filia pulcrior* did not resist so charming a recantation. In the Ode to the *triste lignum* the framework of parody does not seem to be an adequate vehicle for Horace to deal with his feelings, and after the third stanza he allows it to lapse abruptly. The major part of the poem (13–40), a consideration of human mortality and the poet's afterlife, is generally serious despite some lighthearted touches.[61] Moreover, the frequency with which Horace returned to the incident of the falling tree suggests an abiding concern that resisted all attempts to banish it by ridicule.[62]

The Amatory Odes

Horace's amatory Odes, perhaps his most elusive work, have long baffled attempts to relate them to his life. Readers have responded, on the one hand, with elaborate charts of the *amores Horatii.* The staggering numbers of his boasted conquests and confessed defeats have been carefully annotated, and commentators have exercised their knowledge, or intuition, in distinguishing the "truly felt" affairs from the passing fancies. Others—and this is now by far the more common view—have ridiculed all such attempts, denouncing the notion that there is any point in anatomizing Horace to see what breeds about his heart. His declarations they dismiss as faint fictitious flames, reflecting only an imagination well trained in the traditional forms of literary sentiment.[63]

The problem posed by the possibility of two so violently opposed judgments may perhaps be best approached by retaining somewhat formalistic terms for analysis. Nearly all of the amatory poems display Horace's familiar antitheses and shifts of attitude. His imagination was excited less often by the extremes of happiness or despair of lovers than by their self-contradictions, illusions, or deceptions. It was, perhaps, the fact that lovers suffered so abundantly from these that made the subject appeal to him beyond any personal involvement he may have known. The obvious difference between the devious pair in *C.* 3.9 and the adoring Septimius and Acme is itself

61. The heavily solemn *quam paene* (21) seems an incipient return to the burlesque seriousness of the opening. On *C.* 2.13 see below, 315–17.

62. Cf. *C.* 2.17.27, 3.4.27, 3.8.8.

63. For a survey of the attempts to distinguish and rank the various girls mentioned by Horace, see J. G. F. Estré, *Horatiana Prosopographeia* (Amsterdam, 1846), 509 ff., and for a more recent effort, P. Pivo, *Horace, martyre d'amour* (Paris, 1936). An example of those skeptical of all Horace's confessions may be seen in the quotation from H. D. Sedgwick cited above, 100; see also the wholesale indictment of R. Y. Tyrrell, *Latin Poetry,* 192 and 203 ff., and the works cited in n. 77, below.

suggestive. The course of true love never did run smooth in the Odes; there is no equivalent to the Catullan *amant amantur* (45.20). Even in a poem (*C.* 3.7) written ostensibly to comfort the lonely Asterie, Horace retains as profoundly ironic a view of her sex as he did in describing the variable Pyrrha (*C.* 1.5). *Quid fles, Asterie?* She is weeping, it appears, from foolish anxiety lest her absent lover Gyges succumb to the more available charms of his present hostess. After reassuring her that Gyges will remain a *durus puer,* Horace turns suddenly upon Asterie with a warning that she look to her own susceptibilities and remain obdurate to the serenades of her neighbor:

> prima nocte domum claude neque in vias
> sub cantu querulae despice tibiae
> et te saepe vocanti
> duram difficilis mane. [*C.* 3.7.29–32]

> At nightfall close your door and do not look down into the streets at the sound of the plaintive pipe; and, though he often call you harsh, remain unyielding.

When Horace does not surprise us with the shifts of his lovers, he often throws the whole world of love into an antithesis with some alternative existence. Love and war were traditional foils in the *recusatio,* but even when Horace was not directly concerned with begging off from martial themes he found it natural to balance the two. His extravagant protestations of love for Glycera yield for a moment to a brief disclaimer:

> in me tota ruens Venus
> Cyprum deseruit nec patitur Scythas
> et versis animosum equis
> Parthum dicere nec quae nihil attinent.
> [*C.* 1.19.9–12]

> Rushing upon me with full strength, Venus has quitted Cyprus, nor does she allow me to sing of the Scythians or of the Parthian, bravest when his horse wheels about in retreat, or of anything else not to the point.

He is forever reminding us of *quae nihil attinent,* if only to dismiss them. An apostrophe to Lydia (*C.* 1.8) demanding why she is bent on destroying Sybaris with love is actually a catalogue of Sybaris' athletic accomplishments, and we are purposely made more aware of what Sybaris has given up than of what he has gained. In the independent masculine world that Horace conjures up, Sybaris' love for Lydia seems an almost feminine weakness, a suggestion confirmed by the concluding image of Achilles dressed in the robes of a woman. Although the odd and almost fragmentary Ode that is Neobule's lament (*C.* 3.12) reverses the situation, the two poems share the premise that the claims of Venus are best measured in terms of Diana. Now the man is not seduced by a feminine world, but remains happy in his athletic triumphs. The tension between alternative existences is made the more powerful by the fact that it is Neobule herself who proudly describes the masculine world for which her lover deserts her.

In each of these three poems the two lovers are the only figures, yet each poem makes us aware of an opposed world. The tendency to force any situation outward to a more general context is equally apparent in an Ode describing a rivalry for the peerless Nearchus:

> grande certamen, tibi praeda cedat,
> maior an illa.
>
> interim, dum tu celeris sagittas
> promis, haec dentis acuit timendos,
> arbiter pugnae posuisse nudo
> sub pede palmam
>
> fertur et leni recreare vento
> sparsum odoratis umerum capillis,
> qualis aut Nireus fuit aut aquosa
> raptus ab Ida. [*C.* 3.20.7–16]

> Great is the struggle, whether the prize shall fall to you or she prove herself the stronger. Meanwhile, as you draw your swift arrows, and as she sharpens her fearful teeth, the judge of the battle is said to have crushed the palm of victory beneath his bare foot, and to be cooling in the light

breeze shoulders scattered with perfumed locks, such a one as was Nireus or he who was carried off from many-fountained Ida.

The distancing *interim,* confirmed by the gnomic detachment of *fertur,* gently disengages us from the present, and the fierce struggles of the rivals sink quietly to a subordinate clause. Treading the contested palm casually underfoot, Nearchus seems as elusive as the perfume of his floating locks. The comparison with Nireus, fairest of the Greeks after Achilles, and Ganymede, snatched from mortal love to immortal life, bestow upon him a timeless grace. Nearchus' almost divine indifference, emphasized by the ironic echo of *Epod.* 15.9–10, does more than provide a twist to the tale of hot pursuit. It disengages us, too, from the lovers' close present; we move back to view their struggles in a more inclusive perspective. And as we leave the actual world for that of myth, we become aware of the continuity of beauty that lies behind any individual's crystallization of it, no matter how intense the particular emotions he creates.

Horace's specifically autobiographical love poems present a special problem of language. His professions are consistently couched in terms so exaggerated, and so conventional, as to travesty the emotions they record. At the very moment that he proclaims the intensity of his emotions he simultaneously begs us not to believe him.

The Ode to Pyrrha (*C.* 1.5) is a good example.[64] The poise of its structure and the triteness of the image of the lover as a *naufragus* encourage us to feel that Horace's delight in Pyrrha's sea changes outweighs any distress he may have felt. The *insolens puer,* soon to weep (*flebit,* 6) over his mistress' inconstancy, seems not untypical of the lovers of elegy and their *flebiles modi* (*C.* 2.9.9). Horace's language appears to be modeled on that of Catullus, for the warning of broken *fides* and *mutatos deos* reminds us of Catullus' constant invocation of *fides* and of the gods who guard it. Catullus' eighth poem, in particular, is curiously close. Pyrrha's alternations of fair and foul form Horace's version of Catullus' *fulsere quondam candidi tibi soles;* the solemn apostrophe, *miseri, quibus intemptata nites,*

64. On *C.* 1.5 see above, 65 ff.

suggests a detached echo of the specific *miser Catulle, desinas ineptire;* the amused question, *quis multa gracilis te puer in rosa . . . urget?* recalls Catullus' inflamed queries: *quis nunc te adibit? cui videberis bella?*

We may feel that Horace's stylized echoes of Catullus enforce the standard antitheses between the two authors. These have achieved an almost canonical rigidity, recalling those of a confident Dr. Johnson mediating between Dryden and Pope. Catullus is the more sincere, Horace the more artful; Catullus is the more affecting, Horace the tidier; Catullus appeals to the heart, Horace to the mind; the one gives more heat, the other more light; one is more intense, the other more correct—there is little need to rehearse the familiar categories that so cramp an appreciation of either poet. If we briefly consider Catullus' eighth poem without the usual presuppositions, we find that it is not in fact "one of the most naïve utterances of love in all the range of poetry." [65] And this, in turn, may influence us to take a less narrow view of Horace's Ode to Pyrrha, and of the amatory Odes in general.

In 1909 E. P. Morris published an article on Catullus' eighth poem which has received less recognition than it deserves.[66] He demonstrates that the poem, far from being a "naïve utterance," is remarkably sophisticated. He shows the attitudes that Catullus strikes to be intensely literary, derived largely from the antic lovers of Roman Comedy. From this fact Morris concluded that the poem is "all a jest," that it stands as a "light and humorous presentation" of Catullus in the conventional role of the comic lover. His interpretation is a salutary counterpoise to the treatment the poem has been traditionally accorded. Yet, on the basis of the evidence he cites, the poem may still be taken as desperately serious. Catullus casts himself in a conventional role not, surely, for comic effect, but rather for the same reason that he so often adjures himself by name, in order to see himself, psychologically as well as grammatically, as a third person. The very familiarity of the pose he strikes tends to make his emotional

65. T. Frank, *Catullus and Horace* (New York, 1928), 56.

66. *Transactions of the Connecticut Academy, 15* (1909), 139 ff. Morris' interpretation has been taken up, with some additional references, by A. L. Wheeler, *Catullus and the Traditions of Ancient Poetry,* 227 ff.

situation more manageable. The same is true of his famous *Ille mi par esse deo videtur* (51). Acclaimed for its passionate sincerity, the poem is yet a close translation of Sappho. There is nothing paradoxical in this. Clearly, Catullus again seeks a steadying frame for his most intense feelings, and the poem adapts itself to the terms of Coleridge when he defined poetry as "a more than usual state of emotion with more than usual order." Yet had it been written by Horace it would be summarily dismissed as a clever imitation, a charming example of amatory formulas, but hopelessly literary.

If we are to allow such resources to Catullus, whose very name evokes all that is sincere, intense, and affecting in love poetry, it seems unfair to deny them to Horace. Admittedly, Catullus' eighth and fifty-first poems represent rare excursions; moreover, the cumulative force of the other Lesbia poems inevitably, if perhaps improperly, influences us to read these two poems as the record of direct sensuous experience. Horace, on the other hand, consistently casts his amatory Odes into standard literary patterns, and thus there can be no such appeal to a body of other poems as is possible with Catullus. The primary distinction between the two writers is, of course, one of temperament; yet the difference in their dates is also important. In Catullus' time the amatory conventions had yet to harden into as available a form as they would present to the Augustan writers. Horace could draw upon a far greater range of language and attitude —the one which Catullus himself had evolved and handed on to the elegists, where it rapidly became stylized. There is no real reason to deny at least the possibility that in such Odes as that to Pyrrha (*C.* 1.5) Horace may be elaborating upon the technique that Catullus occasionally explored, and using the standard amatory gestures to enforce a sense of the community of feeling, an awareness that no individual's passions and frustrations are ever unique.[67]

Typical of the autobiographical amatory Odes is one to Chloe:

> Vixi puellis nuper idoneus
> et militavi non sine gloria:
> nunc arma defunctumque bello
> barbiton hic paries habebit,

67. Cf. Horace's attitude toward Tibullus, below, 240 ff.

laevom marinae qui Veneris latus 5
custodit: hic, hic ponite lucida
funalia et vectis et arcus
oppositis foribus minacis.

o quae beatam diva tenes Cyprum et
Memphin carentem Sithonia nive, 10
regina, sublimi flagello
tange Chloen semel arrogantem. [*C.* 3.26]

> Recently I was a fit match for maidens, and I fought not without glory. Now my arms and the lyre worn out with battle shall rest upon this wall, which guards the left side of sea-born Venus. Here, here, lay down the shining torches and the levers and the bows that threaten opposing gates. O goddess, you who hold rich Cyprus and Memphis free from all Thracian snows, O queen, touch just once with your uplifted lash Chloe the arrogant.

Horace has withdrawn from the warfare of love; the first word bears the stamp of finality. Yet how does the poem end? Not, as we expect, with a prayer for Venus' blessing in his retirement, but with the request that she flick, just once, the disdainful Chloe and bring her beneath love's sway. Within twelve lines the boast of immunity has become a confession of continuing pursuit, and nostalgia has given way to a revived ambition, even though Horace can be no more successful than before.

Horace's sense of the fragility of a lover's resolves is as marked here as it is in the Ode to Lydia (*C.* 3.9), with whom he stepped through a cycle from recollection to renunciation to reacceptance, awaiting with gentle irony the capitulations that both he and Lydia could foresee. Again the language is consciously stylized.[68] In only three stanzas Horace manages to develop the traditional conceit of the warrior of love, to allude briefly to his role as an *exclusus amator* (6–8), and to include a well-turned invocation. We may feel that

68. With *C.* 3.26 we should compare *C.* 4.1 where the images and language are equally formal, though consideration of *C.* 4.1 is complicated by the Ode's function as an introduction to the fourth book; see below, 295 ff.

the Ode's formal cast betrays his own distance from any real feeling. Or we may feel that here, as in the Ode to Lydia, so ordered a view is itself a comment on the impossibility of ordering the same emotions in life. The delicate tension between form and content gives to the poem an almost paradoxical effect, one that is both its chief charm and, if we are bent on biographical information, peculiarly frustrating.

Though feminine inconstancy was not the unique instance of love's vicissitudes, it was easily the most obvious. We remember the tempestuous Pyrrha, and in Barine (*C.* 2.8) we can recognize a near relative:

> Ulla si iuris tibi peierati
> poena, Barine, nocuisset umquam,
> dente si nigro fieres vel uno
>   turpior ungui,
>
> crederem: sed tu simul obligasti 5
> perfidum votis caput, enitescis
> pulchrior multo iuvenumque prodis
>   publica cura.
>
> expedit matris cineres opertos
> fallere et toto taciturna noctis 10
> signa cum caelo gelidaque divos
>   morte carentis.
>
> ridet hoc, inquam, Venus ipsa, rident
> simplices Nymphae ferus et Cupido
> semper ardentis acuens sagittas 15
>   cote cruenta.

If any punishment had ever visited you, Barine, for your perjured vows, if you were uglier by even the blackening of a single tooth or nail, then I would believe you. But no sooner have you bound your perfidious head with oaths than you shine yet the more fair and betray our youths, a concern to all alike. You find it profitable to swear falsely by the buried ashes of your mother, by the silent constellations of night together with the whole sky around them, and

> by the silent gods who live exempt from chill death. Venus herself laughs at this, I say, the guileless nymphs laugh, and fierce Cupid, forever sharpening his glowing arrows on a bloody stone.

Barine's fair surface (*enitescis,* 6), like Pyrrha's, conceals a darker reality which not the smallest sign (*dente nigro,* 3), betrays to her unwary lovers. The overwrought details of her physical appearance might suggest that Horace was letting his dialectic of fair and foul run away with him, were they not a literary *τόπος*.[69] Barine's own solemn protests echo through Horace's rhetoric (9–12), but only to be punctured by the colloquial sharpness of *ridet hoc, inquam* (12). Cupid's bloody darts (15–16) give the lie to Barine's pale and obscure vows, dramatizing the gap between her words and her deeds. The contrast between *obligasti* (5) and *expedit* (9), which retains something of its primary meaning of "set free," underlines the paradox that Barine presents. The blacker she becomes within, the fairer she shines forth; the more tightly she binds herself by promises, the freer she becomes in her actions. In the final stanzas Horace's sardonic awareness of her duplicity mounts to an eloquent climax:

> adde quod pubes tibi crescit omnis,
> servitus crescit nova nec priores
> inpiae tectum dominae relinquunt
>   saepe minati. 20
>
> te suis matres metuunt iuvencis,
> te senes parci miseraeque nuper
> virgines nuptae, tua ne retardet
>   aura maritos.

> Add the fact that all the young men grow up for you alone, that the ranks of new slaves grow continually, nor do the earlier ones leave the home of their wicked mistress, however often they threaten to. It is you that mothers fear on account of their children, you that parsimonious old men

69. Cf. Theocritus, 9.30, 12.24; Ovid, *Am.* 3.3.1 ff. The story of Pinocchio's nose represents the same kind of fable.

> fear, and virgins just recently married, lest your aura should captivate their husbands.

Adde quod, a prosaic formula unique in the Odes, recalls Lucretius' emphatic repetition:

> adde quod absumunt viris pereuntque labore,
> adde quod alterius sub nutu degitur aetas. [4.1121–22]

> Add the fact that men consume their strength and kill themselves with labor, add the fact that their whole life is spent at the beck and call of another.

Lucretius is describing the evils endemic to all passion, and Horace, we realize, is hardly more specific. That the gods indulged the faithlessness of lovers, and that a woman's words were to be written on the wind and running water, were the most familiar of amatory commonplaces.[70] Barine is, in Horace's solemn phrase, a *publica cura* (8) in literary tradition too. As in the Ode to Pyrrha, Horace may be trying his hand at a standard theme, and in both poems the generic quality of the situation may be an index to his own indifference. Or he may equally well impress so formal a structure in order to achieve a certain distance from his feelings, the familiar lines of the situation themselves lending him a measure of objectivity toward it.

The latter possibility complicates nearly all the personal amatory Odes:

> Mater saeva Cupidinum
> Thebanaeque iubet me Semelae puer
> et lasciva Licentia
> finitis animum reddere amoribus.

70. Cf. Ovid, *A. A.* 1.633: *Juppiter ex alto periuria ridet amantum.* G. Pasquali illustrates in detail the conventional character of the motifs: *Orazio lirico* (Firenze, 1920), 477 ff. The lover perpetually threatening to leave (18–20) was a stock comic character; cf. *S.* 2.3.259 ff. The beautiful fifteenth Epode presents several of the same conventional themes.

Might the last stanza of *C.* 2.8 be a kind of parody of Catullus, 61.51 ff.?

urit me Glycerae nitor
  splendentis Pario marmore purius,
urit grata protervitas
  et voltus nimium lubricus adspici.

in me tota ruens Venus
  Cyprum deseruit nec patitur Scythas
et versis animosum equis
  Parthum dicere nec quae nihil attinent.

hic vivum mihi caespitem, hic
  verbenas, pueri, ponite turaque
bimi cum patera meri:
  mactata veniet lenior hostia. [*C.* 1.19]

The savage mother of the Cupids, and the child of Theban Semele, and wanton License command me to give my heart again to loves I had thought were finished. The beauty of Glycera, shining brighter than Parian marble, inflames me; her welcome forwardness inflames me, and her face, too tempting to look upon. Rushing upon me with full strength, Venus has quitted Cyprus, nor does she allow me to sing of the Scythians or of the Parthian, bravest when his horse wheels about in retreat, or of anything else not to the point. Here, boys, lay the cut turf for me, put the boughs here, here the incense with a bowl of two-year-old wine—the goddess will come more gently once a victim has been sacrificed.

Never has "savage Venus" in her raging onslaught been more politely received. The fires in Horace's breast will not, he makes us feel, consume him. Rather, they seem to afford him the luminous calm that comes with being in the most familiar of literary traditions.[71] He speaks with a poised rhetoric which is chastened even at its most extreme: *urit . . . urit, nec . . . nec, hic . . . hic.* The relevant

71. For the triteness, by the Augustan age, of the conceit of the flame of love, see the references collected by R. Pichon, *De sermone amatorio, s. v. flamma* and *urere.*

deities are carefully included, Glycera's charms are detailed in terms that yet remain generic,[72] and the possibility of entertaining any thoughts save amatory ones is dismissed in the best manner of the elegiac poets. Horace, it would seem, deploys his emotions with the same precision with which he instructs his slave to conduct a sacrifice to alleviate them.

The terms in which Horace describes his predicament are formal to the point of parody. Yet we need not conclude that the situation is necessarily fictitious, or that the only love to which he, in the curiously evocative phrase, "gives his heart again" (4), is his love of dabbling in amatory themes. As in the Ode on Lalage (*C.* 1.22), the absurdity of the attitude he strikes may conceal a certain envy of those so single-minded that they can maintain it unabashedly—an indulgence that Horace morally rejected.[73] The Ode is too compellingly beautiful an image of experience to be dismissed as a mere parody. At the same time that its literary quality distances us, its haunting loveliness draws us in as powerfully as the lambent and provocative promise of Glycera herself.

In an Ode to Lydia (*C.* 1.13), Horace's protestations are equally fervid—and equally stylized:

Cum tu, Lydia, Telephi
  cervicem roseam, cerea Telephi
laudas bracchia, vae meum
  fervens difficili bile tumet iecur.

tum nec mens mihi nec color
  certa sede manet, umor et in genas
furtim labitur, arguens,
  quam lentis penitus macerer ignibus.

uror, seu tibi candidos
  turparunt umeros inmodicae mero
rixae, sive puer furens
  inpressit memorem dente labris notam. [1–12]

72. Fairness (5) and forwardness (7) are characteristic of Horace's girls: *C.* 1.5.4, 13, 1.9.21–24, 1.13.9, 2.4.3, 14, 2.5.18, 2.8.6, 2.12.25–28, 3.9.19, 19, 4.11.5, 4.13.17.

73. See below, 239 ff.

> Lydia, when you praise the rosy neck of Telephus, the waxen arms of Telephus, ah, my raging liver swells with bile I can hardly control. Then my mind is shaken, nor does my color remain constant, and a furtive tear trickles down my cheek, betraying how I am consumed within by slow fires. I burn, whether quarrels made excessive by wine have discolored your fair shoulders, or whether the raging youth has impressed a lasting mark upon your lips with his teeth.

So extreme is Horace's despair as to suggest a parody of the habitual agonies of the elegiac poets. Surely, we feel, his burning passions were kindled less by an actual situation than by Catullus' slender flame:

> nam simul te,
> Lesbia, aspexi, nihil est super mi
> [vocis in ore],
>
> lingua sed torpet, tenuis sub artus
> flamma demanat, sonitu suopte
> tintinant aures, gemina teguntur
> lumina nocte.[74]

> For whenever I see you, Lesbia, then no words are left me, but my tongue falls silent, a fine flame runs down through my limbs, my ears ring with their own sound, and my eyes are covered with twin night.

And beyond Catullus we look back to Sappho, whose φαίνεταί μοι κῆνος (2, Diehl) was praised by Longinus (10.3) for the accuracy and poignancy of its emotions. Longinus could hardly have acclaimed the same qualities in Horace's Ode. Sappho's fused intensity has become a cool awareness of what were by the Augustan age conventional motifs, and of the poet's own skill in handling them. The marks of passion that Lydia bears were stock in elegy and in comedy before it,[75] while Horace's anger is so exaggerated that it recalls the description of *ira* in the Ode to the *filia pulcrior* (*C.* 1.16).

74. Cat., 51.6–12; cf. 35.14–15, 45.15–16; Theocr., 2.106–10; Apollonius Rhodius, 3.960 ff.; Valerius Aedituus, *Frag. Poet. Rom.* 275, 1 (Baehrens).

75. See W. L. Grant, *Studies in Honour of Gilbert Norwood,* 194 ff.

The very brilliance of the Ode's effects tends to confirm the literary quality of its sentiments. Any actual heat in Horace's consuming jealousy all but disappears in his cool variations upon the conceit. Each person seems to kindle the next by an aesthetic rather than an emotional enjambment; we follow from Telephus' rosy neck to Horace's *fervens iecur,* from there to his lingering fires within, and thence finally to Telephus' equal flame, *puer furens.* The startling transformations in Horace's appearance are similarly so submerged in an aesthetic pattern that it is easier to admire the total picture than to respond to its anguished details. Each stanza displays a careful balance of colors: the first, in Telephus' rosy neck and waxen limbs as against Horace's boiling black bile; the second, in Horace's violent fluctuations between pallor and flushed rage, underscored by his transparent tears and raging inner flames; the third, in Lydia's alabaster shoulders covered with livid bruises. Even the sounds are so carefully manipulated that they seem to have a separate life of their own. The opening words could hardly be more poised. The alliterative pattern of initial consonants in *Cum tu, Lydia, Telephi cervicem* suggests the grammatical order of a chiastic Golden Line (*c – t – l – t – c*), and the artifice is prolonged in the echoing arrangement of *Telephi cervicem . . . cerea Telephi.* So ostentatious is the control as to deny, in effect, the disintegration that the lines announce. No less contrived is the balanced alliteration opening the second stanza: *nec mens mihi nec color certa.* Half-rhymes (*difficili – bile, penitus – ignibus, umor – uror, candidos – umeros*) suggest an almost singsong rhythm, and though we may catch Horace's repeated groans in the *ur, er,* and *or* sounds (*iecur, color, umor, furtim, labitur, uror, turparunt, puer, furens*), they seem so heavily portentous as to rouse our amusement rather than our sympathy.

Horace deliberately encourages us to feel that his primary, or even sole, concern was to capture in perfect verse a palpably absurd and palpably conventional situation. Form and declared emotions are so flagrantly at odds that they make the poem seem a purely aesthetic exploration, not an emotional one. But what then are we to make of the last two stanzas?

> non, si me satis audias,
>   speres perpetuum dulcia barbare

laedentem oscula, quae Venus
  quinta parte sui nectaris imbuit.

felices ter et amplius
  quos inrupta tenet copula nec malis
divolsus querimoniis
  suprema citius solvet amor die. [13–20]

> You will not, if you heed me, hope for constancy from one who so cruelly wounds your sweet lips, which Venus has imbued with the quintessence of her own nectar. Thrice blest and more are they whom an unbroken bond holds fast, and whose love, torn apart by no bitter quarrels, will not release them before their final day.

Is Horace's appeal a continuation of elegiac bathos? Does the epic echo in *felices ter et amplius* prolong the parody? Or does it signal a change to high seriousness? The latter alternative seems the more tempting, if only because of the similar structure of the Ode on the falling tree (*C.* 2.13) and that to the *filia pulcrior* (*C.* 1.16), both of which abandon irony for a straightforward statement. Probably Horace intended the poem's close to leave us in uncertainty. He refuses, as he does so frequently, to allow us the satisfaction of restricting him to a single attitude.

In poems as personal as the amatory Odes claim to be, we expect a direct relationship with the author, but Horace invites us to nothing more intimate than a triangular area of experience. We become uncomfortably aware that he stands at a distance from the attitude he professes, and that "I" operates chiefly as a third person pronoun. Speculation as to an author's motives is always suspect, and the tact with which Horace expresses his most private feelings calls for an equal tact in our estimate of them. Yet it is tempting to wonder whether self-parody was not a method of self-protection for Horace. As the ending of the second Epode enables him to indulge a sentimental vision and yet repudiate it, or as the masks of the Satires allow him to pontificate without being himself pontifical, or as the *recusationes* and palinodes of many political poems permit him to essay the grand style without committing himself to it, so the intense stylization of his autobiography baffles ridicule by anticapting it. Only after establishing his own ironic perspective does Horace sometimes allow himself a serious view. The initial parody in poems like that to the *filia pulcrior* (*C.* 1.16), that on the *triste lignum* (*C.* 2.13), or that to Lydia (*C.* 1.13) acts almost as a shield. By hopelessly exaggerating an event's significance he makes it into a joke which he shares with us. Only thus could he forestall possible mockery for giving to his feelings a disproportionate importance, for he knew that to laugh at oneself is the only guarantee of being laughed with as well as at.

By his shifts to a serious tone in *C.* 1.16 or *C.* 2.13, and possibly *C.* 1.13, Horace reveals, at least partially, the feelings underlying each of these Odes. When he sustains a single tone throughout, as in the personal amatory Odes, his intentions remain more obscure, and the mood of the poems more difficult to assess.[76] The very number of girls he addresses begs us to believe that no one of them affected him for very long. In the individual poems, moreover, Horace's withdrawal into the shelter of ostentatiously literary language and sentiments allows him a characteristically elegant elusiveness, for his ironic view of the conventions that he exploits allows him to explore them the more freely. Speaking, as it were, through an elegiac mask of himself, he may indulge the extravagant sentimentality that he never permitted himself in any direct way. Just as we cannot disregard all that Davus and Damasippus say, cannot dismiss Horace's feelings for the country on the basis of the second Epode, and cannot categorize him as a nonpolitical poet because of his nonpolitical declarations, so we should not allow ourselves the easy conclusion that his amatory poems are no more than literary gesticulations. We need not, conversely, suppose that he enjoyed all the "thousand passions" ascribed to him by Damasippus (*S.* 2.3.325). Yet it seems unlikely that he would have been moved to write so many love poems simply by a fondness for displaying his mastery of amatory formulas. The fact that many of the various girls may never have existed, and that their beauty may be that of a composite image, does

76. To the amatory Odes discussed in this chapter (*C.* 1.5, 1.13, 1.19, 1.22, 2.8, 3.26) should be added such poems as *C.* 1.23, 1.30, 2.5, 3.9, 4.1, and 4.10; perhaps *C.* 3.10 should be included as well. Although poems like *Epod.* 3 or *C.* 3.21 sustain a single tone throughout, the impetus behind them seems to be nothing more obscure than the pleasure in playing with set conventions.

not make the emotional experiences he associates with them any less real. His poems, often so obscurely moving, are in a sense addresses to his own feelings about any girl who ever excited, betrayed, or recaptured him. We are in no position to state that "Horace was not of a temperament to make a serious business of love," or that "his indolent detachment prevented him from charging the conventional lyric motifs with even a semblance of emotion." [77] How real Horace's detachment was we have no way of knowing, for we may guess that if he recorded any actual affairs they would take some such shape as those Odes that we confidently dismiss as virtuoso exercises.

To expect a direct relation between a writer's life and his work is to misconceive the function of literature, and with Horace the identification is especially misleading. "No Latin author writes so openly and so winningly . . . he unbosoms himself naturally." [78] Almost never in the Odes does Horace unbosom himself, and if he wins us it is not by his openness. The unwillingness to accept Horace on his own terms may come in part from a too-narrow conception of the kind of verse he wrote. We know him to be a "lyric" poet, and immediately certain presuppositions form in our minds. The term is as hospitably amorphous as "tragic," and is applied with almost equal generosity. Paul Valéry's definition, "le lyrisme est la développement d'une exclamation," has been frequently echoed, and criticism abounds in phrases such as "lyricism being an explosion of ideas and sentiments." [79] The lyric has been made to seem an eminent example of what Wordsworth proposed in defining poetry as "the spontaneous overflow of powerful feelings," a statement that did not, however, prevent him from channeling his own exuberant emotions through successive drafts of his poems. We speak of a "lyric cry" and assign it the type of spontaneity and directness usually associated with the name of Burns, who is often impressed to serve as an analogue for Catullus. So authoritative a scholar as Munro refers

77. C. L. Smith, *Odes and Epodes of Horace,* xxxi; J. I. M. Tait, *Philodemus' Influence on the Latin Poets,* 66. Cf. C. H. Moore, *Horace's Odes and Epodes,* 23; J. B. Chapman, *Horace and His Poetry* (London, 1919), 111; H. D. Sedgwick, *Horace,* 65 (quoted above, 100).

78. J. W. Duff, *A Literary History of Rome* (London, 1953), 391; cf. G. Showerman, *Horace and His Influence* (Boston, 1922), 4.

79. P. Colmant, *LEC, 9* (1940), 418.

familiarly to the "lyric of the heart," which in the next sentence, by an easy transition, becomes "the true lyric." [80]

Catullus is cited as often as anyone to give substance to this concept of the lyric, but how fully he satisfies it need not concern us here. More to the point is the fact that Quintilian does not include him at all among the Latin lyric writers, listing Horace as "almost the only one worth reading" (10.1.96). Quintilian's formal separation of the two poets has exacerbated comparisons rather than alleviated them, for admirers of Catullus seem to bear Horace a certain animus for pretending to something to which Catullus has clearly a stronger claim. Quintilian's canons were, of course, perfectly justified, for "lyric," like most poetic terminology, had at first a technical meaning, and referred simply to songs written to be sung to the lyre. Only because he wrote in the meters so used by the Greek poets is Horace a lyric poet, and it is on this basis that he prays in the introductory Ode to be enrolled among the established *lyrici vates*.[81] He could hardly have foreseen the weight of subjective accretions which the term would draw upon itself during the next two thousand years, and it is futile to hold him responsible to them. Without suggesting that Catullus' poems are truly "explosions" we can, I think, cheerfully grant that his sensibility more nearly approaches what, for want of a better word, we term "lyrical." Two of the most sensitive studies of the two poets implicitly acknowledge the distinction by their titles: E. A. Havelock's *The Lyric Genius of Catullus,* and L. P. Wilkinson's *Horace and His Lyric Poetry*.[82] One appeals to

80. *Criticisms and Elucidations of Catullus,* 235. Cf. J. B. Chapman, *Horace and His Poetry,* 97: "Yet the Odes, on the whole, are not marked by great depth of feeling; the passionate cry which we find in such true lyrists as Catullus and Burns is seldom heard in the poems of Horace."

81. *C.* 1.1.35; cf. *C.* 4.3.13 ff. Since Catullus wrote only a few poems in lyric meters, Horace felt free to consider himself the first Roman lyric poet in a strict sense. It is on his technical feat of transferring to Rome the meters of Greece that he especially prides himself: *C.* 1.26.10–12, 3.30.13–14; *Ep.* 1.19.32–33. We tend to forget how formal the division of genres was at that time; thus Quintilian (10.1.96) names as a lyric poet other than Horace only Caesius Bassus, who, interestingly enough, seems to have written a tract *de metris.* On Horace's claim to be the first lyricist, see J. Ferguson, *AJP, 77* (1956), 1 ff.

82. Both books have interesting sections on the nonlyrical quality, in the modern sense, of the Odes: Havelock, 162 ff.; Wilkinson, 123 ff.

our modern subjective standards, the other to an awareness of historic forms. Each view is equally valid, and we need not dispute between them or seek to impose one upon the other.

Since Horace was not, in the Odes, disposed to open his life to us, and since their form gives us no special right to expect him to, we may as well abandon attempts to reconstruct his biography from them. Remy de Goncourt has argued that it is the poet's duty "to write down himself, to unveil for others the sort of world which mirrors itself in his individual glass." The observation comes not from a plea for autobiographical verse but from the preface to the *Imagist Anthology*.[83] "To write down himself"—the poet is historian only of his imaginative consciousness and not of his worldly career. Where we cannot successfully speculate as to the facts the Odes conceal, we may more profitably attend to the imagination they disclose. The manner in which Horace treats the events of his life tells us more about him than would the events themselves, even if we could be sure that they were actual. We do not know whether, as a tribune, he had a shield to lose at Philippi; nor does it greatly matter. The story remains "true" in the sense that it accurately represents his response to experience, however alien that response may be to our own. In measuring his autobiography against formal patterns, Horace shows the same kind of double vision that characterizes the Odes. His mind runs to intricate structural contrasts and correspondences, to puns and oxymorons, to allegory and parody. Every event or emotion is quickly placed in some more ample context. Though he may on occasion have felt some experience to be the whole of life, he could never forget that it was, finally, no more than a part. His songs of triumph become elegies, his pastorals, satires; his most grandiloquent Odes collapse, and his most modest disclaimers become grandiloquent: even in the Odes that pretend to be his most private statements, the real quality of his feelings eludes any definition. "I'm not confused," Robert Frost enjoys saying, "only well mixed."

83. Cf. T. S. Eliot, *The Sacred Wood* (London, 1953), 56: "The poet has, not a 'personality' to express, but a particular medium, which is only a medium and not a personality, in which impressions and experiences combine in peculiar and unexpected ways."

IV

THE POLITICAL ODES

It is more accurate to speak of Horace's political movement than of his political position. The period in which he was writing, from about 40 B.C. to 13 B.C., spanned crucial years in Roman history. It included the civil wars that culminated at Actium, the change from a Republic to an Empire, and the growth of Octavian from a youth into the most powerful ruler Rome had yet known. Horace, who fought beneath Brutus at Philippi, lived to become the poet laureate of his former enemy, and from the earliest Epodes through the massive Odes of the early twenties to the eulogies of the fourth book, the themes, attitudes, and quality of his work undergo changes that are at once obvious and profound.

Early Work

After the Republican defeat at Philippi in 42 B.C., Horace seems to have retreated from further political commitments. The Satires studiously avoid political subjects, treating public events only as a background to Horace's private life. The journey to Brundisium (*S.* 1.5), for instance, seems hardly more than a social outing. Although it was almost certainly an embassy of some political importance, Horace refers to its purpose only once, and there almost casually:

> huc venturus erat Maecenas optimus atque
> Cocceius, missi magnis de rebus uterque
> legati, aversos soliti conponere amicos. [27–29]

> Maecenas was to join us here, and the worthy Cocceius, both sent as ambassadors on matters of great importance, since they were accustomed to settling quarrels among friends.

In the Epodes, also written during the thirties, only the threat or reality of civil war moved Horace to open comment. The seventh and sixteenth are probably among the earliest of the book.[1] In the latter Horace nowhere finds hope for the Romans, or even the "better part" of them (15), save in abandoning the city to the wild boars and wolves (20) and setting sail for the fabled "Isles of the Blest":

> nos manet Oceanus circumvagus: arva beata
> petamus, arva divites et insulas,
> reddit ubi cererem tellus inarata quotannis
> et inputata floret usque vinea . . . [41–44]
>
> Iuppiter illa piae secrevit litora genti,
> ut inquinavit aere tempus aureum,
> aere, dehinc ferro duravit saecula, quorum
> piis secunda vate me datur fuga. [63–66]

> The encircling Ocean awaits us: let us seek the blessed fields, the fields and blessed islands, where the earth untilled produces corn each year, and where the vine flourishes continually without pruning . . .
>
> Jupiter set aside those shores for a righteous people, when he debased the Golden Age with bronze; with bronze, then with iron he hardened the ages, from which there is a happy escape for the righteous with me as their prophet.

1. *Epod.* 16 may have been written about the same time as the outbreak of the Perusine war in 41 B.C., and *Epod.* 7 perhaps reflects the political situation just before the hostilities with Pompey, around 38 B.C., though both dates are problematic. *Epod.* 16 seems to have been written at about the same time as Vergil's fourth Eclogue, judging from the closeness in language. The priority of these two works has been debated at length; see the bibliography in Kiessling-Heinze's ninth edition of the Odes (Berlin, 1959), and G. Duckworth, *TAPA, 87* (1956), 289–90.

Horace's proposal hardly pretends to actuality,[2] for the pastoral vision he conjures up could be realized only in the fairy realms of poetry. He referred to the *divites insulae* only once again, and then as a symbol of the immortality conferred by the poet (*C.* 4.8.27). The repetition in so alien a context is probably coincidental; certainly it does not justify our supposing that at the time of the sixteenth Epode Horace felt escape from the iron age of the present could come only with death. Yet the fact that he felt free to use the concept again suggests that in the Epode too it referred, at least in part, to the world of art. And it is interesting, if inconclusive, that the perfect peace and perfect plenty of the land set aside for the "pious" is close to the ideal landscape over which Horace's *pietas et musa* preside in *C.* 1.17. Speculation as to Horace's motives is always dangerous, but the beautiful description of the country in the sixteenth Epode—and perhaps we should include the second Epode as well—might proceed from a particular kind of escapism, an attempt to substitute the world of imagination for the world of fact.

In any practical sense the poem is negative; *fuga* is Horace's last word. The seventh Epode is still darker. *Quo, quo scelesti ruitis?* The first line restates with dramatic immediacy the opening of Epode sixteen, *altera iam teritur bellis civilibus aetas*. Not lions or wolves, Horace goes on to say, are so savage: never do they turn on their own kind. His harangue deepens into a stony despair:

> furorne caecus an rapit vis acrior
> an culpa? responsum date.
> tacent et albus ora pallor inficit
> mentesque perculsae stupent.
> sic est: acerba fata Romanos agunt
> scelusque fraternae necis,
> ut inmerentis fluxit in terram Remi
> sacer nepotibus cruor. [13–20]

Does blind rage or some fiercer force or guilt snatch you onward? Give an answer! They are silent, and a white pallor

2. Despite the fact that Sertorius had projected a similar trip (Ps.-Acro *ad Epod.* 16.41; Plu., *Sertorius* 8.571f ff.). See Fraenkel, *Horace,* 49.

> spreads over their faces; their minds are stricken and dazed. Thus it is: bitter fate and the crime of a brother's murder drive on the Romans, ever since that time when the blood of innocent Remus flowed upon the earth, a curse to his descendants.

The concept of a racial guilt is almost that of original sin, and spells out what is only tentative in the sixteenth Epode's reference to "an impious age of accursed blood" (9). In its conviction of predestined fatality, the seventh Epode is as negative as the Utopian fantasy of the sixteenth. Only with the ninth, written immediately after Actium, do we meet something more positive, for Horace's cry of triumph over Cleopatra at the same time commits him to the "care and fear for Caesar's fortunes" (*Epod.* 9.37). And a year later the Cleopatra Ode (*C.* 1.37), despite its revelation of the Egyptian queen's private victory, shows Horace to be identified with Rome's destiny in a new way.

In Horace's movement from retreat to recommitment the so-called "Ode to the Ship of State" stands as a moral weather vane:

> O navis, referent in mare te novi
> fluctus. o quid agis? fortiter occupa
> portum. nonne vides, ut
> nudum remigio latus
>
> et malus celeri saucius Africo
> antemnaeque gemant . . . [*C.* 1.14.1–6]

> O ship, new waves bear you back out to sea! Oh, what are you doing? With all your strength, make for the port. Do you not see how your sides are stripped of oars, how the mast is buffetted by the swift south wind, how the yard-arms groan . . .

For four stanzas, in language that seems innocent of any nonliteral sense, Horace describes the tempest that threatens to overcome the already battered vessel. But the final stanza compels us to abandon a merely narrative context for reading the poem:

nuper sollicitum quae mihi taedium,
nunc desiderium curaque non levis,
interfusa nitentis
vites aequora Cycladas. [17–20]

You who were recently to me a vexatious burden, who are now my love and anxious care, avoid the seas that lie about the shining Cyclades.

Not even Catullus had ventured upon language of such transcendent affection when addressing his *phasellus* (4), and it is clear that Horace has something more in mind than an actual vessel. Quintilian is the authority for the standard interpretation: "The author names the ship for the state, the waves and tempests for the civil wars, and the port for peace and concord" (8.6.44). His construction of the poem is unobjectionable; the metaphor had been familiar since the time of Theognis.[3] Moreover, Horace is imitating some lines of Alcaeus (46A, Diehl) to which a similar allegorical meaning is usually assigned. They describe a storm beating upon a ship—an image, explains the rhetorician Heraclitus, of the political troubles besetting the state. "Who," he asks, "would not immediately conclude from the foregoing image concerning the sea that the fear was the fear of the sea felt by the men who were sailing? But such is not the case. The subject is Myrsilus and a tyrannical conspiracy hatching against the Mytileneans." [4]

Some critics have nevertheless held that Horace's Ode is to be taken literally, and the same objection has been raised against an

3. Thgn., 671 ff.; Archil., 56 (Diehl); Aes., *Th.* 1 ff., 62, 758 ff., 795 ff.; Eurip., *Rh.* 246 ff.; for further references, see D. Page, *Sappho and Alcaeus* (Oxford, 1955), 182, n. 1. By Horace's time the figure of the "ship of state" was common enough to be a textbook example: Demetrius, *Eloc.* 2.78. For the related metaphor of a "wave of war," cf. Tyrtaeus, 9.22 (Diehl); Lucr., 5.1290, 1435; Hor., *C.* 2.7.16; *Ep.* 2.2.47. See also J. Kahlmayer, *Seesturm und Schiffsbruch als Bild* (Hildesheim, 1934). The probability that the sea in *C.* 1.14 is to be taken metaphorically may be increased by the fact that *C.* 1.14 is the first poem in the Asclepiadean stanza after *C.* 1.5, where the sea is clearly metaphorical.

4. Heraclitus Rhetor, *All.* 5. It is probable that Horace was influenced not only by Alc., 46A (Diehl), but by Alc., 119 (Diehl) as well; the latter is also cited by Heraclitus as an allegory of "tyrant troubles."

allegorical interpretation of Alcaeus.[5] In the latter case Heraclitus' eagerness to establish the fact of Homeric allegory is thought to have made him unduly hospitable toward parallels; and in the former, a voyage of Octavian actually took place at a time when Horace might have written about it. It is true that what was termed "allegorical" in Greek literature usually had less to do with the writer's intentions than with the flights of his interpreters. Homer and Hesiod, as Herodotus observes (2.53), gave the Greeks their theology, and a literal reading of either poet would have confounded the staunchest piety. Hence commentators were eager to ferret out the "under-senses" [6] from beneath the text's frequently embarrassing surface: "if Homer did not allegorize he was irreligious in every way," stated the rhetorician Heraclitus.[7] Such reasoning is scarcely convincing, nor are the "allegories" it uncovered any more so. In their ingenuity the interpretations often rivaled the more famous ones of the Church Fathers. Aphrodite's famous encounter with Ares, and their capture in the net of Hephaestus, could be glossed as a conjunction of two planets, a symbolic union of love and strife, or a statement that strong objects are melted by fire into objects of beauty.[8] Or the *impia fabula* that Kronos ate his children might, with the aid of a fanciful etymology, be made to yield a *physica ratio*. Kronos becomes Chronos—and

5. For a literal interpretation of Alc., 46A (Diehl), see Diehl, *ad loc.;* Kiessling, *Q. Horatius Flaccus, Oden und Epoden* (Berlin, 1890), *ad C.* 1.14 (Kiessling's view was revised by Heinze in subsequent editions; see Fraenkel, *Horace,* 156, n. 2). The lines of Alcaeus probably are allegorical; see C. Theander, *Eranos, 41* (1943), 156 ff.; G. Carlsson, *Eranos, 42* (1944), 1 ff. For a literal interpretation of Hor., *C.* 1.14 see the editions of Bentley and Muretus, and, more recently, R. Kukala, *WienStud 34* (1912), 237 ff.; T. Birt, *Horaz' Lieder, 2,* 125 ff.

6. The name ἀλληγορία, "other-saying," replaced the earlier ὑπόνοια, "under-sense"; see Cic., *Or.* 27.94; Plu., *Moralia* 19e. Definitions of "allegory" seldom ventured anything more precise than a hospitable *aliud verbis, aliud sensu;* see *Auct. ad Her.,* 4.34.46; Cic., *De Or.* 3.41.166; *Att.* 2.20.3; Heraclit. Rhet., *All.* 5; Demetr., *Eloc.* 2.99 ff. A similar definition was "continuous metaphor," and "continuous" was interpreted as any number larger than one; see Cic., *Or.* 27.94; *De Or.* 3.41.166; *Auct. ad Her.,* 4.34.46; Quint., 8.6.45.

7. Heraclit. Rhet., *All.* 1; cf. Longin., 9.7. For attacks on the morals of the Homeric gods, see Xenophanes, 11–12 (Diels); Pythagoras (Diogenes Laertius, 8.21); Heraclitus Philosophus, 42 (Diels); Plato, *Euth.* 6a ff.

8. Hom., *Od.* 8.266 ff.; Plu., *Moralia* 19f; Heraclit. Rhet., *All.* 69; Cornutus, *Theol. Gr. Comp.* 19 (Lang).

does not time devour all? [9] If we except the personifications in Hesiod, and such short passages as the description of the Prayers in Homer, the remarkable proem of Parmenides, and Prodicus' "Choice of Hercules," virtually no classical text persuades us it was written as an allegory. Reading, as it were, came before writing, and Hastings' *Encyclopedia of Religion* shows exemplary caution in defining classical allegory as "a form of representation which a reader believes himself to find in a piece of writing which is more or less in need of interpretation."

On general grounds, then, there might be cause to suspect Heraclitus' judgment on Alcaeus. Yet whether or not these suspicions are justified is irrelevant for the interpretation of Horace's imitation. To prove one poet indebted to another is not to convict him of imaginative bankruptcy. Horace might have invested what was merely narrative in Alcaeus with his own allegorical significance; the procedure would not be unique.[10] Equally without force is the other objection to an allegorical interpretation, that Horace is describing an actual voyage. Allegory need not exist in a historical vacuum. Spenser's Una may represent Truth, but she wears the colors of Queen Elizabeth as well. To be sure, Octavian in 30 B.C. sailed from his winter quarters at Samos to Brindisi, where he quieted some rebellious legions. On the way his ship was twice nearly wrecked in storms, losing both rigging and rudder, and after no more than twenty-seven days in port he again put to sea.[11] *O navis, referent in mare te novi fluctus:* the situation adapts itself to Horace's Ode. Yet after Actium Octavian's ship was literally the Ship of State. What was there to prevent Horace from felicitously combining a prayer for the safety of both alike?

9. Cic., *N. D.* 2.24.64; Plu., *Moralia* 363d; Sallust. Phil., 4. The etymology may go back to Pherecydes of Syros; see Roscher, *Lexicon,* 2[1], 1546. Cicero pokes fun at such *enodatio nominum;* see *N. D.* 3.24.62 ff.; cf. Plato, *Charm.* 163d; *Crat.* 384b; Democritus, 2 (Diels). For more general discussion see E. Zeller, *Stoics, Epicureans, and Sceptics* (London, 1892), 354 ff.; F. Wehrli, *Zur Geschichte der allegorischen Deutung Homers* (Borna-Leipzig, 1928); F. Buffière, *Les Mythes d'Homère* (Paris, 1956), 60 ff.; J. Tate, articles cited *s. v.* "allegory" in the *Oxford Classical Dictionary.*

10. Compare Alc., 90 (Diehl) with Hor., *C.* 1.9 (see below, 269 ff.), or Alc., 39 (Diehl) with Hor., *C.* 1.37 (see above, 89 ff.; Fraenkel, *Horace,* 159). Compare also Horace's transformation of the "spring songs" of the *Greek Anthology;* see below, 265 ff.

11. Dio, 51.4; Suet., *Aug.* 17.

Although factual events often provide the germ of a poem they rarely explain it, and a possible reference to Octavian's voyage should not distract attention from the Ode's allegorical significance. It seems to be a palinode recanting Horace's despair of the thirties. His former estrangement from political reality is revealed to be merely a lover's quarrel, not a permanent disaffection: "You who were recently to me a vexatious burden, who are now my love and anxious care." Could we be sure that some further lines of Alcaeus belong to the same poem on which *C.* 1.14 is modeled, Horace's avowal would become still more pointed. In these lines Alcaeus bids farewell to a sinking ship, and turns to his companions: "forgetting these things [I would] be merry with you, and in the company of Bycchis." [12] Where one poet repudiates concern for the ship (of state?) to sport with his favorite, the other declares the ship itself to be his *desiderium.*

If we disregard the possible allusion to Octavian's voyage, the Ode is difficult to place. The *imperiosius aequor* (8) had scarcely been quiet since the murder of Julius Caesar, nor was its serenity clearly guaranteed by Octavian's victory at the battle of Actium. The series of political Odes between 31 and 27 B.C. proves that Horace made some sort of commitment, and shortly before Actium, the date suggested for *C.* 1.14 by most editors, seems as likely a time as any. Rome was then again drifting into civil war—*referent in mare te novi fluctus*—and the weakened fabric of her government—*non tibi sunt integra lintea*—might well have seemed inadequate to another struggle.

R. S. Conway puts the Ode as late as 29 B.C., and the implications of his theory are important.[13] In that year, he reminds us, Dio laid the famous conference to which Octavian summoned Agrippa and Maecenas, in order that he might ask their advice on his next political move (Dio, 52.1–41). Agrippa pressed the ruler to retire, and hand the government over to the Senate, but Maecenas urged him rather to accept a monarchy:

12. Alc., 46B (Diehl). Bowra, Edmonds, and Lobel, in their editions of Alcaeus, accept the lines as belonging to the same poem as Alc., 46A (Diehl); cf. R. Lattimore, *AJP, 65* (1944), 173–74. The erotic vocabulary of the last stanza of Hor., *C.* 1.14 (*desiderium curaque non levis*) may well have been influenced by Alc., 46B (Diehl).

13. R. S. Conway, *Bulletin of the John Rylands Library, 13* (1929), 89 ff.

> And therefore our city, like a great ship manned by a crew of every race, but without a pilot, for many generations now has been borne along in a heavy sea, plunging and veering this way and that, as though she had no ballast. Do not allow her to be beaten by the tempest any longer, for you see that she is filled with water, nor allow her to be shattered against a reef, for she is unsound and will not be able to endure for long. But, since the gods, taking pity on her, have made you her judge and overseer, do not betray your country, so that, just as now she has revived a little because of you, so she will survive in safety for the ages to come. [Dio, 52.16.3–4]

Many of the parallels cited by Conway between Maecenas' speech and Horace's Odes are so conventional as to make any direct borrowing highly problematic. Even if we allow Dio to have been reading the Odes at the time that he wrote his fifty-second book, and even though he may have derived the image of a laboring ship from *C.* 1.14 rather than from any other of its many occurrences in previous literature, we need not conclude that Horace's meaning was that of Maecenas. Dio may have assumed that it was, but his judgment is not definitive. Nothing justifies us in concluding that the danger Horace fears is also "the possible revival of the old regime." [14] The crucial point in Maecenas' image is the necessity for a helmsman; but nowhere in *C.* 1.14 does that idea appear. Indeed, Horace seems to avoid it deliberately, for since Plato's famous treatment in the *Republic* innumerable descriptions of the Ship of State had dwelt upon precisely that point.[15] Since *C.* 1.14 lacks such an emphasis, the contention that Horace writes in a partisan vein falls to the ground. "O Captain" may be Maecenas' cry, but Horace's *tu* is the whole state. He does not renounce his political indifference in favor of a particular party. His

14. Ibid., 100. His judgment has been supported by G. Duckworth, *TAPA, 87* (1956), 285–86 ("Horace may well be supporting the policy of Maecenas here.") So also L. P. Wilkinson, *Hermes, 84* (1956), 495 ff.

15. Plato, *R.* 488; Cic., *Att.* 7.13; *Fam.* 1.9.21, 9.15, 12.25.3. For further references, see Fraenkel, *Horace,* 155. But Fraenkel's emphasis on this aspect of the ship of state metaphor is misleading, inasmuch as such an analogy is quite absent from *C.* 1.14.

concern signals simply the recognition that all the Romans, willingly or not, are caught in the same boat.

One critic ventured that the ship represents not the state, but the poet's own life—the metaphor was scarcely less common.[16] From a cry of national anxiety, the Ode then becomes a resolution to retire to "the quiet life of the philosopher-poet." If such an explanation seems implausible, it cannot be disproved. Nothing in the poem tells us what the ship represents, for allegory, unlike the simile and many metaphors, customarily leaves one term tacit. To say "my love is like a red, red, rose" involves no difficulty, and the statement "my love is a red, red, rose" is hardly more abstruse. But were we to write simply a description of a red, red, rose, readers might justly be excused for failing to grasp its significance, unless they received sufficient hints. Thus Dante's Beatrice has been taken as The Church, Scholastic Theology, Faith, Divine Grace, and finally, Platonic Philosophy.[17]

Fortunately for our peace of mind, allegory as a pure form is something of an anomaly in classical literature. We find, of course, veiled references to contemporary persons or events, particularly in the masks of pastoral or the mirror of satire; and Vergil did not conceive Aeneas without an eye on Augustus. One of the most common forms for such allusions was a reference to the ruler as a god, a symbolism made familiar by the practice, which was especially prominent in the Hellenistic kingdoms, of honoring the ruler as divine.[18] With Ovid the comparison was to become a commonplace of flattery,[19] but Horace is more sparing. He probably refers half humorously to Augustus as Jupiter in *Epistle* 1.19.43, and the same comparison may be hinted at in an Ode that welcomes back to Rome one Pompeius, a former companion in military service: [20]

16. C. W. Mendell, *CP, 33* (1938), 145 ff. He dates *C.* 1.14 as early as *Epod.* 16, and takes its meaning to be roughly the same.

17. E. Panofsky, *Studies in Iconology* (New York, 1939), 100. Similarly, other interpretations of *C.* 1.14 are possible. Ps.-Acro thought the Ode was written to Sextus Pompey, and Porphyrio thought it was to Brutus. Others have taken it as a warning against moving the Roman government to Troy ("avoid the shining Cyclades," 19–20); see W. Leaf, *JPh, 34* (1915), 283 ff.

18. For bibliography and discussion of divinization of the ruler, see L. Cerfaux and J. Tondriau, *Le culte des souverains* (Tournai [Belgium], 1957).

19. See K. Scott, *TAPA, 61* (1930), 43 ff.

20. See Wilkinson, *Horace,* 33–34.

tecum Philippos et celerem fugam
sensi relicta non bene parmula,
  cum fracta virtus et minaces
    turpe solum tetigere mento:

sed me per hostis Mercurius celer
denso paventem sustulit aere,
  te rursus in bellum resorbens
    unda fretis tulit aestuosis.

ergo obligatam redde Iovi dapem
longaque fessum militia latus
  depone sub lauru mea nec
    parce cadis tibi destinatis.

oblivioso levia Massico
ciboria exple, funde capacibus
  unguenta de conchis. [*C.* 2.7.9–23]

With you I suffered Philippi and our headlong flight, my shield ingloriously abandoned, when our strength was broken and menacing hosts touched the base soil with their faces. Swift Mercury sustained me, trembling, in a dense mist, through the enemy's midst; but the wave of battle caught you up and swept you off again into the tempestuous straits.

Then render to Jove the feast that you owe, and rest your limbs, tired from long military service, beneath my laurel, nor spare the casks of wine set aside for you. Fill the smooth goblets with the Massic which dispels memories, and pour forth the unguents from their generous shells.

Although the poem is without express political formulations, the circumstances surrounding it force political overtones upon it. Pompeius, like Horace, had fought on the losing side at Philippi, and has only now returned to his homeland. The Ode is usually assigned to 29 B.C., the year Octavian declared a general amnesty, and Horace's rhetorical question "who has given you back as a full citizen to your fatherland's gods and to the sky of Italy?" (3–4) might logically have "the ruler" as an answer. In this context the "owed feast" (17) that Horace proposes to Pompeius may be not so much a general sacrifice to Jove as an offering of thanks to Octavian. The emphatic position of *oblivioso* (21) suggests that it is not merely a stock adjective, but rather a hint that the time has come for Pompeius to forget, or at least forego, his militant Republicanism, as Horace himself had done.[21] The Ode is essentially hortatory. After Actium a whole generation found themselves in a world they never made and may even have fought against. But Horace knew that a frozen retrospect was futile, and he urges his friend to accept the changes that the years have brought. The feast, so often a token of freedom from the past and fulfillment in the present,[22] loses nothing of its familiar significance in a political context.

The question of Horace's "basely abandoned shield" (10) has attracted nearly as much attention as Falstaff's "better part of valor" at Shrewsbury. It is easy to forget that Horace does not pretend to be a historian, and that his reminiscent anecdote—reminiscent, too, of previous poetry [23]—may have a specific motive. The flippant manner in which he describes his part in the battle is surely intended to place Philippi in a less solemn perspective for Pompeius. In 42 B.C. Horace, a student at Athens, was only twenty-two, and Pompeius, *prime sodalium* (5), was not likely to have been much older. Horace reminds him that Philippi was only an adventure of their youth, or at least he intimates that it was now best so to regard it. He does not

21. *Quiritem* (*C.* 2.7.3) has a distinctly civil, as opposed to a military, connotation; cf. Tacitus, *Ann.* 1.42; Suet., *Caes.* 70. On Horace's political shift as characteristic, see below, 255–56.

22. See my article, *TAPA, 88* (1957), 68 ff.

23. See above, 128. Fraenkel (*Horace,* 164–65) denies that there is any implication in *C.* 2.7 of Mercury's role as patron of poetry (for which, see *C.* 1.10.6, 3.11.1 ff.; possibly *C.* 2.17.28 ff., though even this passage is explained by Fraenkel on astrological grounds; he makes no mention of Faunus in *C.* 2.17.28, on whom, see below, 348 ff.) We could, nevertheless, say that there is at least a suggestion of Mercury's possible connection with poetry in *C.* 2.7, for it seems likely that it was primarily through poetry that Horace found refuge from the waves of civil discord (cf. *Ep.* 1.1.16, 2.2.85) in the decade following the battle of Philippi; see on *Epod.* 16, above, 162–63, and below, 341 ff. In these terms *C.* 1.14 marks Horace's recognition that, at that point, indifference to the waves of political struggle was no longer desirable, or possible.

repudiate the past, as the bold reference to *fracta virtus* (11) proves.[24] But he does declare that the past is finished, and that it should no longer dictate one's attitude toward an altered world.

Longer Odes of the Early Twenties

Horace hardly did more than hint at the comparison between Octavian and Jove in the Ode to Pompeius, but the tacit correspondence between the ruler and a deity was to provide the structure for his most important political work. Usually it functions within the framework of a mythical paradigm. The form is of course familiar: we think of Medea, of the Centaurs, of Ajax, or of Achilles, all the concrete equivalents for abstractions.[25] The Ovidian rambles on the Danaids (*C.* 3.11) or Europa (*C.* 3.27) also ostensibly point a moral, though it is hard not to suspect that their real function is to adorn a tale. Between these two types of mythology lies a third, more elaborate than the first and of greater density of meaning than the second. Paradigms here create a new meaning rather than refresh the explicit one, being allegorical, not merely in the sense that any example may be an "other saying" for an abstraction, but in that they convey something beyond the advice or statement that they formally illustrate. Though neither the thirteenth Epode nor the Ode to Plancus (*C.* 1.7) is strictly political, they deserve parenthetic consideration as samples of the kind of structure Horace was to develop in more complex form for his longest poems about Octavian.

In the thirteenth Epode Horace summons his friends to wine and song while a storm gathers force outside. His invitation borrows

24. Though the meaning of *fracta virtus* may be no more than "when our strength was broken," it seems likely that there is an elegiac reference to Brutus' last words, in which he claimed always to have served ἀρετή; see Dio, 47.49, cited by Orelli, *Q. Horatius Flaccus, Odae* (Berlin, 1886), *ad loc.* Augustus was indulgent toward former Republicans. Sestius (addressed by Horace in *C.* 1.4), who kept images of Brutus around his house, was appointed *Consul Suffectus* in 23 B.C. (Dio, 53.32), and Livy, who debated whether or not the birth of Julius Caesar were a blessing to Rome (Sen., *Q. N.* 5.18.4) was affectionately termed by Augustus his "Pompeyite" (Tac., *Ann.* 4.34.4); cf. Sen., *Clem.* 1.10.1. Fraenkel (*Horace,* 12–13; 360) rightly emphasizes Horace's continuing acknowledgments of his political past.

25. On the *exemplum,* see above, 122 ff.

authority from the tale of Chiron's advice to Achilles on the eve of the hero's departure for Troy:

"invicte, mortalis dea nate puer Thetide,
te manet Assaraci tellus, quam frigida parvi
findunt Scamandri flumina lubricus et Simois,
unde tibi reditum certo subtemine Parcae
rupere, nec mater domum caerula te revehet.
illic omne malum vino cantuque levato,
deformis aegrimoniae dulcibus adloquiis." [12–18]

"Unconquered one, mortal son of the goddess Thetis, for you waits the land of Assaracus, through which the cold streams of narrow Scamander and the swift Simois flow; from there the Fates with their unalterable thread have broken off your return, nor can your sea-born mother bring you back again to your home. Once there, lighten every evil with wine and song, sweet consolations for unsightly grief."

Levato (17) corresponds to Horace's *nunc iuvat levare* (8 ff.), just as the generalized *omne malum* (17) picks up the equally vague *cetera* (7). But instead of providing a parallel the myth takes the form of a parabola, drawing the poem's meaning away in another direction. Had Horace wished simply to inculcate a lesson of cheerful endurance during bad weather, any number of examples would have served as well. Achilles is the prime example of the awareness of death, for in sailing to Troy he renounces the hope of return (15–16). The myth's ultimate implications force the poem to a new context, and we realize that Horace's advice to his friends is of the same seriousness as Chiron's to Achilles. *Rapiamus, amici, occasionem de die* (3–4) does not refer to a single day any more than does *carpe diem*.[26] Horace writes to his friends about youth and age, modified forms of life and death, just as all men are embarked upon a modified form of Achilles' journey.

In the Ode to Plancus (*C.* 1.7) the structure of sermon and *exemplum* is equally identifiable:

26. *C.* 1.11.8; here, too, wine serves as a symbolic answer to death; see below, 264; 273–74; *TAPA, 88* (1957), 71 ff.

albus ut obscuro deterget nubila caelo
  saepe Notus neque parturit imbris

perpetuos, sic tu sapiens finire memento
  tristitiam vitaeque labores
molli, Plance, mero, seu te fulgentia signis
  castra tenent seu densa tenebit

Tiburis umbra tui. Teucer Salamina patremque
  cum fugeret . . . [15–22]

As the fair south wind often clears the clouds from a lowering sky, nor does it always breed showers, so must you, Plancus, wisely remember to put an end to your sadness and to the labors of life with gentle wine, whether now the camps with their gleaming standards hold you, or whether the dense shade of your own Tibur shall hold you. Teucer, when he was fleeing from Salamis and his father . . .

Horace amplifies the paradigm from nature by one from myth, the story of Teucer's exile and his voyage to a "second Salamis" (29). The tale's relevance is emphasized by the echo of *tristitiam* (18) in *tristis* (24), much as the link between myth and present in the thirteenth Epode was enforced by the recurrent *levare;* both belong to the technique of verbal repetition familiar from the Odes discussed in the second chapter. Although the injunction to wine recalls that of the thirteenth Epode, Teucer's journey is to a new life rather than to death. His story was familiar. Cicero, deprecating the evils of exile, recommended Teucer's equanimity: *ad omnem rationem Teucri vox accomodari potest: patria est ubicumque est bene.*[27] Horace's Teucer incarnates the same adaptability, and in the example Plancus could see not merely a vague recommendation to wine, but a more precise reminder that one may survive in any land. In these terms the relevance of the introductory catalogue of towns (*laudabunt alii* . . .) becomes clear; there is no need to split the Ode into two poems.[28]

27. Cic., *Tusc.* 5.37.108. Cicero is probably quoting the lost *Teucer* of Pacuvius. Whether or not Horace knew Pacuvius' play, he almost certainly knew the passage in Cicero; see E. T. Silk, *YCS, 13* (1952), 147 ff.

28. Porphyrio (*ad loc.*) already knew of attempts to split *C.* 1.7 into two

Plancus, styled a "pathological turncoat" by Velleius Paterculus (2.83.1), had shifted his allegiance from Antony to Octavian only shortly before Actium, and it has been plausibly suggested that at the time the Ode was written he was being kept abroad in a kind of disguised exile.[29] Certainly in the years immediately after Actium, Octavian would have wished to have firm supporters at Rome rather than such political reeds as Plancus, whose main value seems to have lain in showing which way the wind was blowing. The promise made by a *certus Apollo* (28) that Teucer will find a new homeland might well be Horace's assurance that Plancus will soon return from his military service (20) to his beloved Tibur. Teucer's journey between two different Salamises is in a sense Plancus' journey between two different Romes. And we may guess that, comforted by the oblique assurance of the myth, Plancus was more ready to accept in the meantime the conventional advice to relax with *molle merum* (19).

Although the story of Teucer seems intended for more specific application than that of Achilles, both poems are structurally alike in that the myth in each case bears the weight of the meaning. Both poems suggest the hand of a mannerist working in classical patterns, for though the familiar paraenetic lines remain, the balance they normally control has altered. In each case the paradigm proposes a new significance rather than merely confirming one already made explicit: it illuminates rather than reflects. And in thus transforming the fable, the simplest of narrative devices, Horace was to find the instrument for some of his most elaborate work.

C. 1.2

When Horace used paradigms involving a divinity he tended to reserve them for the ruler alone. Certainly the distance between the gods and *altus Caesar* (*C.* 3.4.37) was less impressive than was that which separated them from the common run of mankind. Vergil had tentatively hailed Octavian as a god as early as 40 B.C. (*E.* 1.6), and in the years to come such tributes became increasingly common

parts. Some modern editors have suggested that the poem represents two unfinished fragments; see C. H. Moore, *Horace's Odes and Epodes, ad loc.*

29. See J. P. Elder, *CP, 48* (1953), 1 ff.

and increasingly extravagant. It was Horace's distinction to reserve the comparison for strategic rather than adulatory ends. Of *C.* 1.12 it has been observed that Augustus "is declared to be a god." [30] Yet Horace touches upon the similarity of temporal and eternal rule only to emphasize the gap that remains. To Jove he observes *tu secundo Caesare regnes* (51–52), and the emphatic pronouns of the last stanza are still more forceful:

> te minor latum reget aequos orbem:
> tu gravi curru quaties Olympum,
> tu parum castis inimica mittes
>   fulmina lucis. [57–60]

> Beneath you, Caesar will justly rule the wide earth. You with your massive chariot will shake Olympus; you will cast thunderbolts on polluted groves.

And at the same time that the fifth Roman Ode flatters Augustus by a comparison with Jove, it carefully relegates his role as a *praesens divus* to the future (1 ff.).

In the Odes that develop a comparison with a deity at length, the gods provide a mirror for magistrates much as the ignoble figures of the Satires provide a mirror for fools; in each case Horace's intention is hortatory. The same motive underlies even an Ode that is customarily regarded as one of the most baldly flattering, *C.* 1.2. It was almost certainly written during the early twenties, when Horace had already celebrated the victor of Actium (*Epod.* 9; *C.* 1.37), and had urged, or was shortly to urge, Pompeius to come to terms gracefully with the new ruler. It is usually assumed that in *C.* 1.2 Horace makes formal announcement of his allegiance to and enthusiasm for Octavian: "The Ode is fitly placed in the forefront of the three Books, as containing once for all Horace's palinode and 'apologia.' He is professing and explaining his conversion to Caesarism." [31]

30. L. Highbarger, *TAPA, 66* (1935), 229.

31. E. C. Wickham, *Works of Horace,* I, *ad loc.* Cf. C. L. Smith, *Odes and Epodes of Horace, ad loc.;* C. H. Moore, *Horace's Odes and Epodes, ad loc.;* P. Shorey, *Horace, Odes and Epodes, ad loc.* Smith terms *C.* 1.2 a "declaration of allegiance" to Octavian.

The verdict is based primarily on the poem's conclusion, which salutes Octavian virtually as Mercury incarnate. Yet Mercury is but one figure within a larger scheme of contrasts and alternatives; here for the first time Horace explores at length a roughly allegorical use of divine mythology. Only in so elaborate a structure could he find terms to convey the shades of his response, one too complex to be named simply an "apologia" or "palinode."

Standing immediately after the dedicatory Ode, *C.* 1.2 takes on a certain importance from its very position. Our expectations are confirmed by the solemn cadences of the opening:

> Iam satis terris nivis atque dirae
> grandinis misit pater et rubente
> dextera sacras iaculatus arcis
> terruit urbem,
>
> terruit gentis, grave ne rediret 5
> saeculum Pyrrhae nova monstra questae,
> omne cum Proteus pecus egit altos
> visere montis
>
> piscium et summa genus haesit ulmo,
> nota quae sedes fuerat columbis, 10
> et superiecto pavidae natarunt
> aequore dammae.
>
> vidimus flavom Tiberim retortis
> litore Etrusco violenter undis
> ire deiectum monumenta regis 15
> templaque Vestae,
>
> Iliae dum se nimium querenti
> iactat ultorem, vagus et sinistra
> labitur ripa Iove non probante u-
> xorius amnis. 20
>
> audiet civis acuisse ferrum,
> quo graves Persae melius perirent,
> audiet pugnas vitio parentum
> rara iuventus.

quem vocet divum populus ruentis 25
imperi rebus? prece qua fatigent
virgines sanctae minus audientem
carmina Vestam?

cui dabit partis scelus expiandi
Iuppiter? 30

Now enough snow and dread hail has the Father sent upon the earth; hurling down the sacred citadels with his glowing right hand he has terrified the city, has terrified the people, lest there return the awful age of Pyrrha, who lamented strange portents, when Proteus drove his whole marine flock to the high mountains and the race of fish clung to the treetops, formerly the accustomed roost of doves, and the trembling deer swam in the waters that had spread over the land. We have seen the yellow Tiber, with his waves hurled back in violence from the Tuscan shore, go to overthrow the monuments of king Numa and the temples of Vesta, boasting himself the avenger of too plaintive Ilia, and, uxorius river god, overflowing upon the left bank—not with Jove's approval.

Our descendants, made fewer by the sin of their parents, will hear of battles in which citizens sharpened their swords against citizens, swords by which the dreadful Persians might better have perished.

Which of the gods will the people call to the needs of their falling empire? With what prayer will the sacred virgins weary Vesta, oblivious to their hymns? To whom will Jupiter give the task of expiating our crime?

In the first five stanzas Porphyrio saw a description of the portents following the assassination of Julius Caesar, and his interpretation has remained popular. It has much against it. Earliest estimates put the Ode eight years after Caesar's death, while it is probable that as many as fifteen years had elapsed.[32] Would Horace's storm still

32. *C.* 1.2 has been dated as early as 36 B.C. by H. T. Plüss, *Horazstudien* (Leipzig, 1882), 39 ff. Most editors agree upon a date after Actium, though they vary as to the precise date between 29 and 27 B.C. See below, 189 ff.

convey so specific a meaning to his contemporaries? His images of disorder are not markedly similar to the portents recorded by other authors, while he has neglected the most remarkable—volcanos and earthquakes, sweating and weeping statues, wolves in the streets, and speaking cattle.[33] Nor, apparently, did a flood of the Tiber such as Horace describes take place at that time.[34] Debates over the possible applicability of the events of 44 B.C. obscure the fact that if Horace had intended an immediately recognizable description he could easily have produced one. Material was not lacking, particularly after Vergil's catalogue of portents in the first Georgic, which Horace had almost certainly seen.[35] The lines are, rather, deliberately vague enough to include the events after Caesar's death without being so detailed as to restrict themselves to these alone.

To locate a factual explanation is not, in any case, to dismiss the possibility of a figurative one, any more than a citation of Octavian's voyage satisfactorily explains the Ode to the Ship of State. The structure of the first six stanzas of *C.* 1.2 suggests an *exemplum*-sermon relationship, though the linkage never becomes explicit. Quintilian appositely describes a "mixed allegory" as one in which "the ornamental element is provided by the words used figuratively, and the meaning by those used literally" (8.6.48–49). Just as the literal statement opening the last stanza of *C.* 1.14 demands a figurative interpretation for the first four stanzas, so the first twenty lines of *C.* 1.2 must be something more than a weather report if the following four lines are to have any consecutive meaning. In the various aberrations of nature we are surely intended to recognize the civil wars that had for so long beaten upon the Romans. The violence of Tiber's attack—*retortis undis,*[36] *violenter, deiectum*—points to a mili-

33. Cf. Verg., *G.* 1.466 ff.; Tib., 2.5.71 ff.; Ov., *Met.* 15.782 ff.; Dio, 45.17. The Horace editions of Wickham, Page, Plessis-Lejay, Villeneuve, Moore, and Shorey follow Porphyrio in his identification of the events Horace describes with the portents following Caesar's death. But see the sensible comments of Fraenkel, *Horace,* 246.

34. See M. E. Hirst, *CQ, 32* (1938), 7 ff.

35. Ps.-Acro early commented on the resemblance between *C.* 1.2 and Verg., *G.* 1.466 ff., and the details of the similarity have been discussed by C. Franke, *Fasti Horatiani* (Berlin, 1839), 142 ff.; cf. T. Birt, *Horaz' Lieder, 2,* 54 ff.; K. Barwick, *Philologus, 90* (1935), 257 ff.

36. *Retortis undis* (13–14) has caused confusion as to its meaning in terms of the Tiber's actual course; see any commentary *ad loc.* Perhaps Horace used

tary analogy, and the animals and buildings bearing the brunt of the storm are associated with peace. Does and doves represent natural creation, while Rome's topography is confined to the shrine of Vesta, goddess of the hearth,[37] and the Regia, built by Numa the Good and official residence of the Pontifex Maximus. If the *horrida tempestas* gathering in the thirteenth Epode bore a political meaning,[38] the storm clouds are now seen to have broken in full force.

The cause of Ilia's complaint (17 ff.) remains obscure. While a Vestal Virgin she had borne Romulus and Remus to Mars, who might thus be considered the "author" of the Roman race (36). Her plea of the twins' divine parentage was disregarded, and for her sin in conceiving them she was hurled into the Tiber. The river god promptly took her as his wife (thus *uxorius amnis,* 19–20), and his anger at the Romans is probably to be explained by their unjust execution of her. Ilia may also demand punishment for the Romans' murder of Caesar, who as Pontifex Maximus had been her priest.[39] But if the motive for her complaint were crucial it would surely be less equivocal. In the account we should probably see only the general type of excessive revenge—for whether we take *nimium* with *querenti* or *ultorem* (17–18) the sense remains clear—rather than an allusion to a specific crime and punishment. The unholy character of Tiber's vengeance appears even from the buildings he attacks. Jove himself disapproves (19). And in condemning such zeal the father of the gods holds out the first hope that an end to the long continued storm may be at hand.

Ps.-Acro, apparently misunderstanding *partis* (29) as a genitive singular, defined *scelus* as the murder of Julius Caesar: "for indeed,

---

the phrase primarily to suggest violent turmoil in general, rather than with the wealth of geographical detail in mind which editors assume.

37. Vesta is later (26–28) explicitly connected with peace: from her the Romans entreat a savior to end civil wars.

38. See Campbell, *Horace,* 143; J. Stroux, *Philologus, 90* (1935), 325 ff.; G. Giarratano, *Il libro degli epodi* (Pescia, 1930), 89 ff.; V. Pöschl, *Foundation Hardt, Entretiens, 2* (Geneva, 1953), 100.

39. Cf. Ov., *F.* 3.699–700. A further reason for Ilia's anger has been found by invoking a genealogy whereby Ilia, as the daughter of Aeneas, becomes the ancestor of Julius Caesar. Neither of these two causes for Ilia's anger (i. e. that Caesar was her priest, or her direct descendant) is supported by the Ode itself; for references and discussion of further details, see my article, *AJP, 80* (1959), 37 ff.

not all consented to his death."[40] Yet the last of Caesar's murderers was by now dead,[41] and Horace's sense of sin is less localized. By invoking the flood of Deucalion and Pyrrha (5 ff.), Horace insinuates a virtually archetypal context, in which individual crimes are lost in the wickedness of whole generations.[42] During the civil wars all the Romans had shown themselves murderers of a sort. Though Caesar's death may epitomize their culpability it does not exhaust it. In line twenty-three the *vitium* of the Romans is explicitly associated with civil war, and we may surmise the same reference in the mention of their *scelus* (29) and *vitiis* (47). Such words preserve a general sense elsewhere:[43]

> Quo, quo scelesti ruitis? aut cur dexteris
> aptantur enses conditi?
> parumne campis atque Neptuno super
> fusum est Latini sanguinis . . . ? [*Epod.* 7.1–4]

> Where, where, are you rushing, bent on crime? Or why are your swords, once sheathed, now grasped in your right hands? Has not enough Latin blood yet been shed upon the land and sea?

One critic has appealed to the seventh Epode to prove that *scelus* in *C.* 1.2.29 cannot refer to civil war.[44] The Epode, he feels, defines the crime of the Romans (*scelus,* 18) as Romulus' murder of Remus, civil war being rather their punishment. Yet the tragedy of Rome's history lies in the fact that punishment not only fits the crime but is the crime—for what is civil war but expanded fratricide? Civil war, while punishing an original *scelus,* likewise perpetuates it; thus the *scelesti* of the seventh Epode (1) are those contemporaries bent on renewing the past. Though Horace abandoned the doctrinaire aspect

40. Ps.-Acro, *ad C.* 1.2.29. *Scelus* is also taken as referring only to the murder of Caesar by Villeneuve, *Horace, Odes et Épodes, ad loc.;* L. Hermann, *RevBelge, 15* (1936), 983.

41. Velleius Paterculus, 2.87.3; cf. Appian, *B. C.* 5.1.1; Plu., *Caes.* 69.240e–f.

42. Ovid (*Met.* 1.211) names the *infamia temporis* as the cause of the flood. Cf. the flood of Noah, God's punishment for the sins of the whole race.

43. Cf. *Epod.* 16.9; *C.* 1.35.33, 2.1.30; Verg., *G.* 1.468; Luc., 1.37 ff.

44. Zielinski, *AC, 8* (1939), 171–72.

of the scheme, he retained his conviction that the crimes of the Romans were themselves their punishment. Sometimes the "accursed blood" of the Romans causes their wars (*Epod.* 16.9); sometimes the blood shed in the wars is itself the evil to be expiated (*C.* 2.1.5). Vergil proposed a more ancient mythological blood guilt, but only to register the same conviction of a fallen state:

> satis iam pridem sanguine nostro
> Laomedonteae luimus periuria Troiae. [*G.* 1.501–02]

> Already have we paid enough with our blood for the perjury of Laomedon at Troy.

Since the Romans considered themselves descendants of the Trojans, upon them fell the responsibility for Laomedon's fraud in deceiving the gods at the time he founded Troy.[45] In *C.* 1.2 the Romans' murder of Ilia suggests another version of Romulus' crime or Laomedon's, while Tiber incarnates the corresponding divine wrath. Whatever the source of Rome's evil destiny its effects were inescapable. In each case divine anger works through, and is evidenced by, the human crime of civil war. The fusion of crime and punishment may be logically unsound, but in the storm of *C.* 1.2 it achieves symbolic reality.

Horace was not advancing a formula for history, but responding emotionally to the spectacle his generation had witnessed. Ever since the murder of Tiberius Gracchus in 133 B.C. the specter of civil war had haunted Roman imaginations, and had emerged with a desperate clarity in the decade of the thirties. Actium might be seen simply as the culmination of a Hundred Years' War. Punishments were often as bad as the crimes. In 73 B.C. the rulers had revenged themselves upon the followers of the revolutionary Spartacus by nailing them to crosses every fifty yards from Capua to Rome (Appian, *B. C.* 1.14.120). Proscriptions had become almost a commonplace. If not all Horace's contemporaries would remember those of Marius and Sulla, few would forget those of Antony, Octavian, and Lepidus after

45. Hom., *Il.* 21.441 ff. In *C.* 3.3 Horace elaborates this scheme; see below, 214 ff. Cicero (*Marcell.* 6.18) also suggests the possibility of some original sin, though he does not specify it. See also H. Wagenvoort, *Studies* (Leiden, 1956), 169 ff.

Julius Caesar's death. Two thousand Equites and three hundred Senators fell, and Cicero's head was impaled on the rostrum from which he had spoken. After Octavian's successful siege of Perusia, where Lucius Antonius had taken refuge, the unoffending Perusine Senate was executed, though it was found expedient to spare Antonius himself. (One story even had it that Octavian sacrificed a number of the leading citizens to the shade of Julius Caesar.[46]) Philippi in 42 B.C., the naval battle against Sextus Pompey in 36 B.C., and Actium in 31 B.C. combined to make civil war the most compelling fact of recent history.[47] To Horace, who had fought beneath Brutus at Philippi, Caesar's murder was less significant as a moral sin than because of its historical consequences, for the blood spilled on the Senate floor prefigured that which was to flow in the fields and seas of the whole Empire.[48]

In calling a halt to such a downpour *C.* 1.2 marks a turn in the cycle of sin and expiation charted by Horace's political poems. The sixteenth Epode, perhaps the earliest, offered no hope but flight, while the seventh subsided into gloomy resignation. Vergil, writing about the same time as the sixteenth Epode, hailed fantasy as imminent reality, and predicted a Golden Age at Rome itself (*E.* 4). Whatever the priority of the two works, Horace's judgment proved the more immediately accurate. Not until after Actium did the hope of escaping from the spiral of wars become more than sporadic, and even then there were no firm guarantees. Only from the comfortable retrospect of two thousand years does Actium seem so sturdy a landmark, and Horace, well schooled in skepticism by the collapse of each previous settlement, was not likely to fall prey to sudden certainties. Could he be sure that all bloodshed was past, there would be no point to the complicated tenses of the sixth stanza. The past of the future (*audiet*) is the present, and the sinful ancestors (*vitio*

46. Suet., *Aug.* 10; Dio, 48.14.

47. Hor., *Epod.* 7; 16; *C.* 1.35.33 ff., 2.1; Verg., *G.* 1.489 ff. For a survey of the bloodshed of the whole century, see R. S. Conway, *New Studies of a Great Inheritance* (London, 1921), 49 ff.

48. The figure is Horace's own: *Epod.* 7.3; *C.* 2.1.29. Cf. Verg., *G.* 1.491–92; Ov., *Met.* 15.824. For Vergil, as for Horace, the murder of Julius Caesar was less important as an individual crime than as the historical cause of further war: *ergo inter sese paribus concurrere telis* (*G.* 1.489).

parentum) of later generations (*iuventus*) are Horace's contemporaries.[49] An unresolved fear (25–30) brings us from a relation between past and present to one between present and future. We leave exposition for command:

> tandem venias precamur 30
> nube candentis umeros amictus
> augur Apollo;
>
> sive tu mavis, Erycina ridens,
> quam Iocus circum volat et Cupido;
> sive neglectum genus et nepotes 35
> respicis auctor,
>
> heu nimis longo satiate ludo,
> quem iuvat clamor galeaeque leves
> acer et Marsi peditis cruentum
> voltus in hostem; 40
>
> sive mutata iuvenem figura
> ales in terris imitaris almae
> filius Maiae patiens vocari
> Caesaris ultor,
>
> serus in caelum redeas diuque 45
> laetus intersis populo Quirini,
> neve te nostris vitiis iniquum
> ocior aura
>
> tollat: hic magnos potius triumphos,
> hic ames dici pater atque princeps, 50
> neu sinas Medos equitare inultos
> te duce, Caesar.

At long last may you come, we pray, augur Apollo, veiling your gleaming shoulders with a cloud; or you, if you will, smiling Venus, about whom fly Mirth and Love; or you, if

49. Cf. *posteri negabitis* (*Epod.* 9.11), used with present verbs. *Ruentis* (*C.* 1.2.25) emphasizes the immediacy of the danger. For the usage of *ruo* in connection with civil war, cf. *Epod.* 7.1, 16.2; see below, 199.

> you cast a kind glance upon your neglected race of descendants, you who are finally satiated by the, alas, too-long-continued game of war, you who delight in battle shouts and polished helmets, and the bloody face of the Marsian foot soldier turned against the enemy. Or you, winged son of gentle Maia, if changing your form you imitate an earthen youth and endure to be called the avenger of Caesar, late may you return to the sky, and long may you joyfully remain among the Roman people, nor may any too swift breeze carry you from us, angered at our sins. Here may you enjoy magnificent triumphs, here be called father and chief, nor allow the Medes to ride on their raids unavenged, with you, Caesar, our leader.

The catalogue of possible deities mounts to a crescendo which breaks only upon the final word. The savior is Octavian himself, an earthly image of Mercury, *almae filius Maiae* (42–43). Even now, we learn, the hope of the future is present in the still youthful ruler. The savior's task is threefold: to save the falling empire from civil war, to expiate the Romans' *scelus,* and, as we infer from line forty-four, to avenge the death of Caesar. Although Horace does not grant to the last the initial importance of the other two (which are in effect identical), later commentators have emphasized it particularly, seeing in it his repudiation of the Republican cause and his commitment to Octavian.[50] For Sellar the phrase *Caesaris ultor* was sufficient to convict Horace of suggesting that Octavian's "first duty was, as the avenger of Julius Caesar, to crush the remnants of the party for which Horace himself had fought." [51] To such a construction history lends a certain authority. At the battle of Philippi Octavian had vowed a temple *pro ultione paterna,* and the two thousand dead after the proscriptions of 43 B.C. testified to his seriousness. Ovid was to celebrate the revenge Octavian exacted.[52] Might not Horace be doing the same thing?

50. See above, 176 and n. 31.

51. W. Y. Sellar, *The Roman Poets of the Augustan Age: Horace and the Elegiac Poets* (Oxford, 1924), 153.

52. Ov., *F.* 3.707 ff., 5.569; *Met.* 1.200 ff. In *Met.* 1.200 ff. Ovid compares Octavian's revenge with that taken by Jove in the age of Pyrrha. Velleius

If such be the purport of the Ode we should be able to locate it not merely in isolated phrases but in the structure of the whole. Vengeance is indubitably the principal theme, as the repetition of *ultor* insists (18, 44; cf. 51). We hear of Jupiter's punishment of the Romans, and of the river god Tiber's; Mercury is hailed as avenger of Caesar and urged to exact revenge, in an ambiguous identification with Octavian,[53] from the Medes. Yet the idea that vengeance is sweet is less pertinent than the fact that there has been a surfeit of vengeance—for from the opening phrase the theme of excess accompanies that of revenge.[54] The plea for a redeemer ("at last may you come," 30) confirms our sense of a too-long-continued punishment, as does the repetition of *nimium* (17, 37). Jupiter himself officially disapproves the vengeful disruptions caused by Tiber, whether they be for Ilia's murder or for Caesar's. The last of Caesar's assassins had died shortly after Actium, and for Octavian to exact further vengeance would be to perpetuate the sin of civil war rather than expiate it, to renew the past and not redeem it. *Fulmen est ubi cum potestate habitat iracundia,* ran the proverb. Were Octavian to indulge his wrath, the storms from which Rome had so long suffered would surely come again. Horace, we should remember, had fought against Octavian at Philippi, and his home had been confiscated for the triumvir's veterans (*Ep.* 2.2.49–52). He was never to repudiate his Republican friends nor to denigrate the Republican cause.[55] Summaries naming the Ode a panegyric preserve only a half-truth. In *C.* 1.2 Horace has come less to praise Caesar than to bury him, and

Paterculus (2.66.2) excuses Octavian on the ground that he had been compelled to the proscriptions by Antony and Lepidus, though Suetonius (*Aug.* 27.1) claims that Octavian proved more severe in his vengeance than either of his fellow triumvirs.

53. On Octavian's ambiguous "deification" (*C.* 1.2.41 ff.), see Fraenkel, *Horace,* 247–49.

54. The persistent hiss of *s*'s in the first two lines of *C.* 1.2 reinforces the sense of an excessive unpleasantness. The same is true of 21–24; the similarity of sound to 1 ff. underlines the *exemplum*-sermon correspondence of the two passages. For the hissing sound of *s,* cf. *C.* 1.37.26–27, 2.2.13–16, and see Wilkinson, *Horace,* 138.

55. Horace dedicated Odes to such Republicans as Sestius (*C.* 1.4) and Messalla (*C.* 3.21), praised the Republican hero Cato (*C.* 1.12.35–36, 2.1.24), and referred to the Republican defeat at Philippi as *cum fracta virtus* (*C.* 2.7.11); cf. n. 24, above.

while declaring allegiance to Caesar's adopted son and heir he reads him at the same time a warning. The poem's intent might find an epitome in one of the *sententiae* of Publilius Syrus: "He conquers forever who uses mercy" (500, Woelfflin).

The gods whom Horace invokes ratify such an interpretation, for the character of each belies the title *Ultor.* One sometimes receives the impression that in *C.* 1.2 Horace concerned himself only with providing a footnote in the history of the ruler cult. Debates as to whether he thinks Octavian actually a god, metaphorically a god, or merely very like a god, have moved from the confines of the text to the ampler grounds of a comparative religion, sometimes with an almost apocalyptic suggestiveness.[56] It has often been remarked that each of the first three divinities he mentions could claim a connection with the Julian house or Roman race. Apollo (32) was special patron of Octavian, and the ruler's calculated program to identify himself with that god has been amply documented.[57] As mother of Aeneas, Venus (33) was ancestress of the Julian line through her grandson Iulus; thus the *Carmen Saeculare* salutes Augustus as *clarus Anchisae Venerisque sanguis* (50). Mars (36), as father of Romulus, was author of the Roman race itself, and Horace's contemporaries are termed his "grandchildren," *nepotes* (35). Multiplying the possible connections of each of these figures is an intoxicating and frequently indulged right of scholarship, but for the purposes of his poem Horace tells us exactly what he wants us to remember. *Neque semper arcum tendit Apollo:* the god appears not as the warrior of the fourth Roman Ode, but as the *augur* of the *Carmen Saeculare,* presiding deity of Rome's revival. As a model for Venus, Horace may have in mind Lucretius' *Aeneadum genetrix,*[58]

56. Zielinski, *AC, 8* (1939), 179, invokes the Arcadian Hermes and his son Logos, and, incorporating the Gospel according to St. John, emerges with a remarkably hospitable view of Octavian as "le Verbe, Verbe créateur, Verbe, identifié à la seconde personne de la Trinité, Verbe, identifié au Messie." Cf. K. Rupprecht, *WJA, 1* (1946), 67 ff.

57. See F. Altheim, *A History of Roman Religion* (London, 1938), 365 ff.; J. B. Carter, *The Religion of Numa* (London, 1906), 164 ff.; E. H. Haight, *AJP, 39* (1918), 341 ff.; W. Déonna, *RevArch,* 5e série, *11* (1920), 166 ff.; J. Gagé, *Appollon Romain* (Paris, 1955), 479 ff.

58. The Horace editions of Kiessling-Heinze, Shorey, Smith, Plessis-Lejay, etc. note the similarity between Horace's and Lucretius' Venus.

perhaps remembering that for the older poet she was goddess not only of growth but of peace, the Romans' best hope for *placidam pacem* (*Lucr.,* 1.40). As *Erycina ridens* (33), in any case, she stands as the embodiment of gentleness, and her companions *Iocus* and *Cupido* confirm the benevolence implicit in the adjective. Mars is summoned not as god of war but as *auctor* of the race, and the etymological meaning of "increaser" is surely pertinent here. Though delighting in the battles of the Roman foot soldiers (*Marsi,* 39) against the enemy, even he is now satiated by civil war. By turning last and most elaborately to Mercury, Horace has provoked endless arguments as to whether there was in fact a cult of Mercury-Augustus at Rome.[59] The consideration has very little to do with our understanding of the Ode. Horace's views emerge from the poem itself rather than from contemporary cult practice. Perhaps the most important thing about Mercury is the fact that he is never named. *Almae filius Maiae:* the periphrasis is significant. Horace can now introduce the adjective *almus* (which might sit oddly upon Mercury himself), thus suggesting the character that Mercury, and by extension Octavian, is to display. *Alma* was the word Lucretius had used of Venus (1.2), and Horace was later to apply it to the Muses (*C.* 3.4.42). Like both of these divinities, Mercury embodies the twin conceptions of nourishment and peace. Nor was his character inappropriate to the role. As patron of the peaceful arts of commerce and poetry, his statue won admission to the temple of *Concordia,* next to that of the goddess herself.[60] Elsewhere Horace invokes him as god of the lyre and tamer of the *feros cultus hominum* (*C.* 1.10.2); the union of poetry and political harmony that Mercury suggests resembles that represented by the Muses in the fourth Roman Ode.

After emphasizing the peaceful aspect of each of the possible gods, Horace proposes "the son of gentle Maia" as *Caesaris ultor.* His implication is clear. There must be no vengeance. The two halves of the Ode contain, in modified form, *exempla* of revenge, and the structure

59. For references to works on the supposed cult of Mercury-Augustus, see my article, *TAPA, 88* (1957), 48.

60. F. Altheim, *A History of Roman Religion,* 531, n. 49. H. Plüss, *Horazstudien,* 35, appositely cites Ovid's description of Mercury as *pacis et armorum superis imisque deorum arbiter* (*F.* 5.666). The Cadeuceus that Mercury carries on Roman coins is to be understood as a symbol of peace; see F. De Waele, *The Magic Staff or Rod in Antiquity* (The Hague, 1927), 75.

remains identifiably paraenetic. Tiber, "boasting himself" the avenger of Ilia, stands in pointed contrast to Mercury, "enduring to be called avenger of Caesar." Even Mars, *nimis longo satiate ludo*, seems to disparage excesses such as those of Ilia and Tiber. Tiber's vengeance is only in the loosest sense allegorical, for Ilia is not Julius Caesar nor is the river god Octavian. The description does, however, provide a suggestive parable of excessive punishment. The alternate type of revenge, associated with Mercury, is war against foreign enemies:

> neu sinas Medos equitare *inultos*
> te duce, Caesar. [*C.* 1.2.51–52]

The poem's final lines thus seal its logic; they are not an afterthought, as a first reading may suggest. The Medes and the Persians were virtually interchangeable to Horace, and the concluding plea hence echoes a deceptively casual line:

> audiet civis acuisse ferrum,
> *quo graves Persae melius perirent.* [*C.* 1.2.21–22]

Since the stanza is cast into the future the imperfect *perirent* does not rule out hope of fulfillment. Under Mercury's auspices Persians may yet perish by Roman swords, and Medes may yet be avenged.[61] Only if all punishment be turned against foreign enemies may the *scelus* of the past be expiated.[62] Horace could number himself among Rome's *scelesti,* and the Ode may be, as commentators repeat, a *peccavi* for his former Republicanism. Yet it is also a *caveat.* A strategic rather than a confessional bias controls the Ode, for the fact of the poet's past errors was less urgent than the possibility of the ruler's future ones. There were at Rome not only Republicans but Pompeians and Antonines as well. All might have lively fears of reprisal, and in the name of all alike Horace issues a covert plea for mercy. Praise of the godlike victor unites with a prayer for his sinful people.

Many editors suggest the end of 28 B.C. as the date for the Ode.

61. Horace does not make Mercury a symbol of internal and partisan revenge, as is claimed by W. Y. Sellar, *Horace and the Elegiac Poets,* 153, and K. Rupprecht, *WJA, 1* (1946), 70.

62. If, with Kiessling-Heinze and Klingner, we accept the emendation *Marsi* for *Mauri* (*C.* 1.2.39), Mars becomes a kind of miniature *exemplum* of what Mercury also represents. Mars rejoices in the shout and bloody face of the Roman foot soldier (*Marsi*) only when turned *in hostem.*

They assume that Horace protests lest Octavian retire to private life, and chaos come again. With whatever sincerity, Octavian did make such a proposal to the Senate on January 13, 27 B.C., and it is possible that he earlier gave public indications of it.[63] Yet the concern with revenge in the poem's first half, and the sense of expectancy in the second, are inappropriate to such an interpretation and so late a date. Three and a half years after Actium the issue of punishment need agitate no one, while an effusive welcome (*tandem venias*) might seem rather a coy anachronism. A date better suited to the Ode's mixture of joy and apprehension would be either just before or just after Octavian's return to Rome in July of 29 B.C. He had by then completed his triumphal[64] swing through the East, yet a question remained as to what policy he would pursue. Our knowledge of subsequent history inevitably clouds the study of any noncontemporary literature. We assume that since events after Actium proved Octavian's *clementia,* Horace could never have had any doubts about it. Yet he was not clairvoyant, and the past was anything but reassuring. Seneca, we are often reminded, cited Augustus as a paradigm of mildness. Yet it was Seneca, too, who speculated as to whether it were not merely *lassa crudelitas:*

> As a youth he burned with anger and was borne along by his wrath; he did many things which later he was unwilling to look back upon . . . he was moderate and merciful, certainly, after the sea at Actium had been stained with Roman blood, certainly, after both his own fleets and those of others had been destroyed in Sicily, certainly, after the sacrificial altar at Perusia and after the proscriptions. But I at least do not call tired cruelty mercy.
>
> [*Clem.* 1.11.1]

63. Though this seems unlikely in view of the stir that Octavian's announcement created; see Dio, 53.11. For references to various opinions as to the date of *C.* 1.2, see my article, *TAPA, 88* (1957), 52, n. 45.

64. *Triumphos* (49) has been thought to refer to the triumphs Octavian celebrated in August of 29 B.C., thus establishing a *terminus post quem* for *C.* 1.2. It is not necessary, however, to assume that Octavian's triumphs had already been celebrated at Rome; the military facts would already justify Horace in using the word *triumphos.* Cf. Verg., *G.* 1.503, written and read to Octavian before Octavian had returned to Rome; see n. 69, below.

And Velleius Paterculus, Augustus' most convinced apologist, praised the *lenitas ducis* only to regret that he had not shown it earlier.[65] Professor Adcock has compared Augustus to the Sicilian bandit, who, when asked on his deathbed to forgive his enemies, replied, "Indeed I do, father—for I have killed them all." There was the tale of Maecenas' whispered remark to Octavian as the latter was dealing out sentences—"rise, executioner"—and of Pollio's jibe: "I am silent, for indeed it is not easy to write (*scribere*) to the man who is able to proscribe (*proscribere*)." [66] Horace could not have foreseen that, in Ovid's flattering words, the day of battle would end the day of wrath, and that Jupiter would scatter the rain clouds after he thundered.[67] (And Ovid, writing from exile, had a vested interest in proving a tradition of forgiveness.) The power that Octavian held after Actium must have increased any fears. *Potitus rerum omnium,* he describes himself (*Res Gestae* 34), and the vast army under his command guaranteed that the boast was not idle. All his *acta* had been ratified by a Senate eager to please; the whole city was prepared to go out and meet him on his return to Rome. In the East shrines in his honor were beginning to appear, while at the capital his name had been enrolled in the hymns to the gods, and libations to his genius were poured at every banquet, public or private. "It would be quite superfluous," wrote Dio, "to go on and mention the prayers, the images, and all the other honors of the sort." [68] Recent history had sufficiently proved that all power corrupts—what then of absolute power?

The bloodshed of the past, in which Octavian must confess to a

65. Velleius Paterculus, 2.86.2. Augustus himself (*Res Gestae* 3) claimed to have spared all who sued for mercy, a claim viewed skeptically by historians since Tacitus (*Ann.* 1.2 ff.). See R. Syme, *The Roman Revolution* (Oxford, 1939), 299 ff.; K. Scott, *MAAR, 11* (1933), 20. It has been suggested that Vergil and Horace influenced Octavian toward clemency; see R. S. Conway, *Poetry and Government* (London, 1928), 1 ff.

66. Macrobius, *Sat.* 2.4.21.

67. Ov., *Tr.* 2.33 ff. The lines read almost like a commentary on the first five stanzas of Hor., *C.* 1.2.

68. Dio, 51.19.3; cf. Suet., *Aug.* 52; Tac., *Ann.* 4.37. For the religious honors received by Octavian, see H. Heinen, *Klio, 11* (1911), 150 ff.; L. R. Taylor, *The Divinity of the Roman Emperor* (Middletown, 1931), 142 ff.; L. Cerfaux and J. Tondriau, *Le culte des souverains,* 313 ff.

prominent part, the uncertainty of his actions in the future, and the immense power he enjoyed could easily have produced a situation between Actium and his return that would fit the mood of *C.* 1.2. And were it written in 29 B.C., the strong *hic . . . hic* (49–50) might imply a contrast with the East. Horace entreats, or possibly applauds, Octavian's return to the capital to celebrate his victories. Nor would it, perhaps, be extravagant to detect a hint that the time had come for a descent to earth after the virtual divinization that Octavian had received in Egypt. The poem might be seen as a welcome home in the manner of Vergil's *Georgics*.[69] Its closeness to the conclusion of the first Georgic has been often emphasized, yet the differences are also instructive. With *iam satis* Horace acknowledges his debt,[70] but his Ode succeeds, complements, and qualifies Vergil's cry:

> Di patrii, Indigetes, et Romule Vestaque mater,
> quae Tuscum Tiberim et Romana Palatia servas,
> hunc saltem everso iuvenem succurrere saeclo 500
> ne prohibete. satis iam pridem sanguine nostro
> Laomedonteae luimus periuria Troiae;
> iam pridem nobis caeli te regia, Caesar,
> invidet atque hominum queritur curare triumphos,
> quippe ubi fas versum atque nefas; tot bella per orbem, 505
> tam multae scelerum facies, non ullus aratro
> dignus honos, squalent abductis arva colonis,
> et curvae rigidum falces conflantur in ensem.
> hinc movet Euphrates, illinc Germania bellum;
> vicinae ruptis inter se legibus urbes 510
> arma ferunt; saevit toto Mars impius orbe;
> ut cum carceribus sese effudere quadrigae,
> addunt in spatio, et frustra retinacula tendens
> fertur equis auriga neque audit currus habenas.

69. The *Georgics* were read to Octavian on successive days at Atella, where he rested on his way to Rome after landing at Brindisi in the summer of 29 B.C.; see Suet, *Vit. Verg.* 61 (Reifferscheid).

70. Horace often uses the first words of an Ode to indicate his model, and then goes on to develop the theme in his own way; see *C.* 1.9, 1.12, 1.37, 4.12.

> Gods of the fatherland, Heroes, Romulus and mother Vesta, you who guard the Tuscan Tiber and the Palatine of Rome, at least do not prevent this youth from coming to the rescue of an age overturned. Already have we paid enough with our blood for the perjury of Laomedon at Troy; for long already have the courts of the sky grudged you to us, Caesar, complaining that you care for triumphs among men, where, indeed, right and wrong are inverted: so many are the wars covering the earth, so many the forms of evil; nor is any honor paid the plow, and the fields, their settlers snatched away, lie barren, while the curved scythes are beaten into strong swords. Here Euphrates, there Germany, rouses war; neighboring cities, their treaties broken, bear arms against each other; unholy Mars rages over the whole globe —as when the chariots pour forth from the barriers, they add lap upon lap, while the charioteer, pulling in vain upon the curb, is borne along, and the chariot does not obey the reins.

Vergil probably wrote these lines several years before Horace's Ode, for *saevit toto Mars impius orbe* would hardly be appropriate after Octavian's settlement of the East. For Vergil the mere presence of *hunc iuvenem* promises an end to the wars following Caesar's death (489 ff.), and the parallel *satis iam pridem . . . iam pridem* (501–03) implicitly identifies the hoped-for end of an ancestral curse with the arrival of Octavian. For Horace expiation depends less upon the arrival than upon the character of the ruler—for it is with possible characters that the Ode's latter half deals, as Horace seeks a god suitable to endure being called *Caesaris ultor*. Vergil's background is one of undifferentiated chaos while Horace sees foreign wars not as part of an *everso saeclo* but as an alternative to civil wars. One poet thinks in terms of the ruler's presence, the other in terms of his policy. Where the former demands only that a charioteer seize the reins, the latter suggests a course for him to follow. While Horace was still recovering from the Republican defeat at Philippi, Vergil's rustics were greeting Octavian as a god (*E.* 1.6), and the almost baroque fancy of the proem to the *Georgics* testifies to a still increasing enthusiasm.

The dangers of a single ruler presented themselves at this time with greater immediacy to Horace than to his contemporary, and apprehension perceptibly qualifies his praise. Mercy, he suggests, is the tax on power; divinity demands a greater humanity. By reminding Octavian that the hope of the future depends upon his wisdom in the present, the Ode becomes a summons to greatness no less than a celebration of it.

The Ode to the Ship of State (*C.* 1.14) is obscure historically rather than morally, since it is principally our ignorance as to the circumstances in which it was written that makes Horace's intention uncertain. But an inherent doubleness of intent complicates the Ode to Octavian; in this respect it recalls the Cleopatra Ode. As that poem manages to praise Cleopatra even in celebrating her conqueror, this one reminds Octavian not merely of his supernatural greatness but, more importantly, of his superhuman responsibilities as well. "We must speak carefully when addressing a despot," suggests the handbook of Demetrius (*Eloc.* 293). It is impossible to read Horace's poems on the ruler in the same way that one reads those of Ovid. While displaying the characteristics of a paean they frequently betray those of Cautionary Verses. The two elements coexist, and there is no need to choose between them. To the impatient "either-or" of critical logic Horace found it disconcertingly easy to reply "both."

C. 3.4

Res est publica Caesar, wrote Ovid: "Caesar is the state" (*Tr.* 4.4.15). The equation worked both ways, and several of the poems addressed to the people at large are clearly earmarked for a private hearing as well. Such is the fourth Roman Ode, probably written shortly after *C.* 1.2.[71] The longest of the Odes, it is among the most formal in its rhetoric:

> Descende caelo et dic age tibia
> regina longum Calliope melos,
> seu voce nunc mavis acuta,
> seu fidibus citharave Phoebi. [*C.* 3.4.1–4]

71. See R. Heinze, *NJW, 5* (1929), 681 ff.; F. Klingner, *Gnomon, 13* (1937), 41.

> Descend from the sky, Queen Calliope; come, strike up upon your pipe a stately song, or with your clear voice, if you prefer, or with the strings of Apollo's lyre.

For so authoritative an appeal some credentials were necessary. Instances of divine patronage from the poet's past, beginning virtually *ab ovo,* are now paraded before us. We hear of Horace's miraculous protection even as a child, of his escapes from battle, from shipwreck, from natural hazards; he assures us that under the Muses' protection he dares defy any danger. Establishing in this way his own right to speak as one inspired, he passes to the Muses' influence on Octavian:

> vos Caesarem altum, militia simul
> fessas cohortes abdidit oppidis,
> finire quaerentem labores
> Pierio recreatis antro;
>
> vos lene consilium et datis et dato
> gaudetis, almae. scimus, ut inpios
> Titanas . . . [*C.* 3.4.37–43]

> In your Pierian cave you re-create lofty Caesar, who seeks an end to his labors, as soon as he has hidden away in the towns his cohorts tired from military service. You give gentle counsel, gracious ones, and rejoice when it is given. We know how the wicked Titans . . .

Cherishing princes no less than poets, the Muses combine the very functions assigned them by Hesiod (*Th.* 80 ff.). Horace may intimate as much by invoking *regina Calliope* (2), for to the Greek poet it was Calliope who was "chiefest of all the Muses, for she attends on worshipful princes" (*Th.* 79–80). A talent for peace is the substance of the Hesiodic Calliope's gift, and the "gentle counsel" bestowed by the *almae Musae* upon Octavian suggests a similar conception. The scene is curious. When Octavian returned to Brindisi in the summer of 29 B.C., the legions under his command might justly be termed "tired" (38) after nearly three years in the field. More than one hundred thousand of his veterans would soon be "hidden away" in colonies in Italy and the provinces, a visible token that the military *labores* of the past were finished.[72] It is this period of readjustment that provides the Ode's dramatic setting. Perhaps Horace has a specific moment in mind. On the way from Brindisi to Rome Octavian stopped to rest at Atella, where, in the Pierian grotto, as it were, Vergil and Maecenas read to him the four books of the *Georgics*. Here was *lene consilium* indeed, for in Vergil's hymn to the blessings of a peaceful land Octavian must occasionally catch the rhythms of a prayer:

> non ullus aratro
> dignus honos, squalent abductis arva colonis,
> et curvae rigidum falces conflantur in ensem.
> [*G*. 1.506–08]

The tacit condition of Vergil's poem is peace. Swords, in a reversal unprecedented in the poet's lifetime, must be beaten into plowshares, and soldiers must again turn farmers. Vergil is bucolic where Horace is mythological, but the community of intent between the two works is unmistakable.

Possible allusions to Hesiod and Vergil are beguiling rather than necessary, for Horace's image is self-explanatory. Octavian waits in a moment of perfect stillness, halfway between the turmoils of the past and the as-yet-untested order of the future. The *almae Musae* "re-create" him in a very real way; we catch a sense of imminent rebirth. Beneath their nourishing tutelage Octavian revives within the Pierian cave, soon to emerge as the incarnation and the director of Rome's new destiny.

Though the precise meaning of *lene consilium* resists definition, its value is demonstrable. We need only look at the disastrous results that wait upon those who lack it, rebels against Zeus such as the Titans, the Giants, and the Aloedae, or those others who grasped at the prerogatives of the gods, Orion, Tityos, and Pirithous. Commanding examples from myth, Horace brings the Ode, by a somewhat devious route, to the familiar paraenetic formula:

72. *Labores* (*C*. 3.4.39) may have a general meaning, but it probably refers primarily to battles; cf. *S*. 1.1.5; *Epod*. 16.16. For Octavian's settlement of veterans see *Res Gestae* 3, 15.

scimus, ut inpios
Titanas immanemque turbam
fulmine sustulerit caduco,

qui terram inertem, qui mare temperat 45
ventosum et urbis regnaque tristia,
divosque mortalisque turmas
imperio regit unus aequo.

magnum illa terrorem intulerat Iovi
fidens iuventus horrida bracchiis 50
fratresque tendentes opaco
Pelion inposuisse Olympo.

sed quid Typhoeus et validus Mimas
aut quid minaci Porphyrion statu,
quid Rhoetus evolsisque truncis 55
Enceladus iaculator audax

contra sonantem Palladis aegida
possent ruentes? hinc avidus stetit
Volcanus, hinc matrona Iuno et
numquam umeris positurus arcum, 60

qui rore puro Castaliae lavit
crinis solutos, qui Lyciae tenet
dumeta natalemque silvam,
Delius et Patareus Apollo.

vis consili expers mole ruit sua, 65
vim temperatam di quoque provehunt
in maius, idem odere viris
omne nefas animo moventis.

testis mearum centimanus Gyges
sententiarum, notus et integrae 70
temptator Orion Dianae
virginea domitus sagitta.

iniecta monstris Terra dolet suis
maeretque partus fulmine luridum

missos ad Orcum; nec peredit 75
inpositam celer ignis Aetnen

incontinentis nec Tityi iecur
reliquit ales, nequitiae additus
custos; amatorem trecentae
Pirithoum cohibent catenae. 80

We know how he struck down with his descending bolt the wicked Titans and their huge host, he who rules the lifeless earth, the wind-swept sea, the cities of men and the grim regions below, he who alone governs with his impartial power both the gods and the throngs of mortals. That band of youths, bristling with arms and trusting in their strength, brought great terror upon Jove, they and the brothers who tried to pile Pelion on shady Olympus. But what could Typhoeus do, or mighty Mimas, what Porphyrion with his menacing stature, what Rhoetus or Enceladus, bold hurler of the tree trunks he had plucked up—what could they do, rushing against the ringing shield of Pallas Athene? Here stood eager Vulcan, here mother Juno and he who will never put aside his bow, he who bathes his loosened locks in the pure water of Castalia, he who holds the Lycian groves and his native wood, the god of Delos and Patara, Apollo.

Force without counsel rushes to ruin through its own weight, but tempered force even the gods make greater, though they hate force which conceives every kind of evil. Hundred-handed Gyges is a witness for what I say, and Orion, notorious for his attempt on chaste Diana, he who was conquered by that maiden's arrow. Earth, burying her own monsters, grieves and mourns for her offspring cast down to lurid Orcus by Zeus' thunderbolt; not yet has the swift flame eaten through Aetna heaped above it, nor has the vulture left the liver of incontinent Tityos, whose wickedness he guards, and three hundred chains yet hold fast the lover Pirithous.

Of the various rebels against the rule of Zeus the Giants were the most notorious, and it is the Gigantomachia that furnishes Horace with his most elaborate version of ὕβρις. *Vis consili expers mole ruit sua:* the line is at once the poem's official moral and an epitaph for the Giants, rushing (*ruentes,* 58) upon the goddess of wisdom to their own destruction. They lack the *consilium* (65) that the Muses endorse (41), which we may liken to the *vis temperata* approved by the gods (66). Where the Olympians affirm a stable order (45–49), their opponents threaten an unnatural confusion.[73] Uprooting mountains and forests in their struggle (51–56), they represent the same disruptive force as did the rain, hail, and floods of *C.* 1.2. Horace in that poem abandoned his allegory to look elsewhere for a savior, but now he resolves the myth in its own terms: *vis consili expers* . . . Gnomic complacency has replaced the agonized question, *quem vocet divum populus ruentis imperi rebus?* (*C.* 1.2.25–26). The poet speaks no longer as the victim of a deluge, but as the spectator of a revolt.

In turning to so familiar a myth Horace took over the traditionally public connotations it bore. During his student days at Athens he could hardly have avoided seeing the Gigantomachias inscribed upon the east metopes of the Parthenon and emblazoned upon the shield of the goddess Athene within. Though the Olympians' triumph over the sons of earth may at first have signified simply the conquest of a lower order by a higher, or the consolidation of the divine πόλις, subsequent generations read into the image more parochial meanings. It became a contest between civilization and barbarism, and as such could offer the Greeks a tempting analogue for their struggles with the Persians.[74] The myth's obvious sculptural appeal ensured its continuing popularity, while the terms of the conflict were basic enough to remain pertinent historically. In the most comprehensive represen-

73. Thus the emphasis on the Giants' shapeless (*immanem turbam,* 43) and chaotic (*horrida brachiis,* 50) aspect. Horace does not keep the Giants strictly separated from various other rebels against Zeus; thus Typhoeus' revolt was traditionally supposed to have come later.

74. See Aristophanes, *Eq.* 566, and Wilamowitz, *Die Glaube der Hellenen* (Basel, 1956), *2,* 94; E. A. Gardner, *A Handbook of Greek Sculpture* (London, 1929), 242; E. M. Sanford, *CP, 36* (1941), 52 ff.; F. Vian, *La Guerre des Géants* (Paris, 1952), 284 ff.

tation, that upon the Great Altar of Zeus at Pergamum, the forces of Attalus I are seen as the Olympians, and those of the recently defeated Celts as the Giants. Callimachus described the Celts as "later day Titans" (*Hymn* 4.174), and Hellenistic monarchs such as Antigonus and Demetrius may have gone so far as to insert their own figures into representations of the struggle. Lucan too was later able to find in the myth a convenient precedent for the bloodshed preceding Nero's Olympian rule (1.36; cf. 7.144 ff.).

Few of Horace's contemporaries would fail to extract a contemporary relevance from the myth. Octavian had just emerged from a gigantic battle as Rome's supreme ruler, and other writers found it easy to identify the Eastern forces of Antony and Cleopatra with those of strange and brutish gods.[75] By describing Octavian's soldiers as "tired from military service" (37–8) Horace virtually ensures for *scimus* (42) a contemporary rather than an antiquarian object. In the amount of space given to Apollo we may also detect a tactful nationalism. While sculptural tradition assigned him a comparatively minor role in the Gigantomachia, he was the only one of the Olympians to have taken part at Actium. The battle was fought within sight of his temple on shore, and Octavian was quick to claim his support. He encouraged a belief that the victory evidenced Apollo's aid, and in describing the conflict later poets practically ignored the other Olympians.[76]

Where *C.* 1.2 was a study in contrasts, black gloom yielding to a single ray of light, *C.* 3.4 is more luminous throughout. Yet parts at least have darker undertones. In sculptural friezes of the Gigantomachia we sometimes see the upper half of Gaia's body rising from below, hands outstretched to supplicate mercy for her children. Horace's concluding picture of Mother Earth brooding over her

75. Verg., *A.* 8.702 ff.; Prop., 3.11.41–42. Wickham, *The Works of Horace, ad C.* 2.12.6 ff. suggests that these lines also refer to the battle of Actium. Cf. Ov., *Tr.* 2.333 ff.; *Pont.* 1.1.26. The temple of *Juppiter Tonans,* dedicated by Augustus in 22 B.C., probably had a relief showing the battle of the Giants; see Claudian, 28.44–45 (Koch); F. Vian, *Repertoire des Gigantomachies* (Paris, 1951), 24. For Ovid's supposed epic on the battle of the Giants, and for later versions, see S. G. Owen, *Ovid, Tristia 2* (Oxford, 1924), 63 ff.

76. See Verg., *A.* 8.704–06; Prop., 4.6.31 (*solutos crines* here may be an imitation of Hor., *C.* 3.4.62); Ov., *A. A.* 3.390.

fallen sons shows him to have been sensitive to the pathos of the situation. In Pirithous many editors have found a reference to Antony, an *amator* (79) who loved not wisely but too well. The identification is plausible, but more important is the whole mood of the close. We feel no sense of partisan, even though Olympian, jubilation; these *monstra* (73) draw our sympathy in the same way that did Cleopatra, *fatale monstrum* (*C.* 1.37.21). Pirithous, in his only other appearance in the Odes, figures not as an alien monstrosity but as a symbol of man's common fate:

> nec Lethaea valet Theseus abrumpere caro
> vincula Pirithoo. [*C.* 4.7.27–28]

> Nor is Theseus able to break the Lethean bonds that hold his dear Pirithous.

After his return to Rome Octavian was careful to celebrate a triumph over Cleopatra alone, and when he had judiciously distributed part of the spoils from Egypt the Romans "forgot all their unpleasant experiences and viewed his triumph with pleasure, quite as if the vanquished had all been foreigners" (Dio, 51.21.4). The elegiac tone of Horace's close reminds his readers of what was never officially admitted, that many of the fallen shared a common ancestry with the victors.

Horace's vagrant sympathies may be felt to signal simply a recognition that no gain is achieved without loss, and that to establish even the golden rule of Zeus some suffering was inevitable—and deserved. The shapes of myth are archetypal, and a poem such as *C.* 3.4 derives its vitality from the scope as well as from the intensity of its symbols. Yet the virtue of such general symbols lies partly in their capacity to welcome more specialized meanings; we need not cut down the trees in our attempt to see the forest. Recent history could not but have fortified the appeal of Gaia's children to contemporary imaginations, and Horace does not allow the amplitude of myth to conceal intransigent facts. Among the fallen *monstra* Horace could recognize his fellow Romans, and might remember his own position not fifteen years before, *cum fracta virtus et minaces turpe solum tetigere mento* (*C.* 2.7.11–12). The fallen figures of *C.* 3.4 need not be labeled Antonines alone. From Philippi down to the belated conspiracy of Marcus Lepidus, one might find insurgents as various as the rebels against Zeus.[77] All had relied upon *vis consili expers*—or so a discreet recapitulation would term it. Whatever the folly of such movements, their confusion was bloodily apparent. Ovid viewed Octavian's ascendency without compunction,[78] but Horace never adopted so politic an attitude, and his view is more somber. He accepted and celebrated the present as it was, rightly judging that Octavian was the sole guarantee of peace. But never did he undertake to retouch the past.

Divine myth touches ground at two points and here the allegorical intent becomes most precise.[79] The line *vim temperatam di quoque provehunt in maius* must refer to a human *vis* if it is not to become meaningless. Horace reminds Octavian that though he has been compared to Zeus it yet remains only a comparison. The opening lines of the next Ode, as though to correct any possible misapprehension, pointedly relegate Octavian's divinity to the future. In the first of the Roman Odes Horace had been equally careful to put the ruler in his place:

> regum timendorum in proprios greges,
> reges in ipsos imperium est Iovis,
> clari Giganteo triumpho,
> cuncta supercilio moventis. [*C.* 3.1.5–8]

> The rule of dread kings lies over their own people, but over kings themselves is the rule of Jove, famous for his victory over the Giants, controlling all things with his frown.

Jovelike though Octavian may be, and Gigantesque as are his opponents, the dimensions are metaphoric rather than absolute. There

77. Franke, (*Fasti Horatiani,* 189) thought that Horace's rebels represented Egnatius Rufus and Cornelius Gallus.

78. Ov., *F.* 3.707–10; *Met.* 1.200 ff.

79. *C.* 3.4.37 ff.; 65 ff. According to the terms of Quintilian's "mixed allegory" (8.6.48), these lines provide the allegory's "meaning," while its "beauty" would come from the myth: *species ex arcessitis verbis venit et intellectus ex propriis.*

was always the danger that the ὕβρις of the conquered might pass to the victor with the spoils; the temple raised by Cleopatra to Antony was not long in being rededicated to Octavian.[80] Only those who lack *vis temperata* attempt the prerogatives of the gods. And their downfall is its most convincing testimonial.

Lene consilium, like *vis temperata,* had been conspicuous in recent history chiefly by its absence. The various mythical figures can establish its value in negative terms alone: *vis consili expers mole ruit sua.* The embattled Olympians are improbable paradigms of *lenitas,* a quality more appropriate after hostilities are finished. *Bellante prior, iacentem lenis in hostem*—in these terms the *Carmen Saeculare* (51–52) praises Augustus' mildness, but the *Carmen Saeculare* came only in 17 B.C. A dozen years earlier his leniency was more problematic. Still resting from the *labores* of the past, Octavian had yet to give a token of the future, and of the positive effects of the Muses' "re-creation." To read the poem as a clear salute to Octavian's *clementia* or *vis temperata* is to confess a retrospective bias.[81] The Ode is admonitory as well as eulogistic. In recounting the Muses' gift, Horace prescribes it; in describing the "hiding away" of troops—the word has been unjustly emended—he approves it. Probably somewhat later than *C.* 1.2, the fourth Roman Ode is likewise more serene. Yet the differences between the two are to some extent merely tactical. In one case the present is made to appear so tempestuous that Octavian cannot but alter it, while in the other the present becomes potentially so harmonious that he must feel obliged to secure it. But in both poems we sense the same tension between praise and admonition, and if *C.* 3.4 is to receive an epitome we can do no better than to turn again to the words of Publilius Syrus: *perpetuo vincit qui utitur clementia.* And, appropriately, where Octavian-Mercury was in the last lines of *C.* 1.2 exhorted to seek revenge from the Medes, *C.* 3.4 leads into an Ode that opens with the following condition for the ruler's divinity:

80. The temple was dedicated to Octavian together with the goddess *Roma;* see Tac., *Ann.* 4.37.

81. A. V. Domaszewski, *RhM, 59* (1904), 306, thinks *C.* 3.4 to be written in praise of Octavian's *clementia;* S. Pilch, *Eos, 29* (1926), 60, finds in it praise of Octavian's *vis temperata;* cf. G. Strodach, *CW, 29* (1935), 140. Wilkinson, *Horace,* 71, in my opinion more correctly, sees its force as a "plea for a real amnesty"; cf. L. MacKay, *CR, 46* (1932), 243–45.

Caelo tonantem credidimus Iovem
regnare: praesens divus habebitur
Augustus adiectis Britannis
imperio gravibusque Persis. [*C.* 3.5.1–4]

We believe Jove to rule in heaven because we hear him thunder; Augustus will be held a god on earth when he has added to our empire the Britons and the dreaded Parthians.

Editors customarily designate the fourth Roman Ode as one of Horace's most Pindaric efforts, and isolated references direct us most often to the first or eighth Pythian. The similarities between these two poems and the fourth Roman Ode are not those of detail alone. In the first twenty lines of the eighth Pythian, Pindar's hymn to Peace, Horace could have observed his own contrast between *vis* and *consilium.* Φιλόφρον Ἡσυχία . . . : it is the kindly goddess of Peace, daughter of Right, who makes cities great; it is she who holds "the masterkeys both of war and of council." [82] Though knowing with perfect fitness the secret of gentleness, τὸ μαλθακόν (6), Peace knows also how to plunge Hybris into the brine (12). Thus did the rebels Porphyrion and Typhoeus fall, for "violence overthrows the braggart at the last": *vis consili expers mole ruit sua.* From the congruences, not so much of verbal detail as of concept, we may guess that Horace found Pindar's terms apposite, and that his Ode to Octavian is equally a prayer to "kindly Peace, who makes cities great." Actium saw insolence literally "plunged into the brine"; henceforth it will be in *lene consilium,* τὸ μαλθακόν, that the goddess must manifest herself.

By referring to the "gentle voice of song," φθέγματι μαλθακῷ (*P.* 8.31), Pindar ties poetic with political harmony (τὸ μαλθακόν, 6). Where the link is incidental to the eighth Pythian it is central to the first Pythian.[83] After the famous invocation to the "golden lyre,

82. Pi., *P.* 8.3–4. L. R. Farnell, *Works of Pindar, 2* (London, 1932), *ad loc.,* aptly explains the phrase: "for the true object of a righteous war is to secure a lasting peace."

83. Fraenkel (*Horace,* 273 ff.) has magnificently expounded the influence of Pi., *P.* 1 on Hor., *C.* 3.4, though he concentrates on *P.* 1 practically to the exclusion of *P.* 8, mentioned only in one footnote. See also W. Theiler, "Das Musengedicht des Horaz," *Schriften der Königsberger Gelehrten Gesellschaft, 12* (1935), 253 ff.

owned alike by Apollo and the violet tressed Muses," the Ode celebrates the powers of harmony as a kind of ever-widening halo. At the sound of the lyre, Zeus abates his thunderbolt, and his eagle sleeps upon his scepter; even Ares sets aside his spears, warming his heart in repose (*P.* 1.5–12). But all those whom Zeus does not love are struck with terror by the voice of the Muses; such a one is Typhoeus, lying imprisoned beneath Mount Aetna (*P.* 1.13–29). In the Typhoeus of the eighth Pythian we can perhaps discover a political significance,[84] but in the Typhoeus of the first Pythian we cannot avoid it. By extending the Giant's body north from Mount Aetna to Cumae (*P.* 1.17–19), a span unsanctioned by previous tradition, Pindar points to a spot made illustrious by recent history. It was at Cumae that Hiero of Syracuse, whose victory at Delphi the first Pythian formally celebrates, had defeated an Etruscan fleet in 474–73 B.C. The whole of southern Italy was then at stake; no less so, Pindar recalls (*P.* 1.79–80), than at Himera in 480 B.C., where Hiero's brother Gelon had defeated the army of the Carthaginians. During these same years Aeschylus and Simonides were celebrating the fall of the Persians in the East, and in Salamis and Plataea (*P.* 1.76–78) Pindar found a felicitous comparison for the Sicilian triumphs over the barbarian powers of the West. By formally identifying Carthaginians and Etruscans with Ὕβρις (*P.* 1.73), he makes plain the archetypal proportions of the struggle. In scale it is comparable to the confrontation of Ὕβρις and Ἡσυχία in the first Pythian, or of Giants and Olympians in Horace's fourth Roman Ode.

Hiero's victory in the racecourse provided an occasion rather than a motive for the first Pythian, which dwells upon a more lasting accomplishment of Syracuse's ruler. At the games Hiero was proclaimed "Aetnaean" in honor of the city he had recently founded, which his son Deinomenes was to rule. The Ode is a birthday celebration of sorts:

> Zeus, you who bring all things to fulfillment, may the true report of men always give to citizens and to kings alike such fortune as this, by the waters of the Amenas. With your help may he who is the ruler, and who gives in-

84. See H. Wade-Gerry, *JHS, 52* (1932), 214 ff.; Farnell, *Works of Pindar, ad P.* 8.

structions to his son, respect the people and lead them into harmonious peace (σύμφωνον ἡσυχίαν). [*P.* 1.67–70]

The adjective σύμφωνον extends the concept of divine harmony to its earthly counterpart, civil peace.[85] By founding Aetna, Hiero, like Octavian, had crowned his victories of the past with a substantial hope for the future. Yet it was perhaps less the similarity of the historical situation that drew Horace to the first Pythian than it was the quality of the Greek poet's response to the situation. Pindar too was quick to scent the abuses of power, and his praise of Hiero is a prayer as well as a benediction. The man who, Zeuslike, had vindicated civilization against barbarism might find it easy to forget that he was not in fact Zeus, and Pindar's reminder that "from the gods come all the means for mortal exploits" (*P.* 1.41; cf. 48) is as pointed as Horace's *vim temperatam di quoque provehunt in maius* (*C.* 3.4.66–67). Horace could find in the first Pythian not only a vision of "harmonious peace" but also a perception of the qualities that might impair it. Thus Pindar's praise of Aetna's "god-built freedom" (61); thus his injunction to Hiero to "steer your people with the helm of justice" (86); thus, finally, the pregnant reminder that while kindliness guards praise forever green, evil deeds win undying infamy (93 ff.). The kindly Croesus will never lack tribute, but hatred will always cloud the name of Phalaris, whose story must remain forever a stranger to soft (μαλθακάν) song, the symbol of harmony (97–98).

Fraenkel's exposition of the first Pythian illuminates what has long seemed obscure to readers of the fourth Roman Ode, the relation between Horace's elaborate invocation of the Muse and the Gigantomachia. Horace, it is clear, recasts the Pindaric union of celestial harmony and its earthly agents; his poem too celebrates "harmonious peace." Yet the Greek poem confirms rather than reveals the plan of the Latin one, and Horace's long section on the poet and the Muse has its own interior logic. The voices of the two poets are really quite different. Χρυσέα φόρμιγξ . . . *descende caelo:* Pindar's objective salute is a far cry from Horace's subjective command. For Fraenkel the distinction is primarily one of social circumstance.

85. Cf. Pi., *P.* 5.63 ff. (referred to by Fraenkel, *Horace,* 280); *P.* 6.48.

Pindar was performing a task grounded in communal ritual, one that might easily unite public harmony with private. Horace's tones are more lonely. "He does not pretend or even wish to be the mouthpiece of a community such as no longer exists; he is determined to remain the man he is, born in a late and distracted age, walking alone, full of simple strength, with a glad heart and an immense capacity for enthusiasm, and above all, in continual communion with the *μουσικόν* which lifts him up and protects him." [86] The distinction between fifth-century Greece and first-century Rome is cogent, and we forget it at our peril. Yet we may also locate a more precise logic behind Horace's allusive autobiography.

The description of the Muses' patronage is so stylized as to suggest an amalgam of traditional fables. The boast of divine protection (25 ff.) was familiar from the stories about Arion, Simonides, Ibycus, and Archilochus, while for his miraculous childhood (9–20) Horace could have consulted the myths about Aeschylus, Stesichorus, and Pindar. By appealing to these dusty beliefs about the poet's privileged status, Horace invests his calling with something of the antique dignity that it possessed for a Hesiod or a Pindar. He consciously dons the robes of a *sacer vates,* asserting his right to speak as from the holy grove, carried along by an ecstatic vision (1–8). For the Augustan age such ideas were little more than anachronisms,[87] and Horace's adoption of them here suggests a special motive. By parading proof that he is a true spokesman of the Muses might he not hint to Octavian that their *lene consilium* is the Ode itself? [88] Through their inspired poet they give to Octavian "mild counsel" in the form of a mythical allegory. Such a strategic union of poetry and politics elaborates what was merely a suggestion in *C.* 1.2. Mercury too, *almae filius Maiae,* was a patron of poets.[89] And just as the *almae Musae* re-create and instruct Octavian, so Mercury figures as a possible image for him; the two functions are not dissimilar. The presence of the deity can in each case be no more than fanciful, yet through

86. Fraenkel, *Horace,* 284–85.

87. See above, 1 ff., 128.

88. For the usual view, that the link between the Muses and Octavian is a tribute to Octavian's literary patronage, see Campbell, *Horace,* 107. Yet in the poem it is, we should remember, the Muses who are the patrons of Octavian.

89. See n. 23, above.

the work of the poet it achieves reality. The poems themselves act as the earthly manifestation of the deities. Only by heeding the poet's voice can Octavian give evidence of Mercury's influence or of the Muses'. And in each case the poet demands the same things: peace and rebirth, an end to the *fera moenera militiai* of the past and the creation of a new future.[90]

Horace's work invites division into public Ode and private lyric, and the relative merits of the two have long been a subject of lively debate. Whether we hold that he left themes of wine and song only under official command, or that "the erotic Odes are . . . jam round the political pill," [91] the fact of division has seemed clear, and by labeling *C.* 3.1–6 as "the Roman Odes" we bear witness to its persuasiveness. Horace himself supports the distinction, both by isolating these Odes as a coherent group and by reiterating elsewhere the contrast between a *levius* and a *maius plectrum.*

But where subjects are arbitrary, qualities of imagination are not, and in these terms the state Odes refuse to be separated from the body of Horace's work. Their formal relation is clear enough. In shorter poems metaphor proved an architectural rather than decorative device, and the "continuous metaphor" or allegory of *C.* 1.2 or *C.* 3.4, as of *Epod.* 13 or *C.* 1.14, displays the same type of structural dialectic. A tension between figure and reality forms both groups of poems, whether it be to point distinctions (as between war and the war of love) or to elaborate similarities (as between the wars of the gods and the wars of Octavian).

Allied to the metaphorically structured Odes on one side, the political myths look toward parody on the other. Though parody enjoys the distance between some formal concept and reality, while allegory seeks to bridge it, both agree in postulating its existence. The myths of Achilles, of Teucer, of Tiber, or of the Giants, have

90. In explaining *lene consilium* as the equivalent of the Ode itself as a whole, we need not reject the phrase's possible reference to Vergil's *Georgics* as well. The phrase is elastic enough to include both possibilities; and both works, after all, are similar in their sentiments.

91. Campbell, *Horace,* 113. For references to the debate over whether Horace was essentially a political and social poet, or essentially devoted only to light themes, see E. Turolla, *Orazio* (Florence, 1931), 6.

counterparts in the epic farces of the Satires, in the invocation to a Wine Jar, in the *propempticon* to Mevius, and in the outrageous uses to which honored paradigms are turned. The intentions of all three types of verse are distinct, but their assumptions are identical. Each insists that a situation can be seen in terms other than its own. And in each form Horace shows himself equally adept.

The political Odes are as central morally as they are formally. Perhaps the sharpest distinction between the fourth Roman Ode and its Pindaric models lies in Horace's broader sympathies. "Not yet has the fierce flame eaten through Aetna's pile, nor does the vulture leave the breast of incontinent Tityos" (*C.* 3.4.75–78). Horace's fallen sons of earth touch us in a way that Pindar's rebels do not. For those whom Zeus hates Pindar shows only a corresponding hatred; we need not pause over a fallen Carthaginian or Etruscan. But even though Horace officially took his stand with the Olympians, he seems finally to see the scene from below rather than from above. As in *C.* 1.37, song of triumph slides uneasily toward elegy; as in *C.* 1.2, praise of the victor's wisdom is equally a prayer for it. So elusive a response is not the product of historical circumstance alone. It seems to have been instinctive, and might complicate Odes on any subject. We have seen praise of man's heroism turn to reproach of his *stultitia,* pastoral vision become satiric, and satiric love poetry yield to idyllic; epic sinks easily to self-ridicule, and even the *recusatio* occasionally aspires to epic. Such a movement between, and yet reconciliation of, divergent attitudes characterizes *C.* 1.2 and *C.* 3.4. In the quality of their dual response, as in the technique that controls it, they stand as a massive document of the Horatian imagination.

C. 3.3.

When in 40 B.C. Vergil's Meliboeus saluted Octavian as a god he quickly qualified it: "for he will always be a god to us" (*E.* 1.7). A decade later the qualification was gone. Even now, reports Vergil, the constellation Scorpio is drawing in his claws to make room for heaven's new inhabitant (*G.* 1.34–35). Octavian, the *divi filius* of the thirties, was showing signs of outgrowing his youthful titles. The peoples of the eastern Mediterranean had long honored their own rulers as divine, and were prepared, not unnaturally, to transfer the same worship to the Roman who had conquered them. Temples to Octavian—usually to Octavian and the city of Rome—sprang up soon after Actium, and at the capital itself he received religious honors which were unprecedented.[92] In the years that followed, the line between divine likeness and actual divinity became increasingly tenuous. The persistent reminders of Octavian's mortality [93] suggest the difficulty in keeping his godhead within the safe limits of a metaphor, and Horace felt the need for placing it upon a more regular basis. At hand was a conception dating back at least to Euhemerus, whose work had been made available in Latin by Ennius. The gods, Euhemerus held, were no more than unusual mortals who for their services to mankind were honored after death as divine. The Stoic Poseidonius popularized the idea, and Pliny, perhaps translating from him, gave it its classic form: *deus est mortali iuvare mortalem, et haec ad aeternam gloriam via* (*H. N.* 2.5.18). The mortals who had thus achieved "eternal glory" were such as Hercules, Castor and Pollux, Aesclepius, Bacchus, and Romulus.[94] In the second Roman Ode Horace introduces the concept in general form (*virtus recludens inmeritis mori caelum,* 21–22), and in the third he uses it to enroll Augustus among the canonical demigods:

Iustum et tenacem propositi virum
non civium ardor prava iubentium,
  non voltus instantis tyranni
    mente quatit solida neque Auster,

dux inquieti turbidus Hadriae, 5
nec fulminantis magna manus Iovis:
  si fractus inlabatur orbis,
    inpavidum ferient ruinae.

92. See above, 191.

93. *C.* 1.12.51–52, 57, 3.1.5–8, 3.5.1–4.

94. Cicero (*Leg.* 2.8.19) quotes this list of divinities from an old law. Cf. Cic., *N. D.* 1.42.119, 2.24.62, 3.18.45; *Tusc.* 1.12.28 ff.; *Rep.* 1.7.12, 2.2.4, 6.3.3 (Mueller); Tac., *Ann.* 4.38; Wilamowitz, *Die Glaube der Hellenen, 2,* 422–23; P. Wendland, *Die Hellenistische-Römische Kultur* (Tübingen, 1912), 123 ff.; A. R. Bellinger, *YCS, 15* (1957), 93 ff.

hac arte Pollux et vagus Hercules
enisus arcis attigit igneas, 10
quos inter Augustus recumbens
purpureo bibet ore nectar,

hac te merentem, Bacche pater, tuae
vexere tigres indocili iugum
collo trahentes, hac Quirinus 15
Martis equis Acheronta fugit,

gratum elocuta consiliantibus
Iunone divis: "Ilion, Ilion . . .

Not the enthusiasm of citizens urging evil, not the countenance of a threatening tyrant, not the south wind, tumultuous ruler of the restless Adriatic, not the mighty hand of thundering Jove himself, can shake from his fixed resolve the man who is just and steadfast in purpose. If the dome of heaven itself should break and fall, the ruins will strike him unafraid.

Pollux and wandering Hercules, because they possessed such a character, strove and attained the fiery citadels of the sky; between them will Augustus lie, sipping nectar with his purple-stained lips. For the same reason, father Bacchus, your tigers drew you to heaven, bearing the yoke on necks never before broken to the harness; and on account of that same virtue Quirinus escaped from Acheron on the horses of Mars, at the time when Juno addressed these welcome words to the gods gathered in council: "Troy, Troy . . ."

The confident prediction of Augustus' deification marks the distance between this Ode and *C.* 1.2. Where Horace had previously implored some god to take earthly form as the Romans' savior, he may now proclaim that Augustus will earn his own divinity by his deeds. Such a classification had obvious advantages. It at once preserved a belief in the ruler's divinity, while relegating it firmly to the future—*bibet* (12) is emphatic. The idea of a demigod with postponed godhead proved a happy compromise. While tactfully throwing a detour in the way of any overly rapid progress toward divinity, it simultaneously encouraged the ruler to guarantee the future by his present benevolence.[95]

The virtues ostensibly celebrated by the Ode are blanket ones. *Constantia* and *iustitia,* as they are usually termed, correspond to the equally vague *virtus* or *meritum* customary in formulas for this type of apotheosis. The qualities had to be elastic enough to include demigods as various as Bacchus and Romulus (or Quirinus), Hercules and the Dioscuri; we need not seek the specific occasions on which Augustus demonstrated them. The substance of the poem, here as elsewhere, lies not in the statement it makes but in the mythical *exempla* it invokes. Otherwise we must construe the fourteen stanzas on Romulus' apotheosis (15–68) either as being merely decorative or as demonstrating Horace's perverse pleasure in watching the tail wag the dog. Early commentators had no doubts as to the myth's significance: "in this Ode Horace praises Quirinus or Romulus in honor of Augustus." [96] Of all the demigods Romulus provided the clearest prototype for Augustus. "There is nothing," wrote Cicero, "in which men draw nearer to divine than in founding new states or in preserving those already founded." [97] As Romulus had achieved the first, so Augustus had realized the second. His wish to be recognized as Rome's second founder was no secret; indeed, it was practically coeval with his entry into politics. In 43 B.C., when taking the auspices for his first consulate, he re-enacted the famous augury of Romulus, even managing to produce twelve vultures.[98] The Palatine,

95. By the time of *Ep.* 2.1, however, Augustus was recognized as distinct from the other demigods in that he received a modified form of worship while still alive (*Ep.* 2.1.1 ff.; cf. *C.* 4.5.33 ff.; Tac., *Ann.* 4.37–38). For an interesting example of Augustus' own ideas on his divinity, see Dio, 53.9.5.

96. Ps.-Acro *ad C.* 3.3.15.

97. *Rep.* 1.7.12; Cicero uses Romulus as an example: 1.16.25. Cf. *Rep.* 6.3.3, 6.26.28–29. Horace was later to list as conditions for divinity the settling of wars, the assigning of lands, and the founding of towns (*Ep.* 2.1.7 ff.; cf. *Ep.* 1.17.33).

98. Suet., *Aug.* 95; Appian, *B. C.* 3.94. Livy (1.7) and Ovid (*F.* 4.817 ff.), in describing Romulus' augury, seem to have Augustus' imitation of it in mind. The temple of Quirinus, which had Romulus' augury portrayed on the pediment, may have been restored by Augustus, thus keeping the analogy between the two leaders before the people's eyes; see K. Scott, *TAPA, 56* (1925), 91 ff.

where Romulus had lived, became the site of his palace. Coins of the period bear the inscription *Romulo Augusto;* some show Augustus bearing the augur's staff, called the *quirinalis lituus* from its association with Romulus-Quirinus.[99] A politic astrologer arranged that Romulus' birthday should fall on practically the same day as that of Augustus, while after the emperor's death a former praetor declared that he had seen Augustus' effigy rising to the heavens in obvious emulation of Romulus' ascent.[100] Augustus himself made his wishes explicit. "May it fall to my lot to establish the state firm and strong and to obtain the wished-for fruit of my labors, that I may be called author of it, and that when I die I may carry with me the hope that the foundations I have laid may abide." [101]

For the achievement of this pious hope the events of mid-January, 27 B.C., were crucial. At that time Octavian went to the Senate with the avowed intention of restoring the government to the Senate and People of Rome (*Res Gestae* 34). To seal the restoration of power he proposed to retire to private life. The Senate, probably with little real choice, begged him to stay in office, voting him special but strictly legal powers for ten years to come. The extraconstitutional powers of the triumvirs had been abolished together with the edicts they had passed; Octavian's position was at last unimpeachable. Yet his boasted preservation of the *mos maiorum* (*Res Gestae* 6.7) had more to do with form than with substance, and few contemporary or subsequent historians have accepted his claim at its face value.[102] Octavian still controlled the army through his provincial commands, and, in his own ambiguous words, he surpassed all others in *auctoritas*

99. J. Gagé, *MEFR, 47* (1930), 139. More generally, see A. Alföldi, *MH, 8* (1951), 190 ff.

100. Dio, 56.46.2. Dio, not unreasonably, suspects a bribe. Cf. Suet., *Aug.* 100; Sen., *Apoc.* 1.2, 9.5; K. Scott, *TAPA, 56* (1925), 100. On the *Romulusgrab* of Augustus, see E. Kornemann, *F&F, 15* (1939), 425 ff.

101. Suet., *Aug.* 28.2. Suetonius says that Augustus "repeatedly expressed" this wish, and finally formulated it thus in an edict.

102. Dio, 52.41.1, 53.1.1, 53.11.5, 53.12, 53.16.1, 53.17.1; Strabo, 6.4.2, 17.3.25; Florus, 2.34.66; Tac., *Ann.* 1.9; Suet., *Aug.* 28.2. Even the faithful Velleius Paterculus speaks only of a *forma revocata* (2.89.4). See also R. Syme, *The Roman Revolution,* 322–24; E. T. Salmon, *Historia, 5* (1956), 458 ff.; and, for a less cynical view of Augustus' claims, M. Hammond, *The Augustan Principate* (Cambridge, 1933), 2 ff.

(*Res Gestae* 34). A *novus status* (Suet., *Aug.* 28.2) had indeed been born, but it could acknowledge only a single parent.

For the founder of the age a new name was inevitable. There was talk of christening him "Romulus," Octavian's own preference, Dio tells us (53.16.7). The choice was a natural one for the man who was considered *quasi et ipsum conditorem urbis,*[103] but it was rejected as having too much the odor of kingship. "Augustus" was instead chosen, the opportune proposal of Munatius Plancus. The title adopted still had associations with the one that was rejected, if the name Augustus had in fact been suggested by Ennius' line on the founding of Rome: *augusto augurio postquam inclita condita Roma est.*[104] Writers, in any case, dwelt increasingly upon the relation of the two figures. Propertius, perhaps taking a hint from Vergil, saluted Augustus by the name Quirinus, while Ovid characteristically bade Romulus yield to his greater successor.[105]

The appearance of the name Augustus in the third Roman Ode (*C.* 3.3.11) proves it to have been written after, if not in honor of, the events of January, 27 B.C.[106] Never had the example of Romulus been so pertinent. Even the details of Augustus' assumption are calculated to point the flattering parallel. A drink of nectar (11–12) is the token of his immortality, just as it had been for Romulus:

"Ilion, Ilion
fatalis incestusque iudex
et mulier peregrina vertit 20

in pulverem, ex quo destituit deos
mercede pacta Laomedon, mihi

103. Suet., *Aug.* 7; cf. Florus, 2.34.66: *tractatum etiam in senatu an quia condidisset imperium Romulus vocaretur.*

104. Ennius, *Ann.* 502 (Vahlen[2]), quoted by Suetonius (*Aug.* 7), though it may be a gloss; see J. Gagé, *MEFR, 47* (1930), 138. In any case, a popular derivation connected "Augustus" with *augurium* and *augur,* both of which were connected with Romulus; see K. Scott, *TAPA, 56* (1925), 90.

105. Verg., *G.* 3.27; Prop., 4.6.21; Ov., *F.* 2.133 ff.; cf. *Cons.* 243–46. See also R. Getty, *CP, 45* (1950), 5–8; M. Hirst, *AJP, 47* (1926), 347 ff.; L. R. Taylor, *CR, 32* (1918), 158 ff.

106. Heinze plausibly conjectures that Horace composed *C.* 3.3 to celebrate the occasion; see *NJW, 5* (1929), 685.

castaeque damnatum Minervae
cum populo et duce fraudulento.

iam nec Lacaenae splendet adulterae 25
famosus hospes nec Priami domus
periura pugnaces Achivos
Hectoreis opibus refringit,

nostrisque ductum seditionibus
bellum resedit: protinus et gravis 30
iras et invisum nepotem,
Troica quem peperit sacerdos,

Marti redonabo. illum ego lucidas
inire sedes, discere nectaris
sucos et adscribi quietis 35
ordinibus patiar deorum."

"Troy, Troy, has been turned to dust by a fateful and unchaste judge and by a foreign woman, a city which, with its people and its deceitful leader, was handed over for punishment to me and to chaste Minerva, ever since that time when Laomedon cheated the gods of the reward he had promised them. No longer now does that infamous guest dazzle the Spartan adulteress, nor does the perjured house of Priam any longer stave off the Argives through Hector's strength, and the war spun out by our quarrels now has ended. Henceforth I shall give over my fierce wrath, and yield to Mars my hated grandson whom the Trojan priestess bore. I shall allow him to enter the shining seats of heaven, to drink the sweet nectar, and to be enrolled among the serene ranks of the gods."

The poetic parallel between Augustus and Romulus, and the contemporary political identification of the two, make it almost impossible to ignore the allegorical possibilities of Juno's speech. Theodor Mommsen, normally skeptical of such interpretations, allowed that Paris and Helen could not but awaken memories of a more recent pair of lovers.[107] Antony, like Paris, had staked all for love; both had made their beds, and had slept in them. Like Paris, he found the charms of Aphrodite more cogent than those of either wisdom or victory—and again nearly a thousand ships had been launched by a woman's face.[108] In Juno's speech the three hundred years between the fall of Troy and Romulus' apotheosis drop out of sight. The death of the past (*iam nec,* 25) and the birth of the future (*protinus,* 30) seem immediately consecutive. The time scheme is patently designed to fit more recent history. Though the correspondences remain imprecise the similarity of pattern is persuasive. In each case a state founded under evil auspices had engaged in a war involving adulterous lovers, followed by a fresh beginning. Romulus' deification signals a new kind of future for the Trojan people, one free from the *gravis iras* that had pursued them since their city's fradulent foundation. In ringing tones that anticipate the prophecies of the *Aeneid,* Juno outlines a boundless destiny for the Romans. To secure it they need only renounce any return to their fallen state:

"dum longus inter saeviat Ilion
Romamque pontus, qualibet exsules
in parte regnanto beati;
dum Priami Paridisque busto 40

insultet armentum et catulos ferae
celent inultae, stet Capitolium
fulgens triumphatisque possit
Roma ferox dare iura Medis.

. . . . . .

sed bellicosis fata Quiritibus
hac lege dico, ne nimium pii
rebusque fidentes avitae
tecta velint reparare Troiae. 60

Troiae renascens alite lugubri
fortuna tristi clade iterabitur

107. T. Mommsen, *Reden und Aufsätze* (Berlin, 1902), 173.
108. Lucan (10.60–62) compares Helen and Cleopatra. Cf. below, 218.

ducente victrices catervas
coniuge me Iovis et sorore.

ter si resurgat murus aeneus 65
auctore Phoebo, ter pereat meis
excisus Argivis, ter uxor
capta virum puerosque ploret."

"Provided that a broad sea rage between Troy and Rome, let the exiles reign happy wherever they wish; provided that the herds trample upon the grave of Priam and Paris, and the wild beasts hide their young there with impunity, then let the Capitol stand in its glory, and let fierce Rome impose laws upon the conquered Medes . . . But only on one condition do I set this destiny for the warlike citizens: let them not trust to their own power and, all too pious, attempt to rebuild the roofs of their ancestral Troy. Troy's fate, born again under evil auspices, shall again be repeated with dreadful slaughter, and I, the sister and wife of Jove, will lead again the conquering hosts. If thrice the bronze wall should rise under the auspices of Phoebus Apollo, then thrice would it perish, cut down by my Argives, thrice would the captive wife mourn her husband and children."

What is the meaning of Troy? That question beyond all others perplexes commentary upon the Ode. One explanation, distinguished by the names of Mommsen, Wilamowitz, Pasquali, and Syme, holds Troy to be, precisely, a city upon the Hellespont, and Juno's speech a warning against removing there the seat of government. Julius Caesar may have contemplated such a move, though even the amiable Suetonius reports it only as a rumor (*Caes.* 79), and Augustus is surmised to have entertained the same idea. The conjecture lacks any real foundation. Augustus had just finished a war that the Romans were encouraged to regard as a victory of West over East, and he had himself played effectively upon the fear that Antony might move the capital from Rome.[109] For Augustus to do so now would be to

109. See K. Scott, *MAAR, 11* (1923), 44.

fall certain prey to his own propaganda, nor is there any evidence that he ever considered such a step.

Unable to see Horace's Troy in a physical landscape, others have located it in a moral one. Its position has not altered markedly. Though no longer an actual Eastern city, it still stands as an incarnation of Eastern vice, as represented particularly by the adulterous lovers.[110] To think of immorality as inherently oriental has always been convenient for westerners. Yet Antony had proven himself a precocious pupil well before he went to school with the Ptolemies, and Horace, in addressing himself to such themes in other Odes, felt no need to look to Alexandria for examples.[111] Austerity had hardly characterized the declining years of the Republic; the Senate was no longer notable for its Catos. Moreover, Horace does not seem overly concerned in this case with adultery as such, but only in so far as it is a cause of war. The ethical lapses of an Antony or a Paris concerned him less than did their consequences:

> heu heu, quantus equis, quantus adest viris
> sudor, quanta moves funera Dardanae
> genti. iam galeam Pallas et aegida
> currusque et rabiem parat. [*C.* 1.15.9–12]

> Alas, alas, how great the toil at hand for horses, how great for men! What great destruction you are preparing for the Trojan nation! Even now Pallas is making ready her helmet, shield, and chariot, rousing her frenzy.

A pragmatic bias rather than indignation at "oriental" immorality controls his view of the rape of Helen. Whether or not the lines allude to the war with Egypt,[112] Horace's attitude is again not that of a moral censor but that of an implicated historian. Troy's rebuilding, we

110. Campbell, *Horace,* 110; Campbell elaborates the contrast with Roman *virtus.* Wickham, *The Works of Horace, ad C.* 3.3, sees the move to Troy as representing "the *orientalizing* of the Roman empire." Cf. J. F. D'Alton, *Horace and His Age* (London, 1917), 11.

111. Cf. *C.* 2.15, 3.6, 3.24; and the Satires, passim. In *C.* 4.5 and *C.* 4.15 Horace does not identify the immorality of the Roman past with anything alien. Cf. Sallust, *Cat.* 10–13.

112. See the edition of Kiessling-Heinze, *ad loc.* Cf. Plutarch, *Comp. Demetr. et Ant.* 3.957a; Campbell, *Horace,* 110; Wilkinson, *Horace,* 68. One scholiast,

should remember, is in the third Roman Ode associated with only one thing: *tristis clades* (62).

Even more confining is the related thesis according to which Troy represents "the Oriental tradition of unbridled despotism." [113] To write a poem celebrating Romulus, Rome's first king, would be a remarkably devious way to protest a monarchy, even for Horace. And by what obscure equation do we make Troy represent dictatorship? Priam is not a very ominous despot, and nowhere in the Odes does Horace single out Troy's government as its familiar evil. Troy's connotations are less particular. Had the Ode been written three years earlier, while Octavian was still in the East—that is, at about the time of *C.* 1.2—the theory would be more plausible. But upon his return Octavian had quickly outlawed Egyptian rites inside the *pomerium,* and had "most stubbornly" forbidden his own worship in the city.[114] Fears that he might have taken over the habits of the Ptolemies along with their country must have been less lively. By the twenties Horace could not have been so opposed to Octavian as he had been in the forties. During the intervening decade political life must have appeared as a series of lesser evils. Whatever the dangers of a single ruler—and *C.* 1.2 and *C.* 3.4 prove Horace alive to these—that form of government nevertheless offered the best hope for security. The Republic for which Horace had fought at Philippi was a thing of the past; one could only be grateful that Augustus was prepared to preserve its form. Horace was ready to urge the recalcitrant Pompeius to make his peace with great Jove, and in *C.* 3.24, the fullest indictment of Rome's domestic evils, Horace appeals for help to a single *pater patriae,* as Romulus and Julius Caesar had already been titled and as Augustus was later to be. Cicero had conceded the need for a *rector* or *moderator rei publicae,* and even such anti-Augustans as Tacitus and Dio were compelled to acknowledge that a concentration

---

followed in elaborate detail by F. Ritter, *Horatii Carmina et Epodi* (Leipzig, 1856), *ad loc.,* terms *C.* 2.15 an allegory of Antony and Cleopatra; cf. Wickham, *The Works of Horace, ad loc.* The fact that *C.* 2.15 is, as Fraenkel points out (*Horace,* 188 ff.), an adaptation of Bacchylides does not necessarily mean that it can have no contemporary reference, any more than the fact that *C.* 1.14 is an imitation of Alcaeus rules out a contemporary reference for that poem.

113. R. S. Conway, *New Studies,* 61. Cf. L. MacKay, *CR, 46* (1932), 244; K. Strodach, *CW, 29* (1935), 140.

114. Dio, 53.2.4; Suet., *Aug.* 52.

of power was indispensable: "In this way the government was changed at that time [January, 27 B.C.] for the better and in the interest of greater security; for it was no doubt quite impossible for the people to be saved under a republic." [115]

A crucial phrase for understanding the meaning of Troy is *bellicosis Quiritibus . . . nimium pii* (57–58). Strictly, we should understand it as applying only to the citizens rather than to Romulus-Augustus; they, not he, may, in their truculence, seek a return to the past.[116] *Nimium* recalls *C.* 1.2, and the third Roman Ode could be taken as redressing the fears of Octavian's excesses that Horace expressed in that poem. On the other hand, it is perhaps a mistake to insist too rigorously on the terms of the mythical framework. *Quiritibus* could be construed as a glance at Romulus-Quirinus-Augustus, and the phrase *bellicosis Quiritibus . . . nimium pii* would then become a warning that Augustus should not, out of too great filial piety, seek to imitate his father Caesar's type of quasimonarchy. Probably the phrase should not be restricted to any exclusive political meaning. In the fourth Roman Ode, praise of the ruler does not preclude a subdued warning to him, and it is likely that there is an element of admonition in *C.* 3.3 also. Yet Horace addresses himself to the people as well. Augustus had led them from the storms of the past, and now they too must prove their constancy and steadfastness of purpose in avoiding a repetition of these storms. Horace had probably seen early portions of the *Aeneid,* though it is doubtful whether the last book, which makes explicit the break with the Trojan past, had yet been written.[117] *Nimium pii,* coming at the end of the Vergilian vision of Rome's future (42–56), may well be strongly ironic. It seems to caution all the Romans alike against imitating too sedulously an ancestral regard, in the Ode's specialized sense, modeled on that of the *pius Aeneas.*

We need not make Juno a lobbyist in order that her speech have a contemporary meaning. She is less a politician than a prophet. In

115. Cic., *Att.* 8.11; Dio, 53.19.1; Tac., *Hist.* 1; cf. Florus, 2.14.5–6.

116. The theory of Kiessling, *Horatius, Oden und Epoden, ad loc.,* that Troy represents the decadent and unworkable government of the Republic, is perhaps the most plausible if Troy must be viewed as an exclusively political symbol. Cf. H. Plüss, *Horazstudien,* 211 ff.; W. Y. Sellar, *Horace and the Elegiac Poets,* 155–56; Wilkinson, *Horace,* 73.

117. See M. M. Crump, *The Growth of the Aeneid* (Oxford, 1920), 100 ff.

announcing Augustus' coming apotheosis (11–12), Horace sets the mood for the Ode, which, beyond any of the political poems in the first three books, celebrates the future. To make the Ode's meaning depend upon the precise structure of a fallen "Troy" is to falsify its perspective. The idea of redemption is most important, and exactly what it is that the Romans have been redeemed from is secondary. More significant than the political or moral structure of the past is the hope that the past is finished; Juno's salute to the future takes an additional emphasis from her somber warning of the disaster any relaxation will bring. Troy represents no more—and no less—than the weight of all the evil elements in the past. Its significance is confined to no single political party or moral failing. Rather, it embodies the whole concept of the Romans' fallen state, one that was evidenced particularly by the civil wars. The oracular rhythms of Juno's *requiescat* (*ter si resurgat . . . ter pereat*) are apocalyptic rather than specific, and we need not attempt to identify the occasions to which she refers.[118] Her speech is not a cryptogram for history, but rather the mythical expression of a political mood. In earlier poems Horace persistently returned to the idea that Rome labored under some divine curse. The adjective *fatalis,* as applied to Paris (19), already suggests a context larger than that of mere narrative.[119] We remember the *acerba fata* of the seventh Epode, the *devotus sanguis* of the sixteenth, the *nondum expiatus cruor* of *C.* 2.1, and the hope of redemption in *C.* 1.2. By 27 B.C. the cycle has turned decisively, and the third Roman Ode hopefully celebrates the expiation of past evils. A feast is preeminently the image of reconciliation, and it is significant that the apotheosis of both Romulus and Augustus should take that form. Romulus redeems Rome from Juno's *gravis iras;* Augustus, the second Romulus, has all but redeemed it from its *acerba fata.* The Ode dramatizes a feeling only, not a scheme.[120] But in the myth of sin,

118. Campbell (*Horace,* 111), for instance, attempts to find the specific occasions to which Juno refers.

119. Cf. *fatale monstrum* (*C.* 1.37.21). *Fatale,* as applied to Cleopatra, may suggest that the Egyptian war, too, was part of the punishment imposed upon the Romans by their *acerba fata* (*Epod.* 7.17). *Monstrum* also has associations with the idea of something sent by fate; see Fraenkel, *Horace,* 160; cf. *nova monstra* (*C.* 1.2.6).

120. Horace in *C.* 3.3 clearly cannot assign the primal fall to Romulus' murder of Remus, as he does in *Epod.* 7. It is interesting to find, in the years

war, redemption, and rebirth, Horace's generation could find a parable for their own experience, and for their hopes as well. All that was now needed was for Augustus to show his *constantia* and *iustitia* in ruling both his people and himself, thus preventing Rome from drifting once more into the past that she had known.

Modern readers have found it easy to dismiss Juno's command as simply an attempt to save divine face.[121] But among Horace's contemporaries her plea for a break with the past would have found a more responsive audience. Other poets were similarly proclaiming that some decisive grace had been achieved, some watershed attained. Vergil's Aeneas, in many ways a prototype for Augustus, wins remission of Juno's anger and his own semideification as an *Indig*es much in the style of Horace's Romulus. Provided that Trojan name, tongue, and habit be forgotten, stipulates Vergil's Juno, the Romans may expect only divine favor henceforth.[122] Juno's speech answers the despair of the first Georgic (501–02) much as her counterpart in the third Roman Ode replies to the anguish of *C.* 1.2. Each poet, in the later work, proclaims that the tyranny of the past is exhausted. *Iam satis,* no longer a prayer, has become a declaration. Even Propertius

after Actium, a general rehabilitation of Romulus. Vergil assigns the original sin of the Roman race to Laomedon (*G.* 1.502); later he refers to Romulus' murder of his brother only in happy retrospect (*A.* 1.292–93). Ovid tactfully lays the murder of Remus to Celer, presenting Romulus as grief-stricken (*F.* 4.8.33 ff.). Propertius (3.9.50) makes the murder a symbolic myth illustrating the inviolability of Rome's walls. Contrast the older version: Cic., *Off.* 3.10.41.

121. Thus we read that Juno's command against rebuilding Troy, "which saves her dignity and her consistency, is sufficiently explained by the poet's desire to seem true to life"; see C. L. Smith, *Odes and Epodes of Horace, ad loc.* Cf. C. H. Moore, *Horace's Odes and Epodes, ad loc.;* P. Shorey, *Horace, Odes and Epodes, ad loc.;* Fraenkel, *Horace,* 269. The often-compared myths in *C.* 3.11 and *C.* 3.27 are similar primarily in formal terms, all being presented as lengthy addresses. But there is not a comparable density of meaning in *C.* 3.11 and *C.* 3.27.

122. Verg., *A.* 12.794 ff.; cf. *A.* 1.279–82. The line *occidit occideritque sinas cum nomine Troia* (*A.* 12.828) has been often cited, especially since the observations of R. S. Conway (*New Studies,* 60), to corroborate the idea that Vergil, like Horace, is protesting against a removal of the capital to the Hellespont. We need suppose nothing so specific was in Vergil's mind; cf. *A.* 6.62 ff. for a similar theme of war, connected with a foreign marriage, followed by a final peace. Juno's speeches in both Horace and Vergil may go back to that in the first book of Ennius' *Annals* (65, Vahlen[2]); cf. Ov., *Met.* 14.812; *F.* 2.485.

makes at least a perfunctory contribution to the legend: *Troia cades et Troica Roma resurges!* (4.1.87). As early as the sixteenth Epode, Horace, with dim hopes of success, had adjured the *melior pars* of the Romans to break with its present Iron Age.[123] Would they not take an oath never to return? (25 ff.). Juno's demand exactly, but by now the break has become a matter of history rather than a golden potential. The *Carmen Saeculare,* itself a definitive symbol of renewal, repeats the conviction of a renewed destiny. The theme is that of *C.* 3.3, but now the figures are Vergilian, perhaps influenced by the last books of the *Aeneid.*[124] A *castus Aeneas,* in an almost ritualistic purification, leads a band of survivors to a new city founded under more favorable auspices (39 ff.). A *melior pars,* as it were, has made the voyage to the Isles of the Blest, which are now discovered to be in Rome itself (49–60). Vergil had hopefully saluted the same change from Iron Age to Golden in the fourth Eclogue, and by the time of the *Aeneid* he could be certain enough to speak through Jove's own lips.[125]

Though the figures and symbols of the various passages differ, one theme remains constant: Rome's break with the past. The third Roman Ode, one might almost say, is about chronology. From the Epodes to the fourth book of Odes time itself remains an abiding concern. *Altera iam . . .* the first words of *Epod.* 16 define the substance of its meaning: Rome is caught in an accursed past. An equal despair is implicit in the powerful present tense of *quo, quo scelesti ruitis?* (*Epod.* 7.1). No real future exists. There is only an impossible idyll of the Isles of the Blest. In the Ode to the Ship of State the dominance of past over present continues unabated: *O navis, referent in mare te novi fluctus* (*C.* 1.14.1–2). Even Horace's commitment is a *peccavi* rather than an expression of hope: *nuper sollicitum . . . nunc desiderium.* In all three poems the present appears as a continuation of the past,[126] and the same is true of the first half of the Ode to Octavian, *iam satis.* Only with the possible arrival of some

123. *Epod.* 16.65; cf. *dura aetas* (*C.* 1.35.34).

124. Might the last stanza of *C.* 3.3 signal Horace's withdrawal from such grand national themes in favor of Vergil?

125. Verg., *A.* 1.291 ff.; cf. *A.* 6.791; Hor., *C.* 4.2.37–40, 4.5.17 ff.

126. Seen in this sequence, the strong temporal expression *nunc est bibendum* (*C.* 1.37.1) has even greater impact.

redeemer (30 ff.) does the mood of the poem change, though even the future may be tinged by memories of present sins: *audiet pugnas vitio parentum rara iuventus* (23–24). The balance of past and future achieves greater serenity in *C.* 3.4. The Giants have fallen, the conqueror is even now resting from his efforts, and is soon to emerge "re-created" by the Muses. The sense of harmony and expectancy becomes definitive in the third Roman Ode. We hear of Augustus' coming apotheosis, and listen as Juno predicts Rome's future glories. Retrospect has been abandoned for prospect, and the present is seen no longer as an extension of the past but as a preamble to the future. Only a willful turning back will encounter divine wrath again. By the fourth book the limits of the future have been reached. Nothing greater than Augustus can be conceived even if the centuries should bring again the Golden Age:

> quo nihil maius meliusve terris
> fata donavere bonique divi
> nec dabunt, quamvis redeant in aurum
> tempora priscum. [*C.* 4.2.37–40]

> The Fates and benevolent gods have given to the earth nothing greater or better than Caesar, nor will they, even if the ages should return to their pristine gold.

Here is the dream future of the sixteenth Epode, now become present reality. The *arva beata* lie nowhere but in Rome itself—by now the iteration is even somewhat weary.

For the establishment of the *Pax Augusta* and the transformation of the Roman state, the early twenties are crucial years. In Horace's political Odes, the poems of this period, *C.* 1.2, *C.* 3.4, and *C.* 3.3, mark a corresponding division. On one side lie the themes and images of the Epodes and early Odes, on the other those of the *Carmen Saeculare* and the fourth book. The prevailing images for the period from Philippi to Actium are those of wild animals and storm. The sixteenth Epode suggested leaving Rome to the boars and ravening wolves (19–20); the seventh proclaimed the Romans even worse than wolves or lions. In the storm of *C.* 1.14 or the tempest of *Epod.* 13

Horace found an equally somber reflection of Rome's condition. The latter poem left the hope that some god might change things for the better, but by *C.* 1.2 the whole sky seemed rather to have descended. Rome was racked by convulsions unknown since the age of Pyrrha, when peaceful animal creation had been all but destroyed, or perverted into *nova monstra* (6). But now appears the hope that the disruptions of nature may yield to a supernatural control: perhaps some god really will change things for the better. Implicit in "the son of *alma Maia*" are the themes of divinity, peace, and rebirth which henceforth replace those of destruction. In the *almae Musae,* intent on re-creating Caesar, they become still more prominent. The bestial Giants, upheaving all nature in their revolt, have fallen, and in the new harmony even they may be redeemed. By 27 B.C. Augustus' divinity was assured, and the images of an iron past have been relegated to Troy, happily abandoned to wild animals (*C.* 3.3.40–42). Only an act of wanton reversion would make it necessary to hear of them again. The danger was avoided. "Golden Plenty from full horn has poured her fruits on Italy." [127] Themes of fertility and divine favor, most fully realized by the *Carmen Saeculare,* alone remain. Gone are the winter storms of *C.* 1.2, and spring is now the proper emblem for the reborn age and its founder:

> lucem redde tuae, dux bone, patriae.
> instar veris enim voltus ubi tuus
> adfulsit populo, gratior it dies
> et soles melius nitent. [*C.* 4.5.5–8]

> Bring back the light to your land, good leader; for once your countenance, spring's image, has shone upon your people, then day comes fairer, then the sun shines more splendidly.

By the fourth book Augustus has become virtually an incarnation of Lucretius' *alma Venus,* bringing peace and plenty to Rome. The storms of the past have been stilled and even brute creation, no longer a symbol of fallen nature, now gives evidence of divine grace:

127. *Ep.* 1.12.28–29, written in 19–18 B.C. Cf. *C. S.* 59–60; *C.* 4.15.4.

tutus bos etenim rura perambulat,
nutrit rura Ceres almaque Faustitas,
pacatum volitant per mare navitae. [*C.* 4.5.17–19]

The ox in safety wanders the fields, Ceres and nourishing Prosperity increase the crops, and sailors fly over a sea made peaceful.

Later Odes

The thematic clarity with which Horace conveys Rome's national development from a fallen to a redeemed state makes it easy to overlook the change in the quality of his own response. In the years after 27 B.C. there was ever more for him to applaud, yet at the same time there was ever less to appeal to his imagination. When Augustus returned from Spain in 24 B.C., Horace celebrated the occasion by announcing a feast:

dic et argutae properet Neaerae
murreum nodo cohibere crinem:
si per invisum mora ianitorem
   fiet—abito.

lenit albescens animos capillus
litium et rixae cupidos protervae:
non ego hoc ferrem calidus iuventa
   consule Planco. [*C.* 3.14.21–28]

Tell clear-voiced Neaera to hasten and bind her chestnut hair into a knot; but if any delay is caused by a hateful doorkeeper, then leave. My whitening hair mellows a spirit once fond of strife and bold quarrels. I would not have borne such a thing in my hot youth, in the consulship of Plancus.

The "licentious vigor" [128] of these last two stanzas has often been deemed inappropriate in a poem to "Caesar, who holds the earth in

128. T. E. Page, *Horace's Odes and Epodes* (London, 1895), *ad loc.*

sway" (15–16). Yet the lines have a more serious undercurrent. *Consule Planco* is not an innocent elegancy for "the past." Plancus' consulship fell in 42 B.C., the year of Philippi. At that time, Horace wryly recalls, his spirit was quicker to strife—now he is more equable. The banquet, pointedly dissociated from the martial stubbornness of youth, recalls that which welcomed Pompeius (*C.* 2.7). Its significance is now explicit, as Horace views his political shift in terms of a comprehensive decorum of age and natural change.

Into Horace's renunciation of his more impetuous past there creeps an almost wistful note and he seems to falter at the very change he announces. The poem as a whole rings a little hollow. A certain irony glances from his description of Livia as *unico gaudens marito* (5), for the ambiguous meaning of *unicus* must have reminded readers that Augustus was in fact Livia's second husband, and that his courtship had been anything but edifying.[129] No more wars, to be sure; no more revolutions, no need to fear death by violence (13 ff.). Yet it is hard to be enthusiastic about these virtues once they can be taken for granted, and Horace's praise seems negative and mechanical. To compare his reception of Octavian after Actium, in *C.* 1.2 and *C.* 3.4, is to be struck by how pale his response has become. The absorbing promises and dangers of that time have ebbed away leaving only Augustus *tenens terras* (15–16). We feel something of the dissatisfaction that we do at the close of the *Aeneid,* which ends not with the triumphant bang we expect, but with the pathetic death of Turnus: *vitaque cum gemitu fugit indignata sub umbras.* Throughout the poem *res Romanae* become ever more shadowed by *lacrimae rerum,* by what Arnold was to call "the Vergilian cry, the sense of tears in mortal things." The tension between the two is what makes the *Aeneid* so moving; nothing so profound perplexes Horace's later political Odes. Only a vague discontent troubles *C.* 3.14. There was, after all, no political alternative. But at the same time that Horace reaffirms his allegiance to Augustus, his tones suggest that his allegiance was itself becoming jaded.

While Augustus was still in Spain, Aelius Gallus led an expedition against Arabia in which Horace's friend Iccius planned to take part.

129. Augustus had forced Livia, while still pregnant, to divorce her husband Tiberius Claudius Nero and marry him (Suet., *Tib.* 4).

In anticipation of Iccius' departure Horace wrote a short Ode to him (*C.* 1.29), and though not an important poem it is suggestive of Horace's feelings at the time. Again there is a sense of disenchantment with Rome's national progress. To take part in the state's expansion is now, it appears, to choose the less noble path: Iccius had promised better (16). The raid on Arabia was baldly financial, for its "rich jewels" (1–2) had attracted other eyes than those of Horace's friend. Horace's satiric banter is at the same time almost melancholy, and we find a new sympathy for the children soon to be captives:

quae tibi virginum
sponso necato barbara serviet,
puer quis ex aula capillis
ad cyathum statuetur unctis

doctus sagittas tendere Sericas
arcu paterno? [*C.* 1.29.5–10]

Which of the girls, her husband slain, will be your barbarian slave? What boy from the court will, with perfumed locks, serve as your cupbearer, though taught to stretch Seric arrows upon his father's bow?

Possit Roma ferox dare iura Medis, Juno had declaimed. The heroic concept of the Empire's progress has become less winning in its subsequent details.

The coolness incipient in these poems is not, probably, political but imaginative. Horace's prayers for Augustus' safety never falter. Without him a return to chaos would have been certain, and the thought of civil war was enough to overcome any scruples for Arabian children (*C.* 1.35.33 ff.). But if the change that Rome had undergone could still command Horace's allegiance, it could no longer compel his enthusiasm in the same way. From the sober joy of *C.* 4.6, an introduction to the *Carmen Saeculare,* we know how pleased he was to be chosen as author of that work. Written for public performance at the games of 17 B.C., the *Carmen Saeculare* was in effect an anniversary hymn to Rome's growth and renewal. From the author of *C.* 1.12 or

C. 3.3 we might expect an immense response—but our expectations are frustrated. The processional vision of Rome's growth from tenuous beginnings to the world's greatest power fires him briefly:

> Roma si vestrum est opus Iliaeque
> litus Etruscum tenuere turmae,
> iussa pars mutare lares et urbem
>   sospite cursu,
>
> cui per ardentem sine fraude Troiam
> castus Aeneas patriae superstes
> liberum munivit iter, daturus
>   plura relictis:

But after this his descent is dismal:

> di, probos mores docili iuventae,
> di, senectuti placidae quietem,
> Romulae genti date remque prolemque
>   et decus omne. [37–48]

If Rome be your accomplishment, and if Trojan bands hold the Etruscan shore, that part which was commanded to change their household gods and their city by an auspicious path, they for whom untainted Aeneas, the survivor of his own country's downfall, unharmed made a free path through burning Troy, destined to give more than was left behind: then, gods, give wholesome customs to the youth to learn, give peace to placid old age, and give wealth and offspring and every ornament to the people of Rome.

The catalogues ring wooden and dutiful as he celebrates the laws he had himself evaded:

> diva, producas subolem patrumque
> prosperes decreta super iugandis
> feminis prolisque novae feraci
>   lege marita. [17–20]

> Goddess, bring forth our offspring, and bless the decrees of the Senate relating to the marriage of women and to the matrimonial law, fruitful in new children.

The fact that a chorus of boys and girls sang the verses may have improved the effect, and, considering the occasion and function of the *Carmen Saeculare,* it is perhaps unjust to be harsh with it. The organization is admirably symmetrical, the old verities are gracefully invoked, and the appeal to both past and future is satisfactorily sonorous—surely the audience was not disappointed. Yet when we compare this work to such a poem as the fourth Roman Ode the falling off in quality is apparent. By now the state's perpetual growth, even to the attempted enforcement of marriage, had become sobering rather than stirring. Juno's warning had been heeded, and her prophecies fulfilled. But even as Rome had achieved its destiny, that destiny had become somehow less splendid. And the time when Horace felt he could play a significant part in the affairs of the gods was past. Now he was simply their laureate.

The failure of state subjects to quicken Horace's imagination becomes marked in the fourth book. Suetonius (*Vit. Hor.*) asserts that Augustus forced Horace to compose the Odes upon Drusus and Tiberius, the emperor's stepsons. The poems do not discredit Suetonius' statement. The ἐπινίκιον on Drusus (*C.* 4.4), the book's most elaborate work, is, to be sure, deliberately inflated in style. Yet the fact that Horace so planned it does not make it any more winning. He seems to be pulling out a series of standard stops, letting conventionally epic language and similes carry him on. Certainly the parenthesis on the arms of the Vindelici is a grotesquely humorous bit of Pindaric padding:

> videre Raetis bella sub Alpibus
> Drusum gerentem Vindelici; quibus
> mos unde deductus per omne
> tempus Amazonia securi
>
> dextras obarmet, quaerere distuli,
> nec scire fas est omnia . . . [17–22]

> Drusus was seen waging war beneath the Alps by the Rhaetian Vindelici—whence was derived their custom, kept since time immemorial, of arming their right hands with the Amazonian battle ax, I have not asked, nor, indeed, is it right to know all things . . .

"For what is rhetoric," asked Yeats, "but the will trying to do the work of the imagination?"

Though Horace's language is manifestly derivative, he uses it in such a way as to rouse an equivocal response. Drusus is seen as an eagle driven by "love of food and battle" upon the sheepfolds, or as a lion plunging upon the kid still drinking from its mother's udder (9 ff.). "We hate the hawk because he lives ever in arms, and the wolves that go always against the trembling flock," wrote Ovid (*A. A.* 2.147). We need not go so far as "hatred" in order to sympathize with the savage Drusus' victims, the newest prey to Rome's growth. Horace allows his similes to undercut his praise; we remember the description of Caesar in the Cleopatra Ode (*C.* 1.37.17–20). Nor is the tribute to Drusus' ancestors, the conquerors of Hannibal, altogether simple in its emotional effect:

> dixitque tandem perfidus Hannibal:
> "cervi, luporum praeda rapacium,
> sectamur ultro quos opimus
> fallere et effugere est triumphus." [49–52]

> Finally perfidious Hannibal spoke: "Like stags, the prey of rapacious wolves, we follow of our own accord those whom it would be the greatest of triumphs to avoid and flee."

Hannibal becomes a stag fighting against wolves. Even though the metaphor comes from the perfidious Carthaginian—the shift in viewpoint may remind us of Aeschylus' *Persae*—it tends to displace the formal alignment of our sympathies. The following comparison between the Trojan race and a growing tree (57–60) flashes out with momentary beauty, recalling the description of Marcellus: *crescit occulto velut arbor aevo fama Marcelli* (*C.* 1.12.45–46). But then the character of the imagery alters:

> "non hydra secto corpore firmior
> vinci dolentem crevit in Herculem
> monstrumve submisere Colchi
> maius Echioniaeve Thebae." [61–64]

"The Hydra did not grow more strong with each blow of Hercules, refusing to yield, nor did the Colchians or Echionian Thebes send forth a greater monster."

The Trojan stock becomes a monstrous growth, a Hydra, or armed warriors sprung from the dragon's teeth. In opposing it, Hannibal stands forth a Herculean figure; nowhere in previous poems is he so sympathetically viewed. He seems to win Horace's imagination almost in the way Cleopatra or Cato did, a figure of lonely splendor resisting the inevitable. And the fact that the image is Hannibal's own may mitigate its force, but it does not nullify it. Aeschylus' Persians never conceived of Athens in comparable terms.

C. 4.4 is in a way the next generation's fourth Roman Ode. The earlier poem's praise of *vis temperata* (*C.* 3.4.66) reappears in the generalized praise of Drusus:

> doctrina sed vim promovet insitam
> rectique cultus pectora roborant. [33–34]

But training improves inborn power, and proper cultivation strengthens the soul.

Yet the very closeness of language brings out the difference in concept all the more clearly. The poems belong to worlds that are as distinct imaginatively as they are politically. The sense of personal commitment and urgency that inspired the fourth Roman Ode has disappeared, and the union of *vis* with *doctrina* or *consiliis* (*C.* 4.4.24) is now but a discreet compliment to Augustus for wisely educating his stepson's native strength. Only the shell remains of the terms that were so tensely alive in the fourth Roman Ode. The great issues of that earlier period had now disappeared. With them had gone the poet's sense of crucial involvement that had produced a work as vital as *C.* 3.4.

Tactfully placed to succeed the Ode on Drusus is a poem in praise of Augustus, appropriately studded with echoes of Ennius' tributes to Romulus.[130] The serenity Horace evokes is itself a quiet eulogy:

> tutus bos etenim rura perambulat,
> nutrit rura Ceres almaque Faustitas,
> pacatum volitant per mare navitae,
> culpari metuit fides,
>
> nullis polluitur casta domus stupris,
> mos et lex maculosum edomuit nefas,
> laudantur simili prole puerperae,
> culpam poena premit comes. [17–24]

> The ox in safety wanders the fields, Ceres and nourishing Prosperity increase the crops, and sailors fly over a sea made peaceful; faith shrinks from censure, and the chaste home is polluted by no adultery; custom and law have conquered tainted sin, childbearing women are praised for children that resemble their fathers, and punishment presses close upon guilt.

Horace's verse has assimilated itself to the lulling rhythms of a land at peace, and the effect is as saddening in one way as it is brilliant in another. Familiarity had made the *Pax Augusta* less stirring, if no less welcome. In the early twenties, order itself, if only because it had been for so long a stranger, could command the most magnificent of salutes. Fifteen years later the fourth Roman Ode's vision of peace and harmony has had time to subside into a picture of the *tutus bos*. The "Fortune of Rome" had become manifest: "even as Aphrodite, when she crossed the Eurotas, laid aside her mirror and her ornaments and her cestus, and took spear and shield to adorn herself for Lycurgus' eyes, so when, after her sojournings with Per-

130. Compare *C.* 4.5.1–2, 5, 15, with Ennius, *Ann.* 110–14 (Vahlen[2]). Horace's echoes confirm the identification he had hopefully postulated in *C.* 3.3.

sians and Assyrians, with Macedonians, Τύχη approached the Palatine and crossed the Tiber, she laid aside her wings and took off her sandals and left behind her ball, the symbol of fickleness and change." [131] The Golden Age was no longer a fitful gleam but a refulgent reality, and one could only be quietly grateful to the man who had created it. Horace remained alive to the danger of a too lofty ruler longer than most of his contemporaries, and as late as *C.* 1.12 he had reminded Augustus that only Jove was supreme. But that danger had been avoided or assimilated, and now it was easier to acquiesce in the semidivinity that Augustus had won, and join in pouring a libation to him at the second course.[132]

Horace never swerved from the consequences of his political commitment to Octavian, and there is no deep disaffection from the changes that time brought. But there is an unmistakable falling off in the quality of his imaginative commitment. The tough and massive structure of the semiallegorical Odes of the early twenties was necessary to sustain the complexities of Horace's attitude toward an already complex situation. In like fashion, the easy similes and lifeless catalogues of the last book are symptomatic of the relaxed and almost perfunctory response that was by then all that was called for. Gone were the conflicts that beset the years around Actium, conflicts between commitment and withdrawal, between the promise and the perils of the new leader. The stability of a Golden Age does not demand a complicated response. One need not speak very meaningfully to its rulers or citizens, but only loudly, explicitly, and politely. The exaggerated humility of Horace's refusal to Pindarize—*tum meae, si quid loquar audiendum, vocis accedet bona pars* (*C.* 4.2.45–46)—should not lead us to discount the truth that it preserves. His voice was in fact now a representative tribute. The days when the *almae Musae* could preside in an active way over politics no less than poetry were gone, and gone too was the imaginative intensity that brightened them. The time, in effect, had passed for Horace's kind of political verse. Now it was ready for an Ovid.

131. Plutarch, *Moralia* 317f, cited by Wickham, *Works of Horace, ad C.* 1.35.

132. *C.* 4.5.32. It is now Augustus who is *optime custos* (*C.* 4.5.2; cf. *C.* 4.15.17). Contrast Horace's emphatic reminder of Jove's supreme power in an earlier Ode: *gentis humanae pater atque custos* (*C.* 1.12.49).

V

THE WORLD OF NATURE: TIME AND CHANGE

NATURE AS A MORAL METAPHOR

DISCUSSIONS of Horace's treatment of nature have so tended toward the bucolic that the writer whom they present seems more nearly a farmer than a poet. His claim to be a *ruris amator* (*Ep.* 1.10.2) has been singled out for acrimonious debate, with the landscape of the second Epode providing the most common site for scholarly alarums and critical excursions. We are alternately invited to a kindred enthusiasm or to a tolerant skepticism as to the sincerity of his protestations. Sellar and Tyrrell, writing shortly before the turn of the century, assumed conflicting positions, and thus dramatized the issue both for their own and for later generations. By their arguments they seem to have legislated the very vocabulary for subsequent disputes, and charges of artificiality or insincerity are still leveled against the defense of a "keen eye" or "lively appreciation," as Horace is alternately identified with town or country mouse.

The quarrel has obscured the fact that, in the Odes at least, Horace's interest in nature is seldom pure, and that sincerity is often irrelevant. Those championing Horace's love of the country in and for itself have proved jealous defenders. They offer, for instance, the description of a ripening grape in the Ode to Lalage's lover: [1]

1. See W. Y. Sellar, *The Roman Poets of the Augustan Age: Horace and the Elegiac Poets,* 182, and, more generally, J. W. Duff, *A Literary History of Rome* (London, 1953), 394–96.

tolle cupidinem
inmitis uvae: iam tibi lividos
distinguet autumnus racemos
purpureo varius colore. [*C.* 2.5.9–12]

Banish your desire for the unripe grape; soon will many-colored autumn touch the bluish clusters with purple.

The lines are, to be sure, evidence of the poet's susceptibility to nature's beauty. Yet they are also a moral warning against such susceptibility, for the "unripe grape" is a metaphor for a still maturing girl. Horace is less concerned here with paying a tribute to physical nature than he is with making it an attribute of human nature. The two are not, of course, mutually exclusive, and to be aware of the second is not to deny the first. Perhaps the nonliteral character of Horace's interest has been underemphasized because it seems so familiar. Together with myth, nature provided the classical world with a grammar in which it could construe any experience. One appealed to a common tradition, the other to common knowledge, or even common sense. Yet it remains to ask if there is a discernible pattern behind Horace's analogies. What aspects of nature does he characteristically invoke? And what, if anything, does this imply as to his view of human nature?

Insofar as nature is a standard for human behavior in the Satires and Epodes it usually represents a static order. Most common are comparisons with animals, almost proverbial statements of fixed relationships. A frog can never swell himself to the size of a cow, nor an ass race in the Campus Martius; the wolf attacks with its teeth, the ox with its heels; stroke the steed clumsily and it will kick; Horace's anxiety for Maecenas is as natural as a mother bird's for her young, his hatred of an anonymous freedman as inevitable as a lamb's for a wolf; civil war is as unnatural as lions preying on lions. Once the analogies assume the form of ἀδύνατα, the ultimate statement of an unalterable order: the Romans should no more return from the Blessed Isles than rocks should swim, mountains move, rivers run uphill, or tigers lie down with deer.[2] The stable world that such analogies create is natural to the genres of satire and epode, which

2. *S.* 2.3.314 ff., 1.1.90, 2.1.55, 2.1.20; *Epod.* 1.19, 4.1, 7.11, 16.25.

are primarily concerned with asserting forms for human relationships. Their assumptions are social rather than individual; thus death, the most private of all concerns, is rarely mentioned.[3]

The Odes, more personal in their address, appeal to a different nature and a different kind of order. Storm and calm, flowing rivers, the changing moon, growing plants, the seasons—these are the persistent analogies. We leave the world of static relationships for that of alternation, progress, growth and decay, a more private world of change, time, and age. Horace tends to reserve natural images with stable connotations, such as epic similes, for his more public Odes. The Roman youth is a bloody lion in combat; Paris will flee Diomede as a deer the wolf; Drusus will sweep down upon the enemy like an eagle upon the sheepfold.[4] The more private poems use the same kind of simile with quite different intent:

> Vitas inuleo me similis, Chloe,
> quaerenti pavidam montibus aviis
> matrem non sine vano
> aurarum et silvae metu.
>
> nam seu mobilibus veris inhorruit 5
> adventus foliis seu virides rubum
> dimovere lacertae,
> et corde et genibus tremit.
>
> atqui non ego te tigris ut aspera
> Gaetulusve leo frangere persequor: 10
> tandem desine matrem
> tempestiva sequi viro. [*C.* 1.23]

> You shun me like a fawn, Chloe, that through the wild mountains seeks its fearful mother, not without foolish fear of the winds and the forest. For whether spring's approach ruffled the swaying bushes, or green lizards made

3. See above, 87–88.

4. *C.* 3.2.11 ff., 1.15.29 ff., 4.4.1 ff. When Horace uses images relating to weather in the political Odes, the point of comparison is, in general, not the certainty of change but rather the intensity of storm (*C.* 1.2.1 ff., 1.14.1 ff.) or of calm (*C.* 4.5.5–8).

> the bramble crackle, she trembles with fear in heart and limbs. And yet I do not pursue you in order to crush you like some fierce tiger or Gaetulian lion; come now, since you are ripe for a husband, cease at last to follow your mother.

Pursuer and pursued, raging lion and timid fawn: the formulation is an amatory commonplace. Yet Horace touches upon it only to repudiate it (*non ego,* 9). The second stanza already suggests the different use to which Horace turns the conventional simile. Chloe flees to her mother for protection not from a tiger or a lion, but from the spring itself. The lines, often cited as evidence of Horace's sharp eye for external nature, describe as well the springtime of the affections, a period of growth, pubescence, and love. Chloe, whose name is equivalent to "green shoot" (χλόη), is *tempestiva* (12), "ripe," or "seasonable." Bentley's attempt to amend *veris . . . adventus* (5–6) to *vepris . . . ad ventum* ignores the Ode's controlling metaphor, which is a seasonal one. Just as a fawn should forget her mother and take the spring with joy, so should Chloe acknowledge her own seasonable age and leave her mother for a man. The static associations of fawn and tiger are forgotten, and the animal image becomes the vehicle for quite a different statement.[5]

Horace's concentration here on nature's changing aspect is symptomatic rather than isolated. It was, we remember, by an obliviousness to nature's changes, to the black breezes lurking behind the sea's fair face, that Pyrrha's *gracilis puer* marked himself out for emotional shipwreck (*C.* 1.5). The crucial word in that poem is perhaps *insolens* (8). It does not mean "insolent," as we use it, but preserves the radical sense of "unaccustomed." [6] The youth's fond hope that Pyrrha will remain constant is, in the poem's fanciful context, as culpable a blindness to time's transformations as is that of Chloe. We might equally well recall the advice to Plancus:

5. Contrast the conventional use of tiger and deer in *Epod.* 16.31.

6. From *soleo;* thus Milton translates it "unwonted" (see above, 51). Cf. *insolenti laetitia* (*C.* 2.3.3), where the sense is practically "joy not accommodating itself to change." On *C.* 1.5 see above, 66, 144 ff.

albus ut obscuro deterget nubila caelo
saepe Notus neque parturit imbris

perpetuos, sic tu sapiens finire memento
tristiam vitaeque labores
molli, Plance, mero . . . [*C.* 1.7.15–19]

As the fair south wind often clears the clouds from a lowering sky, nor does it always breed showers, so must you, Plancus, wisely remember to put an end to your sadness and to the labors of life with gentle wine . . .

or that to Murena:

informis hiemes reducit
Iuppiter, idem

submovet; non, si male nunc, et olim
sic erit. [*C.* 2.10.15–18]

Jupiter brings back the shapeless winters, but he also takes them away; if things go badly now, they will not always be the same.

Plancus' sullen *tristitia* is as unaccommodating as Chloe's coyness, Murena's single-mindedness, or the fatuousness of Pyrrha's lover. All alike are judged and found wanting in their refusal to adapt themselves to nature's changes.

The elegiac poets tended to move exclusively in the world created by their own emotional fiat. To so insulated a view Horace was instinctively opposed, and in an Ode to the poet Valgius (*C.* 2.9) he sets out to alter it. Valgius is frozen with grief for his dead friend Mystes, and Horace berates him in a series of diagrammatically straightforward analogies. "No rain lasts forever; ice in time melts; winter gales pass—only you never abate your tearful moans. Cease now from bewailing the past, and take up a subject better suited to the present." *Non semper . . . tu semper urges flebilibus modis . . . desine mollium tandem querellarum.* Special reasons for Horace's aloofness toward the elegiac poets have often been discovered, ranging from political disapproval to personal animosity. Yet we need look no further than this Ode to understand his distaste for their *flebiles modi* (9). The elegists treat a part of life as though it were the whole; for them love is the sum of experience and grief an eternal attribute. And in such an attitude Horace saw a perversion of human nature that had no sanction in nature itself.

Tibullus excites the same criticism as Valgius, though Horace's language is more affectionate (*C.* 1.33). *Albi, ne doleas plus nimio memor / inmitis Glycerae, neu miserabilis / decantes elegos.* Tibullus' monolithic melancholy over one "unripe" constitutes a double lapse from nature's standards. Glycera's age makes her an inappropriate match, and Tibullus' unceasing laments affirm the same commitment to a vanished past as did those of Valgius. *Ne doleas plus nimio* voices the same warning as did Horace's *tu semper* to Valgius. The rigid sorrow of both elegists prevents their acceptance of the world as it naturally is; they see life not as a never-ending progress but as a set of static relationships. As though to emphasize the constant paradoxes of love, every stanza of the Ode turns upon an oxymoron: *inmitis Glycerae . . . capreae lupis . . . saevo ioco . . . grata compede.* Instead of fastening steadfastly upon one moment in life's kaleidoscopic pattern, Tibullus should rather yield to its changes, consoling himself with the thought that his disappointment is far from unique. Playing the role of a *praeceptor amoris,* as befits an Ode to an elegiac poet, Horace cites examples to prove the communal character of Tibullus' misfortune, and to rebuke the lack of perspective that Tibullus' excessive grief demonstrates. Lycoris loves Cyrus, explains Horace, and Cyrus, Pholoe; but goats shall sooner mate with wolves than Pholoe yield to Cyrus. *Sic visum Veneri* (10): Horace himself had been initiated into the way of the world when, entangled by the freedwoman Myrtale, he had missed his chance of a happier love:

> ipsum me melior cum peteret Venus,
> grata detinuit compede Myrtale
> libertina, fretis acrior Hadriae
>   curvantis Calabros sinus. [*C.* 1.33.13–16]

> I myself, when a better love sought me out, was held fast in Myrtale's beguiling bonds; a freedwoman, she, more tempestuous than the straits of the Adriatic where it hollows into bays the Calabrian shore.

Pasquali has seen a source for the Ode in a short poem of Moschus [7] which records a similar chain of unrequited loves and ends with the wordly moral that you should love only those who love you. Horace is less immediately practical. He simply presents to Tibullus a picture of the way things are, asking him to accept them as such—*sic visum Veneri*. The sea metaphor (15–16) functions somewhat as it does in the Ode to Pyrrha (*C.* 1.5). There it implicitly reminds the *insolens puer* that the nature of love, like nature itself, is constant only in its vicissitudes, abiding only in its illogic. In the Ode to Tibullus the concluding image similarly lifts the poem from the particular to the general, creating a context that makes static grief seem ultimately at odds with life as it naturally is. The last lines have a distancing effect comparable to the close of Vergil's first Eclogue, where Tityrus replies to Meliboeus' lament:

> et iam summa procul villarum culmina fumant
> maioresque cadunt altis de montibus umbrae.
> [*E.* 1.83–84]

> And now in the distance smoke rises from the housetops,
> and the shadows fall longer from the high mountains.

Horace's parting glimpse of the Adriatic, roughening as it rounds the gulf of Calabria, similarly moves us to a more distant and more inclusive perspective. The straits' perpetual roughness is, to be sure, metaphorically tied to a single incident in Horace's private life; and *curvantis . . . sinus,* obliquely reminding us of Myrtale's charms, emphasizes the physical immediacy of the comparison. Yet at the same time, the scene is also a measure of nature's, and human nature's, continuity. Horace, unlike Tibullus, realizes that the tempestuous Myrtale is herself part of a stable order.

7. Moschus, *Fr.* 2 (Wilamowitz); Pasquali, *Orazio lirico,* 496 ff.

The injunction to Valgius, *desine tandem* (*C.* 2.9.17), repeats that to Chloe (*C.* 1.23.11), and the identity suggests that a single prejudice underlies both. Chloe's fear of spring does not differ radically from Valgius' refusal to abandon winter: neither will acclimate to the fact of change. The broad bias beneath Horace's chastisements is even more apparent if we compare an Ode written to someone equally removed from both Valgius and Chloe, the politician Hirpinus:

Quid bellicosus Cantaber et Scythes,
Hirpine Quincti, cogitet Hadria
divisus obiecto, remittas
quaerere nec trepides in usum

poscentis aevi pauca. fugit retro 5
levis iuventas et decor, arida
pellente lascivos amores
canitie facilemque somnum;

non semper idem floribus est honor
vernis neque uno luna rubens nitet 10
voltu: quid aeternis minorem
consiliis animum fatigas?

cur non sub alta vel platano vel hac
pinu iacentes sic temere et rosa
canos odorati capillos, 15
dum licet, Assyriaque nardo

potamus uncti? dissipat Euhius
curas edacis. quis puer ocius
restinguet ardentis Falerni
pocula pratereunte lympha? 20

quis devium scortum eliciet domo
Lyden? eburna dic age cum lyra
maturet, in comptum Lacaenae
more comam religata nodum. [*C.* 2.11]

Hirpinus Quinctus, cease to worry what the warlike Cantabrian and Scythian, separated from us by the inter-

> vening Adriatic, are plotting; do not search so anxiously into the demands of life, for the things it asks are few. Smooth-cheeked youth and beauty flee behind us, while dry old age is banishing wanton loves and easy sleep. The same bloom does not last forever on spring flowers, nor does the glowing moon shine always with the same face. Why must you with endless worries weary your mind, unequal to them? Why do we not, while we can, drink wine, lying at our ease under a tall plane tree, or beneath this pine, our gray locks fragrant with roses and annointed with Assyrian nard? Bacchus dissipates gnawing cares. What youth will swiftly quench the cups of burning Falernian in the flowing stream? Who will call forth from her home the coy wanton, Lyde? Come, bid her hasten with her ivory lyre, her hair bound in a neat knot, after the Spartan fashion.

Horace's apparent casualness and spontaneity ("under a tall plane tree, or beneath this pine") is a deliberate counterpoise to Hirpinus' anxious attempts to impose order even on the frontiers. The spatial barrier between Rome and its enemies (2–3) is itself a token of the remoteness of Hirpinus' worries from the needs of the present, *poscentis aevi pauca* (5).[8] Where Valgius cares only for yesterday, Hirpinus is absorbed with tomorrow, and nature rebukes the politician's single-mindedness (*non semper . . . quid aeternis?*) as surely as it does that of the elegist (*non semper . . . tu semper*). Horace regarded both attitudes as equally fragmentary; each, he felt, sees a part of life too steadily to see life whole.

Swinburne was predictably fascinated by the similarity between flowers and hours, and Horace found the analogy no less compelling without the encouragement of the couplet. Where Valgius is to take example simply from nature's alternations, Hirpinus can read a more serious warning in its onward movement as well: *fugit retro levis iuventas* (5–6). Formally, the fading of a flower and the phases of the moon are opposed only to the eternal sameness of Hirpinus' worries, *aeternis consiliis* (11–12). But Hirpinus, gray-haired al-

8. With *remittas quaerere* (3–4) cf. *quid sit futurum cras, fuge quaerere* (*C.* 1.9.13), and *tu ne quaesieris* (*C.* 1.11.1).

ready (15), would be dull indeed not to consider the larger implications of nature's progress. The sense of time's flight gives to the Ode a more ominous context, and lends tacit urgency to Horace's invitation. The scene by the river bank is Lucretian (cf. *De Rer. Nat.* 2.29 ff.) in the harmonious ease it proposes, and the crown of flowers worn by the banqueters (14–15) catches a kind of conspiracy between man and nature. Yet, as is the case with nearly all the garlands thus offered by Horace, the conspiracy is moral as well as sensuous: these flowers too cannot keep their bloom. The penultimate stanza maintains a similar tension. As the burning wine is "extinguished" by cold water from the stream that races past, we sense not only the opportunities of the moment but the certainty of their extinction as well. Acceptance of Horace's invitations involves a moral rather than a social commitment. It is in effect to accept the terms on which life is granted to us, to submit to nature's progress no less than to its beauty. In calling Hirpinus from affairs of state, Horace proposes not an evasion of responsibility but a higher responsibility, that to the present itself.[9]

Close in spirit to the Ode to Hirpinus is a heroically proportioned Ode to Maecenas (*C.* 3.29), urging him to leave the "smoke, wealth, and noise of Rome" for a country vacation:

> Tyrrhena regum progenies, tibi
> non ante verso lene merum cado
> cum flore, Maecenas, rosarum et
> pressa tuis balanus capillis
>
> iamdudum apud me est: eripe te morae, 5
> ne semper udum Tibur et Aefulae
> declive contempleris arvom et
> Telegoni iuga parricidae.

9. Cf. the markedly similar invitation to Maecenas, *C.* 3.8. Here is the same summons from political speculation (*mitte civilis super urbe curas,* 17) and the same emphasis on the present (25 ff.). The warning of death is nowhere explicit, but it is latent in the occasion itself, for the banquet to which Horace invites Maecenas takes place on the anniversary of Horace's narrow escape from a falling tree (6–8).

fastidiosam desere copiam et
molem propinquam nubibus arduis: 10
omitte mirari beatae
fumum et opes strepitumque Romae.

plerumque gratae divitibus vices
mundaeque parvo sub lare pauperum
cenae sine aulaeis et ostro 15
sollicitam explicuere frontem.

Maecenas, descendant of Tuscan kings, for you I have long had in store an unopened jar of mellow wine, incense of roses, and balsam pressed out for your hair. Tear yourself from delays, and do not always merely gaze at moist Tibur and Aefula's sloping fields and the ridges of Telegonos the parricide. Leave worrisome luxury and your house that stretches to the very clouds; cease to admire the smoke, wealth, and noise of Rome, so blest. Often the rich are grateful for change, and the wrinkles have been wiped from their forehead by simple meals at the humble fireside of the poor, without tapestries and purple hangings.

Non ante verso, followed by the emphatic enjambment, *iamdudum apud me,* brings out with initial force the sense of passing time, one confirmed by Horace's urgent imperatives: *eripe te . . . desere . . . omitte mirari.* As in the Ode to Hirpinus, it is the unchanging commitment to political plans that Horace reproves: *ne semper . . . plerumque gratae divitibus vices* (13). Even the country at which Maecenas gazes from a distance is described in political terms (8), ones which are, ironically, unpleasant, while Rome's unpleasantness is graced by the adjective *beatus.* The inversion reflects Maecenas' own distorted standards. Opposed to the agitated speculations of the city is the calm of the Sabine farm:

iam clarus occultum Andromedae pater
ostendit ignem, iam Procyon furit
et stella vesani Leonis
sole dies referente siccos; 20

iam pastor umbras cum grege languido
rivomque fessus quaerit et horridi
  dumeta Silvani caretque
    ripa vagis taciturna ventis:

tu civitatem quis deceat status 25
curas et urbi sollicitus times,
  quid Seres et regnata Cyro
    Bactra parent Tanaisque discors.

Now the bright father of Andromeda shows forth his hidden fire, now Procyon burns, and the star of raging Leo, as the sun brings back dry days again. Now the exhausted shepherd with his languid flock seeks out shade and the thickets of rough Silvanus, and the silent river bank is bereft of stray breezes—but you brood over what is best for the state, and, anxious for the city, you worry about the plans of the Seres and of Bactra, once ruled by Cyrus, and of rebellious Tanais.

The sequence *iam . . . iam . . . iam . . . tu* implies as strong a criticism as the *non semper . . . nec . . . tu semper* of the Ode to Valgius (*C.* 2.9). The twice repeated *iam,* and the very stillness of the baked Italian landscape, give to the present a kind of finality which is itself an answer to the uncertainties of the future. Maecenas' worries suddenly seem irrelevant. "A prudent god," Horace reminds him (29 ff.), has sealed the future in darkness: "remember to settle only what is at hand with a tranquil mind; all else is carried along like some river . . ." Like the alternate possibilities of storm and sunshine (43–45), the flowing river, now smooth, now violent (33–41), demonstrates the extremes that await us. As is the case with the fading flowers in the Ode to Hirpinus (*C.* 2.11.9–10), the river is, formally, an image only of the certainty of variations. Yet again there is the same implicit warning. The secure Maecenas must have found the reminder of Fortune's vicissitudes less urgent than the hint that cloudless days mark off the years as effectively as stormy ones, and that the hour itself is "fleeting." [10] The only thing more

10. *C.* 3.29.48; cf. *C.* 2.11.5–6. With *C.* 3.29.32–33, cf. *C.* 2.3.1–4.

certain than the variations of nature is its implacable progress. Violent or calm, the river flows onward, and even the weariest river winds somewhere safe to sea.

Horace's invitations counsel not simply a "return to nature," but rather an acceptance of human nature. He calls Hirpinus and Maecenas to recognize that life is as capricious and yet as constant in its movement as is nature itself. They are accused in the same terms as were Chloe, Plancus, Murena, Valgius, and Pyrrha's lover: *semper, aeternus, perpetuus, mora.* The constancy of Horace's position is remarkable. Although the situations in these Odes are quite different, he sees all as examples of rigidity in a world of change.

The tenor of these poems is by and large kindly, and their impulse positive. His friends have lapsed more from forgetfulness than anything else. On occasion Horace could be less sympathetic, as in two poems to Lydia and Chloris, superannuated courtesans unable to resign themselves to the loss of their charms. These Odes are usually taken either as attacks on particular individuals who had injured Horace, or simply as exercises in the ἰαμβικὴ ἰδέα. Yet Horace's abuse is neither merely personal nor is it that of a casual literary exercise. Rather it illuminates another aspect of the same decorum that dictated the poems above. Even now, he tells Lydia, youths beat more seldom upon her doors at night; soon she will be abandoned altogether:

> in vicem moechos anus arrogantis
> flebis in solo levis angiportu
> Thracio bacchante magis sub inter-
> lunia vento,
>
> cum tibi flagrans amor et libido,
> quae solet matres furiare equorum,
> saeviet circa iecur ulcerosum,
> non sine questu,
>
> laeta quod pubes hedera virenti
> gaudeat pulla magis atque myrto,
> aridas frondes hiemis sodali
> dedicet Euro. [*C.* 1.25.9–20]

> In turn, as an old woman disregarded in a lonely alley you will weep at your lovers' contempt, while the Thracian north wind plays the Bacchant more fiercely on moonless nights, as flaming love, and the lust that sends mares raging, storm about your ulcerous heart, while you complain because youth takes more pleasure in green ivy and dark myrtle, consigning dried leaves to the east wind, winter's companion.

"A picture of terrible reality," comments Kiessling-Heinze, in what looks like a deliberate echo of Goethe's famous judgment on Horace: "eine furchtbar Realität." The dark disorder of the scene, the harsh *c* and *g* sounds, make an image as effective as Catullus' picture of Lesbia, *nunc in quadriviis et angiportis*.[11] Yet the Thracian wind, "playing the Bacchant" (11) as it buffets Lydia through the deserted alleys, is to some extent an inner one as well,[12] and of an equally "furchtbar Realität." The whole Ode, which has such visual authority, is also highly metaphorical. Perhaps even the phrase *sub interlunia* (11–12) has a nonliteral suggestion. In the Ode to Hirpinus it is the changes of the moon that warn of time's passing (*C.* 2.11.10–11), and just as the *avarus* of *C.* 2.18 ignores the moon's warning (15–16), so Lydia can look to no moon overhead. If this allusion is dubious, there can be no question that the *aridas frondes* of the last stanza represent the sere and yellow leaf of life, the equivalent of *arida canities* in the Ode to Hirpinus. The "green ivy and dark myrtle" (17–18) are an equally clear image for youth.[13] The phrase, suggestive of the Bacchic wreath, reminds us of Lydia's inappropriate abandonment to the tempestuous emotions of a Bacchant. In handing

11. Cat., 58.4. It is interesting that Horace's attack on Lydia should echo, whether intentionally or unintentionally, Catullus' attack on Lesbia, just as Horace's first love poem to Lydia (*C.* 1.13) echoes Catullus' description of his love at first sight for Lesbia (51); see above, 153.

12. Cf. Ibycus, 6 (Diehl); Sappho, 50 (Diehl). *Saeviat* (*C.* 1.25.15) halfway preserves the idea of a raging wind; is it too fanciful to suppose that the transition to *matres equorum* (14) may have been suggested by the popular belief (cf. Vergil, *G.* 3.266 ff.) that mares were aroused and even became pregnant from the wind?

13. Cf. *Epod.* 13.4; *C.* 1.9.17, 4.13.6–12; and the beautiful image of passing time in the Epodes: *hic tertius December . . . silvis honorem decutit* (*Epod.* 11.5–6). The basic image is, of course, an old one; cf. Archilochus, 113 (Diehl).

over the dry leaves to the east wind, "winter's companion" (19), to be destroyed, the youths simply obey a natural instinct. Upon Lydia, attempting to defy the decorum of nature, Horace wastes no sympathy. Her *iecur ulcerosum* (15) places her outside the moral pale, where she is accompanied only by the gusts of her own passion, winter's companion.

The broad logic behind Horace's attack becomes still more apparent in a second poem on the same theme (*C.* 3.15). "Wife of penniless Ibycus, finally put an end (*tandem fige modum,* 2) to your wantonness . . . as one near to the fitting time for death cease to play (*ludere,* 5) among the maidens." As one ripe only for death, Chloris is ordered to leave the youthful games allowed to her daughter: *illam cogit amor Nothi / lascivae similem ludere capreae* (11–12). Flowers, wine, and music (14–16), the privilege of those who accept the realities of the present, are denied to Chloris. The fresh ivy and myrtle sought by *laeta pubes* in the Ode to Lydia (*C.* 1.25.17–18) may have some relation to the Bacchic wreath, and now Horace expressly approves the connection between youth and Bacchic revelry:

> non, siquid Pholoen satis,
>   et te, Chlori, decet: filia rectius
>
> expugnat iuvenum domos,
>   pulso Thyias uti concita tympano.
>
> [*C.* 3.15.7–10]

> Whatever becomes Pholoe does not thereby become you too, Chloris; your daughter may more fitly storm the houses of youths, like a Bacchant roused by the beaten timbrel.

If Chloris may not play the Bacchant her daughter may; propriety is not categorical but chronological. Horace reproves not the sport of love, but rather the failure to leave such sport in due course: *nec lusisse pudet sed non incidere ludum.*[14] The warning to Chloris—*tandem fige modum . . . desine*—is the other half of that to the recently matured Chloe: *tandem desine matrem / tempestiva sequi*

14. *Ep.* 1.14.36, where Horace contrasts his youthful pleasure in fine clothes, love, and drinking with his present mature simplicity.

vira (*C.* 1.23.11–12). Chloe must leave her mother, just as Chloris must cease to ape her daughter. Where Chloe refuses to admit that spring has come, Chloris, like Lydia, ignores the fact that it has passed. Biographical causes for Horace's attacks upon Lydia and Chloris are unnecessary, for to understand his attitude we need consult only his conception of the morality implicit in time itself. Attempts to hold to the prerogatives of youth presented themselves to him not as a foible of age but as a cosmic impropriety. It was as though winter were to masquerade in the colors of spring.

"I wish to marry neither a young girl nor an old woman," reads an epigram from the *Greek Anthology:* "Neither sour grape nor raisin would I have, but a beauty ripe for the chamber of love." [15] For Horace the divisions provided matter not for an occasional aphorism but for a comprehensive moral attitude. We may see it in even so slight a poem as the invocation to Venus (*C.* 1.30), a charming prayer that she visit one Glycera:

O Venus regina Cnidi Paphique,
sperne dilectam Cypron et vocantis
ture te multo Glycerae decoram
  transfer in aedem.

fervidus tecum puer et solutis   5
Gratiae zonis properentque Nymphae
et parum comis sine te Iuventas
  Mercuriusque.

> O Venus, queen of Cnidus and of Paphos, leave your chosen Cyprus to come to the seemly shrine of Glycera, who calls you with plentiful incense. Let your passionate son hasten along with you, and the Graces with loosened zones, and the Nymphs, and Youth, hardly charming without you, and Mercury.

"Glycera" is synonymous with "sweetness"; [16] like *tempestiva Chloe* (*C.* 1.23), Glycera is "a beauty ripe for love's chamber." Her shrine

15. *Anth. Pal.* 5.20; cf. 5.124.

16. γλυκερά. Cf. the effect of an oxymoron in *inmitis Glycerae* (*C.* 1.33.2), and cf. *C.* 3.19.28, and below, 260.

is *decoram* (3) in moral as well as external terms, a fit setting for Venus, as she herself is a fit votary. The final request that Venus bring "youth, hardly charming without you," virtually summarizes the Ode. Horace approves the youthful Glycera's submission to love in the same way that he urges love upon Chloe. Theirs is the positive responsibility of the Golden Mean, just as Lydia's and Chloris' is the negative responsibility of one extreme.

The other extreme is illustrated in a poem in which Horace rebukes a friend's—or perhaps his own—importunate desire for the too youthful Lalage:

Nondum subacta ferre iugum valet
cervice, nondum munia conparis
aequare nec tauri ruentis
in venerem tolerare pondus.

circa virentis est animus tuae 5
campos iuvencae, nunc fluviis gravem
solantis aestum, nunc in udo
ludere cum vitulis salicto

praegestientis. tolle cupidinem
inmitis uvae: iam tibi lividos 10
distinguet autumnus racemos
purpureo varius colore.

iam te sequetur: currit enim ferox
aetas et illi quos tibi dempserit
adponet annos; iam proterva 15
fronte petet Lalage maritum,

dilecta, quantum non Pholoe fugax,
non Chloris albo sic umero nitens
ut pura nocturno renidet
luna mari Cnidiusve Gyges, 20

quem si puellarum insereres choro,
mire sagacis falleret hospites
discrimen obscurum solutis
crinibus ambiguoque voltu. [*C.* 2.5]

> Not yet is she able to bear the yoke upon submissive neck, not yet is she equal to the duties of a mate, nor can she bear the weight of the bull rushing into love. The mind of your heifer is given to green fields, as she now seeks relief from the heavy heat in streams, now rejoices to play with the calves in the moist willow grove. Banish your desire for the unripe grape; soon will many-colored autumn touch the bluish clusters with purple. Soon will she follow you: fierce time rushes on, and the years which it exacts from you it will assign to her; soon Lalage with wanton brow will seek a husband, loved by you as shy Chloe never was, nor Chloris, shining with her fair shoulder like the unclouded moon upon a midnight sea, nor Cnidian Gyges, who, should you place him among a band of girls, would, with his flowing locks and indeterminate features, deceive even the most marvelously clever stranger.

Nondum inverts the *tandem desine* to Chloris; Horace banishes the unripe grape as firmly as he does the raisin. The comparison between Lalage and a young heifer recalls the simile used of Chloe, *vitas inuleo me similis* (*C.* 1.23.1), or that applied to Lyce:

> quae velut latis equa trima campis
> ludit exsultim metuitque tangi
> nuptiarum expers et adhuc protervo
> cruda marito. [*C.* 3.11.9–12]

> Who, like a three-year-old filly, plays exultingly on the broad fields and shrinks from any touch, ignorant of marriage and hitherto not ripe for a wanton husband.

In each case the point of comparison is the age of the girl. To look at the poem of Anacreon that Horace in each case seems to have in mind is to recognize how decisively he has reshaped its terms:

> Thracian filly, why do you look at me askance, and so cruelly flee from me? Do you think I do not understand my art? Know that I might bridle you well enough, and holding

> the reins ride you around the turning post of the course.
> But now you graze in the meadows and frolic about, for you
> have not had a clever rider to break you. [88, Diehl]

Of Horace's three Odes, none is so exclusively concerned with the contest of male and female as are the lines of Anacreon. The question of age and maturity is the most prominent. In each, time itself provides the moral element, and though the circumstances differ, Horace's viewpoint does not.

Of the three poems, that to Lalage's lover (*C.* 2.5) is the most interesting in these terms. In the Ode to Chloe Horace's moral judgment and his desires were united, and his perspective remained urbane and undisturbed. But in his address to Lalage's lover there seems a split between the two. The heavy *nondum* stands a staunchly rational bar to passion—yet in the muttering beat of the syllables that follow we recognize a pulsing excitement. The descriptive second stanza seems intended to diffuse the force of the frankly sexual image with which the poem opens. Nevertheless, the picture of Lalage, excitedly sporting through the moist groves in the heavy heat, remains erotic. Not until the third stanza substitutes the less suggestive image of an unripe grape does the initial impetus seem controlled. Fulfillment of desire is firmly relegated to the future, when autumn shall paint the grape with sensuous color. Then will Lalage become the pursuer, as with *proterva fronte*—half way rescuing the animal metaphor—she seeks a husband. In the meantime the cold facts of mathematics must temper her lover's ardor. For each year he loses, Lalage gains one; if he is past the spring of life, she will soon reach maturity. *Ferox* (13) undercuts the rational balance of loss and gain, almost negating the careful equation by which Horace makes time an ally. The whole phrase *currit enim ferox aetas* reminds us, moreover, of the opening picture of the bull rushing into love (3–4), and suggests that Horace is not altogether reconciled to his own advice. But the next stanzas dissipate any lingering rebellion against decorum. We move to a safe distance from the hot immediacy of the opening as the cool light of the moon (18–20) replaces *gravem aestum* (6–7). Our final view (21–24) is of the ambiguous Gyges; desire is baffled, broken, and finally amused by his sexlessness. The very difficulty of the syntax tends to involve us in the lines. We become so absorbed in them that we virtually forget the emotions of the Ode's opening—as the whole progress of the poem urges that we should. We are left, finally, in calm abeyance, all passion frozen, if not spent.

It is a truism that men define themselves by what they describe, and Horace's concern with the weather's alternations, the moon's changes, a flower's bloom and decay, a growing animal, a river's fugitive surface, and the revolution of the seasons suggests that natural change was to his imagination among the most compelling of facts—to his imagination, since images are the product of the imagination and not of biography. Because Horace draws lessons from a ripening grape he is no more proved a farmer than the Ode to the Ship of State (*C.* 1.14) proves him to be a sailor. While the number of poems built upon the union of natural and human progress evidences the idea's fascination, their general fineness indicates how fruitful a creative impulse it provided. Both the quantity and the quality of these Odes suggest that we have to do with a controlling assumption rather than with a display of decorative language. Horace did not, of course, discover the correspondence between the world and the little world of man; it is easy enough to cite precedents ranging from Homer's celebrated comparison between the lives of men and the generations of leaves to Mimnermus' elegiac declaration that we are young but for a season. The various editions of Horace, and the work of Pasquali and now of Fraenkel, keep us properly aware of the tradition within which Horace wrote, and we may be sure that if more of Greek literature were extant the references would multiply correspondingly. Yet the fact that Horace's figures have such firm roots in the past should not lead us to neglect their distinctive ramifications in his own work. It is difficult to find any other author who appeals to one aspect of nature with such consistency, or for whom that appeal is so consistently a moral one. Horace does not simply record that man's life is like that of a leaf, but insists that it should be, and that bud, maturity, and decline be duly observed.

The Ethics of Change

Attempts to fit Horace to a single philosophical system are recurrent. He becomes in turn (or sometimes simultaneously) a Stoic, an Epicurean, a Cynic, or even, in our generosity, a Christian. Most often we solemnly conclude that he was an Eclectic. The assumption behind such attempts is clear, but only rarely is it spelled out: "That Horace was a serious thinker needs no demonstration. . . . If he be a serious thinker he must inevitably have had a metaphysical basis for his thought." [17] To accept the premises of such arguments we need not agree with their conclusions, for Horace was no more amenable than most poets to the "must's" of critics. Instead of postulating the existence of some "metaphysic," and then trying to discover what it is, we might more profitably ask if it is not a physical basis upon which an important part of his thought rests. It is remarkable that even the word *natura,* which is frequent in the Satires and Epistles, occurs but once in the Odes, and there in describing the philosopher Pythagoras (*iudice te non sordidus auctor / naturae verique, C.* 1.28.14–15). By avoiding the word it seems as though Horace were deliberately discouraging us from attempting to impose upon him any of the philosophical systems that took "living according to nature" as an important tenet. Instead, his metaphoric language itself asserts a moral order, and frequently constitutes a moral imperative. The standards that thus emerge from the Odes to various individuals are strikingly consistent, to the point that they tempt us to ask whether they are not equally relevant in more abstract matters.

In the political poems, for instance, we can watch Horace as he moves from Republicanism through a period of political disenchantment to a final espousal of the Augustan cause. His progress can be seen as a logical extension of his private beliefs. In accepting Octavian's rule, and in urging Pompeius to do the same (*C.* 2.7), he shows a bias similar to that which dictates his rebukes to Valgius (*C.* 2.9), to Tibullus (*C.* 1.33), to Lydia (*C.* 1.25), and to Chloris (*C.* 3.15). He knew that elegiac memories of the past could be no

17. W. J. Oates, *Classical Studies Presented to Edward Capps* (Princeton, 1936), 260.

more effective in national affairs than in private ones; to repudiate what the years brought with them would be equally foolish in either case. In 24 B.C., in an Ode welcoming Augustus home from Spain, Horace explicitly links his abandonment of his former pugnaciousness with the progress of age and nature:

> lenit albescens animos capillus
> litium et rixae cupidos protervae:
> non ego hoc ferrem calidus iuventa
> consule Planco. [*C.* 3.14.25–28]

> My whitening hair mellows a spirit once fond of strife and bold quarrels. I would not have borne such a thing in my hot youth, in the consulship of Plancus.

Despite the somewhat melancholy tone of the poem, Horace's position is clear, and his natural wisdom is thrown into sharp relief by the following Ode, which rebukes the obdurate Chloris for her failure to yield gracefully to the demands of time—brawling, even in love (*expugnat,* 9), is proper only to the young. The fact that in the later political work Horace's imagination seems less intensely involved does not detract from the completeness of his idealogical change. We need not say that his private standards directly shaped his political views. But we can be sure that the same conception, or perhaps instinct, underlay both.

The position Horace adopted in contemporary literary disputes is markedly consistent both with his political attitude and with his attitude toward specific individuals. The studies of Varro, *diligentissimus investigator antiquitatis,* gave a powerful impetus to antiquarianism, and during Horace's lifetime the quarrel between Ancients and Moderns became increasingly devisive.[18] When, in the fourth Satire of the first book, Horace criticized Lucilius' stylistic carelessness, he soon found himself involved in that larger debate. His tenth Satire,

18. The description of Varro is Cicero's (*Br.* 15.60). For a survey of the dispute between Ancients and Moderns, see J. F. D'Alton, *Roman Literary Theory and Criticism,* chap. 5.

a defense of his previous strictures on Lucilius, shows him to be aware of their larger implications. The eulogists of Lucilius, he suggests, do their idol no service by admiring even his awkwardnesses. Lucilius himself, had he been born an Augustan, would not have shown himself indifferent to the change in standards:

> si foret hoc nostrum fato delapsus in aevum,
> detereret sibi multa, recideret omne quod ultra
> perfectum traheretur, et in versu faciendo
> saepe caput scaberet vivos et roderet unguis.
> [*S.* 1.10.68–71]

> If by chance he were to come down to this age of ours, he would rub away much from his work and would cut back everything which dragged on beyond the point of perfection, and in making his verses he would often scratch his head and bite his nails to the quick.

In the Epistle to Augustus (*Ep.* 2.1) Horace developed his position into a full-scale attack upon archaism. Some Augustans were prepared to cry up not only Ennius, Naevius, Plautus, and Lucilius, but even the Saliar Hymns and the Laws of the Twelve Tables, simply because of their antiquity (18 ff.). For Horace such an attitude demonstrated a willful blindness to the nature of literature, as of life itself. An excessive attachment to the past, he maintained, could make one only an anachronism in one's own time:

> ingeniis non ille favet plauditque sepultis,
> nostra sed inpugnat, nos nostraque lividus odit.
> [*Ep.* 2.1.88–89]

> That man does not favor and applaud long-dead genius, but he attacks our own, enviously hating us and all that is ours.

In criticizing earlier writers he is really launching an attack upon their devotees for their determination to live in the past. His attitude toward the *fautor veterum* (23) is not unrelated to his reproaches to a Lydia, a Chloris, a Valgius, or a Tibullus. All alike fall within his range because all too rigidly ignore the changes that time exacts.

Another aspect of the quarrel between Ancients and Moderns lay in the sphere of language, where the sides were drawn up under the terms of analogist and anomalist. The former believed language should be static and codified by rule; the latter, that every generation had a right to forge its own terms. Julius Caesar, in his work *De Analogia,* austerely warned readers to "flee an unheard-of and unaccustomed word as though it were a rock." [19] In protesting against this view Horace clarifies the logic beneath the Epistle to Augustus:

> licuit semperque licebit
> signatum praesente nota producere nomen.
> ut silvae foliis pronos mutantur in annos,
> prima cadunt: ita verborum vetus interit aetas,
> et iuvenum ritu florent modo nata vigentque.
> debemur morti nos nostraque: sive receptus
> terra Neptunus classes Aquilonibus arcet,
> regis opus, sterilisve diu palus aptaque remis
> vicinas urbes alit et grave sentit aratrum,
> seu cursum mutavit iniquum frugibus amnis
> doctus iter melius: mortalia facta peribunt,
> nedum sermonum stet honos et gratia vivax.
> multa renascentur quae iam cecidere cadentque
> quae nunc sunt in honore vocabula, si volet usus,
> quem penes arbitrium est et ius et norma loquendi.
> [*A. P.* 58–72]

It was and always will be permitted to coin a word stamped with the mark in use. Just as trees change their leaves as the years go by, the earliest born falling off, so the eldest race of words perishes, and, like youths, those just born flower and flourish. We and all our works are owed to death. Whether the sea, enclosed within the land, protects fleets from the north winds, a kingly work; or whether the swamp-

19. Aulus Gellius, 1.10.4.

land, for so long sterile and fit only for oars, now nourishes the neighboring cities and feels the weight of the plow; or whether a river, taught a better path, now has changed its course so hostile to the crops—mortal things still will perish, and much less shall honor remain to words, and their glory live on. Many words which now have fallen shall be reborn, and many now held in honor shall fall, if usage so ordain, which holds the power of judgment and the law and rule of speech.

To forbid his own generation the freedom enjoyed by previous ones would be an unnatural denial of time itself.[20] The lines *ut silvae foliis . . .* , with their Homeric and Lucretian echoes, are perhaps the most exquisite in the *Ars Poetica.* They resume both the language and the abiding concern of some of the finest Odes, as the seasonal simile brings to bear on an apparently isolated question of linguistics the same decorum Horace applied to life itself.

The theoretical position Horace adopts in the Epistle to Augustus and the *Ars Poetica* has a social corollary in an Ode addressed to an anonymous antiquarian:

Quantum distet ab Inacho
  Codrus pro patria non timidus mori,
narras et genus Aeaci
  et pugnata sacro bella sub Ilio:

quo Chium pretio cadum
  mercemur, quis aquam temperet ignibus,
quo praebente domum et quota
  Paelignis caream frigoribus, taces. [*C.* 3.19.1–8]

You tell us how much time elapsed between Inachus and Codrus, ready to die for his country, and you talk of the race of Aeacus and of the war fought beneath the walls of sacred Troy. But as to what price we should pay for a jar of Chian wine, as to who will warm the water with fire, as

20. Horace practices what he preaches: in the passage leading up to the one quoted he coins the word *cinctutis* (*A. P.* 50). Cf. *Ep.* 2.2.119.

to who will furnish a house, and as to what hour shall see
me free of the Paelignian cold—as to these you are silent.

Sharp inquiries (*quo . . . quis . . . quo . . . quota*) break in upon the lulling sonorities of a mythically distant past as the necessities of the present banish scholarly research. Old Lycus, too aged to please his neighbor, may hear the festivities only from a distance (22–24). Like Chloris (*C.* 3.15), he is forbidden the youthful abandon of the banquet, at which "seasonable" Rhode ("rose") and Glycera ("sweet one") are more appropriate guests. Should the antiquarian whom Horace addresses wish to join such company, he must abandon the past and commit himself to the present.

A similar invitation to a certain Aelius is amiable rather than impatient, but it relies upon the same contrast:

Aeli vetusto nobilis ab Lamo—
quando et priores hinc Lamias ferunt
denominatos et nepotum
per memores genus omne fastus,

auctore ab illo ducis originem, 5
qui Formiarum moenia dicitur
princeps et innantem Maricae
litoribus tenuisse Lirim

late tyrannus—: cras foliis nemus
multis et alga litus inutili 10
demissa tempestas ab Euro
sternet, aquae nisi fallit augur

annosa cornix: dum potes, aridum
conpone lignum: cras genium mero
curabis et porco bimenstri 15
cum famulis operum solutis. [*C.* 3.17]

Aelius, nobly sprung from ancient Lamus—for since people say that both the Lamiae of former times and the whole race of descendants as well, through the recording annals, took their name from him, you trace your origin from that

> founder who is said to have held as prince, ruling far and wide, the walls of Formiae and the Liris river, overflowing the shores of Marica—tomorrow a tempest, coming down from the East, will strew the grove with many leaves and the shore with useless seaweed, unless the aged crow, the prophet of rain, deceives me. While you can, lay in dry wood; tomorrow you will worship your guardian spirit with wine and with a two-month-old pig, while the household slaves are freed from work.

The grand roll call of Aelius' lineage (1–9) founders upon the homely reminder of leaves, seaweed, and aging raven (9–13). After the lofty rhetoric of the first two stanzas, the repeated monosyllable *cras* (9, 14) and the mention of the pig, who can boast a pedigree of only two months (15), are shattering. Domestic details recall Aelius from his visions of ancestral grandeur to the needs of the present much as the insistent *quo*'s of *C.* 3.19 interrupt the Homeric scholar's research. We may guess that Aelius often indulged in reveries over his past, and that Horace's grandiloquence, carried out by the solemn *dum potes* (13), twits him gently. Whatever the details of the situation, its moral outline is clear. Only if Aelius forgets the past may he partake of the promised feast, symbol of present enjoyment.

To change with the times was even more urgent in personal affairs than in literary ones, and many of Horace's ethical pronouncements adapt themselves to these terms. His famous "wonder at nothing" (*nil admirari*) is a formula for accommodating oneself to a changing world, for achieving equanimity before events either better or worse than expected:

> gaudeat an doleat, cupiat metuatne, quid ad rem,
> si, quidquid vidit melius peiusve sua spe,
> defixis oculis animoque et corpore torpet? [*Ep.* 1.6.12–14]

> Whether a man rejoice or grieve, desire or fear, what difference does it make, if, whenever he sees something either better or worse than his expectations, eyes riveted, he grows numb in mind and body?

quem res plus nimio delectavere secundae,
mutatae quatient. siquid mirabere, pones
invitus. [*Ep.* 1.10.30–32]

Anyone unduly pleased by favorable circumstances will be shaken when they change. If you wonder at anything, you will set it aside unwillingly.

The lines abstract the logic beneath his rebuke of Valgius, Tibullus, Plancus or Pyrrha's *insolens* lover, all "shaken" by their inability to adapt to altered conditions. Horace's much publicized Golden Mean is not an invitation to easy compromises, but rather a strategy for weathering life's inevitable extremes. Its proper analogy is not, finally, with the dead weight of gold so much as with a mercurial fluidity:

sperat infestis, metuit secundis
alteram sortem bene praeparatum
pectus. [*C.* 2.10.13–15]

The man whose heart is well prepared for either extreme has hope in adverse circumstances and is fearful in favorable ones.

Aequam memento rebus in arduis
servare mentem, non secus in bonis
ab insolenti temperatam
laetitia, moriture Delli. [*C.* 2.3.1–4]

Remember to keep a tranquil mind amid difficulties, and likewise, when you prosper, draw it back temperately from unwonted happiness, Dellius, for you are bound to die.

Familiar adjectives of praise such as *rectus* and *aequus* do not underwrite an undeviating rectitude or a flat conservatism. Rather they urge a kind of self-regulation, an equable acceptance of fortune or misfortune without surrender to either. The unstable and frequently arbitrary world in which Horace grew up must have fostered such an attitude, and surely the various stanzas on the fickleness of *Fortuna* [21] owed as much to recent history as to traditional maxims. The careers of Julius Caesar, Pompey, and Mark Antony proved the capriciousness of Fortune's wheel with a completeness that was to delight future moralists, and Horace himself must have acknowledged her power in rising from Republican obscurity to Imperial brilliance. His emphasis upon the fixed accomplishments of the past [22] and upon the opportunities of the present is in large part conceived as an answer to the uncertainties of the future. Life, he knew, makes no promises; no one can even be sure of dying where he wishes (*C.* 2.6).

Death, in the words of Shakespeare's Cleopatra, "shackles accidents and bolts up change." In removing the possibility of change it is itself the greatest of changes. Behind the counsel to Dellius to keep an equable mind through each day's vicissitudes (*C.* 2.3.1–3) waits the reminder of his ultimate transformation: *moriture Delli* (4). Though Horace was quick to upbraid those not accommodating themselves to the reverses of life, he reserved his most strenuous warning for those who ignored the certainty of death. Time's progress, belittling all the things of this world, is the ultimate justification for the advice "to wonder at nothing" (*Ep.* 1.6.1). "Go now, gaze upon silver and old marble and bronzes and works of art; wonder at Tyrian robes with inset jewels; rejoice because a thousand eyes are fastened upon you whenever you speak . . . Time will bring forth into the light whatever is under the earth, and it will bury and hide away what now shines so bright. When the colonnade of Agrippa and the Appian way have looked upon you in your fame, it still remains for you to go where Numa and Ancus have gone before" (17 ff.). Or again, "Thus because perpetual use is granted to no one, and heir follows heir just as wave follows wave, what use are estates and granaries?" (*Ep.* 2.2.175 ff.).

In these terms it is possible to understand why Horace considered avarice the worst of all vices (*S.* 2.3.82). It represents the ultimate blindness to the fact of change, the denial of one's own mortality. *Sepulcri inmemor struis domos:* untouched by the warning of the

21. *C.* 1.34.12 ff., 1.35, 3.29.49 ff.
22. *S.* 2.2.126–27; *C.* 1.9.14–15, 3.29.41–48, 4.7.17–20.

moon overhead, the *avarus* aspires to a permanence that he can in fact never realize (*C.* 2.18.15 ff.). Hoarding wine betrays the same fatuity:

> filius aut etiam haec libertus ut ebibat heres,
> dis inimice senex, custodis? [*S.* 2.3.122–23]

> Do you guard it, old man hateful to the gods, so that your son, or even a freedman heir, will drink it up?

The image [23] gathers a special power in the context of Horace's frequent banquet invitations. In all of them we feel the larger dimensions he suggested as early as the first Satire:

> inde fit, ut raro, qui se vixisse beatum
> dicat et exacto contentus tempore vita
> cedat uti conviva satur, reperire queamus.
> [*S.* 1.1.117–19]

> Hence it comes about that only rarely are we able to find a person who can say that he has lived happily, and who, when his time is finished, will leave life content, like a dinner guest who has had his fill.

Life is a banquet that at death we leave. To the Lucretian formula (3.938) Horace gives a characteristic emphasis. Where Lucretius found difficulty in persuading the satisfied man to leave graciously (*cur non ut plenus vitae conviva recedis?*), Horace proclaims how few there are who may call themselves satisfied. His invitational Odes are a summons to life itself, and to hoard wine is thus a perverse denial of the present in favor of the always dubious future.

The situation of a certain Ofellus (*S.* 2.2), a tenant farmer on

23. Cf. *Ep.* 1.5.12 ff., 2.2.190–92; *C.* 4.7.19–20. Horace cites as an example of the wise man one who does not become frantic if the seal of a flask is broken (*Ep.* 2.2.134). In these terms we can feel the moral urgency behind the apparently casual invitation to Maecenas: *tibi non ante verso lene merum cado . . . iamdudum apud me est* (*C.* 3.29.1 ff.). On the importance of wine as a symbol in Horace's poems, see my article in *TAPA, 88* (1957), 68 ff.

the land he once owned, offers a miniature of the proverbial maxim *vitaque mancipio nulli datur, omnibus usu* (Lucr., 3.971). Ofellus, too, offers the best answer to it. He is undisturbed by fortune's reverses, knowing all permanence to be illusory. Soon the land's new owner will fall:

> nam propriae telluris erum natura nec illum
> nec me nec quemquam statuit: nos expulit ille,
> illum aut nequities aut vafri inscitia iuris,
> postremum expellet certe vivacior heres.
> nunc ager Umbreni sub nomine, nuper Ofelli
> dictus, erit nulli proprius, sed cedet in usum
> nunc mihi, nunc alii. [*S.* 2.2.129–35]

> For nature has appointed neither him nor me nor anyone else the proper owner of the land. That man expels us, and either wickedness or ignorance of the law's tricks will expel him, or, finally, a longer-lived heir will be certain to do so. Now the field that was recently said to belong to Ofellus lies under the name of Umbrenus; it will belong to no one for his own, but falls now to my use, now to that of another.

Ofellus speaks from the dinner table which is, for Horace, from a position of strength, not to say *ex cathedra.* He recognizes what nature guarantees, that we are all owed to death, living on borrowed time. And he knows that time is therefore to be spent well, that in such currency the failure to spend is improvidence.

Nature's Decorum and Death

In the Odes on the different ages of man the analogies with nature are generally clear. Often they take shape as a simile, an explicit statement of relationship, while metaphors such as "unripe grape" or "dry leaves" can hardly be called obscure. The direction in which Horace moves is standard in Greek and Latin verse: man is the subject, nature the analogue. In other Odes the point of comparison, or even the fact of comparison, is less obvious. The seasonal poems, and particularly the so-called "spring songs," are customarily assigned to the genre of landscape poetry. A good example of the type, and one frequently cited as a precedent for Horace's work, is a lovely poem ascribed to Meleager: [24]

> Hush'd is the howl of wintry breezes wild;
> The purple hour of youthful Spring has smiled:
> A livelier verdure clothes the teeming earth;
> Buds press to life, rejoicing in their birth;
> The laughing meadows drink the dews of night,
> And, fresh with opening roses, glad the sight.

Nature's renewal produces a corresponding human revival:

> If Earth rejoices, with new verdure gay,
> And shepherds pipe, and flocks exulting play,
> And sailors roam, and Bacchus leads his throng,
> And bees to toil, and birds awake to song—
> Shall the glad bard be mute in tuneful spring,
> And, warm with love and joy, forget to sing?

Horace did not forget to sing, but his songs might have jarred Meleager's audience. Typical is the Ode to Sestius:

> Solvitur acris hiems grata vice veris et Favoni
> trahuntque siccas machinae carinas,
> ac neque iam stabulis gaudet pecus aut arator igni
> nec prata canis albicant pruinis.
>
> iam Cytherea choros ducit Venus imminente luna, 5
> iunctaeque Nymphis Gratiae decentes
> alterno terram quatiunt pede, dum gravis Cyclopum
> Volcanus ardens visit officinas.
>
> nunc decet aut viridi nitidum caput impedire myrto
> aut flore, terrae quem ferunt solutae, 10
> nunc et in umbrosis Fauno decet immolare lucis,
> seu poscat agna sive malit haedo.

24. *Anth. Pal.* 9.363. The translation is that of R. Bland, in J. H. Merivale, *Collections from the Greek Anthology* (London, 1833), 232.

pallida Mors aequo pulsat pede pauperum tabernas
  regumque turris. o beate Sesti,
vitae summa brevis spem nos vetat inchoare longam; 15
  iam te premet nox fabulaeque Manes

et domus exilis Plutonia; quo simul mearis,
  nec regna vini sortiere talis
nec tenerum Lycidan mirabere, quo calet iuventus
  nunc omnis et mox virgines tepebunt. 20

[*C.* 1.4]

At the pleasant change of spring and the west wind, harsh winter is loosening its grip; the tackle is hauling the dry ships down to the water, and the flock no longer rejoices in the stables or the plowman by his fire, nor do the meadows shine white with hoarfrost. Now Cytherean Venus leads forth her dancers beneath the overhanging moon, and the lovely Graces, hand in hand with the Nymphs, strike the earth with rhythmic steps, while glowing Vulcan goes to tend the great forges of the Cyclops. Now it is fitting to bind our gleaming hair with green myrtle, or with the flowers which the loosening earth bears; now it is fitting in shady groves to sacrifice to Faunus, whether he demand a lamb or prefer a kid.

Pale Death with impartial step knocks at the huts of the poor and at the palace of kings. O favored Sestius, the brief sum of life forbids us to enter upon far-reaching hopes. Soon night will press upon you, and the fabled Shades, and the narrow house of Pluto, where, once you have arrived, you will no longer throw dice to gain the lordship of the feast, nor will you wonder at tender Lycidas, for whom all the youths even now are burning, and for whom the girls will soon warm with love.

"*Pallida Mors* has nothing to do with the above!" The angry marginalia at line thirteen is Landor's, and the fact that a poet so learned in classical poetry found Horace's transition incomprehensible suggests how remarkable it is in Greek and Latin literature. Yet behind the Ode is nothing more than the familiar correspondence between nature's cycle and man's life. The poem seems disjointed only because we are accustomed, in ancient poetry, to seeing the analogy from the other side, as in the various Odes on youth and age already discussed. It looks as though Horace, so prone to draw up nature for *exempla* of change and age, came to regard nature itself as a latent metaphor.

The logic of the Ode becomes clear once we sense the tentative correspondence between spring and youth, death and winter. The associations are felt rather than formulated, instinctive rather than doctrinaire; Horace found it an easy step from the progress of the seasons to the equal progress of man's life, culminating in *pallida Mors*. The abruptness of line thirteen acts as a kind of shock treatment, forcing us to recognize that in the midst of life we are in death. Yet its abruptness is more apparent than real. *Grata vice veris* in the opening line hints that spring is only one of the year's changes, and that others may not be so pleasant. If spring comes, can winter be far behind? The Ode is built upon careful antitheses. From the first three stanzas breathes a trembling expansiveness. *Solvitur* (1) dissolves the brittle sharpness of *acris hiems* by its very sound, and *solutae* (10) confirms the earth's release. The ground throws off the frost, ships move from the dry prison of the land, flocks emerge from their stables, the farmer leaves the confines of his cottage, and Venus leads forth her chorus (1–6). All nature quickens with warmth; we glimpse Vulcan's glowing forge (7–8). The almost Arcadian scenes, sensuously alive with Nymphs and Graces dancing beneath the low-hanging moon, with green myrtle and wildflowers, seem to call for the brush of a Titian. But suddenly the measured pace of *pallida Mors,* its authority emphasized by exaggerated onomatopoeia (12), replaces the light dance of the Nymphs and Graces [25]—*et in Arcadia ego.* Paleness shrouds the colors of the preceding stanza like snow mantling foliage. The Ode's growth resembles that of one of the flowers it describes. Its budlike unfolding is halted as though nipped by frost: *iam te premet*

25. *Impedire* (9) suggests, by its sound, a transition between the joyous step of the Nymphs (7) and the tread of death (13). So too the sacrifice, though conventional, may provide an indication of the way the Ode will turn. Celebrating the spring, it could also remind us that, like the spring, we too are sacrificed to the revolving year. Even the low-hanging moon (5), so often associated with change for Horace, may conceivably be a warning of the shift that is imminent.

nox . . . et domus exilis Plutonia. (16–17). *Exilis* has a primary meaning of "narrow" or "cramped"; to translate it "cheerless" is to destroy the spatial sense it shares with *premet,* and hence the contrast with the openness of spring.[26] The warmth that comes with spring is, in the final stanza, associated with youth: *quo calet iuventus . . . virgines tepebunt.* Love's ardors are viewed only from the chill retrospect of the grave, and the perspective suggests that youthful love, like spring itself, will soon be past. The elegiac tone is itself an injunction. While youth remains we should enjoy it, just as we should welcome the spring, our heads decked with the brief flowers it bears. *Nunc decet* (9) simply localizes in seasonal terms the familiar admonition *dumque virent genua et decet.*[27]

The Ode to Sestius finds its antithesis in the Soracte Ode (*C.* 1.9). Where the former moves from spring to death, the latter moves from a winter landscape to a genre scene of youthful love:

Vides ut alta stet nive candidum
Soracte nec iam sustineant onus
silvae laborantes geluque
flumina constiterint acuto.

dissolve frigus ligna super foco 5
large reponens atque benignius
deprome quadrimum Sabina,
o Thaliarche, merum diota.

permitte divis cetera, qui simul
stravere ventos aequore fervido 10
deproeliantis, nec cupressi
nec veteres agitantur orni.

quid sit futurum cras, fuge quaerere, et
quem Fors dierum cumque dabit, lucro
adpone, nec dulcis amores 15
sperne puer neque tu choreas,

26. Horace often uses a contrast of openness and tightness for life and death; see above, 55.

27. *Epod.* 13.4–5, where the correspondence of youth and greenness is almost formulaic.

donec virenti canities abest
morosa. nunc et campus et areae
  lenesque sub noctem susurri
    conposita repetantur hora, 20

nunc et latentis proditor intumo
gratus puellae risus ab angulo
  pignusque dereptum lacertis
    aut digito male pertinaci.

You see how Soracte stands white with deep snow, and how the laboring trees can no longer sustain their burden, and how the rivers stand frozen with the sharp cold. Dissolve the cold, piling wood plentifully upon the hearth, and, O Thaliarcus, draw forth copiously the four-year-old wine from its Sabine jar. Leave all else to the gods; once they have laid low the winds battling over a seething ocean, then neither the cypresses nor the old mountain ashes are shaken. Do not ask what tomorrow will bring, and set down as gain each day that Chance will give; and while you are young spurn not sweet love and dances, for as long as gloomy old age remains at a distance from your green youth. Now seek the Campus Martius and the squares, and soft whispers at the appointed hour of nightfall; now seek the enticing laugh that betrays some girl hiding in her secret corner, and the pledge snatched from her arm or finger, scarcely resisting.

Readers responding to Horace's initial *vides* have often found themselves unable to adjust their gaze to the final picture of a springtime tryst in the Campus Martius, and they have echoed Landor's bewilderment at *C.* 1.4 in inverted terms: "Everyone knows that the dead of winter at Rome is hardly the season for the *campus et areae* and *lenes sub noctem susurri.*" [28] Horace too knew it, and that fact, coupled with the didactic excursion of the central stanzas, suggests that he was

28. R. K. Hack, *HSCP, 27* (1916), 35. Fraenkel too (*Horace,* 177) feels the "incongruity" between winter and spring to mar the Ode.

not concerned with scenery alone. To "leave all else to the gods" (9) is practically equivalent to "seek not to know the future," or, more specifically, "ask not when you will die." Some such meaning is guaranteed by the accompanying recommendation to "set down as gain each day that Chance will give" (14). The queer instance of the gods' power (9–12) bears out the idea that mortality is the poem's real theme. *Stravere* can have the technical meaning "lay to rest" or "bury," and the absolute calm suggests the final peace of death. Cypress and "old" ash trees point the same way.[29] The contrast between the tossing ocean and its prophesied calm is of the same nature as that between the wine flowing before the hearth and the frozen streams of winter (1–8). *Fervidus* (10) is an epithet of which the customary meaning is "warm," though it is usually translated here as "seething." The young men who disdain old Lyce are *fervidi,* and the opposition in that Ode between blooming youth (*virens*) and the snowy hair of age (*nives capitis*) is apposite.[30] In *nive candidum Soracte* we are surely justified in catching a similar suggestion of wintry old age. Though the comparison is only latent, Horace brings it out through his collocation *virenti canities* (17). *Virens* means "youth" only secondarily; its primary meaning is "green" or "blossoming." And *canities,* "age," retains something of its radical meaning of "grayness" or "whiteness." The contrast of abstracts, we realize, is no more than an explication of the scenery itself, of Soracte's boughs laboring beneath the snow.

The Ode, then, yields a rough antithesis between warmth, tossing waters, moving branches, and green youth as against coldness, icing streams, stillness, and white old age. The seasonal inconsistency between the poem's beginning and end is less disconcerting once we recognize that Horace's terms are not exclusively external. *Nunc . . . nunc* indicates the nonliteral direction of his thought, unless we

29. The cypress was *inferis consecrata* (Servius, *ad Aen.* 3.64), and was used on funeral pyres: Vergil, *A.* 6.216; cf. Hor., *C.* 2.14.22–24; *Epod.* 5.18; Pliny, *H. N.* 16.33.140 (Mayhoff). The ash is the tree from which Europa's father suggests that she hang herself (*C.* 3.27.58); in *C.* 2.9.8 it is used in an analogy for Valgius' sadness at the death of Mystes; cf. *steriles orni* (Verg., *G.* 2.111). On *C.* 1.9 in general, see Wilkinson, *Horace,* 129 ff.

30. *C.* 4.13.6, 12, 26. Cf. *florente iuventa fervidus* (*A. P.* 115–16), and the association of youth–warmth–love in *C.* 1.4.19–20.

suppose him guilty of a total aberration and forgetful of what he is writing about. Although he may have begun the poem with nothing more than a vivid image before his eyes, the vision of Soracte's snows seems to have suggested, however obscurely, the old age and death that lie ahead.[31] He is concerned not with a single winter day but with the whole cycle of life. The proposed drinking bout is as generic as that of the thirteenth Epode, or as the *regna vini* of the Ode to Sestius; by addressing himself to Thaliarchus ("master of the revels") Horace indicates how little he wished to limit himself to a specific occasion. His withdrawal from the cold of winter into convivial warmth becomes generalized in the opposition between youth and old age (13 ff.), and *nec dulcis amores sperne puer* enjoins the same seizing of the moment as *benignius deprome quadrimum . . . merum*. Nor is the warning to "flee the future, absorb yourself in the present," merely abstract; rather it inheres in the very texture of the verse. Thus the poem's first word places us at a distant perspective—*fuge quaerere*—and the shrill staccatos of the first stanza make the soft sounds and long vowels of the second, with all it represents, doubly inviting. The distant view of the sea and of the stilled landscape (9–12) pushes us away again, while the last stanzas draw us in as surely as does the second. The sibilant invitation of *lenes sub noctem susurri* (19) beguiles our imagination, while the struggle through the confused syntax of the final stanza itself tends to involve us, as was the case with the final lines of the Ode to Lalage's lover (*C.* 2.5.21–24). And these sensuous contrasts between distance and closeness are, we realize, themselves the equivalent of the explicit moral contrast between future and present.

In an amusing article entitled "No Fire Without Smoke!" Gilbert Bagnani argued that the fireplace described in the Soracte Ode is architecturally impossible, and that Horace was more likely to have written the poem in the midsummer heat of Rome.[32] The reminder is salutary insofar as it encourages us to relinquish an exclusively literal interpretation for the Ode. Yet it would be a greater mistake still to go to the other extreme and suppose the poem to be no more than a code drawn up for the reader to decipher. If it were, few peo-

31. It may be relevant that Soracte was associated with the underworld: Servius, *ad Aen.* 11.785; cf. Pliny, *H. N.* 2.93.207 (Mayhoff).

32. *Phoenix, 8* (1954), 23 ff.

ple would continue to read it: who does a crossword puzzle more than once? Whether or not the poet was actually looking at a mountain is irrelevant. The poem persuades us that he was, and that we are as well. Soracte stands before us, a triumphant fact, with all the authority of the heavy *stet*. Horace conveys an immediate physical experience, and its reality, not the historical reality of his situation, is what matters. In reading such a poem there is a temptation to assign single meanings to the various elements in it, and to consider the poem only in terms of these abstractions. Yet to define Soracte simply as a symbol is to lose the sense of its evocative power. Like the vision of subsiding waves and static trees, the glimpse of Soracte is infinitely suggestive, and a number of responses or interpretations are possible. What is important is that we attend to the poet's voice as he speaks, a voice that is evoking certain feelings, not prescribing categories of thought. The Ode's "meaning" is not defined by what we figure out when we have finished with it, but by our momentary responses as we read. The poem moves by a sequence of moods rather than by strictly logical steps, and its fluid effect escapes any paraphrase to remain with the verse itself, with the progression of sounds, colors, and images. These, and not some gnomic tag that we extract, constitute the moral universe that Horace opens to us.

Succeeding the Soracte Ode after one intervening poem is the better known Ode to Leuconoe (*C.* 1.11). The similarity in theme of the two poems, as well as their proximity, makes it easy to read them as a pair:

> Tu ne quaesieris, scire nefas, quem mihi, quem tibi
> finem di dederint, Leuconoe, nec Babylonios
> temptaris numeros. ut melius, quidquid erit, pati.
> seu pluris hiemes seu tribuit Iuppiter ultimam,
> quae nunc oppositis debilitat pumicibus mare 5
> Tyrrhenum: sapias, vina liques, et spatio brevi
> spem longam reseces. dum loquimur, fugerit invida
> aetas: carpe diem quam minimum credula postero.

Do not seek, Leuconoe, for that knowledge is forbidden, what end the gods have assigned to me, what end to you, and do not experiment with Babylonian calculations. How

> much better, whatever will come, to await it patiently. Whether Jupiter has granted us many winters, or whether this is the last that now with its opposing rocks weakens the Tuscan sea, be wise, strain clear the wine, and prune down long hopes to accord with our brief span. Even while we are talking, envious time has fled: pluck the day, trusting as little as possible to the future.

The poem might almost be a more explicit redaction of the Soracte Ode. Its first words, *tu ne quaesieris,* echo the command to Thaliarchus, *fuge quaerere* (13), and *vina liques* (6) recalls *benignius deprome . . . merum* (6–8). "Strain clear the wine": Leuconoe, "clear-mind" (from λευκὸς νόος), is, like Thaliarchus, urged to leave murky speculations for the lucidity of the present.

The Odes not only have similar themes, but are also built on similar metaphors. "Prune down long hopes . . . pluck the day" matches the Soracte Ode's summons to "green youth" (17). In the Ode to Leuconoe winter is hardly more than a periphrasis for death, and the sea is obviously associated with life. The striking word *debilitat* (5), "lames" or "enfeebles," is better suited to a human than to a natural context, while the inversion that makes the winter cripple the sea with opposing rocks would be quite remarkable in a purely descriptive context.[33] The landscape is charged with a nonliteral meaning, and confirms as well the possibility of a similar significance in the winter and sea of the Soracte Ode.

From the criticism of *C.* 4.12, to a certain Vergil, we might well think the poem to have been written as an exercise for prosopographers. "The chief interest of the Ode centers in the question to whom it was addressed," deposes Wickham, and a body of spirited debate lends substance to his claim. Yet the question of whether or not this Vergil is Vergil the poet should not be more than peripheral, and

33. A. W. Verrall, *Studies in the Odes of Horace* (London, 1884), 113, found the inversion so odd (we would, of course, expect the sea to be wearing down the rocks) that he concluded that Horace must be praising a specific breakwater. He ignores the possibility of a nonliteral interpretation. For a good example of the use of *debilis,* see the fragment of Maecenas quoted below, 287.

we may better examine the imaginative community that the Ode shares with the other seasonal poems.

> Iam veris comites, quae mare temperant,
> inpellunt animae lintea Thraciae,
> iam nec prata rigent nec fluvii strepunt
> hiberna nive turgidi. [*C.* 4.12.1–4]

> Already the Thracian breezes, the companions of spring, that calm the sea, are striking ships' sails, and the meadows are no longer stiff with frost, nor do the rivers still roar, swollen with the winter snow.

The first two syllables recall Catullus' *iam ver egelidos refert tepores* (46.1). *Aemulatio* rather than *imitatio* prompts Horace, for he calls attention to his model only to depart from it. The spring breezes moved Catullus to a sympathetic revival (*iam laeti studio pedes vigescunt,* 8), but Horace could not detach spring more than momentarily from the lugubrious cycle it implied, nor forget the threat of "death's dark fires" (26). The effect of *temperant, inpellunt* (1–2) is almost that of an oxymoron, and prepares us for the paradoxical significance of spring that the second stanza brings out more clearly:

> nidum ponit Ityn flebiliter gemens
> infelix avis et Cecropiae domus
> aeternum opprobrium, quod male barbaras
> regum est ulta libidines. [5–8]

> The ill-fated swallow, tearfully mourning for Itys, builds its nest—that bird who is the eternal disgrace of the house of Cecrops, because she avenged too cruelly the brutal lusts of kings.

Editors often compare the lines to the epigrams of the tenth book of the *Greek Anthology*.[34] All are Catullan in their joyous welcome of

34. Cf. particularly the poem of Leonidas, *Anth. Pal.* 10.1; see also 10.2, 4, 5, 6, 14, 16.

spring, and many hail the swallow as a happy omen of the change. Horace's *infelix avis* is a bird of a different feather. The plaintive *i* and *e* sounds produce a mournful resonance, and we hear none of the joyful notes recorded by other authors. The harbinger of spring is at the same time a bird of ill omen, an "eternal disgrace" whose ancestry is studded with violence and death.[35] Through the next three stanzas the more somber aspect of the seasons' changes remains in abeyance, only to emerge again in the promise of the wine that will be provided:

> spes donare novas largus amaraque
> curarum eluere efficax. [19–20]

> Generous to bestow fresh hope and potent to wash away the bitterness of care.

Cura, as in the Ode to Grosphus (*C.* 2.16.22), seems close to the Lucretian *timor*, the fear of death. The last lines make overt the reminder that has been waiting beneath the Ode's surface:

> verum pone moras et studium lucri
> nigrorumque memor, dum licet, ignium
> misce stultitiam consiliis brevem:
> dulce est desipere in loco. [25–28]

> In truth, put aside your procrastination and your search for gain, and, mindful of death's dark fires, mix brief folly with your projects while you can. Foolishness is sweet in its place.

The moral urgency of the close effectively distinguishes the Ode from the category of invitation pieces such as Catullus' *cenabis bene* (13), which it superficially resembles. In bidding Vergil put aside the "thirst for gain" Horace continues to appeal to his friend's business sense. He reminds him that time is a commodity too precious to

35. The *animae Thraciae* (2) perhaps foreshadow the Thracian events described in the second stanza. *Regum* (8), a generalizing plural, refers specifically to Tereus, prince of Thrace. For some other associations of Thracian winds, cf. *Epod.* 13.3; *C.* 1.25.11.

be wasted even respectably, and summons him from his finances and *consiliis* much as he called Hirpinus from his *aeternis consiliis* (*C.* 2.11.11–12). *Non semper idem floribus est honor vernis:* the warning that Horace spelled out for Hirpinus he leaves Vergil to read for himself in the progression of the seasons. The *morae* (25) Horace bids Vergil put aside are more than each day's practical preoccupations. As in the similar command to Maecenas, *eripe te morae* (*C.* 3.29.5), the word suggests all that prevents us from living in the present. *In loco,* too, refers not to a single moment, but appeals to a more ample sense of what is fitting: ἐν καιρῷ. And *brevem,* like *dum licet,* reminds us that life itself is as brief as the spring.

The reminder of death was of course a commonplace in festive invitations. What is remarkable here is not the originality of Horace's awareness, but the originality of the progress by which he arrives at it. He instinctively associates the changes of the seasons with the changes of human life, and in this he adds a new dimension to the genre of "spring songs." Whenever we speak of Horace's debt to his predecessors we should remember that debts are nearly always repaid with interest.

Housman termed the last of the seasonal Odes (*C.* 4.7) the most beautiful poem in Latin, and few people have been rash enough to quarrel with him. The analogy that remained tacit in the previous poems now becomes explicit:

> Diffugere nives, redeunt iam gramina campis
> arboribusque comae;
> mutat terra vices, et decrescentia ripas
> flumina praetereunt.
>
> Gratia cum Nymphis geminisque sororibus audet (5)
> ducere nuda choros.
> inmortalia ne speres, monet annus et almum
> quae rapit hora diem.
>
> frigora mitescunt Zephyris, ver proterit aestas,
> interitura, simul (10)
> pomifer autumnus fruges effuderit, et mox
> bruma recurrit iners.

> The snows have fled, and already grass returns to the fields and leaves to the trees. The earth puts on her changes, and the rivers flow subsiding past their banks. The three Graces, companioned by the Nymphs, dare unrobed to conduct their dances. Hope not for immortality, warn the year and the hour that snatches off the nourishing day. The snows melt before the west winds, spring is trampled underfoot by summer, itself destined to die as soon as rich autumn has poured forth its fruits, and soon dead winter rushes back again.

The first word suggests that the correspondence between man and nature is already present, since "fleeing" is frequently associated with life's swift passage.[36] The very swiftness of the snow's departure raises mixed feelings. *Mutat terra vices* (3) warns, even more clearly than the prophetic *grata vice veris* in the Ode to Sestius (*C.* 1.4.1), that spring is only one of the year's changes, while the abruptness of the transition at line six indicates how instinctive it was for Horace to make the analogy. Only afterward does he go back and fill in the missing links, using the headlong flight of the year (9–12) to elaborate what is already latent in *diffugere* (1). The savage haste of time (*almum quae rapit hora diem,* 7–8) is intensified by the compressed cycle of seasons. *Mitescunt . . . proterit . . . effuderit . . . recurrit:* summer dies even in its victory over spring; autumn has barely time to pour forth its fruits before the return of winter. Long lines alternate with short to catch the very rhythm of life, a slow opening out and quick contraction; each couplet reproduces the movement of *C.* 1.4 as a whole. The second line of the couplet is catalectic, and the double weight, followed by sudden quiet, that falls upon *iners* (12) makes it lie upon the page heavy as a gravestone. Winter has the last word, rushing back to close the cycle that began with its flight.

In this Ode Horace makes plain what remained unsaid previously, that although our life is and should be like nature's cycle, it cannot share in nature's continuity:

> damna tamen celeres reparant caelestia lunae:
> nos ubi decidimus

36. *C.* 1.11.7, 2.11.5, 2.14.1, 3.29.48; *Epod.* 17.21; *S.* 2.6.40.

quo pius Aeneas, quo dives Tullus et Ancus, 15
pulvis et umbra sumus.

quis scit an adiciant hodiernae crastina summae
tempora di superi?
cuncta manus avidas fugient heredis, amico
quae dederis animo. 20

cum semel occideris et de te splendida Minos
fecerit arbitria,
non, Torquate, genus, non te facundia, non te
restituet pietas,

infernis neque enim tenebris Diana pudicum 25
liberat Hippolytum
nec Lethaea valet Theseus abrumpere caro
vincula Pirithoo.

Yet the swift moons recover their losses; but we are dust and shadow when once we have gone down where pious Aeneas, rich Tullus, and Ancus went before. Who knows whether the gods will add tomorrow to the sum of today? Everything you give to your own soul will escape the greedy hands of your heir. When once you have died, Torquatus, and Minos has pronounced his august judgment upon you, then neither your family, nor your eloquence, nor your piety will restore you to life. Diana cannot free chaste Hippolytus from the shades below, nor can Theseus break the Lethean bonds that hold his dear Pirithous.

Tamen (13) emphasizes the gap between the permanence of man's last change (*non . . . non . . . non te restituet*) and nature's permanence in her everlasting changes (*redeunt . . . recurrit . . . reparant*).[37] We have watched the swift moons as they warned Hirpinus (*C.* 2.11) and the *avarus* of *C.* 2.18, but now nature is less hortatory. The moon's perpetual cycle of death and rebirth is simply Horace's despair. He is concerned not so much with our duty to accept the

37. Catullus achieves a similar effect through elision (5.4). The repetition of *re* in *occidere et redire* is as powerful as Horace's twice repeated *re*.

human condition as with the sadness of the fact that we must. "For there is hope of a tree, if it be cut down, that it will sprout again, and that the tender branch thereof will not cease. . . . But man dieth, and wasteth away: yea, man giveth up the ghost, and where is he?" (Job 14)

One editor found the similarities between this poem and the Ode to Sestius (*C.* 1.4) so compelling that he supposed both to have been written about the same time.[38] Yet the bleakness of Horace's perspective in the Ode to Torquatus distinguishes the poem from that to Sestius, whether we explain the difference by the years that had elapsed between the two or simply by a change in Horace's mood. The Ode to Sestius strikes a balance of sorts between life and death, for the celebration of spring (*nunc decet,* 9) and the image of love and feasts (17–20), even though retrospective, is scarcely less encouraging than the bright imperatives of the Soracte Ode (*C.* 1.9). The Ode to Torquatus grants us nothing so positive. *Nos ubi decidimus* (14) and *cum semel occideris* (21) may remind us of the lines of Catullus:

> soles occidere et redire possunt:
> nobis cum semel occidit brevis lux,
> nox est pepetua una dormienda.
> da mi basia mille, deinde centum . . . [5.4–7]

> Suns may set and rise again, but once our brief light has set, then one eternal night is left to sleep. Give me a thousand kisses, then a hundred . . .

Yet the echo serves only to dramatize the difference between the two authors. Where Catullus rebounds with renewed vigor, Horace moves to a still darker view. Only one couplet (19–20) offers any encouragement, and it is dim and perfunctory at best. The vision of why it is necessary to pluck the day seems to have paralyzed his will to do so.

38. A. J. Macleane, *Q. Hor. Fl. Opera Omnia* (London, 1881), *ad loc.* He thought the Ode to Torquatus was then put away as being too visibly a duplicate of that to Sestius, and brought out again in order to fill up the fourth book.

The beautiful sounds of the final lines hardly mitigate the sternly repeated negatives, as myth adds its weight to nature's movement in forcing death upon us. Our only consolation for dying is, finally, its commonness.

While the fact of death separates man from the gods, the fact of his knowing it distinguishes him from the animals. But although everyone knows he will die, few live as though they did. "I see it feelingly," cries Gloucester, and many of the Odes are dedicated to making man see feelingly his own limits. The truism that all things change is not very compelling until it wins our imaginative allegiance as well as our intellectual homage. Horace intends us to experience the fact of change, and ultimately of death, with the immediacy that we experience a river, a flower, the moon, or the seasons. The difficulty of so many of the Odes does not contradict that immediacy, but is necessary to it: "We hate a poem which has a palpable design upon us," wrote Keats. The intellectual commitment that we must make to understand what Horace is talking about becomes an emotional commitment as well. "Poetry," the contemporary poet Donald Hall has said, "is not a revelation of technique, but a technique of revelation." Only by yielding ourselves fully to the demands of Horace's verse, and thus to the experience it conveys, can his poems say something that is significantly true rather than obviously true. In this way alone is it possible to feel in the Odes the power that Arnold defined:

> The grand power of poetry is its interpretive power, by which I mean, not the power of drawing out in black and white an explanation of the mystery of the universe, but the power of so dealing with things as to awaken in us a wonderfully full, new, and intimate sense of them.

We have often been told that decorum, τὸ πρέπον, is the key to Horace, but we tend to forget that when he himself uses the word he is likely to precede it with a *dum: dum decet.* The logic he invokes is that of a time cycle, not of a rigid right and wrong; "forever," "eternal," "always," and "delay" are likely to be the sternest accusations. It is difficult to see how we can banish "the *carpe diem* of his more superficial teaching" only to claim the Odes as "a secular Psalter for daily and yearly and age-long use." [39] The processional decorum implicit in *carpe diem,* far from being superficial, is central to Horace's thought. Just as he invokes nature in order to comfort Plancus and warn Pyrrha's lover, to rebuke the elegists Valgius and Tibullus and berate the aging Lydia and Chloris, to encourage the seasonable Chloe and caution the lover of unripe Lalage, so he appeals to it in reminding Hirpinus, Maecenas, Vergil, Sestius, Thaliarchus, Leuconoe, and Torquatus that their time is limited. Those not accepting change as the basis of human life, as it is of nature, are to be marked with charcoal as *insani.* All are unhealthy, if health be the natural state.

In the poems to aging women and ripe girls, to melancholy lovers and anxious politicians, Horace by and large stands apart from the ethic he enjoins. These Odes are not, in general, complicated emotionally, since what is proper is as clear as it is in the literary debates of the Epistles. Death does not lend itself to the same objectivity. In the few Satires that touch upon it, and sometimes in the Epistles, Horace treats death practically as an ally in debate, as a final argument against avarice or ambition. And occasionlly in the Odes Horace speaks with a comparable detachment—*C.* 2.18 is an example. Most of the Odes on death are less brisk. We need only compare Ofellus' cheerful citation of the *vivacior heres* (*S.* 2.2.132) with the greedy-handed heir of the Ode to Torquatus. The logical similarity disappears in the emotional gap between the two. Although the submission to nature's progress remains both proper and inevitable, it is not very exhilarating when viewed at first hand. Nature as a moral code collides with the demands of human nature, and reason and emotion stand unreconciled. Spring may be logically no more than a warning to prepare for winter, but by its very warmth and color it makes winter more unacceptable. The wine Horace calls for in the thirteenth Epode is equally disconcerting in its appeal. He specifies a vintage bottled in the year of his own birth; given the context of the poem we cannot help feeling his invitation to signal his acceptance of his own life's momentary consumption. Yet in its very sweetness

39. J. W. Mackail, *Classical Studies* (New York, 1926), 156, 148.

the wine is a protest against what it abstractly implies: Horace's wines are rarely unmixed. So too the feasts that represent an aware acceptance of life's conditions simultaneously attempt to defy them. Wine, incense, flowers, music, and complaisant girls unite in what is a virtual conspiracy of the senses against the blankness of *pallida Mors.*

An Ode to Dellius (*C.* 2.3) shows clearly this pull between intellectual acquiescence and emotional protest. Dellius had the distinction of changing sides three times during the civil wars, and for his acrobatics he earned from Messalla the name of *desultor bellorum civilium.* We might guess that Horace's recommendation of an "equable mind" (1) was intended for very specific application. Yet in addressing Dellius as *moriture* (4) Horace uses an epithet for all mankind, and his *aequam memento . . . mentem* expands into a *memento mori:*

> quo pinus ingens albaque populus
> umbram hospitalem consociare amant
> ramis? quid obliquo laborat
> lympha fugax trepidare rivo?
>
> huc vina et unguenta et nimium brevis
> flores amoenae ferre iube rosae,
> dum res et aetas et sororum
> fila trium patiuntur atra.
>
> cedes coemptis saltibus et domo
> villaque flavos quam Tiberis lavit,
> cedes et exstructis in altum
> divitiis potietur heres. [9–20]

Why do the tall pine and the white poplar love to embrace and create an inviting shade? Why does the fugitive stream strive rushing along in its winding course? Order someone to bring hither wine and unguents and the too brief flowers of the lovely rose, while the state of affairs and time and the black thread of the three sisters allow it. You will depart from the woodlands you have bought up, and from your

> house and from the villa that the yellow Tiber washes; you will depart, and an heir will take over the riches you have piled so high.

The invitation apparently reiterates that to Hirpinus: *cur non sub alta vel platano . . . potamus?* (*C.* 2.11.13 ff.). "The same bloom does not last forever on spring flowers," Horace warned in that Ode (*C.* 2.11.9–10), but the Ode to Dellius makes no such explicit appeal to nature. Instead, the setting is itself the only metaphor. *Consociare amant* (10) would normally be used only of human beings, and the sturdy pine and graceful poplar intertwined with one another present a suggestive picture. In the fleeting stream Horace seems to catch intimations of a different kind; to find books in running brooks has not always been so happy an exercise as it was in the forest of Arden. Several times Horace imagined time's passing in terms of flowing water, whether in random phrases like *fluunt tempora* and *adfluentis annos,* or in the structure of whole poems such as the Ode to Postumus.[40] The laboring stream, trembling along in its devious course, suggests the transience of all human efforts, and complements the beautiful stillness of the trees overhead.[41] The answer to the questions *quo . . . ? quid . . . ?* is then not merely "to provide a pleasant place for relaxation," but "to remind us, as well, of life's possibilities and of its shortness." *Nimium brevis flores* is equally evocative —for why "too brief"? Not, surely, because the flowers may not last the length of the feast. *Nimium* verges on the pathetic fallacy, and Horace's elegiac tone indicates that his concern is not simply horticultural. In their bloom the roses, like the intertwined branches overhead, remind us of the sensuous beauty of life; but in their briefness

40. *Ep.* 1.1.23; *C.* 4.11.19, 3.29.33 ff. On the water imagery of the Ode to Postumus (*C.* 2.14), see C. Dahl, *CP, 48* (1953), 240, and below, 285–86.

41. The connection of *labor* (11) with human life is pervasive, and *vitae labores* is almost a formula; cf. *C.* 1.7.18; *S.* 2.6.21. *Fugax* (12) is used constantly of time (see n. 36, above), and for a striking use of *trepidare* we need look no further than the next poem: *trepidavit aetas* (*C.* 2.4.23; cf. 2.11.4, 3.29.32). Verrall (*Studies,* 138), paraphrases: "Why, the place where we stand being so charming as it is, why does the flying stream (too apt a type of fretful man) still struggle to haste along its sloped course, instead of pausing to enjoy?" On the lines, see also Wilkinson, *Horace,* 128–29.

they urge that the beauty is passing, slipping away like the stream at our feet.

The lines do not have the appearance of deliberate allegory. As in the Soracte Ode, Horace seems to have emerged with a symbolic meaning rather than to have begun with one clearly in mind. Whatever the imaginative progress, the scene communicates a reminder of mortality hardly less explicit than the warning in the stanzas that follow. Yet even in thus forcing Dellius' mortality upon him, Horace seems to react against his own logic. The roses are "too brief": *nimium,* the habitual accusation of human excess, is now turned against nature. Moreover, the vivid fact of the roses' existence makes any lesson we deduce from them seem an impertinence. Their bloom is sensuously so compelling as to negate the logical fact that it must pass. The *amoenae rosae* are as ambiguous, finally, as the "late rose" of *C.* 1.38, where moral symbol and emotional value remain equally unresolved.

A similar tension between submission and resistance shapes the mournful cadences of the Ode to Postumus (*C.* 2.14). "Postumus" may be no more than an eponym for a man born after the death of his father, and hence already launched on the cycle of time that Horace describes. *Eheu fugaces, Postume, Postume, labuntur anni:* the years flow by until they are swallowed up in the streams of the Styx and the Cocytos, where water, the symbol of passing time, becomes the guardian of an eternal sameness. Nearly all of the Odes on death allow us at least a glimpse of a livelier world, if only through their antitheses. Now Horace neglects any dramatic confrontations. Life's brief reign (*brevem dominum,* 24) is not balanced against but subservient to *indomitae morti* (4). The heavy gerundives (*unda enaviganda . . . visendus Cocytos . . . linquenda tellus*), each emphatic in position, leave no room for the brisk imperatives of the Soracte Ode (*C.* 1.9) or the Ode to Leuconoe (*C.* 1.11). A counterpoint still forms the Ode, but it is not a counterpoint of statement, of life's warmth and beauty on the one hand and death's cold emptiness on the other. Rather it is the counterpoint between a single statement and the tone in which it is made. Abstractly the poem is perhaps the most ruthless that Horace wrote, but its accents rescue it. From the opening *eheu* and the extraordinarily rare double vocative, to the repeated *frustra* and the plaintive farewell to wife and child, the poem's mood is at odds with its stern logic, and almost challenges it. The last stanza summarizes the double effect of the whole:

> absumet heres Caecuba dignior
> servata centum clavibus et mero
> tinguet pavimentum superbo,
> pontificum potiore cenis. [25–28]

> A worthier heir will drink up your Caecuban now guarded by a hundred keys, and will stain the tiled floor with proud wine, richer than that drunk at the pontiffs' banquets.

We remember the misers with their hoarded wine in the Satires,

> filius aut etiam haec libertus ut ebibat heres,
> dis inimice senex, custodis? [*S.* 2.3.122–23]

> Do you guard it, old man hateful to the gods, so that your son, or even a freedman heir, will drink it up?

and in these terms we understand why the dissolute heir is "worthier." He at least enjoys the present, not fencing himself from it by a hundred keys. His profligacy is splendid by comparison with the caution of his father. Piety is futile against death (2–7), and the wine, "richer than that drunk at the pontiffs' banquets," represents the more effective piety that directs itself toward this life; it incarnates what is almost a secular sacrament.

Here, then, in all logic, is the compensating *carpe diem* we tend to expect in Odes of this sort. Yet the mood of the lines undercuts so positive a conclusion. *Dignior* is almost sardonic, and both alternatives seem equally futile. The wine is *superbus,* and suggests all our proud responsibilities to the present—yet if the wine is not hoarded it is wasted. At best, life is only squandered. The vivid wine splashing upon the floor is hardly more comforting than the rush of years as they flow away. As in the Odes to Torquatus (*C.* 4.7) and Dellius

(*C.* 2.3), the heir's role is different from that which he plays in the Satires. Logically, he remains part of the cycle Horace brings before us, a triumphant reminder of time's passing. But the poet's tone undermines his logic, and we sense a muted bitterness at the very progress he upholds.

The sadness of the Ode to Postumus, like that of the Ode to Torquatus, is fierce precisely because it is controlled. Horace never descended to the kind of self-pity satirized by Lucretius:

> "brevis hic est fructus homullis;
> iam fuerit neque post umquam revocare licebit." [3.914]

> "Life's rewards are so brief for us poor creatures; soon they will be no more, nor will it ever then be possible to call them back."

Like Lucretius, Horace did not stain time's majesty with complaints. Rather, he reaffirmed the passing of the years most beautifully when, as in the Odes on death, it was to his own loss to do so. Without his austere conviction of the properness of age and death, we would have the indulgence of a Maecenas, which seems merely pathetic: "Cripple my hand, my foot, my hip; make me a hunchback, knock out my gleaming teeth; if only life remains, I am satisfied! Give me this even if I should be upon the cross." [42] Horace may have felt death to be equally intolerable, but his feelings were scaled against the conviction that one must acclimate to the intolerable simply because it was part of the world as it is.

The pull between revolt from nature's laws and acceptance of them is nowhere more clear than in the Ode to Vergil on the death of their common friend Quintilius:

> Quis desiderio sit pudor aut modus
> tam cari capitis? praecipe lugubris
> cantus, Melpomene, cui liquidam pater
> vocem cum cithara dedit. [*C.* 1.24.1–4]

42. *Fr.* 3, *Poet. Lat. Min.* (Baehrens).

What shame or limit should there be to our grief for one so dear? Begin your mournful dirge, Melpomene, on whom your father has bestowed a clear voice together with the cithara.

The opening question seems rhetorical: what conceivable limit should there be to our grief? Horace's feelings appear to be identified with Vergil's, but as we read on a gap opens between them:

ergo Quintilium perpetuus sopor 5
urget; cui Pudor et Iustitiae soror
incorrupta Fides nudaque Veritas
quando ullum inveniet parem?

multis ille bonis flebilis occidit,
nulli flebilior quam tibi, Vergili. 10
tu frustra pius, heu, non ita creditum
poscis Quintilium deos.

quid? si Threicio blandius Orpheo
auditam moderere arboribus fidem,
num vanae redeat sanguis imagini, 15
quam virga semel horrida

non lenis precibus fata recludere
nigro conpulerit Mercurius gregi?
durum: sed levius fit patientia
quidquid corrigere est nefas. 20

And so perpetual sleep presses upon Quintilius. When shall Modesty and incorruptible Faith, the sister of Justice, and pure Truth ever find his equal? He died wept by many good men, but by no one more than by you, Vergil. Pious in vain, alas, you demand Quintilius back from the gods, he who was granted to life on no such terms.

What? If more winningly than Thracian Orpheus you should strike the lyre once heeded by the trees, would then the life blood return to the empty shade which Mercury, unwilling to open the gates of fate in answer to our prayers, has once gathered into his black throng with his ghostly wand? It is hard; but whatever cannot be righted becomes more bearable through patience.

"What man on such an occasion is at leisure to amuse himself with the little plaster images of *Pudor* and *Fides,* of *Iustitia* and *Veritas,* or disposed to make a comparison of Vergil and Orpheus?" asks Landor's Boccaccio (*Pentameron,* 4). The personified reminders of Quintilius' virtues deepen our sorrow at his passing; such praise was conventional in a *consolatio.* Yet, equally important, the catalogue recalls similar lists of the qualities that only the foolish could think to be of any value against death.[43] The double effect of the catalogue is reproduced by the ambiguity of *non ita creditum* (11). Its meaning at first seems to be: "You demand back Quintilius from the gods, to whose safe keeping you entrusted him on no such terms." Yet a less sympathetic and more austere construction fits the lines equally well: "You demand back Quintilius from the gods, Quintilius, who was in fact entrusted to you, and to life, on no such terms." The latter sense of the lines prepares us for the abrupt question opening the fourth stanza, where Horace separates himself decisively from the tearful Vergil. Orpheus failed to rescue Eurydice, and his unremitting laments, as Vergil could remember from his own *Georgics,* were to cause his destruction.[44] The question *quid? si Threicio . . .* itself answers Horace's initial query, *quis pudor aut modus?* Nature's changes are inevitable, and in this case irrevocable; therefore the very futility of grief should limit it. The Ode's second half reconsiders the first, with the emphatic *frustra* (11) a central pivot. The dirges of the opening are themselves seen to be in vain, just as Quintilius' own virtues proved to be. *Conpulerit* (18) stamps with

43. Cf. *C.* 2.14.2 ff., 2.18.32 ff., 4.7.23 ff.; *Ep.* 1.6.25 ff.; Hom., *Il.* 21.106; Lucr., 3.1024 ff.; Prop., 3.18.11 ff.; Ov., *Am.* 3.9.37. For further references see B. Lier, *Philologus, 62* (1903), 462–63; R. Lattimore, *Themes in Greek and Latin Epitaphs,* 250 ff.

44. Horace may well be deliberately reminding Vergil of Vergil's own treatment of the Orpheus story, for *non lenis precibus fata recludere* (17) is close to Vergil's *nesciaque humanis precibus mansuescere corda* (*G.* 4.470). Similarly, the Ode's final two lines may be a delicate reminder to Vergil of Vergil's own praise of *patientia;* see Suet., *Vit. Verg.* 67 (Reifferscheid); Donatus, *Vit. Verg.* 18; cf. Verg., *A.* 5.710.

finality the earlier *urget* (6), while *vanae imagini* (15) and *nigro gregi* (18) substitute less romantic terms for the initial *perpetuus sopor* (5). *Flebilis* and *flebilior* (9–10) suggest the *flebiles modi* (*C.* 2.9.9) of the elegists, but the not altogether unpleasant connotations of the word are ruthlessly crushed by the final *durum* (19). Horace's own sadness makes his address to Vergil very different in tone from his impatient rebuke to Valgius: *tu semper urges flebilibus modis Mysten ademptum . . . desine mollium tandem querellarum* (*C.* 2.9.9 ff.). But his moral position has not altered. His cry of grief yields, by the poem's end, to an assertion of the order that grief defies. Neither is absolute. Only the powerful balance is final: *frustra . . . heu.*

As the seemingly casual reference to white hair in the Ode to Hirpinus (*C.* 2.11.15) reminds us, *carpe diem* is rarely the cry of youth. Those reasonably sure of the future can afford not to formalize the present. It does not call for self-conscious celebration, but is simply there, like the air we breath, which we hardly become aware of until there is danger of losing it. "No young man ever thinks he will die," said Hazlitt. Only once was Catullus moved to a *vivamus* by the prospect of the night ahead (5.1 ff.), and *fugere* is not a word he uses of time. Beyond all distinctions in temperament between the two writers, we should remember that Horace was older when he began to write the Odes than Catullus was when he died. Where love and betrayal produced the most affecting of Catullus' poems, it was death that provided the creative impulse for what is perhaps Horace's finest work. And just as Catullus tends to become most formal when he is most passionately involved, so Horace invokes nature's progress most ceremonially when he is most likely to resist it. The contradictions that Catullus feels within himself arise from a world he cannot accept; Horace's melancholy is born of his determination to accept it. The tension is rather one of mood than of statement, and the confrontations are rarely explicit. Only occasionally do we sense a radical split in the amatory Odes, such as that to Lalage's lover (*C.* 2.5) or those of the fourth book. These, too, are as much concerned with age as they are with love, and in general it is to the poems on death that we must look. The pressures these Odes betray are quite different from the careful contrasts that Horace so often engineers, for they reveal a fundamental conflict in the poet's own attitude. "We make out of the quarrel with others, rhetoric, but of the quarrel with ourselves, poetry," wrote Yeats. That struggle, for Horace as for Catullus, produced his most powerful verse.

Book Four

Ah, when to the heart of man
Was it ever less than a treason
To go with the drift of things,
To yield with a grace to reason,
And bow and accept the end
Of a love or a season?
—Robert Frost, "Reluctance"

Although none of Horace's Odes may be called youthful, there is a perceptible difference between those of the first three books and those of the fourth, which appeared ten years later. The political Odes of the early twenties, and those that came after the *Carmen Saeculare,* owe their differences, probably, to the inevitably altered imaginative response that the changes in the state produced, rather than to a shift in Horace's own political position. But in the more private poems we feel a change in the poet himself. His moral standards have not altered, but he persistently fails to reconcile his emotions with them. The split heretofore largely confined to the Odes on death becomes virtually endemic. The first poem, to Ligurinus, states the terms of the dilemma. The opening lines suggest an example of tranquillity recollected in emotion:

Intermissa, Venus, diu
rursus bella moves? parce precor, precor.
non sum qualis eram bonae
sub regno Cinarae. desine, dulcium

mater saeva Cupidinum, 5
circa lustra decem flectere mollibus

iam durum imperiis; abi,
  quo blandae iuvenum te revocant preces.

tempestivius in domum
  Pauli purpureis ales oloribus 10
comissabere Maximi,
  si torrere iecur quaeris idoneum.

Once again, Venus, you rouse me to battles long interrupted. Spare me, I pray, I pray. No longer am I the man I was in the reign of good Cinara. Forbear, cruel mother of sweet desires, to bend one who is now almost fifty and hardened against your soft commands; go hence, where the winning prayers of youths call you. Borne by your purple swans, you will go more seasonably to visit the house of Paulus Maximus, if you seek a suitable heart to inflame.

Ovid postulated that love and war were fit only for the young (*Am.* 1.9.3–6), and for vindication he might have pointed to Horace, who withdraws simultaneously from both. The poem is virtually a *recusatio* of the affections. Protesting his own unfitness for Venus' service—since he is by now "around fifty" (6)—Horace recommends to her a younger warrior, Paulus Maximus. *Non sum qualis eram:* nature's changes are again the standard of propriety (*idoneum,* 12). Time is as uncompromising in its laws (*tempestivius in domum Pauli,* 9–10) as it was in the complementary Ode to *tempestiva Chloe* (*C.* 1.23).

Horace had ridiculed both Lydia (*C.* 1.25) and Chloris (*C.* 3.15) for their failure to surrender the privileges of youth in their old age, and in applying the same standards to himself[45] his consistency is unassailable. Yet in the Ode's first word there is a latent conflict. *Intermissa* is prophetic, for the poem's end proves that Horace's passion for Ligurinus is not, in fact, gone, but has merely been interrupted. Where Catullus is concerned with betrayal, Horace is more concerned with self-betrayal, and in the last stanzas of *C.* 4.1 his failure

45. Cf. especially *C.* 4.1.31–32 and *C.* 3.15.13 ff.

to abide by his own ideas becomes overt. His rejection of love breaks upon a haunting confession of its renewal:

> me nec femina nec puer
>   iam nec spes animi credula mutui
> nec certare iuvat mero
>   nec vincire novis tempora floribus.
>
> sed cur heu, Ligurine, cur
>   manat rara meas lacrima per genas?
> cur facunda parum decoro
>   inter verba cadit lingua silentio?
>
> nocturnis ego somniis
>   iam captum teneo, iam volucrem sequor
> te per gramina Martii
>   campi, te per aquas, dure, volubilis. [29–40]

> Now neither woman nor boy delights me, nor the credulous hope of finding my love returned; nor do I wish to contend in wine, nor to bind my temples with fresh flowers. But why, alas, Ligurinus, why does a tear every now and again slip out onto my cheek? Why does my tongue, once so eloquent, fall into an ill-becoming silence in the midst of speech? In my dreams at night, now I hold you captive, now I follow you as you flee over the turf of the Campus Martius, now, cruel one, I pursue you through the streaming water.

The emphasis that falls upon *dure* (40) from both meter and position leads us to recall its previous occurrence: *mollibus iam durum imperiis* (7). The word serves as a weather vane marking the Ode's change of direction. *Duri dicuntur qui amorem oblatum respuunt neque precibus conmoventur:* the term was standard in the erotic vocabulary.[46] In announcing himself *durus* to the blandishments of Venus, Horace rejects the whole world of elegiac experience, but in addressing Ligurinus as *dure* he re-enters it, assuming the posture

46. The definition is that of R. Pichon (*De sermone amatorio,* 136), who lists many examples of the use of *durus*. Cf. Hor., *C.* 3.7.32.

of the *miser amator*.[47] The conventional gestures of the penultimate stanza seem a deliberate stepping back after the moving accents of *me nec femina . . .* (29–32). They re-establish the mood struck by the exquisitely formal language of the opening prayer (*parce precor, precor . . . abi*), and beg us to recognize his own ironic detachment from the situation—the technique is familiar.[48] But the tone of the last stanza is quite different. The oxymoron *dure, volubilis* leaves us with the essence of the whole poem, as Horace's hard resolution slides away and dissolves.[49] And the overwhelming sensuousness of the final image [50] irretrievably banishes not only Horace's earlier excuses but the whole atmosphere of stylized complaint as well.

In the Ode to Glycera (*C.* 1.19) Horace found himself forced by Venus to give his heart again to loves he had thought were finished, and he encourages us to remember that Ode by repeating its first line, *mater saeva Cupidinum* (5). Horace's reversal of position in the Ode to Ligurinus also recalls an Ode to Chloe (*C.* 3.26), only five poems before, where his boasted withdrawal from love's service was likewise followed by his re-enlistment. Yet the superficial similarities to these two poems brings out more clearly their fundamental difference from the Ode to Ligurinus. In the two earlier poems Horace offers no reasons for his retirement, and his capitulations to Venus are lighthearted. Now he invokes a more serious context, introducing for the first time the argument of his advancing years. The impropriety Horace feels emerges vividly from the rare elision of the final syllable of line thirty-five. Our tongue must literally "fall" to the next line in an "ill-becoming" manner. In *parum decoro* we catch a reproach based on something more important than social etiquette. By plunging back into love's troubled waters Horace violates the moral decorum that he had so often invoked, and he lays himself

47. Horace's furtive tear and lapses into silence have precedents running back through Catullus 51 to Sappho 2 (Diehl). Cf. Hor., *Epod.* 11.9; Verg., *A.* 4.76; see also, Pichon, *De sermone amatorio,* 181–82, and above, 113.

48. See above, 144 ff.

49. The immediate effect of the conjunction of *dure* and *volubilis* is the same whether *volubilis* be nominative singular or, as seems more likely, accusative plural.

50. In its physical immediacy the image recalls Lucretius' lover thirsting in midstream: 4.1097 ff.; cf. Ov., *Am.* 2.2.43; *Met.* 9.762.

open to the very ridicule that he had leveled at Lydia and Chloris.

One of the things for which Horace upbraided Chloris was her continuing efforts to play upon the lyre (*C.* 3.15.14). Song, like love, is to be left behind with youth. Horace was prepared to practice what he preached, and when he introduced the first book of Epistles, about three years after the publication of the first three books of Odes, he declared his own abandonment of lyric verse:

> Prima dicte mihi, summa dicende Camena,
> spectatum satis et donatum iam rude quaeris,
> Maecenas, iterum antiquo me includere ludo?
> non eadem est aetas, non mens.
> . . . . . .
> nunc itaque et versus et cetera ludicra pono.
>
> [*Ep.* 1.1.1–4, 10]

> Maecenas, celebrated by my earliest song, and worthy to be by my latest, you seek to shut me up again in my old school, even though I have proved myself sufficiently, and have been presented with the wooden foil of discharge. No longer is my age the same, nor my inclination. . . . And so now I put aside verses and all other playthings.

As a man Horace has put aside the things of a child, among them the game of poetry. *Nec lusisse pudet, sed non incidere ludum.* The Epistle to Florus (probably written soon after the first book of Epistles) reaffirms his resolution:

> singula de nobis anni praedantur euntes:
> eripuere iocos, venerem, convivia, ludum;
> tendunt extorquere poemata: quid faciam vis?
>
> [*Ep.* 2.2.55–57]

> The years as they pass steal things from us one by one. They have snatched away jesting, love, feasting, games; now they are bent on twisting away my poems—what would you have me do?

nimirum sapere est abiectis utile nugis
et tempestivum pueris concedere ludum
ac non verba sequi fidibus modulanda Latinis,
sed verae numerosque modosque ediscere vitae. [141–44]

Doubtless it is useful to cast aside trifling and to learn wisdom, and to leave games to youths as more seasonable for them; not to hunt for words to tune to the Latin lyre, but to learn the numbers and measures of a true life.

Mirth, love, feasts, games, and poetry are judged unfit for age. *Nugae* and *ludus* (ambiguously either "sport" or "poetry") are *tempestivum* only for the young. Yet it is not to time's stately progress that Horace yields. In one passage time is a thief (*praedantur*); in the other, *nimirum* gives an almost bitter flavor to the renunciation that follows. Horace no longer seems comfortable with the moral position he has assumed.

The last book of Odes appeared in 13 B.C., after long silence—*ex longo intervallo,* in Suetonius' words.[51] The *intermissa* with which the Ode to Ligurinus opens strikes an apposite note for Horace's resumption of lyric verse, and he must have been aware of the two contexts the word could imply. *Non sum qualis eram* (3) echoes his earlier justification for abandoning lyrics: *non eadem est aetas, non mens* (*Ep.* 1.1.4). And in vainly commanding Venus to go *tempestivius* to the more youthful Paulus (9), Horace uses the same language he did in dismissing the Muse and declaring poetry a sport *tempestivum* only for the young (*Ep.* 2.2.142). The garland of *novi flores* that he unsuccessfully attempts to reject (32) may be primarily associated with youth, wine, and love, but it suggests as well the poet's wreath. The Ode records the capitulation not only of a lover but of the poet. Although Horace may have been pressured into the poems on Tiberius and Drusus, the rest of the fourth book was not composed merely as padding. The fineness and intensity of the private poems make it apparent that Horace was the victim not so much of his official patron as of the charms of verse itself: Augustus makes

51. Suetonius, *Vit. Hor.* 46 (Reifferscheid). Suetonius does not, of course, include the performance of the *Carmen Saeculare* in 17 B.C.

a poor Venus. Horace returned at last to the end he had prayed for and then later renounced, an old age "not lacking the lyre" (*C.* 1.31.19–20).

As though to make up for his defection in the opening Ode, Horace reasserts the validity of nature as a moral standard in a second Ode to Ligurinus. His own position should be more comfortable, for now it is Ligurinus who is remiss:

> O crudelis adhuc et Veneris muneribus potens,
> insperata tuae cum veniet pluma superbiae
> et quae nunc umeris involitant, deciderint comae,
> nunc et qui color est puniceae flore prior rosae,
> mutatus, Ligurine, in faciem verterit hispidam,
> dices "heu" quotiens te speculo videris alterum,
> "quae mens est hodie, cur eadem non puero fuit,
> vel cur his animis incolumes non redeunt genae?"
>
> [*C.* 4.10]

> O you who are still hard of heart, though potent in the gifts of Venus, when the unexpected down shall come upon your proud cheeks, and those locks that now float about your shoulders shall fall, and your color, fairer than the bloom of the damask rose, shall have changed to bristles, then, Ligurinus, each time you see your altered self in your mirror you will say, "Alas, why did I not as a youth have the same desires that I do today? Or why do not those cheeks return unscathed to me now?"

That "beauty is but a flowre, which wrinckles will devoure," was common knowledge to writers of the *Greek Anthology,* and Horace's editors have emphasized the conventional affiliations of the Ode. Yet the tradition it mirrors is less important than the personal perspective it reaffirms. We need not go beyond the first three books of Odes to find precedent for the cycle of ages it comprehends in its movement from green youth to seasonable maturity to dry old age. *Comae* (3) can mean "foliage" as well as "hair," and the tentative analogy with nature becomes more certain with the comparison of Ligurinus' color to that of roses (4).[52] Roses which, as in the Ode to Dellius (*C.* 2.3.13–14), are all too brief; the temporal theme introduced by *adhuc* (1) becomes insistent with *nunc . . . nunc* (3–4). The repetition implies not only the ripeness of the present but its transitoriness, and behind the lines we sense a familiar urgency: *non semper idem floribus . . .* (*C.* 2.11.9).

Although the Ode is thematically close to the Ode to Chloe (*C.* 1.23), the differences are more interesting than the similarities. In both poems nature argues against those who are seasonable but recalcitrant. In the earlier poem Horace's attitude is unclouded, for in the first three books it is not the amatory Odes that give us the reason why we should "as a youth spurn not sweet loves" (*C.* 1.9.15–16). But in *C.* 4.10, Horace's awareness of what is to come all but smothers the possible enjoyment of the present. Where the Ode to Chloe deals with past and present, that to Ligurinus dwells upon the relation of present to future. Starting as a notice of spring's arrival, the poem becomes a prophecy of the fall and winter ahead: *deciderint comae.*

> Or is it that she dimly doth foresee
> Across her youth the joys grow less and less,
> The burden of the days that are to be:
> Autumn and withered leaves and vanity,
> And winter bringing end in barrenness.

When Dowson wrote these lines to his "Lady April" he was in his early thirties; Horace was nearly fifty. In addressing Chloe, Horace stood detached from the seasonal decorum he invoked, but in the Ode to Ligurinus he becomes part of it. He speaks the lines he foresees for his favorite, and their authoritative tones are bought at the price of a certain pathos. Horace's own mirror might even then have told him that such invitations were no longer fitting: *non sum qualis eram.* For every year that Ligurinus gains, Horace loses one. The equation formulated for Lalage's lover (*C.* 2.5.14–15) is not so

52. Bentley's emendation of the peculiar word *pluma* (2) to *bruma* is not really necessary, though tempting. The analogy between Ligurinus' aging and the progress of the seasons is clear in either case.

comforting when seen from the other side. Horace's appeal to nature seems to backfire, and he is no happier in championing its standards than he was in evading them in *C.* 4.1.

In *C.* 4.13, to Lyce, Horace returns to a theme he had treated twice previously, the efforts of old women to remain young:

> Audivere, Lyce, di mea vota, di
> audivere, Lyce: fis anus; et tamen
> vis formosa videri
> ludisque et bibis inpudens
>
> et cantu tremulo pota Cupidinem 5
> lentum sollicitas: ille virentis et
> doctae psallere Chiae
> pulcris excubat in genis.
>
> inportunus enim transvolat aridas
> quercus et refugit te, quia luridi 10
> dentes, te quia rugae
> turpant et capitis nives.

> The gods, Lyce, have heard my prayers, the gods, Lyce, have heard them: you have become old; and yet you wish still to seem beautiful, and shamelessly you sport and drink, and when drunk you attempt with your quavering song to rouse an unwilling Cupid. He keeps watch over the fair cheeks of blooming Chia, skilled upon the lyre. Hastily he flies past dried oaks, and he flees from you, whom yellowed teeth and snowy hair disfigure.

Lentum (6) often means "pliant" or "flexible," though here its sense is "stiff" or "unwilling." The word reminds us of Cupid's customary availability, and its opposed meaning here brings out more forcibly the unnaturalness of Lyce's efforts. In *lentum* there may be also an echo of *letum:* for Lyce, as opposed to the blooming Chia, love is dead. *Inportunus* (9) has a similar double effect. Normally, when used of Cupid, it would be associated with importunate lovers, but here it describes instead Cupid's hasty flight from Lyce. Like *lentus, inportunus* suggests a double standard: Lyce as she would be, and Lyce as she really is.[53]

Horace's triumphant assurances that Cupid disdains withered oaks and snowy locks for "blooming" Chia (6 ff.) propose a familiar standard of behavior—we need only recall the youths in the Ode to Lydia who rightly prefer green ivy to dry leaves (*C.* 1.25.17 ff.). Lyce's failings remind us as well of those of Chloris (*C.* 3.15.3 ff.). Lyce too would sport among the youths and drain the wine cup; even the hiss of *f*'s and *s*'s (2–6) recalls the earlier poem (*C.* 3.15.1 ff.). Yet although the abstract morality is identical with that in the Odes to Lydia and to Chloris, the impact of the poem is quite different. Lyce strikes us as pathetic rather than egregious. The poem's mood is comparable to that of the final lines of the Epistle to Florus:

> vivere si recte nescis, decede peritis.
> lusisti satis, edisti satis atque bibisti:
> tempus abire tibi est, ne potum largius aequo
> rideat et pulset lasciva decentius aetas. [*Ep.* 2.2.213–16]

> If you do not know how to live rightly, then yield to those who do. You have played enough, you have eaten and drunk enough; it is time to leave, lest, when you have drunk more than is right, wanton youth shall properly laugh and push you aside.

Here Horace's brisk logic is imperiled by his sympathy with those properly pushed aside by *lasciva aetas;* the lines read almost like a prophecy of Ovid's success. With the close of the Ode to Lyce the same kind of division in Horace's attitude becomes unmistakable:

> nec Coae referunt iam tibi purpurae
> nec cari lapides tempora, quae semel
> notis condita fastis 15
> inclusit volucris dies.

53. *Pota* (5) by its sound association with *potens* (cf. *C.* 4.10.1) may suggest the same double application.

quo fugit venus, heu, quove color, decens
quo motus? quid habes illius, illius,
quae spirabat amores,
quae me surpuerat mihi, 20

felix post Cinaram notaque et artium
gratarum facies? sed Cinarae brevis
annos fata dederunt,
servatura diu parem

cornicis vetulae temporibus Lycen, 25
possent ut iuvenes visere fervidi
multo non sine risu
dilapsam in cineres facem.

Now neither Coan purple robes nor precious stones can bring back for you those years which winged time has once stored away in the annals known to all. Whither has your beauty fled, whither, alas, your color, whither your graceful movements? What have you now of her, of her, who once breathed forth love and stole me from myself? She who was happy then, after Cinara, and famous for her beauty and lovely arts? But to Cinara the Fates gave brief years, determined to keep Lyce alive until she should equal the years of the aged crow, so that glowing youths, much amused, might look upon the torch fallen into ashes.

Even in its swiftness (*volucris,* 16), time becomes a prison (*inclusit*); the packed order of words itself confirms the hopelessness of Lyce's attempt to escape from the present. The gap between Lyce's pretense to herself (*vis formosa videri,* 3) and reality (*possent ut iuvenes visere,* 26) is final. The moral decorum is clear—yet *eheu fugaces, Postume, Postume,* is no sadder than *quo fugit Venus, heu, . . . illius, illius.* Horace's love for Lyce had been at best an autumnal passion; she came after Cinara, habitually associated with his youth.[54] In looking back to his affair with Lyce, Horace cannot afford the

54. Cf. *C.* 4.1.4; *Ep.* 1.7.28, 1.14.33.

arrogance that informed his attack on Lydia or Chloris. By now he might more readily sympathize with her situation than triumph in it, for he can no longer number himself among the *fervidi iuvenes,* laughing at an old flame, now cold. The *volucris dies* has fled from Horace no less swiftly; the unusual form *surpuerat* (20) reminds us that Horace's own youthfulness (*puer*) has been snatched from him. Though he is still prepared to maintain his austere standards, he finds it increasingly difficult to abide by them. Ridiculing Lyce's attempt to hold to her youth he cannot suppress his own similar attachment to the past. The Ode to Torquatus (*C.* 4.7) made explicit the fatal difference between man's cycle and that of the world around him, and the Ode to Lyce dramatizes the consequences of that admission. No longer is the decorum of nature an absolute; human failings have an equal strength. In the poems to Lydia and Chloris the gap between the two elicited only our ridicule, but now it commands our sympathy.[55]

With Catullus it is a first love that is so affecting, but with Horace it is a last. His Ode to Phyllis (*C.* 4.11) is as beautiful as almost anything he wrote, and its neglect seems little short of perverse:

Est mihi nonum superantis annum
plenus Albani cadus, est in horto,
Phylli, nectendis apium coronis,
  est hederae vis

multa, qua crinis religata fulges;
ridet argento domus, ara castis
vincta verbenis avet immolato
  spargier agno;

cuncta festinat manus, huc et illuc
cursitant mixtae pueris puellae,
sordidum flammae trepidant rotantes
  vertice fumum. [1–12]

55. For a different view of *C.* 4.13, see F. O. Copley, *Exclusus Amator* (Baltimore, 1956), 160, n. 40: "These poems [*C.* 2.8 and 4.13] are even worse than the worst of Catullus, for they display an ugly, vicious temper in place of Catullus' honest, if misguided, attempts at humor."

> I have a jar of Alban wine more than nine years old; in my garden, Phyllis, there is parsley for weaving garlands; there is a wealth of ivy for you to bind your hair and shine forth the more fair; the house is beaming with silver; the altar, bound with sacred leaves, longs to be sprinkled with the blood of a sacrificial lamb. All the band of house slaves is hurrying about; here and there rush the mingled boys and girls; the quivering flames roll aloft the dirty smoke.

Phyllis is associated with light and growth; green ivy is the natural setting for her gleaming beauty (4–5). Horace's description of his household is calculated to entice her there. The garden is filled with greenery, the house glows with polished silver, the altar is bound with vines, and everywhere there is bustling activity. The mingled sexes of the servants (10) suggests, in a minor way, the Ode's erotic intent, while the trembling flames they tend may have something of the conventional associations with warmth, love, and youth.

Yet the picture is not all gaiety. The smoke that rolls aloft is dirty, *sordidum,* and the image of brightness surrounded by darkness sets the mood of the whole. The occasion is Maecenas' birthday:

> ut tamen noris, quibus advoceris
> gaudiis, Idus tibi sunt agendae,
> qui dies mensem Veneris marinae
> findit Aprilem,
>
> iure sollemnis mihi sanctiorque
> paene natali proprio, quod ex hac
> luce Maecenas meus adfluentis
> ordinat annos. [13–20]

> Still, so that you may know to what joys you are called, it is the Ides that you are to celebrate, the day that splits in half April, the month of sea-born Venus, a day rightly honored by me as almost more sacred than my own birthday, because from it my Maecenas reckons his onflowing years.

Horace's comparison of the two birthdays, enforced by the unusual "my Maecenas," suggests that he felt an association more profound than friendship, however close. The *adfluentis annos* are, we realize, his own as well. That both Horace and Maecenas died in the same year is an arbitrary fact, but more pertinent is Horace's prediction that they would:

ibimus, ibimus
utcumque praecedes, supremum
carpere iter comites parati. [*C.* 2.17.10–12]

> We shall go, we shall go, whenever you lead on, prepared to take as comrades the final journey.

The bond Horace feels between their two destinies makes Maecenas' birthday an equivocal joy. Though the day itself marks a happy celebration, it marks off, at the same time, one year more from the total span of life.[56] April, the month of Venus, is the time of love and renewal—so much Phyllis is told. Yet from Horace spring never receives so straightforward a response, and here April seems in a way the cruelest month. His chastened summons to Phyllis brings into bold relief the darker undercurrent of the onflowing years:

age iam, meorum
finis amorum

—non enim posthac alia calebo
femina—, condisce modos, amanda
voce quos reddas: minuentur atrae
carmina curae. [31–36]

> Come now, last of my loves—for after this I shall burn for no other—learn these measures to sing in your lovely voice; black cares are lightened by song.

56. The tension in *C.* 4.11 is similar to that in Propertius' birthday poem to Cynthia (3.10), where the incantatory language seems an effort to project into the future the happiness of the past; see especially line 17.

Although these "black cares" are at first glance Phyllis' unrequited love for Telephus, a lad "not of her station" (22), they are, we recognize, Horace's own as well. From them his ardor takes on a more somber coloring: his emotions seem mirrored in the trembling flames and dark smoke of his hearth. The last stanza's force diffuses itself over the whole poem as surely as do the "black fires" of the following Ode (*C.* 4.12.26). Even more than Ligurinus, Phyllis, the last of Horace's loves, incarnates a part of life that is flowing away from him. And it is his awareness of that fact which gives the Ode its special quality.

Horace's attempt to hold to Phyllis and what she represents results in a curious inversion of his own beliefs. In the only previous poem concerning her, Horace, impressing some portentous examples from myth, warned a friend against being ashamed of loving Phyllis, who was only a slave girl. Horace himself is no more than an onlooker—one already forty, he reassures his friend, can rouse no jealousy:

> bracchia et voltum teretesque suras
> integer laudo—fuge suspicari—
>   cuius octavum trepidavit aetas
>   claudere lustrum. [*C.* 2.4.21–24]

> As one above temptation I praise her arms and features and smooth thighs; cease to doubt me, for now my age is hastening to close its fortieth year.

C. 4.11 has several of the same elements, but the idea behind them is precisely reversed. Here are the same solemn myths (25–28), but now the lesson to be drawn from them is not the democracy of love, but rather the hopelessness and unsuitability of Phyllis' love for one above her. Horace, moreover, now ten years older, has jettisoned the proprieties he had invoked at forty. He himself, he tells Phyllis, is a suitable match. In violating his own convictions he offers not even the excuse that he is compelled by some supernatural force too strong to resist, as he claimed in the Ode to Ligurinus (*C.* 4.1). The pressure of his black cares is itself sufficient to make him seize any light against them.

Editors frequently observe that the Ode to Phyllis repeats the theme of that to Lyde (*C.* 3.28), another summons to a banquet. Yet what ties the two poems is not so much their similarity of form as the sense of passing time that informs each. In the Ode to Lyde it is no more than a hint. Horace reminds her of the *volucris dies,*[57] and the Ode ends, after an invocation to Venus, with a request for a dirge to Night. In the Ode to Phyllis this darker undercurrent becomes more powerful; we might almost describe the poem itself as a dirge to Night. The same quality is shared by the two other invitations of the last book, that to Ligurinus (*C.* 4.10), and that to Vergil (*C.* 4.12). In all Horace sees the present not as a happy opportunity but as part of a continuum in which more is lost than gained.

It is not possible to force all the personal Odes of the last book into an identical pattern, but they do display certain affinities. It was only natural that they should. In the half-humorous capitulation of the introduction, in the protesting cry to Lyce (*C.* 4.13), in the ceremonial regret of the Ode to Torquatus (*C.* 4.7), and in the muted sadness of the invitations to Ligurinus (*C.* 4.10), Phyllis (*C.* 4.11), and Vergil (*C.* 4.12), Horace's resistance to his own decorum is unmistakable. The tension between his detached logic and the emotions it was designed to control makes these poems as affecting as anything he wrote. Here, as in the Odes on death, he faces squarely the most common and most melancholy of all problems. He acknowledges that our profoundest feelings are not finally to be resolved by the mind, and that life never allows us terms in which we can ultimately manage either it or ourselves. The steadiness with which he watches the transformation of his ideas is itself a triumph, and the fine honesty of these poems puts them at the center of his, and our, experience.

57. *C.* 3.28.6; cf. *C.* 4.13.16. Perhaps *volucrem* as applied to Ligurinus (*C.* 4.1.38) has some of the same suggestions of fleeting time and passing youth.

VI

THE WORLD OF ART

In 1916 Laura Riding stated what was to become a commonplace of criticism, that the characteristic subject of modern poetry is poetry itself. Though it may be true that the verse of no other age has proven so persistently introspective, there have been few writers who did not address themselves at some point to the problems and prerogatives of their art. Certainly Horace was not among them. Even if we leave aside the abstract questions debated in the Satires and Epistles we find that an impressive proportion of the Odes are concerned, however obliquely, with poetry. In addition to the ceremonious invocations of the Muse there are a number of poems cast in less formal terms. And in these Horace seeks to convey in more private language his conception of poetry and of himself as a poet.

Horace knew how remarkable his achievement was simply in social terms, and he never tired of pointing to the gap between his origins and his destiny.[1] But he knew, too, that it was remarkable in a more important way as well. The gift of artistic creation is by nature isolated—and isolating: few poets have felt their singularity so sharply. At the same time that Horace glories in his worldly triumph he marks himself off from those who have given it to him:

> me doctarum hederae praemia frontium
> dis miscent superis, me gelidum nemus
> Nymepharumque leves cum Satyris chori
> secernunt populo . . . [*C.* 1.1.29–32]

1. See above, 1.

> The ivy, reward of learned brows, raises me to the gods above. The cool grove and the light bands of Nymphs and Satyrs separate me from the people . . .

His contempt for the *malignum volgus* signals more than an appeal to the judgment of the few. It represents, finally, his conviction that the awareness of the public can never be adequate to the peculiar quality of his own experience. It was, perhaps, his sense of his own inherent isolation that encouraged a sympathy toward something similar in others. If we think of his characteristic heroes we remember the unbending Cato, "all the world else subdued," or Cleopatra, singly thwarting the massed power of Caesar, or Regulus, pushing his way through the resisting crowd to his lonely death, or even Hypermestra, *una de multis*.[2] The price of heroism is aloneness, and Horace felt that his own achievement as an artist marked him off with equal, if distinct, finality. His too was the *virtus* he speaks of in the second Roman Ode, which, "opening the sky for those not deserving to die, essays its journey by a way denied to others, and spurns beneath its fleeting wing the common throng and the moist earth" (*C.* 3.2.21 ff.).

Horace's large sense of his own specialness was one that he could justify both logically and historically. The fact that writing—or some writing—survives indefinitely, and with it some part of the author, makes the poet a double citizen, a *biformis vates* (*C.* 2.20.2–3). An inhabitant of the natural world of time and change, he can also enter the supernatural world of static timelessness. The assumption had been part of Roman literature from the beginning:

> nemo me lacrimis decoret nec funera fletu
> faxit. cur? volito vivos per ora virum.[3]

> Let no one pay tribute to me with tears, nor celebrate my funeral with weeping. Why? Because I fly, still living, upon the lips of men.

2. *C.* 1.37.21 ff., 2.1.23–24, 3.5.41 ff., 3.11.33–36.
3. Ennius, *Varia* 18 (Vahlen [2]).

Ennius' flight offered both a model and a challenge for his successors, one that Vergil was prepared to accept:

> temptanda via est, qua me quoque possim
> tollere humo victorque virum volitare per ora. [*G.* 3.8–9]

> The path must be attempted by which I too can raise myself from the earth and, victorious, fly upon the lips of men.

Me quoque might well have deepened into anxiety had Vergil foreseen the number of those who would claim to be birds of the same feather.[4] But of all subsequent claims Horace's was in its details the most melodramatic. Sprouting swan's down and roughening skin signal his coming flight from sublunar time to eternity:

> iam iam residunt cruribus asperae
> pelles et album mutor in alitem
> superne nascunturque leves
> per digitos umerosque plumae.
>
> iam Daedaleo notior Icaro
> visam gementis litora Bosphori
> Syrtisque Gaetulas canorus
> ales Hyperboreosque campos;
>
> me Colchus et qui dissimulat metum
> Marsae cohortis Dacus et ultimi
> noscent Geloni, me peritus
> discet Hiber Rhodanique potor. [*C.* 2.20.9–20]

> Even now the flesh upon my ankles roughens, and above I am changing into a white swan; smooth feathers appear upon my hands and shoulders. Now, as a melodious swan, more famous than Icarus, the son of Daedalus, I shall go to see the shores of the roaring Bosphorus and the Gaetulian Syrtes and the fields of the Hyperboreans. The

4. Cf. Ovid, *Met.* 15.875 ff.; *Am.* 1.15.41–42, 3.9.28; *Tr.* 4.10.122, 129–30, 3.7.49–50; *Pont.* 2.9.62, 3.2.31–32; Propertius, 3.1.9; Lucan, 9.980–86.

> Colchian, and the Dacian who masks his fear of our Marsian cohorts, and the far-off Geloni shall know me; the learned Spaniard and they who drink from the Rhone shall learn of me.

The lines of Theognis (237 ff.) that seem to be Horace's model similarly describe a distant flight and immortal name, but assign them to the poem's subject, Theognis' friend Cyrnus, and not to the poet himself. In a world where the divine presences cast only a twilight glow, poets were apt to demand their rewards in their own name; here the Roman practice parted from that of the Greeks.[5] By combining Theognis' geographical hyperbole with the self-emphasis of previous Roman poets, Horace caps them both.

The immortality of poets is now so commonplace a proposition—if one not always vindicated in fact—that Horace's assertions seem loud to the point of shrillness. Yet if we remember how profound was Horace's awareness of the transience of all earthly things, it is easier to sympathize with his extravagant pride. As a poet he became the only exception to the laws of nature that he had himself so steadily enjoined. His fancy was always taken, though not always very seriously, by anyone who managed to leave a monument of sorts to himself. There is Icarus, "destined to give his name to a sea" (*C.* 4.2.3–4), or Europa, who receives half the world as a memorial to her rape:

> mitte singultus; bene ferre magnam
> disce fortunam: tua sectus orbis
> nomina ducet. [*C.* 3.27.74–76]

> Cease your sobbing, and learn to bear happily your great destiny: a region of the globe shall take its name from you.

5. If we compare *C.* 3.30 with what seems to be its model (Pindar, *P.* 6.5 ff.), we find the same difference of emphasis—Pindar on the immortality of the subject, Horace on the immortality of the poet himself. For Roman boasts of personal immortality, see n. 4, above. In Greek poetry we find only occasional, and quite tentative, assertions of immortality: Sappho 55, 193 (Lobel and Page); Aristophanes, *Ran.* 868 ff. It is suggestive that the fullest statement of the poet's immortality should come in a philosophical treatise rather than in a poem: Plato, *Smp.* 209.

Yet the rewards of Icarus and Europa are fortuitous; only the poet can willfully compel a lasting image upon the world. "Not I, the son of humble parents, not I, whom you summon to yourself, dearest Maecenas, shall die, nor shall I be enclosed by the Stygian wave . . . as a melodious swan, more famous than Icarus, the son of Daedalus, I shall go to see the shores of the roaring Bosphorus and the Gaetulian Syrtes and the fields of the Hyperboreans" (*C.* 2.20.5 ff.). The claustrophobic sense of death that haunts the second book of Odes here dissolves, as the iron ring of the Styx which awaits Postumus and all mankind (*C.* 2.14.7 ff.) is shattered. Life, according to the Lucretian formula invoked by Horace in that Ode, is given to none on freehold, to all for use.[6] But now Horace qualifies the absolutism of *indomita mors,* stipulating for the poet a lease on eternity.

"Not I, whom you summon to yourself, dearest Maecenas, shall die." The boast seems almost calculated to recall and simultaneously to deny the sentiments he had expressed only three Odes previous (*C.* 2.17). There Horace had assured Maecenas that their two fates were joined (*ibimus, ibimus . . . supremum carpere iter comites parati,* 10–12), but now his exultant *non ego . . . obibo* repudiates that earlier promise. Ironically, the very poetry that wins Horace Maecenas' patronage (*quem vocas, C.* 2.20.6) isolates Horace from him. The progression of poems from *C.* 2.17 to *C.* 2.20 increasingly emphasizes Horace's separateness. In *C.* 2.17, Horace's half-humorous reminder of his divine protection as a poet (21 ff.) merely points the parallel between his own experience and that of his patron. In the following Ode, however, the gap is already apparent:

> at fides et ingeni
> benigna vena est pauperemque dives
> me petit. [*C.* 2.18.9–11]

But faith and a rich vein of genius are mine, and the wealthy seek me out, poor as I am.

6. The maxim is implicit in *C.* 2.14 in the contrast between *brevem dominum* (24) and *indomitae morti* (4); cf. Lucretius, 3.971, and for the topical quality of the maxim, see the notes of C. Bailey, *Lucretius* (Oxford, 1947), *ad loc.* Cf. *S.* 2.2.129 ff.; *Ep.* 2.2.175.

Even as Horace thanks his *potentem amicum* (12) he sets himself apart from him. The Sabine farm (*unicis Sabinis,* 14), itself the gift of Maecenas, becomes virtually a symbol of Horace's unique independence. With the first lines of the next Ode the ultimate privacy of his calling becomes still more evident:

> Bacchum in remotis carmina rupibus
> vidi docentem, credite posteri . . . [*C.* 2.19.1–2]

> On a remote crag I saw Bacchus, teaching his songs—believe me, you who come hereafter . . .

A further remove, into the isolation of nature, succeeds the Sabine farm as a symbolic setting for himself as poet. He appeals to the generations still to come, and his singular right to make such an appeal becomes explicit throughout the epilogue, *C.* 2.20. Here, by recalling Theognis' celebration of Cyrnus only to alter it, Horace forces upon Maecenas the definitive gap that separates the poet from even his most cherished friend. He closes off the one way in which he might have affirmed the similarity of their fates, for he omits any reference to the immortality that the poet can bestow on others. Horace's flight is his alone.

The epilogue to the third book (*C.* 3.30), and to the three books as a whole, is similar to *C.* 2.20, but more felicitous:

> Exegi monumentum aere perennius
> regalique situ pyramidum altius,
> quod non imber edax, non aquilo impotens
> possit diruere aut innumerabilis
>
> annorum series et fuga temporum. 5
> non omnis moriar multaque pars mei
> vitabit Libitinam: usque ego postera
> crescam laude recens, dum Capitolium
>
> scandet cum tacita virgine pontifex:
> dicar, qua violens obstrepit Aufidus 10
> et qua pauper aquae Daunus agrestium
> regnavit populorum, ex humili potens

princeps Aeolium carmen ad Italos
deduxisse modos. sume superbiam
quaesitam meritis et mihi Delphica 15
lauro cinge volens, Melpomene, comam.

I have raised a monument more lasting than bronze, loftier than the royal pile of the pyramids, one that neither the biting rain nor the powerlessly raging north wind can destroy, nor the innumerable file of years, nor the flight of time. I shall not wholly perish, and a great part of me will escape Libitina. Everlastingly shall I grow, renewed by the praise of posterity, as long as the Pontifex climbs the Capitol with the silent vestal by his side; I shall be spoken of where the violent Aufidus sounds, and where Daunus in a parched land once ruled over a rustic people, as one who, rising triumphant from humble beginnings, was the first to weave Aeolian song to Italian measures. Melpomene, accept the glory won by my merits, and graciously crown my locks with the Delphic laurel.

Horace here returns to a meter he had used only once before, in *C.* 1.1, the stately Lesser Asclepiadean. The formal rhetoric of *C.* 3.30 also recalls the opening Ode, so that the two poems stand as a massive frame for the collection, giving it physically something of the monumentality that, in the epilogue, Horace claims for it in figurative terms. Not only the formal structure of *C.* 3.30, but the structure of ideas and emotions as well, make it a more satisfactory epilogue than *C.* 2.20.[7] Horace's boasts that he will be known to the

7. G. L. Hendrickson, *CP, 26* (1931), 1 ff., suggested that *C.* 2.20 was originally intended for the epilogue of a shorter collection of poems. Whether or not this is so, the Ode's position at the close of the second book seems carefully planned. Not only does it stand as the culmination of the three poems preceding it, but it provides as well a link to the Roman Odes opening the third book; see E. T. Silk, *AJP, 77* (1956), 255 ff. *Non usitata nec tenui pinna* (1–2) may suggest the new magnitude of the themes Horace is about to attempt as he leaves behind the *tenuis* style of lighter lyrics (cf. *C.* 1.6.9). Perhaps Horace is a *biformis vates* (2–3) in the sense also that he can add grand themes to his habitual lighter ones.

C. 1.38 functions in a similar way, linking the first and second books.

reaches of the civilized world (*C.* 2.20.13–20) have evolved into something less boisterous but more complex. The land of Daunus (11) is Apulia, Horace's native region in southern Italy. The Theognean vaunt of universal fame that he developed in *C.* 2.20 has subsided into what seems to be provincial pride, an apparent diminution of glory at which many editors have protested.[8] It is local pride, to be sure, but local pride seen *sub specie aeternitatis*. Assured (7–9) that his fame will last as long as Rome itself, *urbs aeterna,*[9] Horace can rest on his Delphic laurels. In the epilogue to the second book he mentions his origins (*pauperum sanguis parentum,* 5–6) only to mark how far behind his flight will leave them, but in the epilogue to the third the details of his mortal life become themselves the geographic hyperbole for his immortality. The reference to Apulia (10–12) conveys both the humbleness of his life and the potency of his art,[10] since the land where he was born is simultaneously the land where he will never die. The lines dramatically compress the equivocal nature of his experience, a man in this world yet not altogether of it.

Although the Ode is complete in itself, there is a relationship between it and the preceding poem nearly as marked as that between *C.* 2.20 and *C.* 2.19. The sequence at the close of the second book is virtually that of cause and effect—poetic inspiration (*C.* 2.19) and the immortality that is its consequence (*C.* 2.20). The progress at the end of the third book is quite different. Both the penultimate Ode and the epilogue treat similar themes, but in the latter poem Horace speaks from the special perspective of the artist. To Maecenas he recommended a stoic indifference:

Horace's banishment of oriental luxury (*C.* 1.38.1) may signal his turning to the Roman themes of *C.* 2.1. And it is interesting that just as *C.* 1.38 (like *C.* 1.37) seems torn between two attitudes (see above, 117), so *C.* 2.1 ends with a kind of recantation.

8. They prefer to take *qua violens . . .* with *princeps deduxisse* rather than with *dicar*. For arguments against the former alternative, see Fraenkel, *Horace,* 304 ff.

9. The phrase was coming into use in the Augustan age; see J. Cousin, *Études sur la poésie latine* (Paris, 1945), 133.

10. *Potens* (12) is surely to be taken as referring to Horace rather than to Daunus; it stands in deliberate contrast to *impotens* (3), which occupies the same position in the line. Cf. *C.* 4.8.26.

ille potens sui
laetusque deget, cui licet in diem
dixisse "vixi". cras vel atra
nube polum pater occupato

vel sole puro; non tamen inritum
quodcumque retro est efficict neque
diffinget infectumque reddet
quod fugiens semel hora vexit.

[*C.* 3.29.41–48]

> That man shall live content and master of his soul who can say each day, "I have lived." Tomorrow let the Father fill the heavens with black clouds or with clear sunlight; still he cannot undo whatever is past, nor can he cancel and deny what once the fleeting hour has brought.

Immunity to each day's vicissitudes and the security of the granted present—here is the best Horace can lay before Maecenas. But as a poet Horace can become immune to time itself, finally secure in what he creates. He is powerful not only over himself and over the *atrae nubes* of this world, but over whatever storms may come: *Exegi monumentum . . . / quod non imber edax, non aquilo impotens / possit diruere.* Immortality can be seen as the dimension of an eternal present. The possibilities of each moment to which Horace in *C.* 3.29 invited Maecenas are, then, canonized, as it were, in art. *Non . . . possit diruere . . . fuga temporum. non omnis moriar . . .* The *fugiens hora* (*C.* 3.29.48) has been arrested, nature's laws overcome, and the watchword *vixi* (*C.* 3.29.43) can become *vivam.*

While the epilogues to the second and third books are the only Odes to state the poet's immortality in formal terms, one other poem treats the theme obliquely. *C.* 2.13, on Horace's escape from the *triste lignum,* masquerades as a beguilingly lighthearted parody, but the underlying concern is serious. In structure the Ode recalls the *propempticon* to Vergil (*C.* 1.3). Again Horace moves by a kind of centrifugal progress from the ostensible subject to the real one, from an incident to the speculation it excites:

quam paene furvae regna Proserpinae
et iudicantem vidimus Aeacum
sedesque discretas piorum et
Aeoliis fidibus querentem

Sappho puellis de popularibus,
et te sonantem plenius aureo,
Alcaee, plectro dura navis,
dura fugae mala, dura belli.

utrumque sacro digna silentio
mirantur umbrae dicere . . . [*C.* 2.13.21–30]

How near I came to seeing the realm of dusky Proserpina, and Aeacus sitting in judgment, and the regions set apart for the pious, and Sappho, plaintively singing on her Aeolian lyre of the girls from her own land, and you, Alcaeus, sounding more grandly with your golden plectrum, telling of the hardships of the sailor, the evil hardships of exile, and the hardships of war. The Shades wonder at both poets alike, for they sing songs worthy of a sacred silence . . .

In singling out Sappho and Alcaeus to represent the underworld, Horace does more than pay tribute to his models in Greek lyric. The timeless popularity of the two suggests, however fancifully, their triumph over, if not escape from, the *inprovisa leti vis* (19–20). If the parody of the first three stanzas is designed to reduce the incident of the falling tree to manageable size,[11] the scene in Hades attempts to answer it directly. Horace's evocation of the two Lesbian poets is not only a fancy spun from his alarm; it is also a tentative antidote to it, for the scene dramatizes the fact that the *magna pars* of any great artist survives. The poem probably dates from 29 B.C., and is almost certainly earlier than either of the two epilogues. Horace was not yet prepared to celebrate the poet's immortality explicitly, or not, at least, in his own name. Yet he must already have begun to hope that he would some day be able to do so. Perhaps his exaggerated reaction to

11. See above, 140.

the *triste lignum* derives in part from a feeling that he had yet to achieve something that would justify his leaving the ranks of the spectators for the company of Sappho and Alcaeus themselves.

In the fourth book Horace makes no mention of his own immortality, whether because he had said all he thought there was to say, or because the idea had by then come to seem a less persuasive comfort. Instead he concentrates on the poet's ability to immortalize others. "The whole earth," declared Pericles in his Funeral Oration, "is the sepulcher of famous men." Yet without the hand of the poet to carve an inscription, the whole earth would be only an anonymous grave. As a spiritual descendant of Pericles was to phrase it, "Antient Bards are both the priest and door-keeper to the temple of Fame." [12] Poets since Homer had been aware of their power, and when Horace praised Pindar for lifting men's golden virtues to the stars (*C.* 4.2.22–23) he added little to what Pindar himself had already claimed. But in the eighth and ninth Odes of the fourth book Horace elaborated upon the idea in a way that Pindar had not, spelling out at length the glories of poetry and of his own power as a poet. The two poems are placed to succeed the somber Ode to Torquatus:

> inmortalia ne speres, monet annus et almum
> quae rapit hora diem. [*C.* 4.7.7–8]

> Hope not for immortality, warn the year and the hour that
> snatches off the nourishing day.

In *C.* 4.8 Horace allows immortality of a sort to those men whose deeds are recorded in poetry. Beyond the cycle of nature, with its inexorably marching seasons, lies the supernatural and unchanging world of art, the "blessed islands" (*divitibus insulis,* 27) of which the poet is guardian: *caelo Musa beat* (29). Horace's tone is at first almost playful, as in the language of the countinghouse he reckons the value of his poetry against that of the other arts:

12. George Washington, Letter to Marquis de Lafayette, May 28, 1788. In Greek literature the concept that poets can immortalize others appears frequently: Theognis, 237; Pindar, *O.* 10.91 ff., 11.4 ff.; *P.* 3.112; *N.* 4.6, 6.30, 7.12; *I.* 1.46, 4.37 ff., 7.16 ff.; *Fr.* 121 (Schroeder); Aristophanes, *Ran.* 1030 ff.; Xenophanes, *Fr.* 6 (Diels); Plato, *Phaedr.* 245a; Theocritus, 16.29 ff., 58 ff.

gaudes carminibus; carmina possumus
donare, et pretium dicere muneri.

non incisa notis marmora publicis,
per quae spiritus et vita redit bonis
post mortem ducibus, non celeres fugae 15
reiectaeque retrorsum Hannibalis minae

[non incendia Karthaginis inpiae]
eius qui domita nomen ab Africa
lucratus rediit clarius indicant
laudes quam Calabrae Pierides, neque 20
si chartae sileant quod bene feceris,

mercedem tuleris.

You rejoice in songs; songs we are able to give, and to set a value on the gift. Not the marble monuments engraved with public inscriptions, through which breath and life return to good leaders after their death, not the swift flight of Hannibal and his threats, driven back upon his own head, [nor the burning of wicked Carthage] show forth more clearly the glory of that man who returned home, enriched by the name he had taken from conquered Africa, than do the Calabrian Muses; nor, if writings made no mention of your good deeds, would you bear off any reward.

Line seventeen has often been suspected because of the serious historical inaccuracy it contains.[13] Horace has merged the elder Scipio Africanus, victor over Hannibal in 202 B.C. and subject of Ennius' poetry (*Calabrae Pierides,* 20), with the younger Scipio Africanus who burned Carthage in 146 B.C., well after the death of Ennius. As all editors point out, for Horace to confuse the two would be virtually impossible. But rather than delete the line might we not conceivably,

13. Line 17 has also been excised because the Ode, as it stands, violates the so-called *lex Meinekiana* (i. e. that all the Odes consist of a number of lines divisible by four.) To preserve the law's validity for *C.* 4.8, one other line must be dropped; usually line 33 is chosen. The *lex Meinekiana* is not, however, generally considered to be absolute; see the editions of Wickham and Shorey, *ad loc.*

or even fancifully, let it stand and take the mistake as deliberate? Horace's error in recounting the elder Scipio's deeds proves those deeds in fact a less certain [14] guarantee of fame than Ennius' poetry. Certainly the fires that Scipio did not light illuminate his fame less clearly than do the *Calabrae Pierides*. To take it one step further, might not Horace be implying that even the name with which the elder Scipio was "enriched" (*lucratus,* 19) in recognition of his deeds proved to be a less valuable acquisition (since it was shared by his grandson) than the reward (*merces,* 22) of verse?

However we explain these puzzling lines, one thought is clear, that the Muse, by preserving the great deeds of the past, still functions as the daughter of Mnemosyne. The same theme is developed even more exuberantly in the lies that follow:

> quid foret Iliae
> Mavortisque puer, si taciturnitas
> obstaret meritis invida Romuli?
> ereptum Stygiis fluctibus Aeacum 25
>
> virtus et favor et lingua potentium
> vatum divitibus consecrat insulis.
> dignum laude virum Musa vetat mori:
> caelo Musa beat. sic Iovis interest
>
> optatis epulis inpiger Hercules, 30
> clarum Tyndaridae sidus ab infimis
> quassas eripiunt aequoribus ratis,
> [ornatus viridi tempora pampino]
> Liber vota bonos ducit ad exitus.

What would the son of Ilia and Mars amount to now, if jealous silence had stood in the way of Romulus' just deserts? The vigor and favor and voice of powerful bards snatched Aeacus from the Stygian waves and consecrated him to the Isles of the Blest. It is the Muse who keeps the

14. *Clarus* can have a double sense, meaning "clear" or "certain" as well as "distinguished." The trick of accomplishing something which he pretends to be merely describing is characteristic of Horace; see below, 324 ff.

> man worthy of praise from death; it is the Muse who bestows the gift of heaven. Thus it is that laboring Hercules has his place at the longed-for banquets of Jove; thus the sons of Tyndareus, bright stars, save battered ships from the depths of the sea; thus Bacchus [temples wreathed with green vine leaves] brings prayers to happy issue.

The epilogue to the second book declared that poets could save themselves from the waves of the Styx, and now Horace adds that poets may confer that privilege on others (25). Although the claim was familiar by the Augustan age,[15] the terms in which Horace makes it are remarkable. For examples he cites not merely famous heroes of the past such as Scipio, but also the accepted canon of demigods: Romulus, Aeacus, Hercules, Bacchus, Castor and Pollux. Traditionally, all these had achieved posthumous divinity by virtue of their great acts while they were still mortals.[16] The third Roman Ode uses substantially the same figures as well as the same image of divinity, admission to the "table of Jove" (*C.* 3.3.12, 34–36). But in that poem Horace makes no mention of the poet's role. We need only compare *hac arte* (*C.* 3.3.9) with *sic interest* (*C.* 4.8.29) to see the difference in Horace's viewpoint. In the first case it is the heroes' own virtue that guarantees their divinity; in the second it is the *virtus et favor et lingua potentium vatum.* The latter seems the more characteristic. In the third Roman Ode, which particularly honors Augustus, it would be undiplomatic for Horace to press claims in his own name, and in omitting the ruler from the list in *C.* 4.8 of those immortalized by poets Horace shows himself equally discreet. His tact baffles speculation as to how far he considered himself responsible for preserving Augustus' divinity. Elsewhere he leaves the matter equally ambiguous:

> quibus
> antris egregii Caesaris audiar
>
> aeternum meditans decus
> stellis inserere et consilio Iovis? [*C.* 3.25.3–6]

15. *Inter alia,* Cat., 68.45 ff.; Cic., *Arch.* 6.14; Verg., *E.* 9.27; *A.* 9.446; Tib., 1.4.65; see also n. 12, above.

16. See above, 210 ff.

> In what caves shall I be heard, intent upon setting the eternal glory of great Caesar amongst the stars and the council of Jove?

Only if we neglect the proleptic force of *aeternum* does the adjective flatter Augustus alone. Not until Augustus' glory is set among the "stars and the council of Jove" will it be eternal. And no one, it seems, but Horace has the power to place it there. Until then it remains caught in sublunary nature, no more secure than Scipio's glory would have been without Ennius.

Although in *C.* 4.8 Horace theoretically asserts the power of all poets, Ennius is the only one he cites. In the following Ode, addressed to Lollius, Horace makes explicit what he left unsaid in *C.* 4.8, that lyric verse such as his own bestows immortality as surely as does the grander genre of epic. Homer may hold the first place, but Pindar, Simonides, Bacchylides, Alcaeus, Stesichorus, and even the slighter Aanacreon (*siquid olim lusit,* 9) and Sappho have left works untarnished by time.[17] In *C.* 4.8 Horace proves his case in positive terms, listing those heroes and demigods whose memory poets had preserved, whereas in *C.* 4.9 he states the obverse proposition that without poetry there is no survival. He spreads before us a curious collection of what might be called negative *exempla,* a catalogue of probable luminaries who remain unknown. Helen was not the first to burn with love for an adulterer, nor Teucer the first to use a bow; many were the Troys that had fallen before Homer's day, many the Hectors who had fought for their wives and children (13–24). With splendid rhetoric the Ode rises to its climax:

> vixere fortes ante Agamemnona
> multi; sed omnes inlacrimabiles
> urgentur ignotique longa
> nocte, carent quia vate sacro. [*C.* 4.9.25–28]

> Many are the great men who lived before Agamemnon, but all lie unwept and unknown, overwhelmed by perpetual night, since they lack a sacred bard.

17. *C.* 4.9.1–12. The inclusion of Anacreon and Sappho pointedly rebukes those who would dismiss love poetry as an inferior type; cf. above, 36, and below, 339.

Unwept, unhonored, and unsung are practically synonyms—but, thanks to Horace, Lollius will escape time's "long night": *non ego te . . . patiar . . . carpere lividas obliviones* (30 ff.). The praise of Lollius with which the poem concludes sounds determined rather than enthusiastic, being little more than a list of conventional virtues.[18] Clearly Horace found a more compelling theme in art's special power than he did in the particular instance that here called it forth. It is, ironically, Horace's declarations that we remember rather than the lines on Lollius that should, rightly, vindicate them.

O fons Bandusiae (*C.* 3.13) has long been a favorite among the Odes, though its connection with poetry has been generally neglected:

O fons Bandusiae, splendidior vitro,
dulci digne mero non sine floribus,
cras donaberis haedo,
cui frons turgida cornibus

primis et venerem et proelia destinat— 5
frustra, nam gelidos inficiet tibi
rubro sanguine rivos
lascivi suboles gregis.

te flagrantis atrox hora Caniculae
nescit tangere, tu frigus amabile 10
fessis vomere tauris
praebes et pecori vago.

fies nobilium tu quoque fontium
me dicente cavis inpositam ilicem
saxis, unde loquaces 15
lymphae desiliunt tuae.

O fountain of Bandusia, gleaming brighter than glass, worthy of sweet wine and flowers, tomorrow you will be given a kid whose forehead, now swelling with its first horns, destines him for love and battle—but in vain, for this offspring

18. Though perhaps Horace's emphasis on Lollius' honesty (*C.* 4.9.37 ff.) may be a kind of vindication, as Lollius was apparently accused of greed; see Velleius Paterculus, 2.97; Pliny, *H. N.* 9.58.118 (Mayhoff).

> of the wanton flock shall dye your cold waters with his red blood. The harsh season of the blazing Dog Star cannot touch you; you provide lovely coolness for bulls tired from the plow, and for the straying flocks. You too will become one of the famous fountains of the world, when I sing of the oak tree set upon the hollow rocks from which your speaking waters leap down.

So familiar is the poem that its true quality tends to be lost in the sentimental echoes it produces. Here, for instance, is Wordsworth's meditation from "Liberty":

> Give *me* the humblest note of those sad strains,
> Drawn forth by pressure of his gilded chains,
> As a chance sun-beam from his memory fell
> Upon the Sabine farm he loved so well;
> Or when the prattle of Bandusia's spring
> Haunted his ear—he only listening.

"He only listening." Horace is less modest, for he pays tribute not only to an obscure fountain but to the poetry that can place it among the most famous fountains of the world. Rather than term the Ode an invocation to a spring, we could equally well name it an invocation to his own art. The limpid water might be viewed as a counter-image to the turbulent stream that represents Pindar's inspired verse (*C.* 4.2.5 ff.). Providing both solace and beauty, *frigus amabile,*[19] the fountain rests immune from the attacks of nature (9–10); we are halfway to the proud declarations of the epilogue (*C.* 3.30.1 ff.).

Readers have often been repelled by the details of the kid's sacrifice (6–8). Perhaps the description is not there for its realistic effect alone. Destined for love and battle, the "offspring of the wanton flock" epitomizes life's comprehensive vitality, and as his warm blood mingles with the lucid water it is easy to sense a suggestion of the trans-

19. For poetry's combination of solace and beauty, cf. *Epod.* 13.9–10, 17–18; *C.* 1.32.13–15, 2.13.33 ff., 4.11.33–36. For the association of *amabilis* with poetry, cf. *C.* 3.4.5, 4.3.14; *Ep.* 1.3.24. With the *fons Bandusiae* we might compare the "cool grove" of Bacchus (*C.* 1.1.30), setting for the poet's most excited emotions (cf. *C.* 3.25.1 ff.).

formation of life into art. In the Odes on poetry the union of vitality and calm is a recurrent theme,[20] one that is not, of course, peculiar to Horace alone. Seen in these terms, the first two stanzas of *C.* 3.13 suggest something akin to what Yeats implied when he called for a poem "as cold and passionate as the dawn."

Horace elsewhere describes the Muses as "you who delight in fresh springs," [21] and the *nobiles fontes* (13) of Greece and Rome were generally those associated with poetic inspiration: Arethusa, Hippocrene, Castalia. But instead of dwelling upon the traditional concept, Horace inverts it. The waters of the spring do not create his poetry; rather, his poetry gives new life to nature. In such a context *loquaces* (15) becomes a loaded adjective, quite different in meaning from Wordsworth's stock epithet "prattling." Horace had, to be sure, heard Bandusia's waters. Yet he knew and quietly insisted that they were to "speak" most significantly through the medium of his own verse.

Several of the Odes commemorating some person or object have a proleptic quality. The pattern is difficult to define but easy to find parallels for. In the fourth Roman Ode the *lene consilium* that the Muses bestow on Caesar seems to be represented by the Ode itself. Similarly, the assurance that *certus Apollo* gives to Teucer is analogous to the assurance given to Plancus by *C.* 1.7 in its entirety. Certain poems, that is to say, which appear only to describe objectively some message, or to make some promise, turn out to be themselves the substance of that message, or the redemption of that promise.[22] Horace's delight in this kind of a double effect may underlie the long poem on the Danaids. The Ode ends with Hypermestra's injunction to her husband, a characteristic addition to the myth:

> i pedes quo te rapiunt et aurae,
> dum favet nox et Venus, i secundo

20. See below, 337 ff.

21. *C.* 1.26.6; cf. *C.* 3.4.25.

22. For other possible examples see above, 52, 74–75. The equivalent in negative terms is the Horatian *recusatio*, where the very disclaimers prove their own falsity; see above, 112 ff.

omine et nostri memorem sepulcro
scalpe querelam. [*C.* 3.11.49–50]

Go wherever your feet and the breezes take you, while night and Venus are favorable; go with lucky omen, and carve upon my tomb an elegy in memory of me.

The Ode might be the very *querela* that Hypermestra requests; certainly she could have hoped for no finer epitaph than *splendide mendax* (35). Horace himself helps to make her "a maiden noble throughout all the ages to come" (35–36). In these terms the poem's supposed disunity is less alarming, for the introductory praise of the lyre and of Mercury, its inventor, becomes eminently, if obliquely, appropriate.

Seen in this way, the invitation that Horace extends to Maecenas (*C.* 1.20) is curiously evocative:

Vile potabis modicis Sabinum
cantharis, Graeca quod ego ipse testa
conditum levi, datus in theatro
cum tibi plausus,

clare Maecenas eques, ut paterni 5
fluminis ripae simul et iocosa
redderet laudes tibi Vaticani
montis imago.

Caecubum et prelo domitam Caleno
tu bibes uvam: mea nec Falernae 10
temperant vites neque Formiani
pocula colles.

You will drink, dear knight Maecenas, cheap Sabine wine from small cups, which I myself stored away and sealed in a Greek cask at the time when such applause was given you in the theater that the banks of your ancestral river and a pleasant echo from the Vatican mountain returned your praises. At home you will drink Caecuban and the grape squeezed from the Calenian press; but neither Falernian vines nor the Formian hills season my cups.

Roman content, Greek container, modest cups, the emphatic *ego ipse*—the phrasing suggests that Horace's real gift to his patron is not so much the promised wine as the poem itself. The anomalous short *i* in *Vaticani* (7) might be explained as having been intended to bring out a punning reference to *vaticinor,* and the "Mount Vatican" that returns the praise of Maecenas may have some suggestions of the poet's sacred mountain. The contrast between opulence and humbleness with which the poem ends reminds us of similar contrasts in *C.* 1.31, *C.* 2.16, and *C.* 2.18, in each of which Horace's poetic talents are closely associated with the modesty of his external life.[23] The structure of the Ode vaguely suggests that of an echo, with the opening *Vile potabis* picked up, after the pause of the second stanza, by *tu bibes uvam* (10), and, in this context, reinforces the idea that the poem itself is a *iocosa imago* (6–8; cf. *C.* 1.12.3–4), a pleasant or humorous echo of the applause Maecenas received. By the time that Maecenas finishes reading the poem he has, in effect, already imbibed Horace's promised tribute.[24]

An Ode to Lamia (*C.* 1.26) presents a more certain instance of Horace's technique of accomplishing what he seems to be merely describing:

Musis amicus tristitiam et metus
tradam protervis in mare Creticum
portare ventis, quis sub Arcto
rex gelidae metuatur orae,

quid Tiridaten terreat, unice — 5
securus. o quae fontibus integris
gaudes, apricos necte flores,
necte meo Lamiae coronam,

Piplei dulcis. nil sine te mei
prosunt honores: hunc fidibus novis, — 10

23. See below, 232 ff.

24. I am grateful to my friend and student Peter Rose for his suggestions on this Ode.

hunc Lesbio sacrare plectro
  teque tuasque decet sorores. [*C.* 1.26]

> Dear to the Muses, I shall abandon sadness and fear to the fierce winds to carry off to the Cretan sea, singularly unconcerned as to what king of the frozen lands under Arcturus we fear, or what dangers Tiridates dreads. O you who rejoice in untouched springs, weave together sunny flowers, weave a crown for my Lamia, sweet Muse. Without you my praises are worth nothing. It is only right that you and your sisters consecrate him in new measures, consecrate him with a Lesbian song.

In imploring the Muse (*Piplei dulcis*) to weave a garland for Lamia and to consecrate him, Horace makes use of a modest periphrasis for poetry's power to immortalize. A garland is a common metaphor for a poem or group of poems; [25] Pindar used the image frequently. But for a more specific antecedent we need look no further than Lucretius:

iuvat integros accedere fontis
atque haurire, iuvatque novos decerpere flores
insignemque meo capiti petere inde coronam
unde prius nulli velarint tempora musae. [1.927–30]

> I love to draw near the untouched fountains and drink from them, I love to pluck fresh flowers and weave a glorious garland for my head from a place whence the Muses have crowned no man's temples before.

For Horace, as for Lucretius, the pure fountains and fresh flowers represent the poet's own original contribution to Latin literature. As Lucretius had broken the paths of the philosophical hexameter, so Horace had introduced Lesbian measures to Rome: *fidibus novis . . . Lesbio plectro*. The garland he requests of the Muses is, then, an Ode in these new measures. Where Lucretius asserts his distinction

25. Thus, for instance, the "Garland" of Meleager, circulated during Horace's lifetime; cf. *Ep.* 2.2.96, where the image is amalgamated with that of the victor's garland.

in his own name, Horace is content with the reflected glory of what he ostensibly hopes to achieve for Lamia. Ostensibly, because his hope is in fact realized by the Ode itself. At the poem's close we suddenly become aware that the prayer that Lamia be consecrated in *fidibus novis* has already been fulfilled in the Alcaic stanzas that state it, that the *apricos flores* are those of Horace's own creating. This in turn explains the connection between the poem's beginning and its end. It is Horace's very discovery and simultaneous proof of his ability to weave an imperishable garland that makes him *unice securus*. He has found a world independent of political change in the unique security of his art. [26]

When Horace wrote of the immortality conferred by verse he was dealing with a concept that was sufficiently evident and sufficiently familiar to present few problems. To describe other aspects of his art proved more difficult, for now the question of language became acute. In a larger way the problem is that of all poets, of finding terms adequate to the precise quality of their experience; thus T. S. Eliot in "East Coker":

> a raid on the inarticulate
> With shabby equipment always deteriorating
> In the general mess of imprecision of feeling . . .

For the classical poet the difficulty was aggravated by the paucity of words available for describing inner emotional states. We are likely to be most aware of that lack in reading Catullus, whose introspective explorations leave us still puzzled as to what exactly was involved in the *sanctae foedus amicitiae* to which he appeals.[27] Horace felt as profound a need to formulate his feelings about his art as Catullus did

26. *C.* 1.26, usually accepted, on metrical grounds, as an early poem, has been plausibly conjectured to reflect Horace's first delight in conquering Greek meters; see Wilkinson, *Horace,* 11 ff. There may be a relation between *C.* 1.25 and *C.* 1.26. In *C.* 1.25, Lydia, the victim of her fears of aging, is represented by the dry leaves of the last stanza, themselves the evidence of mortality. These *aridas frondes* are handed over for destruction to the East wind, the companion of winter. In *C.* 1.26, Horace, by creating an imperishable garland, can hand over to the winds (2–3) all fears of any change.

27. In general, see J. H. Finley, *Address to the Horatian Society* (July, 1955), and on Catullus see F. O. Copley, *AJP, 70* (1949), 22 ff.

about his love, and he experienced as profound a difficulty. When the inner state a poet attempts to communicate is something as extraordinary as his own attitude toward his writing, the inadequacy of normal discourse becomes almost insuperable. How can he find terms that are not so ordinary as to be meaningless to himself, yet not so private as to be meaningful to himself alone?

One approach lay through the figures traditionally associated with poetry: perhaps they could be made the vehicle for a more private meaning. Certainly few poets have been more willing than Horace to impress any myth, convention, or conceit from the literary past. Yet his frequent assertions of inspiration and of his standing as a *vates* rise only infrequently above the level of formalistic gestures, and he reserves them by and large for his more public verse.[28] It is likely that the traditional images had become too widely and too ingeniously discredited by that time to retain much value for him. At best they could be metaphors of his own singularity, the mythological equivalent of his explicit rejections of the *profanum volgus*. To convey something more individual he needed less blurred symbols. Time and again he explored various ways of defining himself, in language ranging from the abstract to that so allusive as to verge upon a private mythology. The passages are not always successful, or perhaps we should say that their success depends on the amount of subjective intuition we allow ourselves. They are necessarily difficult. Yet they arise from something too central to his imagination to be ignored.

In three scattered passages relating to his poetry we can catch something of the difficulty Horace faced:

> di me tuentur, dis pietas mea
> et musa cordi est. [*C.* 1.17.13–14]

> The gods protect me, my piety and my Muse are dear to the hearts of the gods.

> at fides et ingeni
> benigna vena est pauperemque dives
> me petit. [*C.* 2.18.9–11]

28. See above, 16 ff.

But faith and a rich vein of genius are mine, and the wealthy seek me out, poor as I am.

virtus et favor et lingua potentium
vatum . . . [*C.* 4.8.26–27]

The vigor and favor and voice of powerful bards . . .

What do *pietas, fides,* and *virtus* mean in these contexts? They normally refer to morals or religion, and frequently to the public acts rather than the inner states connected with them. Yet here the words are clearly invested with some private value. *Pietas* is virtually synonymous with *musa, fides* with *ingenium,* and *virtus* with *lingua potentium vatum;* the only piety, faith, or virtue they describe is peculiarly that of the artist, "the Power," as Wordsworth despairingly defined it, "so-called through sad incompetence of human speech." Horace, apparently unable to find sufficiently evocative terms in the conventional language relating to art, seems to be wresting words from a different area of experience and forcing them to carry some specialized but still indistinct meaning. His efforts recall Catullus' raids upon a semilegal, semireligious vocabulary in the attempt to define more precisely his relation to Lesbia. Words like *foedus, pietas, fides, sanctus,* and *amicitia* are somewhat anomalous in such a context; yet their cumulative effect does impart Catullus' individual ethic of faith and betrayal. Horace's search through an alien terminology was less successful, perhaps because it was less sustained, or perhaps because the quality of his feelings was even more elusive than that of Catullus'. We can only intuit, and vaguely at best, what Horace means by words like *fides.* They are incantatory rather than expressive; he has only invoked his own experience, not evoked something equivalent in his reader.

Horace must have felt the inadequacy of such formulations, and he resorted to them infrequently. More characteristic is his cataloguing of typical *βίοι* and contrasting them with his own career. The pattern had been standard even in Solon's time,[29] and in the opening Ode Horace pursues it in detail. *Sunt quos . . . hunc . . . illum*

29. See Fraenkel, *Horace,* 231, and above, 105.

. . . *est qui* . . . *me:* athlete, politician, farmer, trader, gentleman of leisure, soldier, hunter—the list is straightforwardly descriptive until Horace comes to his own career. Here the language becomes mythological, though conventional enough to be immediately understood:

> me doctarum hederae praemia frontium
> dis miscent superis, me gelidum nemus
> Nympharumque leves cum Satyris chori
> secernunt populo, si neque tibias
> Euterpe cohibet nec Polyhymnia
> Lesboum refugit tendere barbiton.
> quodsi me lyricis vatibus inseres,
> sublimi feriam sidera vertice. [29–36]

> The ivy, reward of learned brows, raises me to the gods above. The cool grove and the light bands of Nymphs and Satyrs separate me from the people, if only Euterpe does not withhold the flute nor Polyhymnia refuse to tune the Lesbian lyre. But if you place me among the lyric bards, then will I strike the stars with my uplifted head.

From the ivy, sacred to Bacchus, came the poet's wreath: the "cool grove" was an equally familiar τόπος for poetic inspiration. No special significance attaches to the figures of Euterpe and Polyhymnia, for Horace does not departmentalize the distinct spheres of the nine Muses as later writers were to do. *Lesboum barbiton* of course refers to Sappho and Alcaeus, natives of Lesbos; by invoking it Horace suggests the models he will follow. The Ode is gracefully programmatic. Horace asserts a calling, specifies a particular sphere, and concludes with the hope of thus gaining a place among the nine established lyric poets of Greece.

Equally formal is the markedly similar third Ode of the fourth book, addressed to Melpomene. Opening with a brief reference to his own profession, again expressed in a literary-mythological τόπος,[30] Horace passes to a negative roll call. The child touched by Mel-

30. For the glance of the Muse, cf. Hes., *Th.* 82; Call., *Aitia* 1.1.37, and the references of Pfeiffer, *ad loc.*

pomene's favoring glance will be neither athlete, charioteer, nor general:

> sed quae Tibur aquae fertile praefluunt
> et spissae nemorum comae
> fingent Aeolio carmine nobilem.
>
> Romae, principis urbium,
> dignatur suboles inter amabilis
> vatum ponere me choros,
> et iam dente minus mordeor invido. [*C.* 4.3.10–16]

> But the waters which flow past fertile Tibur, and the dense leaves of the groves shall make him famous for Aeolian song. The youth of Rome, first among cities, deems me worthy to be placed among the lovely chorus of bards, and already I am bitten less by the tooth of envy.

Euterpe and Polyhymnia did not withhold their favor, and what was before a tentative hope has now become a demonstrable fact. All Rome has confirmed Horace's expectation of being ranked among the *vates lyrici,* or *vates amabiles,* and again he gracefully assigns his talent to a representative member of the Pierian Muses. Like *C.* 1.1, the Ode is a declaration of professional status, a public claim to equality with the canonical lyric poets. The most interesting passages in the two poems—the enrollment in the Bacchic train in the first, and the tribute to Tibur in the second—are brief, and Horace saved development of them for Odes more private in tone.

Negative comparisons are often a convenience in defining art, and poets frequently find it easier to say what they are not than what they are. An Ode composed for the opening of the temple of Actian Apollo (*C.* 1.31) follows a pattern somewhat similar to that of *C.* 1.1 and *C.* 4.3. Apollo was both the special patron of Octavian and also a traditional inspirer of poetry, the god to whom Horace was later to ascribe his own "art of song and name of poet." [31] But for Horace, Apollo never seems to become more than a representative

31. *C.* 4.6.29; see above, 17.

figure in the poetic tradition; perhaps he had been too widely publicized politically to retain much meaning as a private symbol.[32] The perfect discretion of Horace's prayer contributes little beyond what we could expect in any such occasional poem. "What does the bard ask from the newly dedicated Apollo?" (*C.* 1.31.1–2). Not the wealth of sheep owner, trader, or landholder, but simply some olives and mallows and a healthy old age companioned by the lyre (15 ff.). The prospect seems a little bare. We may suspect that Horace means his prayer to signify something more meaningful, but our suspicions receive scant support from the lines themselves.

The Ode to Grosphus (*C.* 2.16) hardly appears concerned with poetry at all, for its terms are those of an almost overt Epicureanism, a context unpromising if not actually hostile.[33] The Ode's subject is *otium,* that ἀταραξία which Horace, like Lucretius before him, locates in the freedom from fear and desire (15). The prerogatives of wealth and position are trivial beside the tranquillity of soul possessed by the man "who lives well on little, and on whose humble table (*mensa tenui*) shines his father's saltcellar" (13 ff.). The Ode's general progress seems somewhat haphazard, as though Horace had assembled those topics in Lucretius for which he felt a particular affinity, and stripped them of their doctrinaire associations. Only with the last two stanzas does the poem take a decisively personal turn:

> te greges centum Siculaeque circum
> mugiunt vaccae, tibi tollit hinnitum
> apta quadrigis equa, te bis Afro
> murice tinctae
>
> vestiunt lanae: mihi parva rura et
> spiritum Graiae tenuem Camenae
> Parca non mendax dedit et malignum
> spernere volgus. [*C.* 2.16.33–40]

32. See above, 187.

33. Epicurus himself seems not to have approved of poetry; see J. H. Waszink, *Mededeelingen d. kon. nederlandse Akad. v. Wetenschappen, Afd. Letterkunde* (Nieuwe Reeks, Deel 17, No. 8; 1954), 244 ff. But there was, of course, Lucretius, on whom Horace draws heavily in this Ode; see Kiessling-Heinze, *ad loc.;* K. Latte, *Philologus, 90* (1935), 294 ff.

A hundred herds of Sicilian cattle low in your fields, and for you the racehorse whinnies; wool twice dipped in African dye clothes you. To me Fate, sparing yet not deceiving, has given modest lands and the slender spirit of the Greek Muse, and a disdain for the envious crowd.

The opposition of Grosphus' wealth and Horace's humble Sabine farm gives a special point to the earlier contrast (6 ff.) between the wealthy who lack *otium* and the poor man, content with his ancestral saltcellar, who has achieved it. Horace's tranquil withdrawal to his farm balances the picture of those forever in flight from themselves (19–20); his *parva rura* (37) recall the man "living well on little" (*vivitur parvo bene,* 13); and perhaps in *spiritum tenuem* (38) it is legitimate to catch an echo of *mensa tenui* (14). The verbal associations are only tentative, but they are clear enough to show that Horace's reference to his poetry is not an afterthought but an integral part of the poem's progress. To define the special quality of his own life he makes use of a standard philosophical antithesis, as if hoping that the stable and familiar framework would make self-definition easier.

The theme of wealth's inadequacy was one that Horace turned to on several occasions in his attempt to convey the special quality of his art. Where the Ode to Grosphus remains objective up to the last two stanzas, that to the anonymous *avarus* declares its personal bias from the opening sentence:

Non ebur neque aureum
mea renidet in domo lacunar . . . [*C.* 2.18.1–2]

No ivory or gilded ceilings shine in my home . . .

Neither ivory nor gold, not marble columns nor rich gowns woven by clients grace Horace's home,

at fides et ingeni
benigna vena est pauperemque dives
me petit: nihil supra
deos lacesso nec potentem amicum

largiora flagito,
satis beatus unicis Sabinis. [9–14]

But faith and a rich vein of genius are mine, and the wealthy seek me out, poor as I am. I importune the gods for nothing more, nor do I demand anything further from my powerful friend, rich enough in my Sabine farm alone.

The contrast between external riches and some inner value associated with poetry provides the Ode's initial impetus,[34] though Horace then turns to the theme of wealth's futility before death (14 ff.). The first fourteen lines recall the balance struck by the prayer to Apollo or by the concluding lines of the Ode to Grosphus. Again Horace invests the facts of his life—his Sabine farm, his declared poverty—with symbolic value, demanding that they do service for some particular but unspecified private experience. *Fides* (9) is vague enough to include whatever meaning Horace intended, but it does little to help us in discovering what it was.[35] The contrast between worldly riches and the "rich vein" of the poet is tighter than it is in the other two Odes, with the play upon *beatus* (14) emphasizing the financial basis of the comparison. From here it was but a step to the playful ingenuities of the elegists, for whom the plea of special resources became a predictable trump in the game of courtship. Perhaps their endless variations on the theme [36] devalued the contrast beyond the point where Horace could find it meaningful. *C.* 2.18, like the prayer to Apollo and the Ode to Grosphus, is customarily dated in the early twenties, and in later Odes Horace generally abandoned the antithesis of inner and outer riches as a way of defining his poetic gift, reserving the contrast for Odes concerned with more conventional moral

34. Or so we can assume, since as a starting point for *C.* 2.18 Horace took Bacchylides, 28 (Bergk), transferring the contrast between wealth and poverty from a convivial to a moral context. On *C.* 2.18, see above, 79 ff.

35. Might it be a pun on *fides,* "lyre"? W. C. Helmbold, *AJP, 77* (1956), 291 ff., thinks that Horace intended the same pun in *C.* 1.33.4, and the context in *C.* 2.18.9 is even more appropriate.

36. Cf. especially Propertius, 3.2.9–16, which looks like an imitation of Horace's lines. For references to other uses of the contrast, which frequently incorporates the topic of the *dives amator,* see K. F. Smith, *The Elegies of Tibullus, ad* 1.4.61.

problems.[37] For describing his art he was to find terms more positive and less familiar.

The Odes cataloguing different ways of life and those contrasting wealth and art show Horace rejecting familiar worlds in the effort to attach a clearer reality to his own. Yet his semiprofessional, semi-social classifications of his calling fail to communicate anything very satisfactory. We know more of what he avoided than of what he achieved, more of what his poetry did not involve than of what it did. Logical distinctions can never be very helpful in dealing with something that is ultimately a matter of feeling, and Horace imparts a more meaningful image of his experience through the attributes and effects that he ascribes to poetry and to the figures associated with it.

To connect poetry and immortality is logical, but to join poetry and order seems to be instinctive. In an influential study of Shakespeare, G. Wilson Knight pointed out that the polar images of the plays tend to be those of storm and music.[38] Though the antithesis may be peculiarly apt for Shakespeare, the connotations of the two are virtually archetypal. Running through the whole of Greek literature we find the storm as an image of violence, upheaval, and unpleasantness, and music as one of repose, beauty, and peace. But beyond these generic and nearly inevitable associations, Horace found in music an ideal significance to which none of his contemporaries and few previous poets save Pindar responded with equal intensity. His feelings are most fully realized in the *almae Musae* of the fourth Roman Ode, dispensers alike of poetic inspiration and "gentle counsel." Although his vision was not again to achieve a comparable scope, the union of poetry and peace was fundamental to his thought. Apollo's lyre holds out the promise of serenity to Murena (*C.* 2.10.18), a symbolism its early history was well adapted to. Mercury, inventor of the lyre, is said to have "tamed the fierce habits of men" with his songs, while the magic of Orpheus' music is rationalized as the ability to dissuade men from bloodshed.[39]

37. Cf. *C.* 2.2, 3.1, 3.16, 4.9. Horace continued to use financial imagery in speaking of the gift of immortality that he could bestow (as in *C.* 4.8), as did the elegists. But that is quite different from the concept of the poet's own inner riches.

38. *The Shakespearian Tempest* (Oxford, 1932).

39. *C.* 1.10.2; *A. P.* 391 ff. Cf. *S.* 1.3.103 ff.

The union of poetry and order assumes its most dramatic form in the figure of Bacchus. In his train Horace enrolls himself in the opening Ode, and it is in Bacchus and the closely related Faunus that he finds the most expressive symbols outside of the fourth Roman Ode.[40] Bacchus was traditionally the most violent of the gods associated with poetry, but Horace emphasizes another aspect as well, linking him with such deities as the Muses, Venus, Cupid, and the Graces.[41] Occasionally, as in *C.* 1.20, wine, Bacchus' earthly manifestation, seems to be itself a token of poetry. In *C.* 3.21, written in honor of the literary patron Messalla, Horace invokes a wine jar born the same year as himself: *O nata mecum consule Manlio* (1). Here, as in the thirteenth Epode, it is easy to feel a special significance in the correspondence of ages, though the themes of the two poems could hardly be more different. The adjective "sacred" (*pia testa, C.* 3.21.4) functions not only in terms of the parody, but suggests as well the same poetic associations as *pietas mea et musa* (*C.* 1.17.13–14) or *pios lucos* (*C.* 3.4.6–7). The effects attributed to the *pia testa* fall roughly into two groups: it can give renewed strength, and it can bestow calm. The elements, although admittedly very general, approximate poetry's union of vitality and order.

Bacchus, the inspirer of poetry, represents a somewhat similar reconciliation of opposites. In an Ode that seems a study in the dithyramb (*C.* 2.19), Horace describes his feelings under the spell of the god:

> Bacchum in remotis carmina rupibus
> vidi docentem, credite posteri,
> Nymphasque discentis et auris
> capripedum Satyrorum acutas.
>
> euhoe, recenti mens trepidat metu 5
> plenoque Bacchi pectore turbidum

40. On Bacchus as connected with poetry, see E. Maass, *Hermes, 31* (1896), 375 ff. Aside from the ritualistic connection with Greek tragedy, Bacchus, or Dionysus, does not appear often in previous literature as the inspirer of poets; see O. Falter, *Der Dichter und sein Gott,* 52.

41. *C.* 1.32.9 ff., 1.18.6, 3.21.21 ff. In *C.* 1.12.21–22, Bacchus appears between Athene and Diana in the catalogue of gods whom Horace honors, and in *C.* 3.3.13, 4.8.34, and *Ep.* 2.1.5, he is ranked among the chief benefactors of mankind.

laetatur, euhoe, parce Liber,
parce gravi metuende thyrso.

fas pervicacis est mihi Thyiadas
vinique fontem lactis et uberes 10
cantare rivos atque truncis
lapsa cavis iterare mella.

On a remote crag I saw Bacchus—believe me, you who come hereafter—teaching his songs to the listening Nymphs and the goat-footed Satyrs with their pointed ears. Evoe, my mind trembles with fear still fresh, and in its turmoil rejoices, for my breast is filled with the god. Evoe, Liber, spare me, spare me, you who are fearful with your dread thyrsus. I may sing of the unwearying Bacchants, the fountains of wine and the rivers flowing with milk, and tell again of the honey dripping from hollowed trees.

The stanzas present a dramatic image of the experience that the introductory Ode merely sketches (*C.* 1.1.30–32). The scene, *in remotis rupibus,* gives a more evocative meaning to the opening poem's flat *secernunt populo,* and in the supernatural fertility that Bacchus compels upon the land (10–12) we feel a suggestion of the poet's own lonely and passionate creativity beneath the god's spell. Here, in a more richly developed form, is the previous Ode's declaration of "a rich vein of genius" (*C.* 2.18.9–10).

There follows a brief hymn celebrating Bacchus' violent power over human beings and nature alike (13–20), climaxed by a description of his part in the defeat of the Giants:

tu, cum parentis regna per arduum
cohors gigantum scanderet inpia,
Rhoetum retorsisti leonis
unguibus horribilique mala;

quamquam choreis aptior et iocis 25
ludoque dictus non sat idoneus
pugnae ferebaris; sed idem
pacis eras mediusque belli.

> When the evil army of the Giants attempted to climb through the sky to the realm of father Jupiter, you thrust down Rhoetus with the claws and teeth of the lion shape you had assumed. Although you were said to be better fitted for dancing and jesting and sport, and unsuited for battle, you were in the forefront of war as of peace.

"A surprising feat for this particular god," comments Fraenkel.[42] Bacchus' role in the Gigantomachia is almost without precedent, but its significance here is clear. Animal energy submits itself to a principle of order—the union is similar to that suggested by the wild tigers yoked to Bacchus' chariot (*C.* 3.3.13–15). The balance struck by the qualifying stanza, *idem pacis . . . mediusque belli,* approximates that in Horace's praise of Alcaeus (*C.* 1.32.6 ff.). Both passages suggest the double capacity in which Horace himself served, poet both of convivial themes and of such gigantic historical dramas as the fourth Roman Ode. The fact that Horace so emphasizes the compatibility of these two elements both in his poetic model and in his poetic inspirer should give pause to those who would argue a definitive split between them in the Odes.

But there is a more important union suggested in *C.* 2.19. The Ode closes with what is virtually a Gigantomachia in miniature:

> te vidit insons Cerberus aureo
> cornu decorum leniter atterens
> caudam et recedentis trilingui
> ore pedes tetigitque crura. [29–32]

> And when, magnificent with your golden horn, Cerberus looked upon you, he did you no harm, but, gently brushing you with his tail, he licked with his triple tongue at your legs and feet as you departed.

Editors point out that the "intentional dullness" of the last stanza, after the excitement of the poem's opening, agrees with Horace's

42. Fraenkel, *Horace,* 200. Traditionally, Bacchus had appeared as a lion only on board a ship: *Hom. Hymn* 7.44. Bacchus' appearance in the Gigantomachia is extremely rare in previous literature; see Euripides, *Ion* 216–18; *Cyclops* 5.

fondness for a dying close. Yet the structural function of the lines does not negate the fact that the image was independently a pregnant one for Horace. Twice again he uses something similar, both times to describe the power of music. Here he is speaking of Alcaeus' songs in the underworld:

> quid mirum, ubi illis carminibus stupens
> demittit atras belua centiceps
> auris et intorti capillis
> Eumenidum recreantur angues?
>
> [*C.* 2.13.33–36]

> What wonder, when the hundred-headed monster, dazed by these songs, lowers his black ears, and the snakes twined in the hair of the Furies fall calm?

And here he addresses the lyre itself:

> tu potes tigris comitesque silvas
> ducere et rivos celeres morari;
> cessit immanis tibi blandienti
> ianitor aulae. [*C.* 3.11.13–16]

> You are able to lead tigers and trees in your train, and you can make the swift rivers stand still; to your persuasive strains the huge gatekeeper of hell yielded.

Descriptions such as these are likely to lead us too far into what George Eliot termed "that tempting range of relevancies." Yet in these scenes we are surely justified in finding something more important than the familiar maxim that "music hath charms." Inherent in poetry is the ordering of formless power, as personified by the brute Cerberus. The figure of Bacchus does not suggest simply two types of verse, the martial and the festive; he incorporates a more profound tension. The inspirer of the most turbulent feelings, he also exerts a stern control. These two aspects of his nature convey the two elements of the art of which he is patron, "a more than usual state of emotion with more than usual order," in Coleridge's words. Horace's reconciliation of the two qualities in Bacchus suggests that the anomaly of his own position is no more than superficial, that the tight preciseness of his verse, far from refuting his claims to extravagant emotion, is the necessary complement to it.

The harmonious order inherent in poetry extended, for Horace, into the life of the poet himself. His art becomes itself a world, and at the same time that it isolates him from the *malignum volgus* it provides an alternative to it. "Dear to the Muses, I shall abandon sadness and fear to the fierce winds to carry off to the Cretan sea, singularly unconcerned as to what king of the frozen lands under Arcturus we fear, or what dangers Tiridates dreads" (*C.* 1.26.1–6). Horace is rarely so explicit. Possibly, the invitation to Pompeius to retire *sub lauru mea* (*C.* 2.7.19) suggests that the shade of the poet's wreath offers a special kind of immunity to partisan politics. And in the Ode to Grosphus (*C.* 2.16) Horace seems to stop just short of formulating his own particular peace of spirit. The vague parallels there between the man "living well on little" and Horace himself suggest that the *otium* which is ascribed to the former belongs to the latter as well. Through his "slender spirit of the Greek Muse" and his *parva rura* Horace enjoys a serenity that Grosphus' wealth can never bring him.

Horace's frequent claims of divine protection might be seen in the same way. In general, it is easy to suspect that Horace is most personal when his language seems to be the most abstract or the most stylized, and the fact that in the passages boasting a special immunity his tone is often literary to the point of fancifulness does not mean that the passages are necessarily unserious:

vestris amicum fontibus et choris
non me Philippis versa acies retro,
devota non extinxit arbor
nec Sicula Palinurus unda. [*C.* 3.4.25–28]

Dear to your fountains and choruses, I was harmed neither by the rout at Philippi, nor by that accursed tree, nor by the sea near the headland of Palinurus.

Although his claim has a primary motive in the particular structure of this Ode,[43] the number of parallels in other poems indicates something more pervasive. Horace elsewhere ascribes his escape from Philippi to Mercury (*C.* 2.7.13), and his protection from the *devota arbor* to Bacchus (*C.* 3.8.7) or to Faunus (*C.* 2.17.28), all gods associated, at least in part, with poetry. Even the playful Ode on Lalage (*C.* 1.22) catches something of the same feelings. The portentous wolf that flees from Horace as he sings of Lalage might be the victim not only of the power of Horace's love but of the power of his art as well. Horace's promises of eternal devotion to his mistress are curiously close to his declarations to the Muses in the fourth Roman Ode.[44] The vanquished wolf, too, recalls Cerberus, overcome by Orpheus (*C.* 3.11.15), Alcaeus (*C.* 2.13.33–35), or Bacchus (*C.* 2.19.29); the wolves on Horace's farm are similarly rendered harmless by his *musa et pietas* (*C.* 1.17.14), and by Faunus (*C.* 3.18.13). These resemblances between *C.* 1.22 and other Odes on poetry may be no more than fortuitous. Yet there is the further fact that *C.* 1.22 is addressed to a literary critic, Aristius Fuscus, while even the name Lalage is suggestive.[45] Lalage herself is described but once: *dulce ridentem, dulce loquentem* (23–24). Her only attributes are, as it were, the combined parody and serious statement of the Ode itself.

In *C.* 3.29, the elaborate invitation to Maecenas, Horace never mentions his poetry. Yet though he is not explicitly *Musis amicus,* the images in which he describes himself convey the sense of one who is *unice securus.* His concluding assertion (53–64) of independence from Fortune's whims—*mea virtute me involvo*—can easily strike us as "a rather priggish emphasis on virtue." [46] Yet may not *virtus* (55) have less to do with conventional morality than with something more private, something comparable to his proclaimed *fides* or *pietas?* His glad betrothal to *probam pauperiem* (55–56)

43. See above, 207.

44. Cf. especially *C.* 1.22.17 with *C.* 3.4.29 ff. On *C.* 1.22, see above, 130 ff.

45. It comes from λαλαγέω, "to prattle" or "chatter"; we might compare Simonides' use of the related λαλέω: "painting is a silent poetry, poetry a speaking (λαλοῦσα) painting" (Plu., *Moralia* 346f). Lalage is *dulce loquentem,* and it is interesting that of the eight other uses of *loquor* in the Odes, six are connected with poetry.

46. Wilkinson, *Horace,* 45.

recalls not so much the ostentatious morality of *C.* 3.16 as the blend of physical simplicity and the inner resources of the poet in the Hymn to Apollo (*C.* 1.31) and the Odes to Grosphus (*C.* 2.16) and the *avarus* (*C.* 2.18). In *C.* 3.29, the Sabine farm, a not inconsiderable establishment, is described in terms that recall the home of Baucis and Philemon. The image that Horace conjures up to lure Maecenas from Rome (*mundaeque parvo sub lare pauperum cenae,* 14–15) matches, in its drastic simplicity, his reference to his *parva rura* (*C.* 2.16.37), his description of himself as *pauper* (*C.* 2.18.10), or his chastened claim to feed on olives and mallows (*C.* 1.31.15–16). Horace's exaggerations are deliberate, and suggest that he is trying to find a means of dramatizing the essentially undramatic quality of inner serenity. The end of the Ode to Maecenas, describing Horace's tiny skiff riding out a storm (*C.* 3.29.62–64), conveys a comparable sense of his safe removal from the vicissitudes of Fortune. In this, the lines anticipate the final security from all nature's storms which is asserted in the following poem (*C.* 3.30.3–4). Horace's *biremis scapha,* like his declared poverty or his shielding *virtus,* seems the token of some private tranquillity at which the terms of rich and poor can only hint.

In one of the Epistles Horace speaks of the country as "giving me back to myself" (*Ep.* 1.14.1). The phrase confirms what so many of the Odes suggest, that the Italian countryside, particularly the Sabine farm, represents for Horace not only a physical environment but also a local habitation and a name for certain ideal values. The idyllic landscapes to which he invites his friends are calculated to "give them back to themselves," to call them from the arbitrary to the essential, from the search for political or financial advantage to an awareness of the limitations and possibilities of human life. And, in some of the Odes still more private in their concern, the country, we might say, gives Horace to himself as an artist. With its gods Bacchus and Faunus it expresses the possibilities Horace found in poetry itself—possibilities of isolation and commitment, of freedom and security, of creativity and peace.

The early poetic traditions of sacred groves and springs indicate how instinctive it was to link artistic inspiration with the isolation of the country. Although the mythological justification for the poet's withdrawal had disappeared by the Augustan age, there remained the self-evident fact that these myths had enshrined, that writers need solitude to compose. So Aper rationalizes in Tacitus' *Dialogus:* "Poets, if they are to produce anything worthy, must leave the conversation of their friends and the charms of the city, and leaving every other function they must, in their own words, go into the woods and groves (*in nemora et lucos*), that is, into solitude" (9). Horace says virtually the same thing in protesting against the difficulties of composing in the city:

> scriptorum chorus omnis amat nemus et fugit urbem,
> rite cliens Bacchi somno gaudentis et umbra.
> [*Ep.* 2.2.77–78]

> The whole chorus of writers loves the forests and flees the city, rightly votaries of Bacchus, and delighting in sleep and shade.

In the practical terms of this Epistle, to be a follower of Bacchus involves no more than a preference for quiet surroundings. In the Odes, Bacchus and the country he presides over represent something more vital. *Secernunt populo* in the introductory poem (*C.* 1.1.32) describes more than a bucolic retreat, just as *gelidum nemus* (30) implies more for the god's votary than "sleep and shade." In his Hymn to Bacchus (*C.* 2.19) Horace elaborates the ideas to which the opening Ode merely refers. The wild isolation of the scene (*in remotis rupibus,* 1) evokes that part of his life that lies beyond the comprehension of society. But despite the Ode's descriptive immediacy and its half-whimsical vow of accuracy—*credite posteri*—its landscape remains almost as literary as that of *C.* 1.1. A second Ode to Bacchus (*C.* 3.25) blends realism and symbolism more powerfully:

> Quo me, Bacche, rapis tui
> plenum? quae nemora aut quos agor in specus
> velox mente nova? quibus
> antris egregii Caesaris audiar

aeternum meditans decus 5
  stellis inserere et consilio Iovis?
dicam insigne, recens, adhuc
  indictum ore alio.

Whither, Bacchus, are you carrying me off, filled with your spirit? Into what groves or caverns am I driven, swift with fresh inspiration? In what caves shall I be heard, intent upon setting the eternal glory of great Caesar amongst the stars and the council of Jove? I shall sing something noble and new, never before uttered by another mouth.

Horace withdraws from the world, but only to re-create it in his own terms. If politics are left behind, it is only so that the greatest of political figures may become the subject of his verse. So far the landscape is quite formal. The caves and groves to which Horace feels himself transported are a shorthand for his poetic potential, while *mente nova* (3) suggests not only the physical immediacy of inspiration but also his literary originality in undertaking to immortalize Caesar.

The lines that follow are less stylized and more directly personal:

non secus in iugis

exsomnis stupet Euhias
  Hebrum prospiciens et nive candidam 10
Thracen ac pede barbaro
  lustratam Rhodopen, ut mihi devio

ripas et vacuum nemus
  mirari libet. o Naiadum potens
Baccharumque valentium 15
  proceras manibus vertere fraxinos,

nil parvum aut humili modo,
  nil mortale loquar. dulce periculum est,
o Lenaee, sequi deum
  cingentem viridi tempora pampino. 20

> Just as the sleepless Bacchant stands upon the ridges, struck dumb with wonder, looking out over the Hebrus and Thrace gleaming with snow, and Rhodope, tracked by barbarian feet, so, wandering, I love to gaze in wonder upon the banks and the deserted groves. O you who rule the Naiads and the Bacchants, strong enough to rip up huge ash trees with their hands, nothing humble or of lowly measure, nothing mortal shall I sing. Sweet is the peril, O Lenaeus, to follow in the train of the god, girding my temples with the green vine.

The banks and groves among which Horace wanders (13) represent not merely the practical refuge sought by the *cliens Bacchi* (*Ep.* 2.2.78) nor the formal symbolism of the introductory Ode (*C.* 1.1.30–32). Rather, the scene blends the domestic with the mystical, the Italian landscape with the Dionysiac experience. Something similar appears in the description of the poet in the Ode to Melpomene:

> sed quae Tibur aquae fertile praefluunt
> et spissae nemorum comae
> fingent Aeolio carmine nobilem. [*C.* 4.3.10–12]

> But the waters that flow past fertile Tibur and the dense leaves of the groves shall make him famous for Aeolian song.

The wedding of literary tradition and local detail makes of Tibur's groves and waters an inner experience as much as an outer one.[47] The beauty of the lines seems to lie half in the scene itself, half in the poet's response to it, and we sense a harmonious interchange between the land that creates such poetry and the poet who re-creates the land in his verse.

In the Ode to Bacchus, Horace suggests more dramatically the special significance of the land around Tibur by comparing his response to that felt by the Bacchant (8 ff.). The incongruity of the

47. Cf. *C.* 3.4.6 ff. and *C.* 4.2.29 ff. for a similar mingling of actual and symbolic scenery.

simile is apparent rather than real. Having his existence in the natural world, yet preternaturally aware, the poet shares the Bacchant's exultation, a mixture of ecstasy and peace. The frozen distance surrounding the Bacchant marks no greater remove than the isolation Horace feels in the domestic country around Tibur, while the Bacchant's rush of energy, enabling him to alter the face of nature (16), is matched by the poet's supernatural power to "place Caesar among the stars" (6). Although Horace claims that it is his new attempt to immortalize Caesar that inflames him, he seems captivated less by Caesar's "immortal glory" than by his own power to create it. He stands, we might say, in the same relation to his art as the Bacchant does to Bacchus. As the Bacchant becomes identified with the god, so the poet becomes identified with his art: "How can we know the dancer from the dance?" A mortal, he yet creates *aeternum decus* (5), and thus can lay claim to divinity of a sort: *nil mortale loquar* (18). The ambiguity of the Ode's last line may well be intentional, and we should not refer it categorically to Bacchus. Normally we would take *cingentem* with the god's follower, whether as subject or as object, rather than with the god, and only a parallel from a later Ode influences us against it.[48] Why should not Horace, *plenus dei,* put on the attributes of Bacchus? His ability to "set the eternal glory of Caesar among the stars" (5–6) is the equivalent of Bacchus' apotheosis of Ariadne: *beatae coniugis additum stellis honorem* (*C.* 2.19.13–14). Author, inspirer, and subject are webbed together, though their precise relationship and the divinity with which each is endowed remains somewhat obscure.[49] The Ode is not an anagram of the poetic experience. A construct of the feelings rather than of the mind, it simply evokes the sensations of creation. In his relationship with the *ripas et vacuum nemus* of his native countryside as touched by the spell of Bacchus, Horace found the most satisfactory

48. *C.* 4.8.33. And here, to confuse things further, Bacchus is one of the gods who have been made immortal by poets—which is, roughly, the state projected for Caesar in *C.* 3.25. On *cingentem* (*C.* 3.25.20) see the notes of Kiessling-Heinze, *ad loc.*

49. Although *C.* 3.25 seems, as Fraenkel (*Horace,* 259) emphasizes, a kind of prelude for poems such as the Roman Odes, we should not assume that Bacchus is simply a symbol for Caesar. Bacchus, after all, had been associated in Octavian's own propaganda with Antony as a symbol of un-Roman debauchery; see K. Scott, *MAAR, 11* (1933), 44–46.

language for the qualities vaguely stated in so many of the Odes on poetry. We can catch something of the isolation, the excitement, the power, and the intoxicating peace that as a poet he had achieved.

The almost surrealistic quality with which Horace charges the landscape of this Ode to Bacchus has no parallel. Yet even when the countryside remains placidly local it sometimes takes on a comparable significance. "Often swift Faunus leaves Lycaeus for lovely Lucretilis, and ever wards off the fiery heat and rainy winds from my goats." From the first sentence of the Ode to Tyndaris (*C.* 1.17) we are in an atmosphere compounded equally of reality and of fantasy. The Sabine farm [50] lies halfway to mythology, competing with Arcadia for the god who dwells there. Horace identifies Faunus, Latin god of the countryside, with the Arcadian Pan, son of Mercury, follower of Dionysus, and inventor of the pipe.[51] It was the same god, "guardian of the men of Mercury," who warded off the falling tree from the poet's head (*C.* 2.17.28–30). From the fact that Horace elsewhere credits his escape either to Bacchus (*C.* 3.8.7) or to the Muses (*C.* 3.4.27), we can infer that Faunus was less important to him in his customary role as god of the country than he was as one of the various deities associated with poetry.

In the description of the Sabine farm Horace develops several of the elements he only hints at in the picture of the *fons Bandusiae* (*C.* 3.13). The farm is also immune to the assaults of nature, and associated with it is a similar union of vitality and peace:

Velox amoenum saepe Lucretilem
mutat Lycaeo Faunus et igneam
  defendit aestatem capellis
    usque meis pluviosque ventos.

inpune tutum per nemus arbutos — 5
quaerunt latentis et thyma deviae
  olentis uxores mariti
    nec viridis metuunt colubras

50. *Lucretilem* (1) signifies the area in which Horace's farm was located. *Lycaeus* (2) was a mountain in Arcadia.

51. On the identification of Pan and Faunus, see C. Bailey, *Religion in Virgil* (Oxford, 1935), 144 ff.

nec Martialis haediliae lupos,
utcumque dulci, Tyndari, fistula 10
valles et Usticae cubantis
levia personuere saxa.

di me tuentur, dis pietas mea
et musa cordi est. hic tibi copia
manabit ad plenum benigno 15
ruris honorum opulenta cornu.

hic in reducta valle caniculae
vitabis aestus et fide Teia
dices laborantis in uno
Penelopen vitreamque Circen. 20

hic innocentis pocula Lesbii
duces sub umbra, nec Semeleius
cum Marte confundet Thyoneus
proelia, nec metues protervum

suspecta Cyrum, ne male dispari 25
incontinentis iniciat manus
et scindat haerentem coronam
crinibus inmeritamque vestem. [*C.* 1.17]

Often swift Faunus leaves Lycaeus for lovely Lucretilis, and ever wards off the fiery heat and the rainy winds from my goats. In safety the mates of ill-smelling consorts wander through the peaceful grove, seeking the arbutus that lies hidden there, and the kids fear neither green snakes nor the wolves of Mars, whenever the smooth rocks and sloping valleys of Ustica have echoed to the sweet pipes of Pan. The gods protect me, my piety and my Muse are dear to the hearts of the gods. Here an abundance of the glories of the country will flow to the full for you from an opulent horn of plenty. Here in a withdrawn valley you will escape the heat of the Dog Star, and upon the Teian lyre you will sing of Penelope and of Circe, clear as crystal in her beauty, both stricken with love for the same man. Here, in the

> shade, you will drink cups of harmless Lesbian wine, and Bacchus, the son of Semele, will not join in conflict with Mars; nor will you fear the gaze of bold Cyrus, lest he should cast incontinent hands upon you, who are no match for him, and tear away the garland clinging to your hair, and rip your undeserving gown.

Though Horace's farm is complete even to evil-smelling goats (7), the bucolic details are submerged in a reality of a different sort. *In reducta valle* (17) names not so much a physical location as a spiritual one. The land that Horace conjures up for us has its truest existence in the private and inherently isolated world of the poet's imagination, like the *remoti rupes* and the *vacuum nemus* in the Odes to Bacchus, or the empty woodlands of "fertile Tibur" in the Ode to Melpomene.[52] All are scenes of chill withdrawal—we think as well of the *fons Bandusiae* (*C.* 3.13) or the *gelidum nemus* to which Horace retreats in the introductory Ode (*C.* 1.1.30). In each scene we feel that the hot sun of life has been shaded and cancelled—but only in order that the poet may reclaim it on his own terms, recreating in his verse all that is hot, heavy, sharp, and violent.

The supernal peace that Faunus bestows upon the Sabine farm is both a tribute to, and an attribute of, Horace's special experience: *di me tuentur, dis pietas mea / et musa cordi est.* The calm created by Faunus' Panpipes (5–12) is reminiscent of that compelled upon the beasts of the underworld by Alcaeus, Orpheus, or Bacchus.[53] Upon the human world falls the same fiat of harmony, in deference to Horace's "piety"—or his Muse. If Tyndaris will come to the Sabine farm she can forget her fears of drunken brawls and of the bestial Cyrus (21–28). The only wine served will be that of Lesbos (21), and the wreath Tyndaris wears will remain immune and inviolate (25–27). Horace's art is the condition upon which such a world rests, and the sunny stanzas that create the scene are themselves an invitation to understand what is meant to be *unice securus.* By comparison, his vague citations of *parva rura,* of *unicis Sabinis,* or of

52. *C.* 2.19.1, 3.25.13, 4.3.10.
53. *C.* 2.13.33 ff., 3.11.15, 2.19.29 ff.

mundae sub lare pauperum cenae are fragmentary and unevocative.[54] Here, in its most beautifully realized form, is the ordered peace that he alone could command.

The land's serenity is equalled only by its perfect fertility: *hic tibi copia manabit . . .* (14–16). The words, intertwined and abundant as the cornucopia itself, pile upon one another with the profusion that they describe; *copia* verges upon a rhetorical term. The stanza is as thickly textured as the second, where the confusing order of words makes the thyme lie hidden much as it lies hidden from the goats. The verbal density of both passages reminds us that the scenes exist only in the world of words. The lines do not so much describe as create the land. Its reality upon the page is, finally, its only reality.

The description of the coming banquet (14–16) is, to be sure, conventional in invitations.[55] Yet here it is not the preparations of the banqueters that are at issue, but rather the opulence of the land itself, which in its preternatural creativity rivals the endless wealth of the cornucopia, and recalls the wild profusion brought by Bacchus (*C.* 2.19.10–12). The "glories of the country" that Horace offers to Tyndaris stand as both the product and the image of his own creativity, of that "rich vein of genius" [56] that he often states but never so sensuously conveys. In thus combining peace and fertility the Ode strikes a familiar theme—we think of the cold waters of fertile Tibur in the Ode to Melpomene (*C.* 4.3.10), or of the cool groves and hot energy associated with Bacchus in *C.* 1.1, *C.* 2.19, and *C.* 3.25.

The Ode to Tyndaris and that to Bacchus (*C.* 3.25) are in a way complementary, emphasizing distinct but overlapping elements of Horace's art. In the frozen ecstasy of the Bacchant, Horace captures the instant of the creative act, an instant guaranteed permanent validity by the eternal beauty it creates, but itself momentary in duration. The Ode to Tyndaris is calm where the other is violent, time-

54. *C.* 2.16.37, 2.18.14, 3.29.14.

55. Fraenkel, *Horace,* 204 ff.

56. *C.* 2.18.9–10 (*ingeni benigna vena est;* cf. *benigno . . . cornu*); cf. *C.* 4.8.5; *Ep.* 2.2.121; *A. P.* 409.

less where the other is evanescent. Faunus' visits are a constant certainty (*saepe . . . usque . . . utcumque*), and the poem dwells less upon the definitive act of creation than upon the serenity that the latent power of creation makes possible. The present tenses emphasize not an immediate action (*Quo me, Bacche, rapis . . .*) but a permanent state (*di me tuentur*). Tyndaris, though she is ostensibly invited to Horace's farm for a specific occasion, seems virtually an attribute of the landscape. Her name reminds us of Helen, the paradigm of perfect beauty. As subjects for her songs Horace suggests Penelope and Circe, both wrung with emotion (19), but both removed from the actual world to that of myth.[57] Tyndaris, too, half belongs to a world that is real only through poetry. The atmosphere of the Ode is comparable to that of Catullus' Septimius-Acme poem (45). There the lovers' boasts of undying devotion are not so much the expression of a possible future as they are a way of intensifying the perfection of the present. The only real action in the poem is Cupid's sign of blessing. So, too, the only action in the Faunus Ode is an intensification—the sound of the Panpipes, or of Tyndaris' lyre. As one poem creates an ideal world of love, the other creates an ideal world of art.

Most of Horace's invitations are haunted by a kind of nostalgia for the impossible, for a lasting world of sweet wine, beautiful women, and ever-fragrant flowers. His banqueters achieve what is in effect a state of secular grace, but in the Ode to Tyndaris, for almost the only time, that state becomes more than a possibility of the moment. No *dum licet* boxes the occasion; the banqueter's usual garland of "too brief roses" has become the poet's wreath. Here is the timeless world of art, of creativity, and of order—and of the peace possible within it. In the luminous spell of this Ode, and in the excitement of the Ode to Bacchus, we feel and understand most fully Horace's sense of his identity as a poet.

57. The combination of *laborantis . . . vitream* (19–20) is not unlike the mingling of the kid's hot blood with the cool Bandusian fountain, *splendidior vitro,* in *C.* 3.13.

REGISTER OF POEMS OR PASSAGES CITED FROM HORACE

(Italicized numbers indicate pages on which a poem or passage is quoted or discussed.)

ARS POETICA: 42–43, 48
A. P. 1 ff.: 98
15–16: *97*
23: 58
27: 39
46: 82
58–72: *258–59*
77: 33
97: *39*
115–16: 271
136: 38
140–42: *4*
261: 32
268–69: 26
289–94: *47*
295: *22*
333 ff.: 48
388: *32, 47*
391 ff.: *18, 103, 336*
408 ff.: 27, *43*, 351
416–18: 45
438 ff.: *44*, 45

CARMEN SAECULARE: 33, 223, 228–30
C. S. 50: 187
51–52: 203
59–60: 225

CARMINA
C. 1.1: 117, *313, 330–31,* 351
1.1.3 ff.: 105
29 ff.: *18–19, 307*
30: 350
30–32: 338, 344, 346
35: 158
1.2: 33, *175 ff.*, 199, 200, 208, 211, *221 ff.*
1.2.1 ff.: 237
1.3: *118–20,* 125
1.3.1: 67
9–12: *52–53*
34: 67
1.4: 59, 186, *267–69, 280*
1.4.1: 278
13–14: 87
17: 82, 83
19–20: 271
1.5: *65 ff.*, 72, *144–46,* 164, *238*
1.5.1–3: *51–52*
4: 152
13–16: *52*
18: 152
1.6: 34, *70–72, 88*
1.6.9: *102*, 313
9 ff.: 7
13–16: *114–15*
1.7: 59, *115, 173 ff.*, 324
1.7.1 ff.: 105
15–19: *239*
18: 284
23: 126
1.8: *143*
1.9: 59, 166, *269–74,* 280, 285
1.9.13: 243
14–15: 263
15–16: 298
17: 82, 248
21–24: *53–54,* 152
1.10.2: 188, 336
6: 171
13 ff.: 126

CARMINA (*cont.*)
C. 1.11: *273–74,* 285
1.11.1: 243
7: 278
8: 173
1.12: *176*
1.12.3–4: 326
21–22: 337
35–36: 186
51–52: 210
57: 210
1.13: *152–55,* 156, 248
1.13.9–12: 69
1.14: *163–69,* 171, 179, 194, 208, 219, *223–24,* 254
1.14.1 ff.: 237
1.15.4 ff.: 136
9–12: *218*
29 ff.: 237
1.16: *136–39,* 140, 155, 156
1.16.22: 276
1.17: *348–52*
1.17.13–14: *329,* 337, 342
21–28: 69
1.18.6: 337
1.19: *150–52, 294*
1.19.9–12: *142*
1.20: *325–26*
1.22: *131–36, 342*
1.23: 156, *237–38,* 292, *298*
1.23.1: 252
11: 242
11–12: 249–50
1.24: *287–90*
1.25: *247–49,* 255, 292, 300, 328
1.25.1–8: 129
11: 276
1.26: *326–28*
1.26.1–6: *341*
6: 12, 324
10–12: 158
1.27: *72 ff.*
1.28.1–4: *54–55*
1.28.7 ff.: 123
14–15: 255
1.29: *227–28*
1.30: 156, *250–51*
1.31: *17, 115–16,* 326, *332–33,* 343
1.31.15–16: 343
19–20: 297
1.32.4 ff.: 36, 111, 339
9 ff.: 337
1.33: 33, *240–41,* 255
1.33.2: 102
4: 335
1.34.12 ff.: 263
1.35: 263
1.35.33 ff.: 181, 183, 223, 228
1.37: 33, 35, *89 ff., 116–17, 163,* 166, 209
1.37.1: 223
17–20: 231
21: 221
21 ff.: 308
26–27: 186
1.38: *117–18,* 285, *313–14*
2.1: *109,* 183, 221, *314*
2.1.13: 53
23–24: 186, 308
30: 181
37 ff.: 18, 34, 111
2.2: *75 ff., 88,* 336
2.2.13–16: 186
15 ff.: 84
2.3: *283–85,* 287
2.3.1–4: 246, 263
3: 238
13–14: 298
17 ff.: 82, 87
2.4: *305*
2.4.3: 152
14: 152
23: 284
2.5: 156, *251–54*
2.5.9–12: *236*
14–15: *105, 298–99*
2.6: 263
2.6.5–12: *105–06*

CARMINA (*cont.*)
C. 2.7: *170–72,* 255
2.7.11: 186
11–12: 201–02
13: 342
16: 164
19: *341*
2.8: *148–50,* 302
2.9: 33, *239–40,* 255
2.9.8: 271
9: 144
9 ff.: *290*
17: 242
2.10.2: 67
9–20: 187
13–15: 262
15–18: *239*
18: 336
2.11: *242–44,* 279
2.11.4: 284
5 ff.: 81, 246, 278
9–10: 246, 284
10–11: 248
11–12: 277
13 ff.: 284
15: 290
2.12: 34, *72*
2.12.1 ff.: *114*
6 ff.: 200
25–28: 152
2.13: *139–41,* 155, 156, *315–17*
2.13.8: 137
31 ff.: *340,* 342, 350
2.14: *87, 285–87*
2.14.1: 278, 301
2 ff.: 289
4: 311
7 ff.: 311
11 ff.: 87
22–24: 271
2.15: *85 ff.,* 218
2.16: 326, *333–34, 341,* 343
2.16.37 ff.: *37–38,* 41, *102,* 343, 351
2.17: *311*
2.17.28 ff.: 171, 342, 348
2.18: 59, *79 ff., 86 ff.,* 279, 282, 326, *334–35,* 343
2.18.9 ff.: 1, *311–12, 329–30, 338,* 343, 351
14: 351
15 ff.: 248, 264
29 ff.: 87
32 ff.: 123, 289
2.19: 31, *314, 337–40,* 351
2.19.1 ff.: *312,* 344, 350
10–12: 351
13–14: 347
29 ff.: 342, 350
2.20: *309–13*
2.20.2–3: 308
5–6: 1
3.1: 336
3.1.1–4: *16*
5–8: 210
16: 53
33–36: 82
3.2.11 ff.: 237
13 ff.: *105*
21–22: 210, *308*
3.3: *110–11,* 182, *209 ff., 224–25,* 232–33
3.3.9: 320
12: 320
13: 337
13–15: 339
34–36: 320
40–42: 225
69 ff.: 18, 34, *223*
3.4: 33, 59, *194 ff.,* 224, 225, 230, 232, 324, 336
3.4.1 ff.: *17*
6 ff.: 337, 346
25: 324
25–28: *341–42*
27: 348
29 ff.: 342
31: 67
37: 175
42: 188

CARMINA (*cont.*)
C. 3.4.49 ff.: 123
3.5: *111–12*
3.5.1 ff.: *176,* 210
13 ff.: 123
41 ff.: 126, 308
3.6: 33, 111, 218
3.7: *111, 142*
3.7.1: *16*
32: 293
3.8: *244*
3.8.7: 342, 348
3.9: *55 ff., 141–42,* 147, 156
3.9.19: 152
3.10: *129–30,* 156
3.11: *172,* 222
3.11.1 ff.: 171
9–12: *252*
13–16: *340*
15: 342, 350
33 ff.: 308, 325
49–50: *324–25*
3.12: *143*
3.13: *322–24,* 348, 350, 352
3.14: 59, *226–27,* 256
3.15: *249–50,* 255, 256, 260, 292
3.15.1 ff.: 300
8 ff.: 129
14: 295
3.16: 336, 343
3.16.1 ff.: *103*
22 ff.: *104–05*
28: *102*
38: *105*
3.17: *260–61*
3.18.13: 342
3.19: *259–61*
3.20: *143–44*
3.21: *126–27,* 156, 209, *337*
3.21.11–12: 137
3.22: 127
3.24: *33, 87,* 218
3.24.1 ff.: *82, 87*
36 ff.: *119*
3.25: 31, *344–48, 351–52*
3.25.3–6: *320–21*
13: 350
3.26: 129, *146–48,* 294
3.26.1 ff.: 69
5: 67
3.27: 172, 222
3.27.58: 271
74–76: *310*
3.28: *306*
3.29: *244–47, 314–15, 342–43*
3.29.5: 277
14: 351
33 ff.: 284
48: 298
49 ff.: *54,* 263
3.30: *310, 312–15*
3.30.1 ff.: *16,* 323, 343
12: 1
13–14: 120, 158
4.1: 156, *291–97,* 305, 306
4.1.1–2: 69
4: 301
15–16: 69
4.2: 59 ff.: 72, *224*
4.2.3–4: 310
5 ff.: 323
22–23: 317
25: 53
27 ff.: 36, 49
29 ff.: 346
31 ff.: 34
37–40: 223, *224*
45–46: *234*
4.3.1 ff.: 105
10: 350–51
10 ff.: *346*
13 ff.: *19–20,* 158
24: 9
4.4: *231–33*
4.4.1 ff.: 237
5 ff.: 46
33: *46*
4.5: 218, *233–34*
4.5.2: 234

CARMINA (*cont.*)
C. 4.5.5 ff.: *225*, 237
17 ff.: 223, *226*
32 ff.: 212, 234
4.6: *17*, 228
4.6.29: 9
4.7: *277–81*, 286, 302, 306, *317*
4.7.13 ff.: 82
15 ff.: 87, 123
17 ff.: 263
25 ff.: 123
27–28: *201*
4.8: *317–20*
4.8.5: 351
26–27: *330*
33: *347*
34: 337
4.9: *321–22*, 336
4.10: 156, *297–99*, 306
4.10.1: 300, 306
4.11: *302–06*
4.11.15: 67
19: 284
4.12: *274–77*, 306
4.12.26: 305
4.13: *299–302*, 306
4.13.6: 271
6 ff.: 248
12: 271
16: 306
17: 152
26: 271
4.15: 218
4.15.1 ff.: 7, *34–35*
4: 225

EPISTLES
Ep. 1.1.1–4: *295–96*
10: *295–96*
16: 171
23: 284
59 ff.: *102*
1.2.1–30: 123
1.3.10: 12
14: 39
1.4.1: 33
1.6.1: *263*
1.6.12–14: *261*
17 ff.: *263*
20 ff.: 87
25 ff.: 289
1.7.28: 301
1.8.12: *105*
1.10.2: 235
3–4: 135
30–32: *262*
1.12.28–29: *225*
1.14: *105*
1.14.1: *343*
33: 301
36: 44, 249
1.16.73 ff.: 87
1.17.33: 212
1.18.86 ff.: 104
1.19.1–14: *29–30*
25: 124
31: 124
32–33: 120, 158
43: 169
1.20: *102*
1.20.3 ff.: 41
20–22: 1, *105*
2.1: 257
2.1.1 ff.: 212
5: 337
7 ff.: 212
50 ff.: 32, 47
76: *39*
88: 49
88–89: *257*
114–17: *45*
119 ff.: *18*
165–67: *47*
166: 9
170 ff.: 47
175–76: 41
225: 46
250 ff.: *113–14*
2.2.47: 164
49–50: 186
55 ff.: 44, *295–96*
77 ff.: *344*, 346
85: 171
96: 327
99–100: *34*

EPISTLES (*cont.*)
Ep. 119: 259
120: 40
121: 351
124: *44*
141–44: *296*
175 ff.: 87, 263, 311
201 ff.: 104
213–16: *300*

EPODES
Epod. 1.19: 236
2: *106–07*
3: *122–23,* 140, 156
3.9 ff.: 137
4.1: 236
5.18: 271
6.13: 124
7: *161–63, 181,* 183, 221, *223*
7.1: 184
11: 236
17: 221
9: *163*
9.11: 184
11–16: *94–95*
10: *124–26,* 209
11.5–6: 248
9: 294
19–22: 129
13: *172 ff., 180,* 208, *224, 282–83,* 337
13.3: 276
4–5: 248, 269
11 ff.: 53, 123
14.6: 7
15: 150
15.9–10: 144
16: *161–62,* 183, 221, *223*
16.2: 184
9: 181
16: 196
25: 236
31: 238
65: 223
17.21: 278
42 ff.: 136

SATIRES
S. 1.1: *87*
1.1.1 ff.: 104
5: 196
68 ff.: *103*
90: 236
101 ff.: 104
117–19: *264*
120: 108
1.2: *103–04*
1.2.23–24: *103*
1.3: 108
1.3.103 ff.: 336
138: 108
1.4.7 ff.: 47
9 ff.: 40
12: 47
13 ff.: *41*
19–21: *108–09*
38 ff.: *42*
46: 9
60–61: 31
1.5: *160*
1.5.51–54: *120–21*
1.9.23–24: *41*
71 ff.: 135
78: *128*
1.10.1 ff.: 47
19: *45*
37: 44
43–44: 71
50 ff.: 40, 47
61 ff.: *40*
68–71: *257*
71: 21, 45
72 ff.: 41, 42, *46*
81 ff.: 33, 41, 135
2.1.10–15: *113*
55: 236
75: 47
121: 136
2.2: *264–65*
2.2.1–4: *108*
53 ff.: 104
126–27: 263
129 ff.: 87, 282, 311
136: 53
2.3: *108*

SATIRES (*cont.*)
S. 2.3.1–2: 41, 46
50: *104*
82: *263*
122–23: *87, 264, 286*
142: *102*
259 ff.: 150
314 ff.: 236
321–22: *30*
325: 156
2.4.52: 39
2.5: *87*
2.5.40–41: *39*
2.6.13–15: *37*
21: 284
40: 278
80: 126
93–97: *121*
100–102: *121–22*
2.7: *108–09*
2.7.28–29: 105
117: *30*

GENERAL INDEX

(Italicized numbers are citations to works; roman numbers are pages in this book.)

Acro: *ad C. 2.18,* 82; *C. 1.2,* 179–80
Actium, 91 ff., 166–67, 171, 182–83, 192, 200, 204
Addison, Joseph, 27
Aeschylus, 28, 38, 205, 207, 231
ἀδύνατα, 236
Agrippa, 71–72, 167
Alcaeus, 28, 123, 166 ff., 316–17, 331; *Fr. 46a,* 164 ff., *46b,* 164 ff., *119,* 165
Alexandrianism, 24 ff., 31 ff.
allegory, 120, 164 ff., 179, 202, 208
ἀλληγορία, 165
Altheim, F., 17
Amphion, 103
Anacreon, 28, 321; *Fr. 43,* 73, *88,* 252–53
analogist. *See* anomalist
Ancients and Moderns, 256 ff.
anomalist, 258
Antigonus, 29
Antimachus, 38–39
Antipater, 29
Apollo, 18, 187, 200, 332–33
'Αραί, 124 ff.
Aratus, 24
archaizing, 31, 257 ff.
Archilochus, 28, 207; *Fr. 79,* 124 ff.
ἀρεταί, 126
Arethusa, 12, 324
Arion, 207
Aristius Fuscus, 135, 342
Aristophanes, 28; *Pax 700 ff.,* 28; *Ran. 868 ff.,* 310
Aristotle, 22, 30, 68, 102
Arnold, Matthew, 227, 281
ars, 20 ff., 43 ff. *See also* τέχνη
Auctor ad Herennium, 26, 68–69, 112
Auden, W. H., 101
Augustus (Octavian), 5, 14, 18, 31–33, 46, 62 ff., 89 ff., Ch. 4 passim, 256, 296, 320–21

Bacchus, 18, 74, 320, 331, 332, 337 ff., 344 ff.
Bacchylides, 335
beatus, 77, 81, 102, 335
Bentley, Richard, 238, 298
βίοι, 330
Blake, William, 116
Browne, Sir Thomas, 49
Brutus, 172, 183
Burns, Robert, 157

Callimachus, 7, 9, 13, 21, 24, 28, 31, 34, 36 ff., 42, 71; *Aitia 1.1.17 ff.,* 36–37; *Fr. 400,* 125; *Hymn 4.175,* 200
Calliope, 195
Calvus, 25
Campbell, A. Y., 16, 18, 35, 59, 111, 117, 207, 208, 218, 221
carmen, derivation of, 46
Cassius Etruscus, 40
Catullus, 5, 25, 26, 33, 38, 41, 45, 57–58, 88, 106, 132 ff., 144 ff., 157 ff., 248, 290–91, 328–29; *5.4 ff.,* 279–80; *7.3,* 55; *8,* 144–46; *8.3,* 67; *13,* 276; *27.6,* 30; *34.21–22,* 127; *45,* 57–58, 132–34, 141–42; *46.1,* 275; *51.6–12,* 153; *61.51 ff.,* 150; *68.45,* 7; *95.10,* 39
Charisius, 71
Cicero, 4, 22–23, 25–28, 31 ff., 68, 174; *Off. 3.26,* 11; *Par. 42 ff.,* 77; *Rep. 1.7.12,* 212; *Tusc. 3.19.45,* 31
Cinna, 25, 26, 32, 39
Cleopatra, 89 ff., 117, 163, 221

Coleridge, Samuel Taylor, 47, 98, 146, 341
Comedy, Roman, 69, 145
Conway, R. S., 84, 167–68, 222
Cornificius, 25
country, as setting, 244 ff., 343 ff.
craftsman, poet as, 21, 23 ff., 42 ff.
Cratinus, 28
Critias, 22
criticism, ancient, 26 ff., 67 ff.

Dante, 60, 169
death, treatment in Satires and Odes, contrasted, 87, 237
deductum, 38
Demetrius, 27, 194
Democritus, 8, 22
Demosthenes, 24
De Quincey, Thomas, 98
Dio Cassius, 168
Dionysius of Halicarnassus, 24, 27
Dioscorides, 125
Dirae, 124 ff.
dives amator, 14, 335
divine protection of poet, 41, 195, 207, 341 ff.
divinization of ruler, 5–6, 169, 175 ff., 187 ff., 203–04, 209–11, 320–21
doctus, 26, 45 ff.
Dowson, Ernest, 298
Dryden, John, 30, 47, 53, 145
Duff, J. W., 157, 235
durus, 142, 293

Elegiac poets, 31 ff., 132 ff., 239 ff., 335
Eliot, T. S., 44, 159, 328
Empedocles, 81
Ennius, 9, 31–32, 53, 214, 222, 308–09, 318
ἔνθεος, 22
ἐνθουσιασμός, 22
Epicharmus, 22
Epicureans, 22, 255, 333
ἐπινίκιον, 230
Erinna, 24
Euhemerus, 22, 210
Euphorion, 25
Euripides, 21, 38, 119
exclusus amator, 129–30, 147
exempla, 122–23, 179, 186, 189, 212, 268. *See also* παραδείγματα

Faunus, 171, 337, 343, 348 ff.
fautor veterum, 258
fides, 132, 144, 330, 335
Fortuna, 54, 263
Fraenkel, E., ix, 74, 124, 166, 168, 171, 172, 204, 206–07, 219, 254, 270, 314, 339
Frost, Robert, 54, 159, 291
Furius Bibaculus, 25, 53

Gallus, 5, 25, 134
Gigantomachia, 119, 199 ff., 339
Goethe, 248
Golden Age, 64, 183, 223, 224, 234
Golden Line, 53, 154

Havelock, E. A., 36, 135, 158
Hazlitt, William, 290
Helicon. *See* poet's mountain
Heraclitus, 81
Heraclitus Rhetor, 164 ff.
Herodotus, 165
Hesiod, 2, 9, 16, 21–22, 195, 207
Ἡσυχία, 204 ff.
Hippocrene, 12, 324
Hobbes, Thomas, 8
Homer, 2 ff., 15, 21, 27, 71, 121, 128–29, 165, 259
ὕβρις, 199, 204
ὑπόνοια, 165
hymnic form, 18, 126–27, 137, 338
hypermetra, 61, 294

ἰαμβικὴ ἰδέα, 247
Ibycus, 207
immortality, of poet, 308–17; bestowed by poet, 317–24
Ingenium, 20 ff., 45. *See also* φύσις
invocations, 3 ff., 126–27, 194–95, 206–07, 331–33
Isles of the Blest, 162, 317
Isocrates, 23

Jonson, Ben, 44
Julius Caesar, 183, 185, 217, 219, 258
Juvenal, 6

καὶ γάρ, 123
Keats, John, 281
Knight, G. W., 336

Landor, Walter Savage, 5, 59, 110, 267, 289
Leonidas, 275
lex Meinekiana, 318
Livy, 172, 212
Longinus, 9, 27, 68, 153
Lucan, 6
Lucilius, 26, 40, 42, 46–49, 256–57
Lucretius, 10–12, 27, 97, 101–02, 188, 225, 259, 264, 327, 333
Lycophron, 25
lyric, 157–59

Macaulay, Thomas, 58–59
Maecenas, 13, 19, 20, 34, 35, 114, 127, 167–68, 196, 211–12, 244–47, 287, 303–04, 311–12, 314–15, 342–43
Martial, 6
Meleager, 125, 266, 327
Melpomene, 19–20, 331–32
Menander Rhetor, 125
Mercury, 128, 171, 177, 188 ff., 203, 207–08, 325, 336, 342, 348
Messalla, 127–28
Mevius, 124 ff.
Milton, John, 51–52, 116
Minnermus, 254
miser amator, 294
Mommsen, Theodor, 215, 217
Morris, E. P., 145–46
Moschus, 12, 241
Munro, H. J., 132–33, 135, 157–58
Murray, J. M., 97
Muse, 2 ff., 17, 195, 324, 331, 336, 337

Naevius, 257
namque, 123
narratur, 126
natura, 22 ff.
nature, treatment in Odes and Satires, contrasted, 236–37
Nero, 6
Neoptolemus, 27
νεώτεροι, 25 ff.
Nicaenetus, 29
Nicolson, M., 9
Nietzsche, Friedrich, 50, 52, 112

occultatio, 112
Octavian. *See* Augustus
ὀλίγος, 38
order of Odes, 16, 65, 115, 117, 127, 164, 202, 256, 273–74, 311–12, 313–14, 314–15, 317, 328
Orpheus, 18, 103, 289
Otis, Brooks, 32
Ovid, 15, 100–101, 169, 185, 234, 292; *Am. 3.8.23 ff.,* 15, *3.9.25,* 12; *A.A. 1.637,* 14, *2.147,* 231, *3.547–50,* 14; *Tr. 3.13.14,* 8
oxymoron, 54, 101–02, 120

Pacuvius, 174
palinode, 109 ff., 136, 155
παραδείγματα, 122–23, 126, 132, 137, 140, 172 ff. *See also exempla*
παρακλαυσίθυρον, 129–30
Parmenides, 166
Parnassus. *See* poet's mountain
Parody, 120 ff.
Parthenius, 25
Pasquali, Giorgio, 35, 150, 217, 241, 254
pater patriae, 219
Peerlkamp, H., 58, 64
Pericles, 23, 317
Permessus, 12
Persius, 6–7
Petrarch, 7
Petronius, 8, 42
Philetas, 13, 24, 25
Philodemus, 56
φύσις, 22 ff., 61
pietas, 132, 162, 330–37, 342
Pindar, 2 ff., 17, 20–23, 43, 45, 48, 59 ff., 69, 123, 128, 204 ff., 317,

Pindar (*cont.*)
323, 336; *N. 2.1 ff.*, 43, *3.1*, 8; *O. 2.86*, 21–22, 61, *9.107*, 21; *P. 1*, 204 ff., *6.5 ff.*, 310, *8*, 204 ff.
pius, 126–27, 162, 337
Plato, 14, 46, 48, 310
Plautus, 49, 257
Pliny, 210
Plutarch, 92
πνεῦμα, 8–9
poeta, 14
poet's grove, 343 ff.
poet's mountain, 9 ff.
πόλις, 24
Pope, Alexander, 47, 136–38, 145
Porphyrio, 42, 58, 73, 179 ff.
Poseidippus, 127
praeteritio, 112
πρέπον, τό, 48, 281
priest. *See vates*
Prodicus, 166
propempticon, 118, 125–26
Propertius, 5, 12–13, 17, 33–35, 134–35, 304; *1.8.41*, 7; *2.1.3–4*, 5; *2.1.13–14*, 5; *2.2.25–26*, 12; *2.34.32*, 9; *3.1.3*, 12; *3.1.5–6*, 13; *3.1.9–10*, 8; *3.1.17–18*, 11; *3.3.5–6*, 13; *3.3.51–52*, 13; *3.10.1*, 7; *3.11*, 35; *3.11.55–56*, 94; *3.16.11–18*, 134; *4.6*, 35
prophet. *See vates*
Protagoras, 21
πρῶτος εὑρετής, 120
Publilius Syrus, 77, 187, 203
puns, 101–02, 120, 326, 335
Puttenham, George, 68

Quintilian, 36, 158, 164, 179, 202
Quirites, 171

recusatio, 13, 35, 62, 71, 112, 142, 155, 292, 324
Reincke, G., 88
Reitzenstein, R., 35
Republicans, addressed, 172, 186
Reynolds, Sir Joshua, 44
Riding, Laura, 307
Romulus, 214 ff., 233

sacerdos, 14, 16
sacred lover, 134–35
sailing, condemnations of, 119
Sallust, 82, 218
Sappho, 310, 316–17, 321, 331; *Fr. 2*, 153, *27*, 105
scelus, 181
Scipio Africanus, 318–19
Sedgwick, H. D., 99–100
Sellar, W. Y., 185, 235
Semonides, 66
Seneca, 6; *Clem. 1.11.1*, 190
Sertorius, 162
Servius, 3
Shakespeare, 27, 88, 95–97
Ship of State, 163 ff.
Simonides, 205, 207, 342
Simylus, 24
Snell, Bruno, 21, 38, 105
Solon, 45, 330
Sophocles, 28, 119
Spartacus, 182
Spenser, Edmund, 22
Stendhal, 97
Stesichorus, 128, 136, 207
Stoics, 22, 77, 108, 210, 255
Suetonius, 217, 296
Swift, Jonathan, 48
Swinburne, Algernon, 243
Syme, Ronald, 191, 213, 217

Tacitus, *Dial. 9*, 344, *9.3*, 14
ταπείνωσις, 71
tenuis, 38, 65, 71, 313, 334
τέχνη, 23 ff., 61
Theognis, 310, 312
Tibullus, 5, 33, 88, 146, 240–41; *1.2.25–30*, 134; *2.5.111–12*, 4; *2.5.113–14*, 15
tristia, 136, 139
Troy, 217 ff.
Tyrrell, R. Y., 58, 77, 107, 235

Valerius Aedituus, 153
Valerius Maximus, 123
Valéry, Paul, 157
Valgius, 33, 239–40
Varro, 4, 256

vates, 13 ff., 25, 46, 207, 329
Vergil, 3, 5, 8, 16–17, 32–33, 35–36, 106, 118–20, 196, 216, 220, 222–23, 227, 274–77, 287 ff.; *Aeneid 12.828,* 227; *Eclogues 1.6,* 193, *1.7,* 209, *1.83–84,* 241, *4,* 161, 183, *6.3 ff.,* 37–38, *6.64 ff.,* 12, *10.64 ff.,* 134; *Georgics 1.34–35,* 209, *1.466 ff.,* 179, *1.498 ff.,* 192–93, *1.501–02,* 182, *2.175,* 12, *2.490 ff.,* 60, *3.8–9,* 309, *3.10–12,* 10, *3.291–93,* 10, *4.470,* 289
Ps. Vergil, *Cat. 9.61 ff.,* 38, 41
Verrall, A. W., 274, 284
virtus, 210, 308, 330, 342

water, connection with poetry, 11 ff., 40–41, 60 ff., 323–24
water-drinkers, 28 ff.
Wilamowitz (-Möllendorff), Ulrich von, 210, 217
Wilkinson, L. P., ix, 36, 91, 158, 168, 342
wine, 87, 173, 244, 249, 260, 264, 282, 286, 326, 337
wine-drinkers, 28 ff.
Wordsworth, William, 23, 98, 157, 323, 330

Yeats, William Butler, 231, 291, 324